Cities of Culture

In memory of Fred and Rachel Holland

Cities of Culture

Staging International Festivals
and the Urban Agenda, 1851–2000

JOHN R. GOLD
Oxford Brookes University

and

MARGARET M. GOLD
London Metropolitan University

ASHGATE

Published by
Ashgate Publishing Limited
Gower House
Croft Road
Aldershot
Hants GU11 3HR
England

Ashgate Publishing Company
Suite 420
101 Cherry Street
Burlington, VT 05401-4405
USA

Ashgate website: http://www.ashgate.com

British Library Cataloguing in Publication Data

Gold, John Robert
    Cities of culture: staging international festivals and the urban
    agenda, 1851–2000
    1. Exhibitions – Social aspects 2. Exhibitions – Economic aspects
    3. Exhibitions – History 4. Sports tournaments – Social aspects
    5. Sports tournaments – Economic aspects 6. Urban economics
    7. Festivals – Social aspects 8. Festivals – Economic aspects 9. Concerts –
    Social aspects 10. Concerts – Economic aspects
    I. Title II. Gold, Margaret M.
    907.4

Library of Congress Control Number: 2004006877

ISBN 1 84014 285 5

Printed on acid-free paper

Typeset in Sabon by Bournemouth Colour Press, Parkstone, Poole.
Printed and bound in Great Britain by A Rowe Ltd, Chippenham.

Contents

Figures

Tables

Preface and Acknowledgements

More than twenty years ago, we were shown sketchbooks belonging to an architect who designs stage sets for musicians for a living. He was then in the early phase of a career that has helped change the way that popular music is presented to live audiences in large venues. The sketchbooks themselves were a revelation. There, with a wonderful parsimony of line, were designs for concerts to be held in different parts of the world over the next two years. Although the sketches related to auditoria of greatly varying size and were commissioned by acts performing in styles ranging from heavy metal to Indian folk music, the sets depicted had a single integrating theme. In each case, they tempered their clients' wishes for memorable spectacle with an approach that retained relevance to the music, and would supply a fresh experience for the audience over and above what they might have gained by buying the record. Although strobe lights and laser shows had been part of stadium rock since the late 1960s, the use of giant inflatables, video displays, the building of huge walls across the stage, three-dimensional banners, fireworks and other pyrotechnics took the experience a stage further. Moreover, these effects were not added patronisingly to keep the kiddies happy, but as legitimate parts of the apparatus of spectacle that the designer believed would enhance the audience's appreciation of the music.

That, of course, was not a new message. Since the dawn of recorded history, festivals, fairs, plays, masques, processions and tournaments have all harnessed spectacle to enhance the staging of cultural attractions. Most often, however, the prime aim was to enhance the reputation and aura of 'magnificence' attached to a dynasty or boost the authority of a spiritual or secular regime. The years since the early 1980s have brought important changes. The rapid growth of what is now termed the 'cultural sector' has been accompanied by a marked increase in the number of music and arts festivals vying for audiences, with founders working overtime to locate the germs of tradition on which to base new events. There has been an enormous proliferation of museum, arts and theatre complexes, with new ones created and old ones expanded and restyled architecturally to add visual excitement. Spectacular sports complexes are often created on the back of attracting so-called mega-events, like the Olympics or football's World Cup. These events are also widely believed to be golden opportunities for ambitious city authorities to initiate far-reaching regeneration plans. It may be an exaggeration to say that promotion of culture has become the preferred route for regenerating ailing economies, but its importance cannot be minimised. Not surprisingly, the large festivals for which cities compete are now the targets of intense, sustained, expensive and, sometimes, bitter campaigns.

Our aim in this book is to explore this territory from a historical and cultural perspective. Although working in different subject areas, we share an interest in the cultural life of cities, in issues such as urban spectacle and exhibition design and, in particular, in the uses made of large-scale, showcase events like international festivals and fairs. Over the years, we have found it extremely difficult to find suitable literature to recommend to students. What was available primarily comprised narrowly focused essays on individual events, widely scattered in academic journals. Their contents were broadly polarised between, on the one hand, heavily theoretical essays in which the empirical context seemed largely gratuitous and, on the other hand, researchers offering detailed, but poorly conceptualised, case studies. There was little that covered a sufficiently broad span of material or that offered comparative insight. In addition, a surprising number of writers positively radiated disapproval for their subject matter. Authors commonly approached showcase events with a sense of detachment tinged with condescension. Such events are accused of misrepresenting social reality, commodifying culture, preserving cultural hegemony, and trading in 'spectacle' – apparently a bad thing – in which audiences are relegated to the role of uninvolved onlookers rather than being active and creative participants. Even those willing to recognise the pleasure that these events convey often seem gnawed by a feeling that their audiences are somehow being duped into expressing enjoyment.

To some extent the critics are right. International festivals do purvey values and work that support the dominance of some groups over others. There is also great value in a style of critical analysis that has effectively sharpened our understanding of mega-events and their relationship to culture, technology and ways of seeing. Yet there is more to staging these events than the operation of naked self-interest, strategies for place promotion, reinforcement of competitive advantage, and opportunities for urban regeneration. Idealism, pedagogy, community reconciliation and even just 'wanting to put on a good show' are also normally part of the agenda when staging international festivals.

If our approach in this book seeks to avoid *a priori* distaste for such festivals, we also seek to avoid the current city managers' perspective that primarily sees them as unequivocally desirable events, well worth capturing. Historically at least, the staging of international festivals has often been characterised by muddle and indecision, chronic financial problems, impractical designs for stadia and auditoria, and severe problems in converting facilities to their post-festival use. Varying degrees of commitment by changing political regimes has often led to logistical problems, retrenchment and shortage of resources. These problems, in turn, have led to profound modifications during the preparation stages of the festival, resulting in enormous differences between initial plan and the end product. Although this is often a difficult subject on which to gain information, we try throughout to throw light on the business of plan implementation as well as discuss statements about underlying vision and intent. That type of emphasis, perhaps inevitably, has led us to make use of case studies in order to seek greater depth of analysis.

As usual, we have built up a list of debts in writing this book, intellectual and otherwise, that are a pleasure to acknowledge here. Thanks must also be recorded to the following libraries and their staff for their assistance: the British Library, National Library of Scotland, Senate House (University of London), the Canadian Centre for Architecture (Montreal), the Special Collections Archive at Harvard University's Graduate School of Design, the Library of the British Olympic Association in Wandsworth (London), the Royal Institute for British Architects, Oxford Brookes University and London Metropolitan University. The School of Social Sciences and Law and the former School of Planning at Oxford Brookes University have provided finance and other assistance that facilitated this work. Colleagues and students at Oxford Brookes University and London Metropolitan University have provided ideas and encouragement. The Urban Morphological Research Group at Birmingham University has constantly supplied a welcoming and stimulating environment for the exchange of ideas about urban form and society. The staff at Ashgate has, as ever, been a pleasure to work with – even for authors who try their patience as extensively as we have. Thanks also go to Mary F. Daniels, Robert Elwall, Mark Fisher, Brian Goodey, Dennis Hardy, Bob Jarvis, Peter Larkham, Curt Noel, George Revill, Stephen Ward and Jeremy Whitehand.

copyright holders would contact us, whereupon we would be pleased to settle matters. A special debt of gratitude goes to Jennifer and Iain for perforce having to find solace by using the microwave. Finally, this volume is dedicated with great fondness to the memory of Fred and Rachel Holland.

West Ealing
December 2003

CHAPTER ONE

Introduction

After the Midway, Grace and I decided to take a
gondola ride. A maze of canals wove through the
exposition to create an illusion of Venice – a sweet-
scented, idealized Venice, and after the Midway a
haven of peace. We glided beneath carved bridges
decorated with classical sculpture; we passed hanging
gardens and miniature waterfalls. The exposition's
extravagant Spanish Renaissance architecture
surrounded us in a riot of colours, from red to warm
ivory. ... Was it beautiful, this city of the imagination
brought to life? From here on the gondola it was.
From here it seemed eternal; there was no sense that it
was merely a plaster stage set that in six months
would be bulldozed back to farmland.

Lauren Belfer (1999, 317–18)

In July 2002, athletes from 71 countries assembled in Manchester in
northwest England to attend the seventeenth Commonwealth Games.
Although less prestigious than premier sporting festivals like the
Olympics or football's World Cup, the Commonwealth Games are still
events of some pedigree. The current series was inaugurated as the
British Empire Games at Hamilton (Ontario, Canada) in 1930 and,
apart from the break caused by the Second World War, has been held at
four-yearly intervals ever since. The Empire Games were themselves
effectively heirs to the sporting competitions that started at the Festival
of the Empire in London (1911). Those, in turn, traced their origins
back to 1891 when John Astley Cooper, an Australian living in London,
proposed the establishment of a periodic Pan-Britannic festival to
celebrate the industrial, cultural and athletic prowess of the Anglo-
Saxon race (Moore, 1991; see also Chapter 6).

This brief genealogical sketch indicates that, like many other such
events, the Commonwealth Games occupy a distinct niche in
international affairs that transcends sporting contests. Although some
would see its rationale as part of a former colonial nation's attempts to
preserve its past dominance by surrogate means, the Games
undoubtedly bolster links between a geographically disparate group of
states with little in common other than their imperial past.
Accompanying symbolism reinforces these ties. Like all major sporting
festivals, the Commonwealth Games have embedded protocols.

Manchester's opening ceremony, for example, featured the arrival of a special baton that had left Buckingham Palace, the Queen's London residence, on Commonwealth Day 2002 (11 March). The baton then toured the territories of member countries in Africa, the Caribbean, the Americas, Europe, Oceania, and Asia before arriving theatrically at the stadium on 25 July.[1] The speeches, the unfurling of flags, parades and general spectacle testified to the rhetoric of an 'international family' assembling for its regular four-yearly meeting. Eleven days later, Queen Elizabeth II declared the Games closed. A prominent part of the rain-lashed closing ceremony – which included concerts, parades, and the inevitable fireworks – was the solemn promise that the participants would convene again in Melbourne (Australia) in 2006. The next family gathering thereby firmly entered the diary.

Ancillary activities enhanced the occasion. As with the Olympics, with which they share a close affinity, the Commonwealth Games grew out of a philosophy that regarded sports, the arts, technology and culture as interrelated enrichments of human life (see also Chapter 6). The sporting events were but the centrepiece of a multifaceted international cultural festival. Manchester entertained the twelfth Commonwealth International Sport Conference just before the Games (19–23 July 2002), which included the Annual Conference of the British Association of Sport and Exercise Sciences, and the eighth International Congress on Kinanthropometry. Elsewhere, the city's burgeoning arts sector, with its swathe of new museums, theatres and galleries, ran extensive programmes to cater for any spare time that visitors might have on their hands. Tourist and heritage attractions put on special events and gala evenings. Taken together with the Games, these activities substantiated the idea, at least in the minds of the city's planners, of Manchester as an important city of culture for 2002 and beyond.

This packaging of events around a major focus is now a common strategy. For Manchester 2002, staging the Commonwealth Games offered opportunities to boost the city's employment prospects and improve its potential for gaining inward investment. More specifically it provided a chance to initiate the regeneration of east Manchester – a 2800-acre (1120-hectare) area immediately east of the central business district that contains some of the city's most deprived districts. The Games required a new 38 000-seat venue to house the athletics events that, in turn, would convert into a state-of-the-art 50 000-seat football stadium.[2] Manchester itself would gain from improvements to roads and other communications. More generally, there was the possibility of boosting the city's standing in the world. Although it bid in vain for the right to host the 1996 and then the 2000 Olympic Games, Manchester was nominated as the City for Drama in 1994 and selected as the location for the follow-up congress to the Rio Earth Summit (Girodano and Twomey, 2002, 52). Victory in the bidding process for the 2002 Commonwealth Games reinforced the city's growing confidence about its ability to compete on an international stage.

A survey[3] carried out immediately after the Games argued that most of these objectives had been met. Construction and preparatory work generated substantial short-term economic returns, with northwest England witnessing the strongest growth in new industrial orders in the United Kingdom during 2001–2. The Games directly created 6000 temporary jobs and brought in £600 million in investment. Chris Clifford, regional director for the Council of British Industry, noted that:

> Local companies have benefited from a huge procurement programme in all sorts of areas, ranging from the provision of uniforms to fencing, security and food. On top of that, there was a big upsurge in confidence, as businesses took pride in what Manchester and the northwest could achieve.

The survey concluded that the city gained a permanent legacy of improved transport, extra sporting facilities and a higher profile – a combination thought likely to attract 300 000 extra visitors a year to the region.[4]

Some months later, although dissenting voices questioned the underlying approach to policy (for example, Peck and Ward, 2002), the prevailing assessment remained dominantly positive. Unusually for such events, the seventeenth Commonwealth Games made a profit, some of which was returned to the bodies that donated the original funds. The British Government received around £2 million, Manchester City Council £3 million and Sport England £4 million. More generally, the Games had given 'a headstart' to the regeneration of east Manchester and imparted a lasting sense of achievement in the city as whole.[5] When talking about the Games in advance, Manchester's political leaders were fond of using a sporting metaphor, which held that the city had to be as competitive as the sporting competitions that it sought to attract (Ward, 1998, 233). With critical reaction generally affirming that the goal had been accomplished, they had grounds for asserting that any future bids that Manchester made for international festivals would, at least, be taken seriously.

That sentiment had significance beyond Manchester. London, bidding for the 2012 Summer Olympics, had suffered a series of reverses that threw doubt on the United Kingdom's commitment to compete for such events. These included, among others, the failure to build a new athletics stadium at Pickett's Lock in the Lea Valley, which meant relinquishing the nomination to host the 2005 World Athletics Championship; repeated delays in rebuilding the national football stadium at Wembley, with endless wrangling over finance and design; and the high-profile financial failure of the Millennium Dome (see Chapter 9). Evidence of a city within the United Kingdom organising a successful event could only help the national cause. As one observer noted: 'The Manchester Games helped reverse the idea that Britain was incapable of providing the kind of tip-top facilities and support required by international sporting events.'[6]

International Festivals

Sporting events of this type, in turn, have a wider historical context. The last 150 years have seen exponential growth of large-scale, prolonged and spectacular celebrations of human achievements in the arts, sport and science (Bassett, 1993; Bianchini and Parkinson, 1993; Carreras, 1995). These 'international festivals', the term that we use here, are roughly equivalent to what other authors have called 'mega-events' (Roche, 1992, 2000; Spezia, 1992), 'meta-spectacles' (Bergmann, 1999, 13), 'hallmark events' (C.M. Hall, 1989), 'landmark events' (Hiller, 1990) or 'world festivals' (Proudfoot et al., 2000). They include gatherings ranging from sports meetings, garden festivals, song competitions, and arts festivals to major trades fairs, awards ceremonies, and scientific congresses. Some are held regularly in the same city. Others are ambulatory, rotating in a fixed sequence from city to city or staged in whichever city has successfully bid to hold them.

   Yet although they may have different origins, the practices and protocols adopted cannot be seen in isolation. The organisers of major festivals seldom start from scratch when planning their programmes, but draw directly on the accumulated experience of previous festivals and, increasingly, also on the practices of related attractions such as modern theme parks. This broader context, of course, constrains as well as empowers. The consensus that underpins many festivals generally favours a predictable blend of pedagogy, family-oriented entertainment and spectacle as the formula for attracting sufficient numbers of visitors. Repeated applications of this tried and tested formula, however, stiffen the criteria for judging the performance of each succeeding festival. Creating memorable spectacle, for example, becomes difficult without providing ever-larger investment. Mark Fisher,[7] the Creative Director of the show performed at London's Millennium Dome (see Chapter 9), summarised a prevailing trend when, jokingly, he anticipated that to be effective the show would need to be: 'grand, spectacular and fabulously expensive'. As the record shows, that is a burden that sponsors and other backers may be unwilling to bear.

This discordant note needs further emphasis. International festivals enjoy a reputation for being versatile events, to which enthusiastic promoters attach often extravagant expectations of the benefits likely to flow from inward investment, urban regeneration, infrastructural improvement and boosts to a city's international standing. Yet for every city that has enjoyed an unquestionably successful festival, several can be found that have experienced adversity on a scale ranging from disappointment to complete disaster. The story of international festivals is littered with cases in which organisers have blithely offset their initial costs against wildly optimistic visitor forecasts, subsequently leading to crippling debts and bankruptcies. Poorly-conceived events, the withdrawal of sponsors, political boycotts, and heavy cost overruns on stadia or facilities – which may remain incomplete years after the festival is over – are some of the commoner reasons for such outcomes.

The associated infrastructural and renewal projects are even more prone to severe problems in the game of roulette that masquerades as festival-led urban regeneration. Temptations to use festivals as the stimulus to 'fast track' major investments in road, rapid transport or underground systems have overloaded many projects and undermined their cost base. Festival sites do not always convert easily to other uses. Stadia, especially those designed for elite sports, may struggle to find post-festival users; athletes' villages do not always generate marketable, or even desirable, housing; showgrounds and pavilions may languish in increasingly decrepit states of repair. Designating specific areas to receive selective investment can stimulate active opposition from unfavoured areas. It can also cause lasting damage to community relations within regenerated areas if existing residents suspect that their interests are secondary to an ill-defined 'public good'. For their part, regenerated neighbourhoods recurrently fail to match planners' expectations. Newly opened large-scale hotels, especially those that are part of luxury hotel chains, frequently change hands after the festivals when local managements fail to attract either tourists or the anticipated conference trade. Even successful festivals may suffer if visitors or the media find the event tainted by triumphalism or over-commercialism. It is not unknown for city authorities to mount promotional campaigns to try to counter the *damage* done to their reputation by badly designed, ineptly organised or socially divisive international festivals.

Aims and Scope

This book proceeds against this background. It examines the staging of international festivals in western cities from 1851 to the start of the twenty-first century, particularly exploring the relationship between the festival and the host city. *Staging* is the key word. It expresses production, intentionality and, to a large extent, theatre – the conscious creation of scripted, dramatic spectacle to elicit a favourable response from an audience that is increasingly global. Yet despite the record of problems encountered, all the world apparently wants to be the stage. Enthusiasm to participate in international festivals now permeates the agendas of cities throughout the world. What was once left to groups of enthusiasts in different countries cooperating over festival arrangements and raising money by subscriptions is now an enterprise that can only be attempted with the support of the public purse or powerful public–private collaborations. Culture has become an increasingly contested sector. Nations and their nominated cities bid against their rivals for the right to stage festivals and then seek to maximise the impact of those festivals to win lasting acclaim and kudos.

In the text that follows, we principally focus on three types of festival: the international expositions, otherwise known as Great Exhibitions, *Weltausstellungen*, World's Fairs, *Expositions Universelles* or just plain Expos; the modern Olympic Games; and the European Cities of Culture (which from 2005 will become the European Capitals of Culture). They are in themselves separately conceived and organised events dating from very different periods, but they share four important characteristics. First, they are large-scale events with an elongated *production cycle*, a term that includes the entire life history of the project. Progress from the original proposals to the completion of the festival's venues can take anything up to six years. This stage may require dealing with mechanisms of public consultation, negotiation with sponsors, recruitment of specialist staff, land and property acquisition, creation of transport links, building stadia or auditoria, and provision of hotels and competitors' accommodation. Transferring the site to its post-festival state takes a further extended period of time. Festival buildings are often ill suited for subsequent uses. The organisers may need to find new owners or tenants, dispose of assets, dismantle some buildings, convert others, and undertake whatever landscaping is necessary. Not surprisingly, this process needs a budget that can withstand the commitment of resources over a long period in the expectation of returns that accrue from a short-lived event that occurs near the end of the cycle. That invariably involves risk. The length of the production cycle is sufficient for dramatic changes to occur in economic circumstances and the replacement of political regimes by others that might have less sympathy for the festival project. Not surprisingly, therefore, there have been many instances when international festivals are plagued by cash flow and logistic problems.

Secondly, we focus on recurrent international festivals controlled by bodies with sole prerogative to select the host nation and city. These bodies are often internationally constituted. The Lausanne-based International Olympic Committee, for example, supervises the Olympic Games; the Fédération Internationale de Football Associations, located in Zurich, runs football's World Cup; and the Paris-based Bureau International des Expositions gives its official seal of approval to events that meet its criteria. These agencies usually have a permanent secretariat and an executive responsible, nominally or otherwise, to a general assembly of delegates appointed by member countries. The organising body invites applications from aspiring hosts and selects the winning bid – an activity that encounters growing calls for transparency of decision-making given the rewards at stake and the inevitable possibilities for corruption. Once awarded, primary responsibility for financing and organising the event then rests with the host.

The third feature shared by the international festivals studied in this book is that they are extraordinary rather than routine occurrences in the life of a city. Places that have regular music, film, arts or horticultural festivals (for example, Edinburgh, Glastonbury, Roskilde, Chelsea or Salzburg) have designated festival arenas and employ a core of permanent staff who routinely organise the festival. By contrast, the nature of the selection process for the events studied here means that a city only normally receives the nomination to act as host once – even if there are instances when a second nomination has been secured after the passage of many years.[8] This process has profound consequences for the organising city. Any host city can learn from the experience of its predecessors, but it must essentially assemble from scratch the teams required to tackle the planning, organisational and construction tasks that bring the festival to fruition.

Finally, all three types of festival are noted for the ease with which they can represent many different agendas. The international expositions, for example, were conceived as universal gathering places, but their development was shaped by the rivalries of European nations in the ages of industrialisation, colonial expansion and Cold War ideological conflict. The late-nineteenth century revival of the Olympic Games saw initial idealism progressively deflected by political ideology and, later, rampant commercialism. The European Cities of Culture programme embodied a collective need to stimulate the non-economic dimension of the European Union and promote its greater cohesiveness, but provided individual cities and nations with an opportunity to proclaim their cultural leadership. All three events have been taken as opportunities for cities to introduce infrastructural improvements, boost their cultural sectors, attract tourists, create employment, regenerate blighted areas, and score points over their rivals. Indeed, it is precisely this characteristic of being able to group many different advantages into one package – the balance of which frequently changes over time – that makes staging of international festivals perceived as such a desirable activity.

Key Terms

Almost any terms relating to cultural phenomena are notoriously open to dispute. This applies particularly to four key terms that recur constantly in this book, namely: 'culture', 'place promotion', 'festivals' and 'spectacle'. Each is frequently used in the literature about international festivals, but their meanings vary according to context, the period being studied, and the understandings shared by their users.

Culture

The Latin origins of the term 'culture' link it to 'cultivation', both in the sense of agricultural tillage and the philosophical sense of the training or improvement of the faculties.[9] Over time, culture became increasingly conflated with related words, such as 'cultivated', 'civilisation' and 'civilised'. Possessing culture was a mark of breeding, class or worth that set individuals and groups apart from others in society who lacked such refinement. At another level, claims to possess culture served to justify the territorial ambitions of Europe's colonial nations. From the sixteenth century onwards, military expeditions claimed large territories in the Americas, Asia and Africa, rationalising subjugation of 'primitive' peoples by being self-appointed carriers of civilisation to an uncivilised world. Academic usage of the word 'culture', itself intimately intertwined with wider usage of the term, began in earnest in the nineteenth century. The British anthropologist Sir Edward Burnett Tylor (1871), the first Anglophone academic to define the term, stated that culture was: 'that complex whole which includes knowledge, belief, art, morals, law, custom, and any other capabilities and habits acquired by man as a member of society'.

It was a definition, however, that begged more questions than it answered. More than eighty years later, Kroeber and Kluckhohn (1952) charted the exponential growth of research centring on culture, grouping the enormous range of available definitions into six categories: descriptive, historical, normative, psychological, structural and genetic. They, in turn, were trying to hit an ever-moving target. Further developments in the fields of sociology, archaeology, political studies, cultural studies and, especially, anthropology[10] made broadly consensual definitions even harder to find. Culture is clearly what people learn, particularly through socialisation during childhood, and sometimes also what they do and make – although even that seemingly straightforward statement uneasily hovers between what a culture *is* and what it *does* (Kessing and Strathern, 1998, 16; Bal, 2003, 18). Perhaps the best approach, therefore, is to acknowledge the essential pluralism of the term 'culture' by recognising that it comprises two different, but overlapping levels of phenomena: creative achievement and social heritage.

Culture as *creative achievement* conjures up an image of 'the higher things' (Hall, 1993, 132) – especially works that testify to intellectual, spiritual and aesthetic development in philosophy, literature, poetry, sculpture and the arts (Bal, 2003, 18). A present-day view, however, might expand this definition to recognise the creative output of the so-called 'cultural industries', which include broadcasting, film, publishing and recording. In the first place, including them within the definition recognises their economic significance as well as their importance as outlets for creative endeavour. Table 1.1, for instance, shows that the cultural industries employed around 633 000 people in Great Britain in 2001, generating revenues of £113.2 billion (more than 5 per cent of the nation's gross domestic product). Secondly, including the cultural industries highlights the continuing intimate links between cities and culture. Cities have long served as crucibles for cultural formation,[11] housing museums, galleries, concert halls and, more generally, supplying opportunities for creative exchange unavailable elsewhere. As groups

Table 1.1   Cultural industries in Great Britain, March 2001

Sector	Employment	Revenue (£ billion)	Exports (£ billion)
Advertising	93 000	3.0	0.774
Architecture	21 000	1.7	0.068
Computer and video games	21 000	1.0	0.503
Design	76 000	26.7	1.000
Designer fashion	12 000	0.6	0.350
Film and video	45 000	3.6	0.653
Music	122 000	46.0	1.300
Publishing	141 000	18.5	1.650
TV and radio	102 000	12.1	0.440

Source: *Financial Times*, 13 March 2001

gather in one place, they establish supportive networks of associations, pressure groups, informal meeting places and formal venues (for example, galleries, theatres, stadia) in which performance and display take place. This process, which has traditionally contributed to the growth of the fine arts, also encourages the growth of the cultural industries. Often developing out of clusters of small premises in specific neighbourhoods, over time the cities concerned have developed pools of creative talent, sources of specialist finance and networks of dealers who trade in the products of artistic endeavour. As these industries become established, they steadily accumulate advantages that are hard to replicate elsewhere, with multiplier effects continually operating to reinforce cultural leadership.

Culture as *social heritage* relates to a social group's shared values, customs, norms, ways of life, typical patterns of behaviour, cognitive constructs, rules, systems of meaning and modes of discourse.[12] The hallmark of culture in this sense is its ordinariness (Couldry, 2000, 23), comprising the taken-for-granted background to everyday life. Ordinariness, however, is not synonymous with insignificance. Among other things, culture supplies a frame in which individuals make sense of the world around them and forge their identity; differentiating those who are part of a cultural group from others within society who are not. Partly due to these characteristics, culture frequently serves as a conservative force that assimilates new circumstances to the old rather than vice versa. Accepted meanings and understandings, with all their implications, may be challenged (for example, see Allan, 1998; Ray and Sayer, 1999), but the established tenets of culture frequently prove tenaciously enduring.

Place Promotion

'Place promotion' is primarily an expression of the interests of groups who have power in a city, region or nation. It refers to the activity of consciously communicating selectively chosen and positive images of specific geographical localities or areas to a target audience (Gold and Ward, 1994, 2). Historically, place promotion originated in support given to schemes for colonial expansion, but was later used by towns and cities to promote themselves to tourists, potential residents and industrialists (Ward, 1998). With economic and social change, especially in the inner city, came new uses of place promotion as part of strategies to rebrand and regenerate blighted areas as cultural quarters, loft apartments and marinas. More recently still, the attractions of regional shopping centres and claims for cultural leadership have been added to the list of issues addressed by place promoters, with new and imaginative forms of tourism based around recycling the industrial legacy as heritage. Very often, these increasingly slick aspects of promotional work have become fused together as part of the strategy of urban entrepreneurialism, in which the interests of the municipality and the private sector, particularly the business community, converge in the activity of 'selling' the city to the outside world (Hall and Hubbard, 1996). As such, place promoters generally treat the city as a multifaceted product, in which the key selling proposition rests on the distinctive blend of advantages that the city in question is said to offer. Of particular interest here is the tendency for the promotional message to be accompanied by 'a relentless emphasis on vibrancy, as if the city was host to a continual series of festivals and other celebrations of culture' (Ward, 1998, 209).

Looked at analytically, place promotion is essentially a communication process involving four interrelated elements (see Table 1.2). First, there are the *producers*, or communicators, who create the content (or message). Once an endearingly amateur activity undertaken by local government officials who had no training whatever in publicity and advertising (Gold, 1974), place promotion increasingly draws in marketing specialists and media consultants. Their budgets often come from partnership between the public sector and private bodies, such as key local firms, industrial corporations, trades unions, employers' organisations, conference bureaux and tourist agencies. The partnership approach here, as in many other sectors of contemporary urban development, recognises the mutual interests of all parties in 'selling' the city more effectively (Ward, 1998, 196). The *content* with which they work traditionally took the form of printed, graphic, moving image or radio broadcast materials, but now these are more often supplemented by internet websites and digital materials. Likewise, the *media* employed to communicate this content comprise the old staples of brochures, posters and press advertising; the more expensive options of radio, television and cinema advertising; the production of promotional videos and gifts; and the increasingly ubiquitous use of information technology. Finally, the *audience* is a term for all who consume this material, ranging from potential tourists and residents to conference organisers and the business community.

In identifying these four elements, there is no suggestion that linear chains of cause-and-effect link production to consumption, since feedbacks occur at many levels. For example, those who produce material for tourists are invariably themselves consumers of such materials at other times and feed that experience into their promotional work. Nor is meaning confined to what is explicitly stated. The product of place promotion is sometimes a compromise between interested

Table 1.2 Elements and actors in the process of place promotion as communication

Producers	Content	Media	Audiences
Local authorities	Written/Print	Brochures	Potential visitors
Regional authorities	Graphic images	Posters	Potential residents
State-appointed agencies, e.g. tourist boards	Moving images	Radio	Conference organisers
	Radio broadcast	Television	Media production teams
Interest groups	Computer interactive	Film	Industrialists
Charitable trusts		Video	
Private businesses		Gifts	
Advertising agents		Internet	
Marketing agents			
Freelance writers			

Source: Based on Gold and Gold (1995, 23)

parties, more revealing for what it says about place-marketing campaigns than for the specific place narratives that they seek to promote (Ward, 1996, 53). Moreover, any act of communication takes place against many other acts that can reinforce, countermand or even neutralise the impact of the specific message (Gold, 1980).

Festivals

The word 'festival' derives from the Latin noun *festum* meaning a feast-day or holiday observed in honour of a god. The festival was an important and widespread expression of culture in the ancient world and has remained central to the organisation and articulation of many cultures.[13] Functionally, a festival is 'a public themed celebration which is concentrated in time and delivered with a clear purpose' (Getz, 1991; Evans, 2001, 237). The word 'themed' is significant, since festivals are always events at which something specific is being celebrated. The most common themes are celebrations of the arts (for example, music, dance, cinema and theatre), feasts, carnivals (stressing fun, games and role playing), heritage celebrations and milestone events, such as centenaries and anniversaries (Hall, 1992; Getz, 2001, 4). They vary in scale and can either be part of the official round of civic events or supported by groups that lie outside the establishment. The sponsorship and purpose of events can change over time. The voluntary staffing that previously characterised the arts festival, for example, has succumbed to the need for greater organisational professionalism and funding. By contrast, most events run by religious or ethnic groups tend to retain their original purpose, indigenous involvement and sacred or profane roots (Evans, 2001, 237).

Sometimes, as with religious or political commemorations, festivals can incorporate solemn ceremonies surrounded by *ritual* – fixed sequences of words and activities performed in a specific gathering place 'designed to influence preternatural entities or forces on behalf of the actors' goals and interests' (Turner, 1972, 1100). Ritual is a schematic device since, as Mary Douglas (1966, 63; quoted in Duncan, 1995, 11) suggests: 'A ritual provides a frame. The marked off time or place alerts a special kind of expectancy, just as the oft-repeated "Once upon a time" creates a mood receptive to fantastic tales'. The Olympic Games, for example, have an established sequence of procedures for gala opening, medal and closing ceremonies. Shaped by modern readings of classical rituals and from more contemporary addenda, the purpose of Olympic rituals is to dignify proceedings, commemorate achievement and model the notion of shared humanity that is an essential ingredient of the ideology that surrounds the Games (see Chapters 6 and 7). They also supply an aura of contrived continuity, a sense that the accomplishments of today comprise merely the latest in a sequence that dates from a heroic age.

Ritual solemnity, however, rarely negates all opportunity for conviviality and enjoyment. Many solemn festivals are preceded or concluded by rejoicing, merry-making, celebration and, indeed, 'festivity', just as Mardi Gras precedes Lent or Eid concludes Ramadan. The presence of boisterous celebration has sometimes posed problems for political or spiritual leaders: the former worried about standards of behaviour, the latter about the pagan roots of many festivals and the ever-present possibility of licentiousness and depravity. Nevertheless, those in authority usually fought shy of imposing outright bans unless prohibition was absolutely necessary and the outcome could be guaranteed. Paradoxically, feast-days often guaranteed acceptable behaviour: 'for the excesses they authorized served as a safety valve: they prevented intemperance from spreading to daily life and throughout the body as a whole' (Ozouf, 1988, 1). Even when those in authority found traditional festivals ideologically or morally repugnant, they felt bound to replace them with new versions more to their taste rather than declare festivals a thing of the past. Torn between tolerance and control, those in authority generally weighed their wish to maintain order against the need for a measure of forbearance of public merry-making. As the lawyer Claude de Rubys noted on witnessing the excesses of the Charivaris festival in early seventeenth-century France: 'It is sometimes expedient to allow the people to play the fool and make merry, lest by holding them in too great a rigour, we put them in despair' (quoted in Davis, 1971, 41).

Spectacle

'Spectacle', like the other key terms defined in this chapter, is frequently used and fiercely contested: 'a stock phrase in a wide range of critical and not-so-critical discourses' (Crary, 1989; quoted in Pinder, 2000, 361). The idea of spectacle is central to recent debate about the relationships between vision, imagery and representational forms, where spectacle is linked to the presumption that modern Western society is 'ocularcentric' – dominated by, or perhaps under the hegemony of the visual.[14] Spectacle is applied to an enormous range of phenomena. Among other things, one can talk about the spectacle of empire, discourse, politics, democracy, race, punishment, violence, terrorism, or even death.[15] It can reside in the built environment, in nature, in the street or in human suffering.[16] It can be pleasing, dubious, gendered or ideological.[17] It can express power or affirm collective, especially national, identity.[18] Spectacle has been identified as a defining feature of the contemporary city. Chisholm and Brazeau (2002, 3), for example, argue that: 'The city is the spectacular centre of metropolitan modernity: a mass theatre where progress is staged in scenes of radical innovation, casting the illusion that society is advancing with the installation of new architectures and technologies.' It is even suggested that spectacle defines modern society as a whole. As Pinder (2000, 357) notes, when prefaced with 'society of the ...', the word 'spectacle' is often loosely used to indicate a shift towards an image-saturated world where electronic media, advertising and other cultural industries increasingly shape everyday experiences.

Spectacle stems from the Latin verb *spectare* meaning 'to look at carefully, contemplate, observe or watch, sight' or 'the act or faculty of looking at or viewing'. The related word *spectaculum* also carried connotations of the place in which spectacle occurs, since it additionally meant 'a performance, especially of gladiators or similar, devised for entertainment' or 'the places occupied by spectators in a theatre'.[19] Spectacle, therefore, immediately suggests not just something that is seen but also an imposing scene. It is best understood as any form of public display put on for the entertainment and benefit of a large crowd of spectators. It is created by consciously manipulating space, landscape or objects to produce displays that draw a powerful emotional response from an audience of spectators. Spectacle can take place in the open air, in an enclosed auditorium, or some mixture of the two, as exemplified by the showgrounds of international expositions, with their pavilions set in landscaped exterior spaces with eye-catching sculptures and statuary. It can be designed for purposes of conspicuous display, public education, punishment, military pomp or civic ceremony. It may appeal to several senses, but remains predominantly visual. In this way, we refer to vistas of scenic splendour as spectacle but not 'dawn choruses' of birdsong; to circuses as 'spectacle' but seldom orchestral performances (MacAloon, 1984b, 243). Understandably, not all sights constitute spectacles since, to qualify for that description, an event needs to have a sufficient scale. This can come from the number of participants (performers, vendors, suppliers, sponsors), the dramatic qualities of the proceedings, vibrancy of colours, the intensity of special effects or the grandeur of the setting (the building, the stadium, the scenery).

Although there may be elements that trigger instinctive response, spectacle works primarily within a cultural frame and is subject to prevailing modes of perception that observers bring to bear.[20] In saying that, we stress that creation of spectacle is neither a universal nor even an inevitable expression of culture, but is a strategy *commonly* used by people from many different cultures to address specific needs. The task of creating spectacle has been likened to creating new works of literature; where writers normally feel bound by the rules and traditions of their genre, yet need to show sufficient originality to impress their audiences. By extension, spectacle is produced by working with the grain of a particular culture, blending the innovative with the established. Thus anyone deploying spectacle may draw on a repertoire of techniques and conventions developed from previous festivals or related activities,[21] but imitation is not enough. Spectacle must also be spectacular. A spectacle has to amaze spectators, outdoing previous efforts if it is to become part of the collective memory of those who witnessed and participated in it (Edmondson, 1999, 77).

Some would argue that spectacle has become so commodified that spectators lose the sense of participating. Henri Lefebvre (1991), for example, juxtaposed spectacle against its supposed opposite, the spontaneous festival. Lefebvre's analysis reflected a school of thought rooted in the work of Jean-Jacques Rousseau, who advocated the simple rural festival as a way of criticising the artificiality of the theatre (Starobinski, 1988; see also Chapter 2). Lefebvre saw spectacle as an expression of the insidious powers of the state to present superficial representations that hid the darker side of social reality. By contrast, the festival was considered a truly spontaneous and participative expression of popular culture (Bonnemaison, 1998, 347; Gregory, 1994).

Another trenchantly negative portrayal of spectacle, also from the ranks of French critical theory, came from the Situationists, who firmly linked spectacle to modernity. The Situationists were heirs to an intellectual tradition that saw urban life as a disconnected and never-ending whirl of new phenomena only superficially understood as 'appearances' (Berman, 1983, 169; Collier, 1985). To Guy Debord (1967: 1995, 12), for instance, the 'whole life of those societies in which modern conditions of production prevail presents itself as an immense accumulation of *spectacles*'. Debord believed that people in modern societies live in a world so dominated by images that the latter are effectively regarded as prime agents in the reshaping of social relationships. This judgment relegated the experience of everyday life to passive consumerism and regarded the spectacle as: 'a tool of pacification, depoliticisation and massification that "distracts" and "seduces" people using the mechanisms of leisure, consumption and entertainment as ruled by the dictates of advertising and commodified media culture' (Gotham, 2002, 1737). To offset its adverse consequences, Debord and his colleagues in the Situationist International tried to provoke the public into abandoning their acquiescent acceptance of spectacle and create 'situation' – in which the structure of society, the rules for its perpetuation, and the possibilities for action and desire are exposed (Lindner, 2001).

This style of analysis has understandably drawn considerable criticism for its universalising tendencies. As Tomlinson (2002, 55–6) summarised, it trivialises human agency, arrogantly dismisses historical variability, inadequately conceptualises spectacle, and 'puts forward a culturally pessimistic worldview with the antidote being a specific form of revolutionary practice' (ibid., 56). In this text, therefore, we choose to see spectacle as special event rather than the everyday outcome of processes of commodification; as the expression of conscious thought and contrivance rather than as a consciousness-numbing feature of ordinary life. Working on this basis, two approaches have considerable promise for understanding the process by which spectacle is staged.

The first views spectacle as *drama*. As with any theatrical representation of objects, events and their interrelationships in space and time, drama is selectively constructed rather than expressing some mythical state of objective reality.[22] The audience and performers participate in a form of interaction governed by tacit understandings about the nature and limits of what will take place (Beacham, 1991, 1). For example, the opening ceremonies of major sporting events such as the Olympic Games and football's World Cup mirror the princely pageants of the Middle Ages in the extent that they feature scripted performance. They create lavish spectacles to enact narrative and convey historical continuity. They demand movement, action, change and exchange from the human actors who are centre stage and expect involved response from the onlookers (MacAloon, 1984b, 243). They dramatise myths and codify the place of sport in the social order. Other types of cultural festival incorporate drama through their handling of space and sequencing of movement. For example, the organisers of expositions often arrange their showgrounds thematically, inviting spectators to reflect on a sequence of profound ideas concerned with, say, faith, the future of the environment, community or world peace. As with the opening ceremonies of games, what is at stake in the dramaturgical approach is 'reflexivity', in which people are encouraged 'to distance themselves from their own subjective experiences, to stand apart from and to comment on them' (MacAloon, 1984a, 11; also Turner, 1984).

The second approach views spectacle in a similar manner to place promotion; namely, as a *medium of communication* that operates within a particular cultural frame (see Table 1.3). From this perspective, individuals or groups (*producers*) create extravagant or startling displays to convey specific *messages* by recognisable *media* to the audience (*spectators*) who consume the spectacle. As Table 1.3 shows, the range of authorities that commission and design spectacle include local authorities (particularly the councils of larger cities), regional authorities, state-appointed agencies such as tourist boards, and international agencies. They seek assistance in those tasks from an array of specialists, including event consultants, who specialise in tasks such as firework displays, concert sound systems, exhibition design, and arena construction. The messages that they convey might be pedagogic, entertainment, religious, ideological, hegemonic, or boosterist; they may be overtly stated or implicit within the communicated content. The media involved include exhibitions, ceremonies and rituals, light and laser shows, concerts, staged performances, historic re-enactments, and explorations in virtual reality. The spectators can come from many different geographical areas. They may be day visitors, short-stay tourists or longer-stay holidaymakers. They may pay for admission, be admitted free or be recipients of corporate hospitality. Whatever their reasons for coming, spectators experience a show that may include spoken language, music, mime and text, but normally communicates its primary message through visual imagery.

Table 1.3   Elements and actors involved in spectacle-as-communication

Producers	Media	Messages	Spectators
Local authorities	Exhibitions/ Artefacts	Pedagogic	Local inhabitants
Regional authorities		Family entertainment	Day trippers
	Ceremonies/ Ritual		
National governments	Light/Laser shows	Religious	Weekend or vacationing tourists
State-appointed agencies, e.g. tourist boards	Concerts	Ideological/ Political	Corporate
International agencies	Staged performance/ Re-enactments	Power/ Prestige	
Event consultants		Boosterist	
	Virtual reality	Hegemonic	

Applying this type of perspective again demands care. As before, roles of producers and consumers overlap. Spectators also need not be passive consumers. Although traditional approaches regard the phenomenon of spectacle as orchestrated, contained and consumed by a captivated audience, research on spectatorship strongly suggests that spectators bring streams of associations to an event through which its meaning is mediated (Hansen, 1991, 13; Allen, 1995; Denzin, 1995). Whether or not spectators respond as producers intend depends on whether they share the same understandings of what is on offer. In addition, the audience is inextricably part of the spectacle. The experience of attending a spectacular sporting event or fireworks display, for instance, is often diminished if few other people have turned up to watch it or if others who are present are thoroughly unimpressed by what they see. In addition, the 'gaze' of particular spectators at an event can be mediated by knowing that others are simultaneously gazing on them. This inevitably affects the experience that one takes from the event, which may not always be pleasurable (Walker and Chaplin, 1997, 97; also

Mayne, 1993). Finally, any specific situation in which spectacle is used takes place against the background of many other acts of communication that mediate the impact of the event in question. Again, therefore, the links between different elements of communication are seldom direct and linear.

Structure

The eight chapters that follow begin with a historical overview (Chapter 2) that identifies the city's role in staging showcase cultural festivals and the use made of spectacle. Festivals often reveal remarkable longevity, a point recognised at many places in this chapter, which looks in turn at their role in the Age of Antiquity, the towns of medieval Europe, princely pageantry and revolutionary spectacle. Chapters 3–5 examine the experience of staging international expositions. Initiated in 1851 by London's Great Exhibition and held at irregular intervals until the present day, the expositions occupy a central position in any analysis of international festivals. They established patterns of practices that have influenced how subsequent events have been organised and, to a large extent, experienced. In these chapters, we make no attempt to summarise the already voluminous literature on expositions.[23] Instead we provide contextualised analyses of three specific expositions that span more than a century. Chapter 3 examines the Great Exhibition of 1851, showing its origins in prevailing interest in science-as-display and in the national industrial exhibitions pioneered in continental Europe. Chapter 4 considers New York's World's Fair of 1939, tracing its roots in the American history of World's Fairs. Chapter 5 focuses on Montreal's Expo 67 (1967), arguably the high-water mark of the international exposition's appeal and popularity in the postwar period. The final part of this chapter looks at more recent experience, which suggests that this type of international festival has now essentially lost its rationale.

Chapters 6–7 turn the spotlight on to the Summer Olympic Games, with very different conclusions. The revival of the modern Games was heavily overlain with the values of nineteenth-century sportsmanship and from the outset sought to place sport in its wider cultural context. Chapter 6 deals with the series of Olympics between Athens 1896 and Berlin 1936, analysing the principles and pan-artistic thinking that lay behind the revival of the Games and the experience of organising key Games held before the Second World War. Chapter 7 looks at subsequent development from the London Games of 1948 to Atlanta 1996, a half-century that saw growing acceptance of the economic importance and general promotional significance of the event for the host cities. In each case, we emphasise the elements and processes involved in staging these events, drawing attention to the much neglected cultural as well as sporting dimensions of the Olympics.

Chapter 8 examines the European Union's Cities of Culture programme. This stemmed from an initiative originally proposed by the Greek Minister of Culture, Melina Mercouri, who suggested that member states should award an arts festival each year to one city in Europe. This chapter examines the varying experiences and implications of being a European City of Culture, starting with the designation of a first round of twelve cities, from Athens in 1985 to Copenhagen in 1996. We then consider the changing patterns in the second round, concluding the analysis with Weimar 1999. In the process, we note how what began as a small affair, lasting a few months, developed into an important, versatile and sought after annual cultural festival.

Chapter 9 completes our account by focusing on the year 2000. The dawn of the third millennium saw all manner of commemorative events, from the brief pyrotechnics of New Year's Eve celebrations to lengthy reflective festivals. The date and its significance gave an added dimension to the international festivals held that year. After setting the scene, the three main parts of this chapter review the staging of Expo 2000, the Sydney Olympics, and the extraordinary nine-centre European Cities of Culture festivals. These allow us to gain a comparative snapshot of the state of the art at the start of the twenty-first century. They also permit us to reiterate this book's key theme, namely, that these events owe much of their longevity and pervasiveness in modern society to the extent that they are malleable to the changing agendas of the cities that host them.

Notes

1   The baton toured all parts of Great Britain as part of Queen Elizabeth's Golden Jubilee celebrations.
2   It became the home of Manchester City Football Club in August 2003.
3   As reported in the *Financial Times* (7 August 2002). The Confederation of British Industry and Experian Business Strategies, a firm of consultants, jointly carried out the survey.
4   Ibid.
5   *Financial Times* (29 October 2002).
6   *Guardian Education* (27 March 2003), 58.
7   Personal communication.
8   London, for example, hosted the Olympic Games in both 1908 and 1948 and nurtures hope that it might one day do so again (see also Chapter 6).

9   *Oxford Latin Dictionary*, vol. 1, 1968, p. 466. See also Williams, 1976.

10   See, for example, Hodder, 1991; Jacobs, 1997; Kupar, 1999; Worsley, 1999; Smith, 2001. Anthropologists also draw attention to the distinction between *culture*, embodied in individuals, and *cultures*, embodied in the superorganic properties of groups (Handwerker, 2002, 106).

11   For more on the nature and articulation of the relationship between the city and culture *per se*, see Mumford, 1961; Hannerz, 1980; Agnew et al., 1984; Jackson, 1989, 25–46; Borden et al., 1996; Zukin, 1996; Westwood and Williams, 1997; Hall, 1998; Miles et al., 2000; Fox, 2001; Lindner, 2001.

12   We have included modes of discourse within this second level of definition, rather than argue that culture, as 'cultural discourse', comprises a separate level of definition (for example, see Heller, 1999, 128–34; also Habermas, 1989).

13   The links between festivals and folk culture lie beyond the scope of this text. For more information, see Manning, 1983; Falassi, 1987; Handelman, 1990; Steinberg, 1990; Schelling, 1999. It is worth noting, too, that such festivals in their modern state are conscious forms of cultural production that draw upon the building blocks of earlier events: see Bauman et al. 1992, 1.

14   Various forms of evidence supposedly support this view. Perceptual theorists, for example, identify sight as the dominant human sense, with over 90 per cent of the information that we receive about the outside world being received through our eyes (Dodwell, 1966). Visual information is also held to be more precise and detailed than that received from the other senses, with thinking being 'thought of in terms of seeing' (Arendt, 1978, 110–11; Urry, 2000, 72). Linguistic theorists note the importance of visual metaphors in everyday speech in English, French and German (Turbayne, 1971) and, by implication, the thought patterns that underpin language in the Western world (Walker and Chaplin, 1997, 26). In passing, it is worth noting that a substantial weight of theoretical discourse opposes the ocularcentric bias of Western culture (for example, Howes, 1991; Jay, 1993a, 1993b; Heywood and Sandywell, 1999; see also Hanawalt and Reyerson, 1994a; Lury, 1996; Messaris, 2001).

15   See, respectively: Morris, 1982; Bruss, 1982; Edelman, 1988; Maxwell, 1995; Schwarcz, 1999; Garber et al., 1993; Merback, 1999; Mason, 2002; Chase and Levenson, 2000; Islam, 1976.

16   See, for example: Boyer, 1994; Green, 1990; Kellum, 1999; Spierenburg, 1984, and Flynn, 1994.

17   For example, see Lloyd, 2002; Glenn, 1997; Arvidsson, 2000.

18   Relevant sources here, in turn, include Bergmann, 1999, 9; Tomlinson, 2002, 48; Bramen, 2000.

19   *Oxford Latin Dictionary*, vol. 2, 1968, p. 1800. Its plural *spectacula* was the original term for the amphitheatre and could thus signify the venue itself. The dedicatory inscription at Pompeii's amphitheatre, for example, refers to it as a *spectacula* (D'Arms, 1999, 301). See also MacAloon, 1984a.

20   Various concepts offer insight into the nature of the shared mind set

(attitudes, beliefs) that observers belonging to the same culture bring to bear on spectacle. Although detailed discussion of this point lies beyond the scope of this book, the interested reader should consult Berger, 1972, with regard to his notion of 'ways of seeing', Metz (1977, 1982, 61–3; see also Jay, 1993b; J.A. Smith, 1999) on 'scopic regimes' and Urry (2002; drawing on Foucault, 1973) on the question of 'gaze'. Jay, 2002, usefully draws attention to the possibility of over-emphasising cultural relativism when analysing visual experience.

21 This would include previous experience of similar events or borrowings from the work of respected pioneers from other fields. A good example of the latter would be the theme parks pioneered in the USA by Walt Disney Productions, notably Disneyland at Anaheim, California (1956) and Disney World, Florida (1965). For more on the general principles involved, see Lyon, 1987; Winsberg, 1992; and Boniface, 1994.

22 We leave aside here the issue of whether or not urban spectacle is a misrepresentation of reality. For more discussion, see Mitchell, 1991, and Bonnemaison, 1998.

23 See, for example: Allwood, 1977; Rydell, 1984; Baculo et al., 1988; Greenhalgh, 1988; Canogar, 1992; Galopin, 1997; Mattie, 1998; Rydell et al., 2000; and Burris, 2001.

CHAPTER TWO

The Place of Spectacle

> Urban life had begun in Greece as an animated
> conversation and had degenerated into a crude *agon*
> or physical struggle. Under a succession of royal and
> imperial conquerors, the conversation ceased – it is
> the slave's lot, observed Euripides, 'not to speak one's
> thought'. With that the struggle likewise came to an
> end. What was left of the old urban drama was a
> mere spectacle, a show staged before a passive
> audience, with professional freaks, contortionists, and
> dwarfs usurping the place once occupied by self-
> respecting citizens.
>
> Lewis Mumford (1961, 228)

> Societies and people define themselves through
> spectacle.
>
> Bettina Bergmann (1999, 9)

Whatever disagreements exist about the general significance of spectacle as an element in urban affairs, few commentators deny its role as a readily identifiable thread in the cultural history of Western cities. This chapter samples this diverse, if fluctuating, tradition, providing a historical overview from Antiquity through to the early nineteenth century. There are four main sections. We begin by recognising the interplay of spectacle and cultural festivals in the Age of Antiquity, focusing on the public games, theatre and civic ceremonies of ancient Greece and Rome. The next part examines the round of festivals, fairs and ceremonies that enlivened and, in some respects, mitigated the hardships of everyday life in medieval Europe. The ensuing section considers the splendour and ambition of princely pageantry from the thirteenth through to the nineteenth century, examining a genre of consciously orchestrated events that harnessed spectacle to address vital interests of the ruling political elite. The final part of the chapter continues the ideological theme, by examining the revolutionary festival in late eighteenth-century France, focusing on the work of Jacques-Louis David, the pageant-master of the First French Republic.

23

Classical Spectacle

Interpreting the role and significance of cultural festivals in the ancient world is plagued by stereotypes that are integral to our modern perceptions of the Age of Antiquity, particularly courtesy of Hollywood film adaptations (Putnam, 1990, 108; see also Walton, 1987; Winkler, 1991, 2001; Green, 1994; Wyke, 1997). What is readily apparent is that festivals already existed at the dawn of recorded history, with biblical and Sumerian sources providing accounts of established civic and religious celebrations. The archaeological record – in the forms of building remains, pieces of costume, ceremonial artefacts and pictorial representations – shifts the chronology back even further, showing that sporting spectacles and ritual were a feature of life in the Bronze Age or even earlier (for example, Parpola, 1993; Barrett, 2000). Moreover, as far as can be determined, such festivals appear linked to the social order, with all this implies for use of resources and the display of power. Games and theatre readily illustrate this theme.

Games

Sporting and artistic contests were an integral part of Roman and Greek society, often conceived as reflections of the exploits of the gods and of legendary heroes. The festive calendar of ancient Greece was punctuated by four regular cycles of pan-Hellenic Games: the Pythian Games, which honoured Apollo, held every four years at the oracular shrine at Delphi; the Isthmian Games at Poseidon's sanctuary, but also honouring Palaemon, held on the isthmus of Corinth in alternate years; the Nemean games honouring Zeus at Nemea every other year; and the Olympic Games held at Olympia, on the west coast of modern Greece about 90 miles (150 kilometres) west of Athens. Of these, the Olympic Games, held in honour of Zeus, were the oldest and the most important of the sequence. Olympia had already assumed the status of a sacred site by 1100 BC, when the flourishing agricultural community of the Alpheios Valley used it as a centre for the worship of Gaia. Over time, its associations with the mythological hero Pelops, the goddess Hera, and the presence of the shrine and oracle to Zeus reinforced its sanctity.[1] Founded before 776 BC, the date from which the first victors' list is available, the Olympics were a panegyris or a 'festive assembly of the entire people' (Sinn, 2000, 24). As such, they attracted athletes, artists, scholars, and speakers from far afield as the festival came to occupy a central consolidating role in Greek culture. In the fifth century BC, for example, the historian Herodotus came to Olympia to recite his narratives as he saw this as a way to secure his fame by the 'quickest and least troublesome path' (ibid., 27).

The Altis, the sacred enclosure, was situated on level land at the foot of a hill (Cronos) at the confluence of two rivers, the Cladeios and Alpheios (Quennell and Quennell, 1957, 157). The enclosure steadily expanded with Olympia's increasing fame. The Cladeios was diverted in the seventh century BC so that the festival site could expand on to reclaimed land. Further extensions occurred after the military campaigns of 480–479 BC, when much of the credit for the Greek success, despite being heavily outnumbered by the Persians, went to the Olympic seers, who advised the Greek forces in the field. The ensuing Olympic festival in 476 BC, the Jubilation Games, cemented the pre-eminence of the Olympics.[2] The Olympic complex now housed a festival lasting for five days in July or August.[3] The stadium, located to the east of the Altis, contained earth banks that could hold 40 000 seated spectators.[4] Visitors converged on a huge tent-city on the banks of the River Alpheios from all parts of the Greek world, which then extended to Asia Minor, the Black Sea, Egypt and North Africa, Italy and Sicily and Spain. They, like the athletes, benefited from the declaration of the truce announced three months before the start of each festival. This gave safe passage to and from Olympia, and was scrupulously observed despite the often turbulent political relations between the Greek states (Toohey and Veal, 2000).[5]

The participants represented their home states, which vied with one another for sporting glory much as nations do in the modern Olympics. The games themselves mixed athletic competition with religious observance, music, singing and orations, with competitions for trumpeters and heralds as much as for athletes and boxers. Processions, prayers, animal sacrifice and feasting accompanied chariot races, foot races, the pentathlon (discus, long jump, javelin, sprint and wrestling), boxing, pancration (a particularly violent form of wrestling) and hoplite (racing in armour). To compete, participants had to be Greek, freeborn and male, but not necessarily amateur.[6] A class of professional athletes gradually emerged that travelled to compete in all the major Greek sporting festivals.

Nominally the four-yearly sequence of classical Olympic Games lasted for around twelve centuries, until the Roman emperor Theodosius the Great ordered the closure of places of pagan worship in AD 393.[7] This apparent longevity, however, belies the steady decline in the cultural significance of the games during the period of Roman rule. The Olympic Games lost their intimate connections with the fabric of Greek society. Moreover, the Roman penchant for the crueller aspects of arena contest, with wild beast fights and human gladiatorial contests, increasingly permeated Greek festivals. Track and field activities declined relative to the more dramatic spectacle of violent, combative events. After abolition, the site at Olympia was abandoned, with frequent flooding gradually burying the site under some 13–16 feet of sand (Sinn, 2000, 129).

Theatre

If the cycle of games provided a forum for the expression of civic and inter-state rivalries, then theatre supplied a medium for articulating the values and ideology of those in political power. The Greek word for theatre, *theatron*, was related to various words for seeing, including *thea* (sight or spectacle). The spectacle provided by early theatres was, in fact, the sight of the dramatically formed valley-and-plain landscape native to Greece. Built into hillsides, theatres were always left open so that a wide arc of distant landforms surrounded spectators. Indeed, this is the first example of the landscape acting literally as 'scenery' (Crandell, 1993, 32; Gold and Revill, 2004). The naturalistic and ritual meanings that initially infused theatre, however, largely disappeared around the fifth century BC. Social upheavals led to new sponsorship, with powerful individuals instead of the *polis* (city-state) now actively creating theatrical spectacle. The ritual functions of performance gradually diminished, being replaced by secular entertainments that often served political ends. With this came changes in the acting profession. Actors joined professional guilds and were employed by wealthy patrons. They travelled to international festivals and performed before huge audiences in spacious new auditoria. In the process, the relationship between performers and spectators changed, with the audience arriving in the expectation of 'being dazzled by a good show' (Pollitt, 1986, quoted in Bergmann, 1999, 10).

Rulers increasingly used theatre as a way of representing themselves to the public. Previously, elected leaders wore plain clothing and behaved modestly before a crowd, only switching to resplendent garments at times of special festivity. Gradually, however, the citizens of the Hellenistic kingdoms saw their rulers script and shape public spectacle to glorify their regimes (Kuttner, 1999, 110). Personal behaviour and dress became vital parts of self-presentation, as did use of tableaux and stage props. Alexander the Great, for example, performed parts from stage plays, slipping into the guise of gods.[8] Antiochus III, surrounded by his friends, gave dance performances.

These associations with the central functions of the state also became a feature of the Roman world, providing a specific place and time where the citizenry saw the dramas facing Roman society played out in symbolic form (Parker, 1999, 163).[9] From more humble beginnings, theatrical spectacle became a medium for conveying the essence of the

Roman state and, in particular, for charting its transformation into an empire. Military and civic leaders actively promoted the development of theatrical venues where they might present favourable images of themselves and their pre-eminence to the public. In 55 BC, for example, the consul Pompey (Pompeius Magnus) sponsored the city of Rome's first stone-built theatre. Capable of seating 40 000 spectators, it acted as a venue for carefully crafted displays that graphically asserted its founder's political prominence.[10] Subsequently, Roman emperors themselves became providers of and participants in such spectacles, which served to present imperial ideology to Roman citizens and subjects (Beacham, 1999, ix, 62). For example, Augustus, the first Roman emperor, paid careful attention to the 'theatricalisation of use of urban life and through the provision of sumptuous and monumental buildings for mass entertainment' (ibid., 130). He circumspectly deployed drama as a medium of propaganda to legitimise and stabilise his regime (Purcell, 1999). By the end of his reign, a single integrated system of imagery had evolved that encompassed in victory celebrations, the ruler cult, presentation and glorification of the emperor, and honorific monuments (Zanker, 1988; quoted in Beacham, 1999, 139).

The Roman Festive Calendar

Theatre and games, key ingredients in ancient Greek life, were just two elements in the enduring cycle of spectacular entertainments of imperial Rome. Others included commemorations, animal displays, gladiatorial contests, triumphal entries, ritual humiliations of miscreants, theatrically staged funerals, mock sea battles in specially constructed aquatic arenas (*naumachiae*), and circuses. Festivals or games were staged at public expense throughout the year to coincide with specific holidays, many in honour of the gods (Kondoleon, 1999, 321). These followed a common timetable throughout the empire after Julius Caesar's regime synchronised the calendar in the mid-first century BC (Bergmann, 1999, 22; Mitchell, 1990). In addition, there were special events such as lavish funerals and 'triumphs' – where returning commanders and their troops processed through the city displaying dazzling trophies of war and captured enemies (Beacham, 1999, 39). Understandably, the different forms of spectacle on offer sometimes competed with one another. Theatre managers, for example, knew only too well that if given the opportunity their audiences would decamp to other, more instantly gratifying events, such as the circus games (*ludi circenses*). It was therefore important to schedule events carefully to avoid competing for spectators.

The cycle of festivals and entertainments lasted more than 500 years.

Many were recurrent events involving rule-bound procedures and performances that defined the social relationships and status of watcher and watched (Feldherr, 1998, 13). Festivals gained strength from repetition of visual formulae combined with enduring individual or community identification with participants. Popular interest in chariot racing, for instance, was fostered by the existence of factiones – teams with their supporters' clubs – based in Rome and elsewhere: the albata (whites), veneta (blues), prasina (greens) and russata (reds) (Vickers, 1989, 111). Gladiatorial contests also drew groups of passionate supporters, identifying themselves with one of the three differently equipped groups of combatants fighting for their lives in the arena.[11] Their appeal, of course, extended well beyond just the locality. As with the Graecian games, the larger Roman festivals drew spectators from far afield. Given the extensive road system developed for trade and administration and the political stability within the empire, wealthy citizens felt free to travel widely to visit festivals with established reputations and experience the spectacle on display (Casson, 1974).

Violent, unnatural death is often considered a defining feature in Roman spectacle, but there was a long history of capital punishment that influenced the creation of arena sport. The Law of the Five Tablets in the fifth century BC, for example, had prescribed execution as the penalty for a range of crimes. Publicly administered and protracted execution by drowning, beating to death, burning alive and crucifixion gave audiences familiarity with excruciating punishment. In addition, many arena entertainments began as sacred or sacrificial rites, rather than as theatre of cruelty. In the third century BC, icons were carried in special litters from their temples to the games, at which they had special places from which to watch over proceedings (Beard et al., 1998, 40–1). Equally, while gladiatorial combat latterly saw prisoners-of-war or enslaved people fighting for their lives for the sake of public entertainment, its original purpose was linked to the rites associated with funerals as duties or tributes to dead ancestors (Kyle, 1998, 43). The gladiatorial games (*munera*) were initially intended to pacify spirits through entertainment, to flatter them with special attention, to give them a share of the energy expended in competition, and to fortify the living. The last of these objectives linked sports to military training, warfare and to the occasion of possible death (Plass, 1995, 17). These underpinnings remained significant in subsequent developments of arena combat. Gladiatorial combat provided a perspective on death *per se* and found a larger social purpose in the military utility of staged violence. The individual deaths of marginal people were considered unimportant (Plass, 1995, 30; Futrell, 1997).[12]

Festivals and commemorations required venues, which served to anchor spectacular events within the time-space framework of Roman city life. Larger Roman towns and cities routinely contained auditoria, arena, stadia and theatres, varying in size from small, temporary constructions built for a specific occasion to grand, permanent structures like Rome's Colosseum and the huge Circus Maximus, which could seat 50 000 and 250 000 spectators respectively. Festival venues were more than neutral containers, since the art of architecture worked in concert with the performing arts to enhance the audience's experience and to convey central values about the society (Fleming, 1990). The external design and seating patterns reflected divisions and observances central to the conduct of Roman life. By their construction, theatres and other venues could change the nature of the spectators' gaze. A semi-circular shaped theatre, which focused attention on the stage, embraced different assumptions than an amphitheatre that exposed performers to view from all around and made the spectators face each other. Yet, the nature of provision was subject to the prevailing views of the time. Several Roman stone theatres were demolished in 154 BC when it was alleged that, by permitting mass viewing, theatres endangered public morals and encouraged riots (North, 1992; also Goldberg, 1998).

Spectacle existed at various scales. At a micro-scale, wealthy patrons could enjoy shows in the theatre or arena and then return home to domestic interiors that recreated an 'environment of spectacle', with 'privileged close-ups of gladiatorial combats on mosaic floors or wild beasts being hunted on painted walls' (Bergmann, 1999, 15; Kondoleon, 1999). More generally, the presence of festival venues coupled with a cityscape filled with monuments and processional routes influenced the meaning of urban space. Foundation myths and cosmological beliefs could endow aspects of the site on which the city stood with special properties (Rykwert, 1976, 42–71). Hills, crossing points, grid lines and boundary ditches became settings for commemorative services, especially if reinforced by animistic beliefs in localised spirits. Each served to energise particular topographic features or routeways with a particular history, imbued with a *genius loci* (Favro, 1999, 205) and gave them meaning within the cultural and temporal rhythms of Roman society.

Medieval Festivals and Fairs

The sack of Rome undermined the recurrent cycle of festivals and the ready availability of resources necessary to support it. While religious festivals and displays of courtly splendour survived in the eastern part of the empire based on Constantinople (Byzantium), the staging of spectacular cultural festivals gradually unravelled in the west after the systemic collapse of the western empire. The animal displays continued but the gladiatorial combats, as the most expensive and infrequent spectacles, rapidly declined (Kyle, 1998, 55). Even so, there was no uniformity in the passage from classical to medieval Europe; no incremental replacement of the ordered festivities associated with Rome by 'Dark Age' chaos. Settlements such as York (Eburacum) continued much as before, whereas in others all traces of Roman rule quickly disappeared. Yet festivals per se remained. Most societies retained some religious observances and these were supplemented by the growth of fairs.

Fairs were not new inventions. It is argued, for example, that the Neolithic 'camps' of England's chalkland ridges were effectively fairgrounds where gatherings of farmer-hunters traded pelts and primitive tools (Cameron, 1998, 12). More dependable evidence shows the existence of fairs in the classical civilisations of Sumeria, Greece and Rome. Written records show that fairs commonly existed in England at the start of the third century (Bancroft, 1893). Some fairs founded in Antiquity, like that at Troyes (Augustobona) in the Champagne region, continued into the medieval period, but changing patterns of trade and cultural contact steadily fostered new venues. Indeed, the existence of fairs served as weathervanes of economic and social vitality throughout the Middles Ages.

Historically, fairs were closely associated with markets, but differed in three important respects. First, markets catered weekly for the basic needs of local householders and were broadly concerned with commodities produced for subsistence. By contrast, fairs were larger, well-publicised events that mainly convened once a year.[13] They made trade possible through barter and pecuniary transactions. Often located on trade routes, they provided meeting points where buyers and sellers converged to trade in livestock, produce (particularly cloth), handcrafted commodities, and promises of labour. Most were small events, but the fairs at places like Geneva, Antwerp, Burgundy, Lyons, Bordeaux, Madrid, Leipzig and Novgorod drew participants from considerable distances (Walford, 1883). The extensive Sturbridge Fair, held near Cambridge in eastern England, provides a good example. Founded in 1211 as a cloth and wool fair, it attracted merchants from as far afield as Iceland, Arabia, Africa and eastern Europe by the late thirteenth century.

Secondly, while the market was normally held in the town centre near the church and the key institutions of civic life, fairs were generally established on farmland or common grazings at the margins. As a temporary tented settlement that appeared and soon vanished, the fair often stood apart from the regular rhythms and regulations of the town. Its physical marginality was therefore paralleled by cultural marginality, which included a degree of licentiousness that would never have been tolerated elsewhere. The presence of large numbers of people with unusual amounts of disposable cash in their pockets quickly stimulated the establishment of nefarious entertainments (Cameron, 1998, 53). Sideshows and amusements developed; the latter, depending on the moral climate of the times, steadily catering for all the major vices. Indeed the pleasure function often outstripped trade.

Thirdly, and despite their later commitment to principles of pleasure, many early fairs had a spiritual function that was quite different from that of the market. Seventh-century Arabic sources speak of the significance of fairs as places where normally hostile tribes came together and maintained a truce. These meeting places would prove significant in the consolidation of Islam, the reinforcement of a shared language and the development of a common identity. In England, there was a close relationship between the fairs and the Christian ecclesiastical calendar, since many were connected with acts of pilgrimage. The earliest fairs stemmed from throngs of pilgrims assembling at abbeys and cathedrals on the feast days of their enshrined saints. As the religious houses were usually unable to cope with the number of pilgrims arriving, tented communities sprang up initially in any available space in the graveyards and then on adjacent land. Recognising the opportunities presented, merchants set up stalls catering for their needs.

Over time, as noted above, fairs discarded their religious origins. The Church itself was not above exploiting the economic benefits from the proliferating trade. England's cathedrals, and the Church generally, grew exceedingly rich from fairs and from the contributions from pilgrims processing to the relics of their favourite saints (Cameron, 1998, 30). It was not unknown for the Church's authorities to promote the merits of recently canonised or neglected saints to generate new revenue. The Church also recognised that fairs were fertile places for raising funds where necessary. For example, when needing funds to complete the building of St Peter's Cathedral in Rome in the sixteenth century, the Catholic Church sent out salesmen to regional fairs and pilgrimage sites to sell indulgences. Sacred and secular interests frequently coincided (Weinreb and Hibbert, 1993, 280).

Recognition of the economic significance of staging fairs led to their rapid proliferation in medieval Europe. Landowners, church authorities and the burghers of towns and cities throughout Europe competed to establish fairs that would maintain, or indeed enhance the comparative importance of a centre. Their rulers also understood the benefits available from granting licences. They added to patronage wielded by the ruler and contributed handsomely to the income of their dominions. In the mid-thirteenth century, for instance, the Counts of Champagne organised a sequence of six fairs, starting with Lagny-sur-Marne in January and ending with the fair of Saint Remy in Troyes in October. Each fair lasted from three to six weeks, a timing that provided a continuous cycle for trading between January and December. In England, King John's cash-hungry regime granted large numbers of royal charters in the early thirteenth century. His successor, Henry III, granted charters at a similarly prodigious rate and actively promoted a fair at Westminster to raise additional funds. In the words of Matthew of Paris (1248, quoted Anon., 2003):

> The king then declared it as his pleasure, and ordered it to be proclaimed by herald throughout the whole city of London, and elsewhere, that he instituted a new fair to be held at Westminster, to continue for a fortnight entire. He also strictly interdicted, under penalty of heavy forfeiture and loss, all fairs which usually lasted for such a length of time in England; for instance, that of Ely and other places, and all traffic usually carried on at London, both in and out of doors, in order that by these means the Westminster fair might be more attended by people, and better supplied with merchandise.

Although difficult to provide exact figures,[14] it is estimated that nearly 5000 English fairs and markets received royal charters between the thirteenth and fifteenth centuries (Cameron, 1998, 19). Some gave legal status to events long established by custom; others were new foundations.

From this complex fusion of secular and spiritual, commerce and culture, came the intricate network of fairs that helped structure the flow of time, consolidate the roles of town and country and regulate the trading life of Europe (Ozouf, 1998, 1). For periods ranging from a few days to several weeks, the speedily assembled tents and booths of the fair transformed otherwise unremarkable and empty spaces. The bustle of trade and the assorted entertainments that fairs attracted added colour and light to the lives of impoverished people and compensated somewhat for the grim realities of living conditions of the time. The famous Bartholomew Fair at West Smithfield (London) provides a case in point. Founded in 1133 as a cloth fair in the grounds of the Church of St Bartholomew the Great, it began as a two-day fair celebrating the Feast of St Bartholomew (24–25 August). Over time it became a pleasure fair that, by the reign of Charles I, lasted for two weeks. Its stalls were a maze of mountebank theatre booths, gambling dens, beer shops, menageries and penny shows.[15] When William Wordsworth toured it seven centuries later, he provided a timeless panorama in *The Prelude* of its spectacle (Wordsworth, 1850, VII, 679–94):

All moveables of wonder, from all parts,
Are here – Albinos, painted Indians, Dwarfs,
The Horse of knowledge and the learned Pig,
The Stone-eater, the man that swallows fire,
Giants, Ventriloquists, the Invisible Girl,
The Bust that speaks and moves its goggling eyes,
The Wax-work, Clock-work, all the marvellous craft
Of modern Merlins, Wild Beasts, Puppet-shows,
All out-o'-the-way, far-fetched, perverted things,
All freaks of nature, all Promethean thoughts
Of man; his dullness, madness and their feats
All jumbled up together to make up
This Parliament of Monsters. Tents and Booths
Meanwhile, as if the whole were one vast mill,
Are vomiting, receiving, on all sides,
Men, Women, three-years' Children, Babes in arms.

The Bartholomew Fair also featured extensive opportunities for debauchery, drunkenness and promiscuity, although it was far from unique in this respect. Indeed its reputation was perhaps surpassed by some of its London counterparts, including the Tottenham, Greenwich, Southwark, Camberwell, Bow, May and St James's Fairs. For example, Greenwich Fair, notorious for the boisterous behaviour of the thousands of Londoners who travelled there by road and river, was described by Charles Dickens in *Sketches by Boz* as a 'sort of spring-rash: a three days' fever which cools the blood for six months afterwards' (Dickens, 1912, 83). Suppression eventually occurred, sometimes through explicit concerns over morality but more often through the gentry's complaints about noise and nuisance. Many fell foul of efforts by Georgian aldermen and magistrates to stamp out 'rude and demoralising amusements' (Marsh, 1999, 278–9). Tottenham Fair was abolished in the mid-eighteenth century, Southwark in 1762, and the May Fair in 1764 (Cunningham, 1977, 164). The Bartholomew Fair became limited to three days instead of a fortnight. In 1855, the Corporation of the City of London finally responded to Victorian sensitivities and closed it after more than 700 years of existence.[16] Its counterpart, Greenwich Fair, quickly followed in 1857.

Fairs complemented a profusion of private, semi-public and civic rituals and ceremonies that operated to draw the population together. Although sometimes romanticised, large-scale festivals required active participation from most segments of the city's residents, whether by adopting special dress, preparing ceremonial foods or decorations, or simply turning out to support their community. In the medieval European city, for example, each guild of artisans or merchants had its place in ceremonial pageantry, which 'had to be coordinated to effect a unity symbolic of the whole city' (Eames and Goode, 1977, 233). On occasions, as with the 'King-of-Fools' festivals, the social order could be inverted, with the aristocracy participating in festivities that 'crowned' a pauper king for a day. Many English towns and urban parishes had annual 'beating the bounds' processions around their boundaries to affirm their civic jurisdiction and identity. Attended by municipal officers, clergymen, local youth and sometimes town companies, they were often sustained by alcoholic beverages and a subsequent feast (Borsay, 1984, 231).

Religious festivals, following the feast days of the Christian calendar, also generated festivities that demanded observance from the community as a whole. The doorway to the church was not a barrier and religious festivals spilled out on to the street (Hanawalt and Reyerson, 1994b, xiii). Church processions and other forms of commemoration took place in European cities at New Year, Twelfth Day (the Feast of the Epiphany), Candlemas (the Feast of the Purification of the Virgin Mary), Lady Day, Shrovetide, Easter, Ascension Day, Whitsunday, Corpus Christi,[17] Trinity, St John the Baptist, Michaelmas, All Saints, Christmas and miscellaneous saints' days. Their practices clearly revealed the early church's policy of assimilating the timing, and sometimes the festive intent, of pagan antecedents. For example, Candlemas celebrations appropriated the old Roman custom of parading through the streets with lighted candles in honour of the goddess Februa and her son Mars. The Shrovetide or Mardi Gras carnival parades that preceded Lent probably originated in the classical Roman Saturnalia, Lupercalia, and Bacchanalia feasts, which similarly gave occasion for raucous processions, street theatre and music.

Over time, particularly in Northern Europe, the rise of puritanical strains of Protestantism proscribed many longstanding festivities associated with the Catholic Church – in Lord Macaulay's ringing words, waging war 'against the lighter vices ... with a zeal little tempered by humanity or common sense' (Macaulay, 1906, 129). At the turn of the seventeenth century, for example, the City of London's Puritanic authorities clamped down on theatrical performances, moved to have theatres pulled down, and equated actors with thieves and vagabonds. Only the Crown's protection prevented acting companies being disbanded. Further prohibitions by the English authorities saw the banning of public amusements ranging from masques, horse racing and wrestling matches to rope dancing, puppet shows and bear-baiting. Severe penalties attended infringement of these rules, with sound whippings favoured for refocusing the mind on healthier pursuits (ibid.).

By contrast, the spectacle of suffering and punishment gave the authorities far less problem. As the seats of courts and assizes, for example, medieval towns and cities provided sites where the public, in large numbers, cheerily witnessed scenes of brutal torture and execution. For lesser crimes, this involved pillorying and ritual humiliations, brandings and whippings. For more serious crimes, the law invented atrocious punishments. At the apex of the system was capital punishment, with its rituals treated as 'spectacular plays with a moral' (Huizinga, 1924, 3). Executions were surrounded by the theatre of preparing the criminal for the scaffold and the rituals associated with torture and execution. Like Roman crucifixions, executions sought to dramatise the power of the state to inflict pain. Killing machines like the rack or wheel delayed death as long as possible so that spectators could see the victims' muscles ripping apart and hear their screams. The main difference with Rome lay in the purpose that the process was designed to serve. These procedures were rooted in Christian notions of penitence and retribution, in that the torture afforded the criminal a last opportunity to confess and avoid eternal damnation.[18] As Merback (1999, 19–20) observed:

> Meditative devotions to the Passion of Christ required a form of contemplative immersion in the grisly details of His affliction from one Station of the Cross to another. Legends of the glorious abjection of Christian martyrs played to the same fascinations. And because it was not uncommon to look upon the suffering convict as a pseudo-martyr, and thus Christ-like, physical pain at the scaffold stood within this very same constellation of beliefs and feelings. It was an ambivalent sign that could point one of two ways. The pain of a guilty malefactor who showed no remorse, refused confession or resisted altogether communicated to spectators the utter alienation of the soul from God; his visible sufferings revealed the criminal as a living *exemplum* of despair, since his last moments on earth were but a foretaste of hell's endless torments. But for the confessed criminal who took refuge in God's grace, admitted guilt (*culpa*), accepted penance, prayed for forgiveness and made a good end ... pain signalled purgation and expiation ... .

Relief of conscience was not the criminal's only possible motive. The act of penitence was sometimes the result of plea-bargaining, where the convict might receive burial after execution or be granted a quick and secret death during the execution process in return for expressing penitence and remorse. The English authorities, from Tudor times onwards, actively encouraged the condemned to address the public with a moralistic story, saying how they had sinned and deserved their punishment. The Dutch allowed the condemned to pray aloud or sing a psalm, but not make a speech (Spierenburg, 1984, 63). In death as in life, there were rewards for fulfilling the obligations of spectacle.

Court Spectacle and Princely Pageants

The realm of court spectacle sat above, and yet was also part of, the annual round of festivals and celebrations. The court comprised not just the palace where the royal household resided but also the community of courtiers and staff that surrounded the ruler. It was at the centre of affairs and revolved around the person who was the fount of all power, honour and patronage (Weir, 2002, 24).[19] Over time, Europe's royal courts developed patterns of observances and ritualistic practices that served to define precedence and etiquette, celebrate key days in the calendar, and keep members of the court entertained and occupied. Entertainment was an adjunct to diplomacy. Elements of lavish spectacle, including hunts, masques, feasts and plays, materially helped the business of arranging marriages, celebrating alliances, and cementing dynastic survival. Some of this activity took place in the interior spaces of the palace, its great hall, courtyards and grounds. Special events might involve purpose-built settings, including mock fortresses and auditoria. Whether or not these events were presented to a wider public varied with the court's attitude towards display[20] and the scale of the event. Displays of princely splendour frequently spilled out beyond the semi-seclusion of the palace and its grounds. Events such as weddings, christenings, knightings, the signing of treaties, royal entries and the reception of foreign dignitaries were accepted as requiring a wider setting and involvement – even if sometimes becoming uncomfortable affairs for the rulers. While it was difficult to exclude the populace from spectacular events of great civic importance, their rulers were normally more concerned to impress rival regimes and consolidate local aristocratic support rather than please their subjects (Hale, 1993, 503). In the event, the best means to achieve their ends was to impose highly structured ceremonial formats that specified the roles that all spectators played, circumscribed their freedom of movement and, to some extent, directed their gaze. As Zorzi (1986, 128) points out: 'Lookers-on and looked-at were equally involved. Everyone was aware of (their) role, and of the social divisions obtaining in the town.'

This was certainly true with regard to the extravagant pageants that were an occasional feature of life in West European cities from the fourteenth century onwards.[21] During Pentecost in 1313, for example, Philip IV of France ('Philip the Fair') organised *La Grant Feste*, an elaborate week of celebrations in Paris to celebrate the knighting of his three sons. Calculated to rival all historical precedents in lavishness, the festival had both private and public elements. The crusading ceremonies, banquets and craft feasts were restricted to select gatherings, with attendance by the nobility and crowned heads of Europe, but there were feasts, extensive musical performances and theatrical entertainments in the streets of Paris that were open to all. These included dramatic representations of biblical scenes and popular tales, sometimes involving the general population as actors and at other times as spectators. Brown and Regalado (1994, 56) read the event as at once establishing the primacy of royal power and forging the bond between king and subjects:

> Organized by the king, the celebration of knighting and crusading vows may be read as an elaborate spectacle whose purposes were political and personal and whose lavishness displayed kingly largesse and royal power. On the other hand, the costly grandeur of street decorations, costumes and entertainments provided by the Parisians staged their independent role within the body politic. The display of urban wealth and splendour dramatised the aspirations and power of the bourgeois while the tableaux they sponsored offered counsel intended to maintain the political and spiritual health of Philip's reign. Spectacle thus joined king and city in a festive experience of *communitas*.

Pageants, however, reached their zenith in the fifteenth and sixteenth centuries when great opulence brought corresponding demonstrations of conspicuous consumption. Expectations about the appropriate extent of courtly splendour and its associated pageantry changed over time, taking on new dimensions from the late fifteenth century onwards when sumptuous displays became an indispensable part of international relations. The Italian city-states and principalities, for example, led Europe in the extent to which they deployed spectacle to boost status and influence. Venice, Florence, Siena, Lucca, and Genoa, the papal court of Rome, duchies such as Ferrara and Urbino, vied with one another to put on the most impressive shows. Their rulers regarded themselves as heirs to the fund of social memory supplied by classical Rome and invested heavily in magnificent architecture and corresponding celebrations. The expense was readily widely accepted as part of the obligation of wealth (Holme, 1988). Humanists such as Leonardo Bruni and Leon Battista Alberti, themselves from distinguished families, cited St Thomas Aquinas and Aristotle in support of costly display. Aquinas had classified magnificence as a virtue; Aristotle in the *Nicomachean Ethics* had identified great expenditure as bringing with it greatness and prestige (Strong, 1973, 72). Magnificence was indeed a prerequisite of worth in the public arena: 'for only the rich were presented with the opportunity of using money virtuously and for the public good' (Cole, 1995, 17). Cities regularly became the tableaux on which poets, architects, painters, sculptors and musicians united to inscribe culturally significant messages through the media of tournaments, ballets, state entries, fireworks or waterworks, alfresco fetes, intermezzi, masques and masquerades. As Roy Strong (1973, 16–17) notes:

> In Venice, in 1574, Tintoretto and Veronese collaborated to decorate an arch designed by Palladio for the entry of Henri III en route from Poland to France; in England, in 1533, Holbein designed a pageant of the Muses for the coronation entry of Anne Boleyn into London; earlier, Leonardo da Vinci had devised both Louis XII's entry into Milan and Francis I's into Pavia; Inigo Jones was to expend forty years of his life in supervising the court entertainments of the Stuart kings; and the entry of the Archduke Ferdinand into Antwerp in 1635 was made under the artistic direction of Peter Paul Rubens. Writers involved range from Ben Jonson and Thomas Carew to Pierre Ronsard and Jean Dorat; and musicians from Orlando di Lasso to Claudin Le Jeune, and from John Dowland to Claudio Monteverdi. Even the philosopher Descartes devised a ballet for his mistress, Christina, Queen of Sweden.

The purpose of elaborate and expensive spectacle transcended interstate prestige, since it also touched on the fundamental relations between rulers and their citizens. Such spectacles were essential vehicles in a ritualistic and symbolic society, surrounding rulers with the mystical aura of authority that helped legitimise their power over their subjects (Jarvis, 1994, 182).

The Visit to Edinburgh of George IV (1822)

Such events, however, were not only a feature of the Middle Ages, since monarchies had recourse to pageantry well into the modern era. In 1822, for instance, the British authorities sought by means of George IV's carefully presented visit to Edinburgh to achieve key national objectives.[22] The position of the monarch in Scotland had been problematic since the Union of the Crowns of England and Scotland in 1603. The Scottish King James VI left for England where he was crowned James I, after which the monarch became increasingly an absentee. George IV's visit in 1822 was the first time a reigning monarch had come to Scotland since 1633[23] and was intended to tackle a diverse set of political goals.[24]

The ensuing visit turned into a two-week pageant held between 15–29 August 1822 in Scotland's capital Edinburgh (see Table 2.1). George sailed from Greenwich (London) to Leith (Edinburgh's port) on the royal yacht, the *Royal George*, leaving on 10 August and arriving four days later with an imposing squadron of ten boats. After delaying embarkation until noon on the next day due to inclement weather, the King arrived in a flotilla of barges at Leith Quay to commence a slow triumphal entry into Edinburgh. George IV then participated in a

Table 2.1 Key events in George IV's visit to Edinburgh

Monday 12 August	Ceremonial removal of regalia from Edinburgh Castle to the Palace of Holyroodhouse.
Wednesday 14 August	Arrival of royal squadron at Leith; Sir Walter Scott welcomes King.
Thursday 15 August	King's landing at Leith; triumphal entry procession into Edinburgh; presentation of keys of city; ceremony of the regalia.
Saturday 17 August	Levée at Holyroodhouse at which highland dress is worn.
Thursday 22 August	Procession back to castle to redeposit the regalia.
Friday 23 August	Review of volunteer cavalry and yeomanry at Portobello Sands.
Saturday 24 August	Redepositing of regalia in crown room at castle; banquet with city dignitaries.
Sunday 25 August	Commemorative service, St Giles's Cathedral.
Monday 26 August	Grand ball.
Tuesday 27 August	Performance of *Rob Roy* at Theatre Royal.
Thursday 29 August	Knighthood ceremonies at Hopetoun House; George IV's departure from Port Edgar.

fortnight's activities that included the Scottish regalia (the crown and ceremonial jewels), a levée at Holyroodhouse,[25] a military spectacle at Portobello Sands, a religious service at St Giles's Cathedral, a grand ball, a theatrical production and a knighting ceremony (Finley, 1981, 65).

Sir Walter Scott, the novelist and historian, conceived these events. Scott was assigned the task of creating regal spectacle in a country that effectively had had no royal presence for almost two centuries (Burnett and Tabraham, 1993). He had unrivalled credentials to do so. His writings and their underlying narratives had already shaped how Scotland, the Scots and their history were presented to the world. His standing in Edinburgh society allowed him to gain speedy cooperation from all the key interest groups in the city. Moreover, his researches and campaigning had been instrumental in relocating the regalia in 1818.[26] He was now effectively given the chance to bring his novels to life; to take his knowledge of the 'lost' past and revive whichever parts of it he wished as parts of a unified programme in which the king was an active participant. It was an opportunity that Scott fully grasped.

Scott saw the royal visit as a chance to restore Scottish pride and identity, breathe life into old customs and finally heal the rift between Jacobites and Hanoverians by presenting George as both the heir of the Stuarts[27] and the recipient of their lingering charisma. Creating the appropriate setting for the political theatre of pageantry was all-important. The city's authorities rapidly overhauled Edinburgh's urban fabric. Workers repaired the streets, painted shop fronts, built triumphal arches, constructed galleries and stands, and levelled ground where necessary as, for example, outside the county rooms so that the judges and others could view the royal procession. The city would be illuminated on the evening of the king's arrival, with lights placed in every window facing a street. Gas lighting was provided in the area around Holyroodhouse and an immense bonfire was lit on Arthur's Seat (a prominent local landmark). The interiors of key public buildings were transformed, the population appropriately dressed, and their actions stage-managed. To meet these objectives, Scott employed friends to advise on various aspects of the project, notably William Murray, the actor-manager of the Theatre Royal, who advised upon pageantry and interior design, the actress Harriet Siddons who advised on style and fashion, and Colonel David Stewart of Garth who organised the Highland element.[28] Leading artists of the day, including Turner and David Wilkie, were given special viewpoints so that they could record the scene.

Scott's unerring instinct for spectacle underscored the invention of a set of ceremonies surrounding the regalia. Three days before the visit formally started, an escort of Highland troops conveyed them in procession from the castle to the Palace of Holyroodhouse, where they remained for the duration of the king's stay. Scott visited the king when he arrived on the royal yacht and presented him with a silver and bejewelled St Andrew's cross ascribed with a Gaelic motto that translated as 'Long life to the King of Scotland'. Welcoming banners and heraldic emblems lined the three-mile route to the Palace of Holyroodhouse, which passed through ceremonial arches at St Bernard Street, Constitution Street and Union Place. Estimates placed the crowds at 300 000 people – roughly equivalent to one-seventh of the entire population of Scotland. James Simpson, an onlooker, reported on the sight of the parade 'in all its gorgeous length of chariots and steeds, plumed heads and shining mantles, tabards and bannered trumpets, rich liveries, romantic tartan, military scarlet and naval blue'. He continued:

[The King's] countless subjects were marshalled in stedfast [*sic*] and deep alignment on both sides of his route, compacted in gallery, balcony, and scaffold, without end, stationed in every window, perched upon every house top, and more ambitious yet, crowded upon every height from which a view could be caught of this most ambitious of spectacles. The whole way for three miles to the shore from the palace, was one mass of hope and joy, all engrossed with one object, and responding on one pulsation.[29]

The organisers of the grand procession relentlessly hammered home the new identity sought for the monarchy. Banners along the route welcomed the king to the land of 'his ancestors'. The tollhouse was decorated with a crown and legend 'Descendent of the immortal Bruce, thrice welcome' (Finley, 1981, 9).[30] On arrival at Holyroodhouse, George IV formally received the major emblems of state – the crown, sceptre and sword – as symbols of his rule over the nation. Just over a week later, another grand procession returned the regalia to the castle.

Celebrating Revolution

Political revolutions habitually create circumstances by which new regimes and their strategists look afresh at things that previously were taken for granted. For the leaders of the French Revolution of 1789, all aspects of life were legitimate targets for scrutiny to see if they harboured counter-revolutionary purpose or intent. As such, the traditional diet of festivals celebrated by the ancien régime was an obvious early subject for attention and reform. Paris had no less than 32 feast-days in 1789 commemorating royal celebrations, religious feast-days and popular holidays – each effectively representing the instruments of social memory. Each festival affirmed the existing social stratification and 'with exemplary rigidity, articulated the hierarchy of rank between corporate persons and bodies' (Ozouf, 1988, 3). To the serious revolutionary mind, too, these ancient festivals had lost their freshness, rationale, and their ability to convey moral or spiritual values. For such people, in this enlightened age:

The popular festival meant the senseless din of coal shovels and pans; crowds obstructing the streets and public squares; barbarous 'sports' like shooting birds or tearing a goose limb from limb; the veiled threat of masks; the disgusting spectacle of people fighting over loaves of bread or sausages. In short, popular excitement disconcerted, or worse 'offended', reason. (ibid.)

As with many earlier regimes, abolition was not considered a realistic answer to the problem. Although prone to asceticism, most revolutionary thinkers recognised the value of festivals as a safety valve and as an intrinsic part of the ties that bound the community together. If pre-revolutionary festivals were proscribed, new festivals were needed. An early innovation was the Festival of the Federation on 14 July 1790, celebrating the storming of the Bastille the previous year. The festival saw 300 priests officiate at the Altar of the Nation, built in the Champs de Mars on the banks of the Seine in Paris. Wearing tricoloured girdles over their vestments, the priests prayed for God's blessing on the Revolution. Although apparently mild compared with subsequent developments, some commentators argue that the idea of honouring France in this way helped create a cult of faith in the motherland (Anon., 2002a; Furet, 1981).

The secularisation drive brought new festivals. The Festival of Reason saw the Church of Notre Dame de Paris become a Temple of Reason on 10 November 1793. The Festival of the Supreme Being, intended as a full-blown deistic alternative to Christian feasts, was held in the Champs de Mars on 8 June 1794. Other additions to the calendar included the Festivals of Labour, Republican Reunion (Feast of Unity and Indivisibility), Youth, Victories, Old Age, the Sovereignty of the People, Spouses, and Liberty (Ozouf, 1988, 13). The new schedule of festivals covered most eventualities. Some recycled the practices of older festivals with a new veneer but most, and certainly the larger state occasions, consciously looked beyond the recent past to reconsider the lessons of a previous heroic age, namely, classical Greece and Rome. The organisers of revolutionary festivals aimed to combine the best of the ancient world with celebration of the new order in festivals that were at once nostalgic and forward-looking. The most notable iconographer and stage manager of these events was the painter Jacques-Louis David.

As an ardent critic of the ancien régime's Royal Academy of Painting and Sculpture and supporter of the new civic virtues of stoical self-sacrifice, devotion to duty, honesty, and austerity, David had an inherent sympathy with the Republicans. They, in turn, put his artistic skills to good use in their pageantry. David, for instance, arranged the fete that accompanied the reinterment of Voltaire's body in Paris on 11 July 1791.[31] This was the first of a series of pageants that saw the bodies of heroes of the Revolution removed from their previous resting places and reinterred in the Pantheon, a church newly rededicated as a shrine in their honour.[32] Voltaire was the first beneficiary.[33] David choreographed the final part of his remains' journey from the Abbey of Scellières, one hundred miles (160 kilometres) south-east of Paris, in a manner designed to 'emulate the pomp [and] grandeur of the Greek apotheoses and the Roman consecrations' (quoted in Dowd, 1948, 48). The estimated 100 000 spectators lining the route saw a lavish procession headed by a cavalry troop, selected delegations from schools and clubs, workers who had participated in the demolition of the Bastille, actors carrying a golden statue of Voltaire and banners inscribed with the names of his major works, a golden case containing those works in 92 volumes and a full orchestra. The sarcophagus was pulled on a carriage by twelve white horses. The casket was decorated with theatre masks and the statement: 'Poet, philosopher, historian, he made a great step forward in the human spirit. He prepared us to become free' (Anon., 2002b). Groups drawn from the National Assembly, the judiciary and the municipality of Paris completed the procession.

The display was not without its critics, particularly over the modes of observance and aesthetics that David favoured,[34] but David's growing experience of handling crowds and creating visual effects made him the regime's trusted pageant-master. This role culminated in his work for the Festival of the Supreme Being (8 June 1794). The festival had a decidedly pastoral theme. It began with a speech by Robespierre outside the Tuileries palace, after which he set fire to an effigy of Atheism to reveal a statue of Wisdom. There then followed a vast procession along the decorated streets, led by a chariot drawn by teams of oxen that carried sheaves of corn, agricultural implements and a statue representing natural abundance. An artificial mountain awaited them in the Champ de Mars. Made from plaster and cardboard, the structure was strong enough to allow the deputies of the convention to sit at the summit for speech-making and other ceremonies (Dart, 1999, 112). The mountain was carefully positioned next to a tall tree that met the practical requirement for a canopy of shade over the gathering as well as symbolising the Tree of Liberty. After speeches, the festival ended with hymns and choral songs in praise of the Supreme Being.

In some respects, the French Revolutionary festivals bore similarities to the princely pageants staged by the Italian city-states. Decorations and temporary structures transformed the buildings and spaces of the city, thereby constructing transitory topographies (Jarvis, 1994). The main difference lay in the role of the people, since in David's view, the Revolution's national festivals were 'instituted for the people; it is fitting that they participate in these with a common accord and that they play the principal role there' (quoted in Jarvis, 1994, 183). This creates an immediate difference, which emerges:

> when comparing engravings of Renaissance and French Revolutionary public celebrations; not only are they peopled, but the boundaries of audience and celebrants are not always immediately apparent. The Revolutionary festivals were also carefully choreographed propaganda events on an urban scale, but not only were they educational – they also had to be *re*-educational,

to instil, inspire (and often revise) a rapidly changing revolutionary agenda, and redirect attention away from old religious and royalist associations (ibid., 183–4).

Conclusion

The Revolutionary festivals immediately attracted international attention through the reports, sympathetic and otherwise, of foreign observers (for example, Williams, 1929, 138–44). They, like the French people, recognised that what was occurring had implications far beyond France's borders. In the fullness of time, too, the prototype supplied by the Revolutionary festivals proved persuasive for other revolutionary regimes from left and right of the political spectrum, all keen to appropriate the mixture of dramatic spectacle, pedagogy and re-education as their own. During the interwar period, for example, the state parades and party rallies held in Mussolini's Italy, the Soviet Union and Third Reich made more than a passing nod to the experience of Revolutionary France (Frampton, 1978; Tolstoy et al., 1990; Atkinson and Cosgrove, 1998; Arvidsson, 2000).

Yet if David's pageants captured the imagination for the extent that they harnessed spectacle to the service of ideology, another, arguably more significant, development was also apparent. In 1798 the French staged the first officially sponsored national industrial exhibition in Paris (see Chapter 3). Although held in the last months of the First Republic, it was an event that made connection to the past and the future. On the one hand, it linked back to the ancien régime through the identity of its organisers and the nature of their endeavours. At the same time, it embraced the spirit of the new economic and political order then emerging in the western world. While conflict in the European arena would slow matters, the rise of industrialisation, the growing interconnection of the global economy and the scramble for empire in the nineteenth century seemingly demanded new forms of festivity and commemoration. The hour of the international exposition was at hand.

Notes

1   The grave of Pelops is said to be at Olympia. Pelops, a legendary king of the city of Mycenae, gave his name to the Peloponnese, the peninsula south of the isthmus of Corinth that makes up the southern half of Greece. The oracle to Zeus advised the Greeks on military matters and even

accompanied forces on the battlefield. It also advised groups of Greek colonists moving westwards into Sicily. Success in these endeavours led to Olympia growing rich from votive offerings and helped to reinforce the four-yearly Olympic festival that brought the former colonists back to Zeus's sanctuary.

2   Olympia became the venue for an arbitration court designed to nurture and preserve the pan-Hellenic cooperation and harmony that had been so important in the victories over Persia (De Sainte Croix, 1972). At this time, too, work commenced on a second and much larger temple that contained the great statue of Zeus by Pheidias – fixed in European memory as one of the seven wonders of the ancient world.

3   The precise timing varying according to the exact date of the second full moon after the summer solstice (Milns, 2000).

4   Elaborate stone seats were later added to some parts of the stadium (Quennell and Quennell, 1957, 157). The stadium itself was so called because its length was one stadion, a measurement of length equivalent to 606 feet (185 metres).

5   The rewards for success in competition were considerable. For the athlete, there was the religious significance of victory, with the olive wreath and the celebrations and ritual at the games themselves. There was also considerable material gain, augmented by honours and wealth from the athletes' home cities, including gifts in kind, trading concessions and relief from taxation. Successful athletes were idolised and gained immortality by having victory odes dedicated to them by poets like Pindar (these survive until the present day).

6   Women were not participants in these sporting festivals. They were not part of the athletic culture that had been developing since the seventh century BC or the 'public sphere' of oratory and politics that surrounded the festivals. They were not even allowed on to the festival site during the games. However, there was a separate festival for women at Olympia in honour of Hera (the sister and wife of Zeus). This even included a foot race for unmarried girls, but women were expected to concern themselves with the domestic sphere (Barney, 1996, xxxvi).

7   The last known victor was the Armenian boxer Barasdates in 393 AD.

8   The status of *isotheos*, or of being like a god, lay at the heart of the kingship theology (see Kuttner, 1999, 111).

9   There is no suggestion in this of a seamless transfer of ideas and practices between Greece and Rome. Indeed there could often be a deep cultural divide between the two (for example, see Vickers, 1989, 122).

10   Pompey's work again points to the close link between theatre and religion, as with the combined theatre and temple complex that he commissioned on the Campus Martius in Rome. This was dedicated in 55 BC to Venus Victoria (Beard et al., 1998, 122).

11   These were 'Semites', who had a rectangular shield and short sword, 'Thracians', armed with a curved sword (*sica*) and scaled armour, and *retiarii* or net-fighters who were armed with tridents.

12 In passing, it is worth noting that violence in the ring could be matched by violence outside. For example, the riot that broke out at a gladiatorial show in Pompeii in 59 BC between local residents and visitors from nearby Nuceria led to the proscription of such gatherings for ten years (Moeller, 1970, 84–95).

13 They were sometimes more frequent. Surveying the history of English fairs, for example, Cameron (1998, 18–19) noted that:

> Fairs did not always come singly, as once-a-year affairs. At times there was an embarrassing plurality. Four was remarkably common, but Tamworth had five; Newcastle under Lyme had six a year 'for the sale of horses, cattle and woollen cloths'; Leek, in the same region, had seven 'chiefly for cattle and pedlars' goods' and neighbouring Longnor, like Berkshire's Newbury, claimed the right to stage eight. Northern Northallerton's, on the other hand, were too numerous to count – and came close at times to being continuous.

14 Many functioned long before the granting of royal charters or other enabling proclamations regularised their existence (Cameron, 1998, 14).

15 The fair illustrated that the gulf between the 'popular culture' of Smithfield and Southwark and the 'elite culture' of Covent Garden and the Haymarket was not very great. The fairground booths drew their actors from the royal theatres and the theatre managers constantly searched for new ways to please the crowd (Inwood, 1998, 203).

16 The City of London was latterly the fair's landlord. The fairground was redeveloped after the fair's suppression as Smithfield Market in 1856. A cattle fair had been held alongside the cloth fair since 1150.

17 The feast of Corpus Christi only originated in the mid-thirteenth century, but was generally accepted by the mid-fourteenth century and became the Roman Catholic Church's principal feast day in the fifteenth century.

18 See Sennett, 1994, 298. This pattern of spectatorship lasted until the eighteenth or even nineteenth century, when 'modern rituals of execution' worked in favour of 'the disappearance of the spectacle and the elimination of pain' (Foucault, 1973, 10–11). The last execution at Tyburn in London, for example, was 1783.

19 Contemporary opinions about the court were decidedly mixed. The court, as defined by Cesare Ripa in 1603, was 'a company of well-bred men in the service of a distinguished superior' although, to his contemporary Tommaso Garzoni da Bagnacavallo, it was also 'the haunt of wicked foxes and the most abject hangers-on, schools of corruption and dens of iniquity' (quoted in Bertelli, 1986, 8).

20 The Spanish and English courts, for example, were profoundly different in the way that they gave access to visitors and others who were not part of the courtly circle to witness the splendours of majesty (for example, see Adamson, 1999).

21 Laconic entries in medieval accounts and chronicles suggest that imposing urban spectacles occurred at an earlier date (Hanawalt and Reyerson, 1994b, ix–x).

22 This section draws on a fuller account in Gold and Gold, 1995, 71–4.

23 Charles I had visited Scotland in 1633 for a coronation ceremony. Charles II was crowned at Scone in 1651, shortly before his defeat at Worcester and exile in France.

24 For the king, there were advantages in travelling north to Scotland given that, after his coronation in 1821, George IV already had visited his dominions in Hanover and Ireland to consolidate his position there. The Monarchy, too, needed to improve its poor standing in the light of the royal divorce and the recent death of Queen Caroline. The Establishment wished to defeat the radicals, countering their protests against worsening economic conditions with an orchestrated upswell of loyalty to the government in the person of the monarch. Lords Castlereagh and Liverpool wanted a royal engagement that would preclude the king from attending the Congress of Nations at Vienna. Landowners wanted to enhance their position since they were beginning to attract criticism over their land policies. A possible visit from the king supplied them with an opportunity to present themselves in a paternal role as clan chiefs owing their allegiance to a Hanoverian chief of chiefs. The city of Edinburgh wished to reassert its credentials as a royal capital, a status severed by default by the union of the Crowns but by no means irretrievably lost.

25 A levée is an assembly held by the sovereign to which only men are invited. A 'drawing room', an equivalent assembly for women, was held at Holyroodhouse on Tuesday 20 August.

26 The regalia, otherwise known as the 'Honours of Scotland', were only rediscovered in a sealed room of Edinburgh Castle in 1818, where they had resided since the Treaty of Union in 1707.

27 The death of Prince Charles Edward Stuart in 1788, followed by that of his brother Henry in 1807, meant that there were no longer any legitimate heirs of James II.

28 Stewart had founded the Celtic Society of Edinburgh in 1820 to promote use of Highland dress and had produced a monograph (Stewart, 1822) claiming that tartan displayed 'the distinctive patterns of the different clans, tribes, families and districts'.

29 Simpson, 1822, 46–7, quoted in Finley, 1981, 9.

30 Scott (1822) consolidated the liberties taken in interpreting genealogy in a shilling pamphlet, originally published anonymously under the rubric of coming from 'an old citizen'. This gave information about the visit, advice to both sexes on what to wear and about etiquette and behaviour generally. It is readily apparent from this pamphlet that Scott wished to put on a dignified and orderly show, historically correct in detail but that '… this is not an ordinary show – it is not all on one side. It is not enough that we should see the King; but the King must also see us'.

31 Understandably, one focuses on the large set-piece events in the French capital, but they were part of a much wider national pattern of observances. As Mona Ozouf (1988, 13) remarked: 'We tend to speak of *the* Festival of the Federation, *the* Festival of the Supreme Being, forgetting that, duplicating and echoing the celebrations in Paris, there were thousands of festivals of the Federation, thousands of festivals of the Supreme Being.'

32   Mirabeau, Voltaire, Marat and Rousseau were the principal figures to receive this treatment.

33   When Voltaire died in May 1778, the authorities forbade either obituaries in Parisian newspapers or the customary service for the death of a member of the French Academy. Fearing that he would not be allowed a proper burial, Voltaire's friends secretly took his body to the Abbey of Scellières, one hundred miles from Paris, where he was quickly given an honourable burial with full Christian rights. The order banning that procedure only arrived after the funerary rites were completed.

34   These tensions were shown in the rival festivals of Châteauvieux and Simonneau that were instituted in 1791 by different political factions within the state. The former was a festival of liberty intended to honour the Swiss of Châteauvieux who mutinied in August 1790; the latter, a festival of the law to honour a mayor who died upholding the law during a food riot. The polarity between the underlying sentiments – one effectively honouring rioters, the other venerating the victim of a riot – spilled over into the aesthetics brought to the pageantry. David, the organiser of Châteauvieux, favoured realism and bare ornamentation based on classical prototypes. Quatremère de Quincy, the organiser of the Simonneau festival, favoured lavish, escapist decoration and use of allegory (Ozouf, 1988, 66–79). In the event, however, the approach favoured by David prevailed (see Dowd, 1948; Sennett, 1994).

CHAPTER THREE

The Great Exhibition, London 1851

'Talking of Exhibitions, World's Fairs, and what not', said the old gentleman, 'I would not go round the corner to see a dozen of them nowadays. The only exhibition that ever made, or ever will make, any impression upon my imagination was the first of the series, the parent of them all, and now a thing of old times – the Great Exhibition of 1851, in Hyde Park, London. None of the younger generation can realise the sense of novelty it produced in us who were then in our prime ...'

Thomas Hardy (1894, 165)

If in retrospect the Great Exhibition aroused fond memories, at the time it evoked extravagant certainties. For many, it awakened a passionate national pride sufficient either to obliterate temporarily the host of social and political problems that had surfaced in the 1840s or, more positively, to pronounce them solved (Billinge, 1993, 103). Those holding such views construed the Great Exhibition as, among other things, a triumph for the British realm, the monarchy (through the involvement of Prince Albert), Protestantism, national genius and democracy. The nation, the argument ran, had taken upon itself the task of rewarding publicly 'the meritorious sons of each individual nation' for their industrious creativity (Berlyn, 1851, 8–9). This reflected the country's standing in the world. Britain 'stood erect in hale composure' while all around had just experienced a 'frightful series of convulsions' (Anon., 1851). There might well be worries about the visitor seeing the capital's seamier side (Cumming, 1851), but Britain alone could offer itself on display as a secure and tranquil gathering place for the world's progressive industrialism. The transparency of the exhibition pavilion, the so-called 'Crystal Palace', seemed a metaphor for the obstructionless free trade that would guarantee this new era of peace (Buzard, 1999, 438).

The sentiments surrounding these 'great new rituals of self-congratulation' (Hobsbawm, 1995, 32) quickly filtered through to the historiography of the Great Exhibition. Understandably those closely involved in the exhibition lionised their own achievements. Sir Henry

Cole, probably the moving spirit behind the Great Exhibition, set the tone: 'The history of the world, I venture to say, records no event comparable in its promotion of human industry, with that of the Great Exhibition of the Works of Industry of all Nations of 1851' (quoted in Gibbs-Smith, 1981, 7). Thomas Hardy referred to it as 'a precipice in time' (quoted in Fay, 1951, 26). Modern historians developed similar themes, regarding it as a compelling focus for a host of narratives united simply by seeming 'to have occurred for the first time in the same place' (Purbrick, 2001, 1). Occurring in both a census year and at virtually the mid-point of the nineteenth century, the Great Exhibition has provided a point of departure for accounts of the history of architecture, art, design, politics, tourism, consumption, curatorship, education, and social trends. Its contents were scrutinised to uncover nineteenth-century precedents for twentieth-century phenomena, or to provide insight into the ordering and disordering of Victorian society at a time of profound change, or to symbolise the modernisation of Britain, the depth of its industrial resources and ingenuity, and the strength of its imperial power. As far as historians are concerned, it was an event that included something for almost everyone (Auerbach, 1999, 2–4).

This chapter starts our analysis of international expositions with the staging of the 1851 Great Exhibition, its cultural legacy and its lasting significance for London. Proceeding cautiously against the prevailing historiographic background that views the Great Exhibition as a watershed, we argue that its creators drew much of their inspiration from attaching the exhibition to pre-existing ideas and practice. We therefore begin by briefly considering the climate of ideas prevailing at the time in which celebrations of the new industrial economy emerged. Early sections of this chapter emphasise a general enthusiasm for science and technology as spectacle in London well before 1850 and the important lessons learned from the French national exhibitions. Yet there is also no doubt that the Great Exhibition supplied the first truly international frame for attracting exhibitors, participants and tourists to a specific host city for a lengthy period of time and initiated the typical production cycle for these events. We then examine the organisation of the Great Exhibition, emphasising the varying response to the proposed exhibition in Hyde Park from London's disparate municipal authorities and from different sections of the city's society. The closing section points to the direct and indirect legacy of the Great Exhibition for London, including the removal and reconstruction of the exhibition structure to Sydenham Hill and the use of the surplus funds to create cultural infrastructure in South Kensington.

Science as Display

London's traditional diet of leisure pastimes changed rapidly during the eighteenth and early nineteenth centuries. The rising law-and-order lobby cut a swathe through popular entertainments, such as cock fighting, bear- and bull-baiting. Local watch committees and like-minded civic dignitaries charged playhouses with lewdness and immorality. New legislation in 1822 gave power to abolish unchartered fairs and limit the hours of chartered ones. Pleasure gardens, however, proliferated. Some, like Ranelagh and Vauxhall, charged substantial entry fees and observed dress codes, which kept out potential artisan users. Others, like the Pantheon in Spa Fields, New Wells in Clerkenwell and Marylebone Gardens attracted working-class clienteles (Schwartz, 2000, 657). Assembly rooms, picture galleries and libraries catered for those of the middle and upper classes that wished to be refined (Brewer, 1997, 59).

In tune with Enlightenment preoccupations, the city's showmen freely dispensed knowledge, suitably packaged as organised spectacle, to anyone who could afford the entry price. Zoos and menageries presented glimpses of the world's fauna. The Royal Menagerie in the Tower of London, that had housed the Royal Collection of Wild Beasts since 1235, met competition from Edward Cross's Exeter Change Royal Menagerie, which opened near Charing Cross in 1773 (Hahn, 2003). As approaches associated with the new science of natural history gained popularity, both collections of curiosities were superseded by the Zoological Society of London's zoo in Regent's Park, which opened in 1828.[1] Ethnographic shows turned to their human equivalent, with North American Indians, Eskimos, Lapps, Polynesians, Zulus and Kalahari Bushmen as fashionable attractions (Malcolmson, 1973). Exhibitions of models and waxworks recreated the sights of Egypt, the Holy Land, Southern Africa, South America and other far distant places. Lest this be considered too fragmentary, the world itself was rendered in miniature form in 1851. Seeking to pick up trade from the hoards of visitors swelling London to see the Great Exhibition, James Wyld MP commissioned the building of a gigantic scale model of the world in Leicester Square. Designed at a scale of ten miles to the inch, the globe's interior contained four storeys of galleries showing the world's geographical features.[2]

The establishment of art galleries and museums gave a further boost to the codification and display of scientific knowledge.[3] Initially, their practices were all-inclusive, as befitted an age characterised by the compilation of encyclopaedias. Art galleries, like the National Gallery (founded 1824) and its grand house predecessors, began collecting

omnivorously, essentially hanging their paintings according to decorative principles (Prior, 2002). Museums developed in much the same way. John Tradescant's Ark in Lambeth included natural history objects, antiquities and ethnography. The Hunterian Museum, on Leicester Square, offered exhibits ranging from anatomical specimens and electromechanical novelties to Old Master paintings. Intended primarily for teaching purposes, it opened for two months a year to 'noblemen and gentlemen' (Altick, 1978, 28). The Leverian museum, a collection of natural history exhibits displayed nearby in Leicester Square's Holophusikon, operated a similarly unforthcoming admission policy through its high entry costs.

The longer-lived British Museum at Montagu House in Bloomsbury, founded in 1753, embraced similar collecting and access policies. Initially comprising a cabinet of curios designed to show 'the plenitude of the world represented in the microcosm of a single room or space' (Crane, 2000, 67), the museum granted admittance in groups of no more than five. Unenthusiastic or diffident under-librarians or assistants escorted visitors around the collections in a specified order (Wilson, 2002, 54). They also obliged visitors to submit their credentials for inspection prior to admission, which was granted only if found to be 'not exceptionable' (Bennett, 1996, 92; also Duncan, 1995). Their caution was not completely unfounded. Riots in 1765 culminated in the siege of the house belonging to the Duke of Bedford, the museum's next-door neighbour in Bloomsbury Square. The anti-Catholic Gordon Riots in 1780 saw troops placed in the museum's garden and part of the building. While there was no sense that the museum itself was a target, the possibility of collateral damage from riots remained (Wilson, 2002, 49–50). Access policies gradually relaxed only as fear of the mob subsided. The first opening during a public holiday, on Easter Monday 1837, passed off without a single breach of the peace. Thus fortified by evidence that the general public could control their passions when confronted by antiquities or natural history, the museum's trustees and curators hesitantly overcame their exclusionary instincts and accepted the desirability of more liberal admission policies and longer opening hours.

If museum galleries offered static displays, other exhibitors started to display science in action. During the late eighteenth century Adam Walker, a peripatetic lecturer on astronomy, gave lectures at London venues accompanied by elaborate orrery devices (Altick, 1978, 81). From 1801 through to the 1880s, inventor-educators like Davy, Faraday and Tindall provided audiences at the Royal Institution with displays of popular science (Marsh, 1999, 285), often presenting the spirit of an industrial and scientific age as entertainments akin to conjurers' tricks.

The Adelaide Gallery, founded in 1832, offered working machines, models and visual dramatisations of elementary scientific principles, which arguably made it 'the first direct English progenitor of the modern science and technology museum' (Altick, 1978, 379). The Regent's Street Polytechnic Institution, established in 1838, offered lay audiences illustrated lectures on contemporary scientific advances (Marsh, 1999, 285). Faced by the new competitor, the Adelaide Gallery transformed itself from museum to amusement hall, giving patrons the chance to submerge in a diving bell, witness a water-powered machine gun, and see practical demonstrations of photography. Other entrepreneurs attracted enthusiastic paying audiences to exhibitions of mechanical ingenuity involving steam-powered gadgetry, elaborate automata, or effects created by inflammable gas or electricity. Pavement exhibitors placed telescopes and mechanical figures alongside the old staples of peepshows, puppetry and trained animals (Marsh, 1999, 278). Specially constructed theatres offered hydraulic shows, imaginatively recreating Noah's flood as well as natural disasters of recent memory. Others employed pyrotechnics to simulate historic volcanic eruptions.

Shows exploiting the latest optical technologies[4] presented images of famous leaders and great battles that far surpassed the illusions available from conventional painting (cf. Samuels, 2002, 82). Burford's Panorama in Leicester Square, a circular building with a 90-foot diameter, showed a panorama of London from the vantage point of Albion's Mills on the south bank of the Thames. Built in 1794, it would retain its position as *the* show to see in London until rivals appeared in the 1820s. In 1824, for example, the 112-foot-high Colosseum near Regent's Park opened, showing panoramic views as if from the top of St Paul's Cathedral. The Colosseum's neighbour, the Cyclorama, used interacting revolving cylinders to create the illusion of moving images. In 1848, it offered shows 'where four times a day customers could experience the sensational sights and sounds of the Lisbon earthquake of 1755' (Marsh, 1999, 289).

By an 'immutable law of London showmanship' (Altick, 1978, 202), these visual novelties quickly turned up at the fairs still remaining in business. Between 1807–23, Richardson, the Bartholomew Fair's veteran theatrical impresario, added sets of 'grand panorama views' of the world's cities and natural splendours to the abridged melodramas and variety acts that comprised his normal show. The 1831 Bartholomew Fair featured a 'moving panorama', showing a voyage from Brighton to the Mediterranean and ending with the Battle of Navarino. In 1836, a stall offered animated pictures of battle scenes and scenic views from around Europe.

Exhibiting Industry

Taken together, these developments in public entertainments underlined a sense of the world being brought to London and of Britain as a hub of the global economy. Exhibitions that brought manufactured products and industrial technology before the public's gaze as educational spectacle were a natural corollary of these developments. The idea of the industrial exhibition itself was not new. There had been exhibitions of machinery in Paris (1683), Weltrus (1754), Geneva (1789) and in Prague (1791). Around Europe, associations were formed to promote the understanding and appreciation of the industrial arts (Davis, 1999, 3). The Society for the Encouragement of Arts, Manufactures and Commerce, normally foreshortened to the Society of Arts, was founded in London in 1754, quickly followed by the Societé d'Encouragement de l'Industrie National in Paris (1764), the Gesellschaft zur Beförderung der Künste und nützlichen Gewerbe in Hamburg (1764), and the k.k. patriotisch-ökonomische Gesellschaft in Prague (1767).

All favoured exhibition activities. The Society of Arts, initially a pan-artistic body, first held an art exhibition in 1760 in its own premises, followed by an industrial exhibition in 1761 in a rented warehouse.[5] The former, devoted to living British artists, had curiously lasting consequences, not least for the Great Exhibition. The society continued its policy of enhancing the pedagogic value of exhibitions by making entry free and linking profits to the sale of catalogues. This imparted an educational spin to proceedings, but created a split in the British artistic community. As Davis (1999, 4) explains:

> this emphasis on the educational and informative conflicted with the immediate interests of the artists involved in the project, who sought their own advancement and that of their profession. The insistence by some that there should be an increase in the price of the catalogue and that its purchase should be a condition of entrance forced a split. Those who parted company with the Society of Arts included William Chambers, whose influence with King George III would lead to the alternative Royal Academy exhibitions begun in 1769. Importantly, however, those who remained in the Society formed a rump of artists in an organisation overwhelmingly committed to production techniques rather than fine arts. This would be crucial in 1851.

The arrival of state-sponsored national industrial exhibitions gave the endeavour official sanction. The first was the Exposition Publique des Produits de l'Industrie Française, staged in Paris in September 1798.[6] The exhibition drew together 110 participants, chiefly from the Paris region. It was housed in buildings comprising a square arcade, of some sixty arches, around a central temporary pavilion called the 'Temple of

Industry'. Backed by the Ministry of the Interior and coinciding with celebrations of the anniversary of the Republic's foundation, the three-day exhibition was in every way a prestige event. Military bands entertained its visitors and there were also athletic competitions, parades, balls and nocturnal illuminations. The exhibition site, the Champs de Mars, was the same location as that selected for key revolutionary festivals and, more recently, was the chosen venue for Bonaparte's triumphant return from his Italian campaign. The uncompromising opening speech by the Minister François de Neufchâteau (quoted in Greenhalgh, 1988, 5), suggested that industrial progress could help France's progress in the battle for European supremacy:

> The French have surprised Europe with the rapidity of their military exploits, and must advance with the same ardour on the paths of commerce and of peace. ... This is not merely an episode in the struggle against English industry, but also the first stone in a mighty edifice which time alone can complete and which will be adorned each year by the joint efforts of industry and commerce.

Paris, as ever the heart of French economic and cultural life, dominated industrial exhibitions in the same way that it later dominated the staging of France's international expositions. Although never managing annual exhibitions, the city staged a second national industrial exhibition in 1801. This had double the number of exhibitors compared with the 1798 show and this time attracted them from across France. Other exhibitions followed at intervals until the eleventh and last in 1849 (Fay, 1951, 2). The venues perforce changed as the exhibitions became larger. Until 1827, the organisers used the courtyard and interior of the Louvre,[7] then a site in the Place de la Concorde, with the last three exhibitions held in the Champs Elysées. The 1849 exhibition involved extensive temporary wooden buildings consisting of:

> two enormous longitudinal galleries, about 800 feet long by 90 broad, and of four traverse, which enclose three court-yards: the central one containing flowers, fountains, horticultural equipment, and ornaments of all kinds; the two lateral, one a reservoir of water in case of fire, and the other a collection of large iron-castings and metal-work. In addition to all this space, still more temporary building has been provided, to receive the objects connected with agriculture, which this year are exposed for the first time.[8]

The same reporter noted that this 'great temple of industry' was 'peculiarly rich in metal works, ribbons, silk, lace, Mulhausen and other garment prints, paper-hangings and furniture'.[9] Significantly, by 1839 the French national exhibitions had acquired an atmosphere of cultural pageantry that made them far more than simply a trade show.

Other countries followed the French model, with national exhibitions held in Munich (1818), Ghent (1820), Stockholm (1823), Tournai (1824), Haarlem (1825), Dublin (1826), Madrid (1827), New York (1828), Moscow (1829), St Petersburg (1829) and Brussels (1830).[10] By contrast, the idea of exhibiting industrial products remained sporadic and low key within Great Britain, despite being the heart of the Industrial Revolution. The Mechanics Institutes – bodies established at the start of the nineteenth century to provide practical support for workers and artisans seeking scientific education – staged occasional exhibitions in the Midlands and the north of England and in the Scottish city of Glasgow. Most were small scale, including exhibits on local geology and natural history alongside manufactured products.[11] The Royal Dublin Society mounted triennial exhibitions of Irish agriculture, arts and manufactures from 1827–50. A large exhibition of manufactured goods was held in the grounds of Birmingham's Bingley Hall in 1849 to coincide with the annual meeting of the British Association for the Advancement of Science. Staged in a purpose-built temporary pavilion providing 10 000 square feet of exhibition space, the organisers looked to gain foreign participation even though, in the event, no overseas exhibits materialised.

London scarcely figured as an exhibition location until the late 1840s. Attempts in 1828 to found a permanent 'National Repository for the Exhibition of New and Improved productions of the Artisans and Manufacturers of the United Kingdom' in the Royal Mews, then located in Trafalgar Square, petered out by the mid-1830s. An exhibition held at the Society of Arts building in December 1844 attracted a handful of exhibitors and a mere 150 visitors. This compared unfavourably with the 3040 and 3940 exhibitors that, respectively, participated in the Zollverein (German Customs Union) exhibition and the tenth French industrial exhibition in the same year. Only in March 1847 did London stage a national industrial exhibition of any consequence, with around 300 exhibitors and 20 000 visitors attending the Society of Arts' first 'exhibition of select specimens of British manufactures and decorative art'.

From this point, interest escalated sharply. Succeeding exhibitions in 1848 and 1849 drew so many participants that they no longer fitted into the premises of what was now the Royal Society of Arts. A large exhibition of artefacts from the French national exhibition opened in Hanover Square in November 1849.[12] By this stage, however, thinking was moving towards planning an *international* exhibition that would bring the world's nations together at one place to exhibit industrial arts and design. If successful, it would involve an enterprise combining the characteristic eighteenth-century passion for the organisation of knowledge with nineteenth-century optimism about the benefits of industrial development (Mainardi, 1996, 884). It would also represent an authentic extension of so much that could be found in the cultural life of the British capital before 1851 even though, unlike Paris, there were no regularly-used showgrounds for such an exhibition nor any established festival committees to take charge of it. Moreover, the scale of effort required to stage an international exhibition had to be qualitatively different from anything previously attempted. The 1849 French national exhibition had 4530 exhibitors from within France. By contrast, the Great Exhibition had 14 000 exhibitors from 28 different countries.

Unlike France, too, that effort would be accomplished without significant direct involvement from the municipality. London in 1851 had matured into a densely built city of 2.36 million people radiating some three miles from Charing Cross (Hebbert, 1998, 37),[13] but lacked any consolidated political structure. Having outgrown its medieval boundaries, city politics revolved around the separate jurisdictions exercised by the City of London, the City of Westminster, the former surrounding villages, and the county councils. Each had its own 'conditions of existence – physical, moral and political' (*The Spectator*, 1849; quoted in Young and Garside, 1982, 20). Despite some faltering steps to establish some cross-city bodies,[14] there were still no well-oiled party machines able to mobilise public opinion, no arenas for city-wide discussion, and no centralised voices empowered to speak or act for London. 'No one', mourned one writer, 'asks in our time what London thinks, or what London is going to do. She is politically a cipher ...'.[15] Not surprisingly, the local political bodies and their representatives were virtual bystanders in the sequence of events that promoted and staged the Great Exhibition.

Equally, Central Government offered little support. British governments were wedded to laissez-faire; acting to create and regulate the conditions for trade but not actively intervening in industrial matters. In this instance, Parliament somewhat reluctantly assisted the exhibition through the establishment of a Royal Commission that effectively ran the Great Exhibition. Yet despite this and the key role played by Prince Albert, the exhibition was not state sponsored in any strict sense but relied on voluntary labour and public subscription. Those attributes would normally be a recipe for organisational weakness and insecure financing, but the Great Exhibition overcame many tribulations to open on time and generate a surplus that had a lasting impact on London's cultural infrastructure. How the organisers achieved this outcome and how the exhibition fitted into the life of London are issues to which we now turn.

Gestation

The Great Exhibition was, in Asa Briggs' words, 'a culmination, not an advent; it had a long and tangled history behind it' (Briggs, 2000, 17). The official history highlights the battles fought to create the Great Exhibition by a group associated with the Royal Society of Arts in the late 1840s. These included the civil servant Henry Cole, the engineer John Scott Russell, politician Charles Wentworth Dilke, London property agent Francis Fuller, patent lawyer Thomas Webster, silk merchant Thomas Winkworth, pioneer of telegraphy William Fothergill Cooke, and Queen Victoria's husband Prince Albert (Davis, 1999, 16). Between them, these individuals were charged with promoting and overseeing an undertaking, unprecedented in its scale and financial demands, in the face of parliamentary indifference, civic inertia and the hostility of local residents.

Their task, however, was made easier, first, by the readily receptive climate for displays of technological innovation and, secondly, by the experience of industrial exhibitions elsewhere. Many Britons had attended the French national exhibitions and seen how the organisers handled the steadily increasing number of exhibitors and visitors. Henry Cole, Matthew Digby Wyatt and Francis Fuller enthusiastically visited the French national exhibition in 1849. Moreover, despite the pervasive hostility that soured Anglo-French relations, Cole freely credited the French Minister of Agriculture and Commerce, Louis-Joseph Buffet, with the idea of holding an international exhibition. Cole noted that in a speech to the French chambers of commerce in 1848, Buffet had remarked that:

> It has occurred to me, that it would be interesting to the country in general to be made acquainted with the degree of advancement towards perfection attained by our neighbours in those manufactures in which we so often come in competition in foreign markets. Should we bring together and compare the specimens of skill in agriculture and manufactures now claiming our notice, whether native or foreign, there would, doubtless, be much useful experience to be gained; and, above all, a spirit of emulation, which might be greatly advantageous to the country (quoted in Cole, 1853, 421).

Cole, however, felt the lack of a free trade policy in France meant that ideas about international expositions remained abstract notions for debate rather than practical realities (Cole, 1853, 423; Davis, 1999, 9). By contrast, post-Corn Law Britain had taken a decisive step towards the expansion of markets under free trade. While protectionists still opposed the idea of an international exhibition or anything else that smacked of free trade, an ascendant middle-class economic and cultural consensus was alive to the prospects that reduction of trade barriers offered (Buzard, 1999, 452). Admittedly with copyright protection still inadequate, many manufacturers were reluctant to reveal their products to the scrutiny of foreign competitors for fear of piracy. Yet if the untrammelled logic of free trade and international capitalism was insufficient to persuade wavering participants, then the offer of substantial prizes might help tip the balance of advantage behind accepting the invitation to exhibit.

The various stages involved in creating the Great Exhibition have been discussed sufficiently elsewhere for a brief account to suffice here.[16] It had a production cycle that spanned five years from a planning meeting at Buckingham Palace chaired by Prince Albert on 30 June 1849 to the re-erection of the Crystal Palace (the exhibition's redundant pavilion) at Sydenham Hill in June 1854. The participants at the June 1849 meeting had decided that the proposed exhibition should incorporate the entire realm of the arts and industrial design into the same event rather than a series of events. Working on the assumption that British industry could withstand comparison with the products of other nations, the steering group argued that the exhibition's focus should be international, by virtue of the undesirability of imposing limitations on the display of 'productions of machinery, science and taste' (quoted in Davis, 1999, 26). The exhibits would be organised into three nominal categories – the raw materials of industry, the products made from them, and the art used to adorn them (Allwood, 1977, 19). Initially, it was decided that prizes should be offered to encourage participation, although this was later switched to the award of medals. Funds would come from voluntary public subscription rather than from the state. It was hoped that Parliament would establish a Royal Commission to organise an event of such national significance rather than leave the matter to the Royal Society of Arts. The exhibition would be housed in a temporary pavilion rather than in permanent premises. Finally, Hyde Park, long favoured as the potential venue for the exhibition,[17] was confirmed as the favourite against a list of alternatives that eventually included Regent's Park, Battersea Park, Victoria Park, Primrose Hill, Wormwood Scrubs, the Isle of Dogs, Somerset House and Leicester Square (Luckhurst, 1951, 97; Auerbach, 1999, 42).

Hyde Park was one of nine royal parks on the northern and western edges of London.[18] Although originally land set aside for royal deer hunting parties – an activity that continued until 1768 – the public had gained varying degrees of access since 1637 (Cox, 1911, 235). Yet despite a tradition of being available for major public events and being increasingly fringed by estates of fashionable town houses, the park remained a walled and gated enclosure with its western parts retaining a rural feel. This certainly applied to the site proposed for the Great Exhibition, a 26-acre plot of flat land on the south side of the park parallel with, and between, Kensington Drive and Rotten Row. Although easily accessible from London's West End and from the major rail termini that would bring visitors to the capital, the site remained on the edge of the built-up area. Like the fairs of old, it brought new life to a site previously marginal to urban affairs and, like those fairs, the use of the land was fiercely contested.

Although obtaining the Crown's permission to use the land was a formality given Prince Albert's involvement, the decision to hold an immense exhibition in a purpose-built pavilion aroused local antagonism. At one level, politicians and others expressed xenophobic fears about foreigners as carriers of disease or as political subversives, able to capitalise on the unrest already created by the Chartists. At another level lay more localised concerns about damage to the park, the potential inconvenience and annoyance to local property-owners from the arrival of vast numbers of visitors, the possibility of brothels being set up around Hyde Park to cater for them, and concern over the exhibition building becoming a permanent fixture. In turn, those antagonistic to the principle of the exhibition capitalised on these issues of local significance to provide tactical rallying points for their resistance.[19]

The first serious manifestations of opposition came from a debate in the House of Lords in March 1850, when claims about damage to the park were blunted by a declaration by Lord Carlisle that the exhibition building would be temporary and removed after the closure of the exhibition. More sustained opposition developed over the design of that building. In the spring of 1850, the Royal Commission established to organise the exhibition had invited architects throughout the world to submit proposals for the design of the main exhibition hall. The response was enormous, with 245 different proposals arriving by May, of which 128 were by London architects. These were displayed at the Institution of Civil Engineers on 10 June 1850. On 17 June, Colonel Charles Sibthorp, the Member of Parliament for Lincoln, asked a question in the House of Commons about the possible removal of ten elm trees that stood in the way of the exhibition building. The answer proved embarrassing, given that the Royal Commission had permitted all but one to be felled. Although a seemingly trivial issue, it prompted a wave of hostility. As Davis (1999, 73) notes:

> As Sibthorpe [sic] had hoped, the opposition to the Hyde Park site
> began to grow in volume – not least because the Kensington lobby
> consisted of many influential people from the *beau monde* and the

newspaper world. *The Times*, which even two weeks previously had been chastising the country for its failure to subscribe, perhaps now seeing that the protectionist cause was beginning to gain the upper hand, suddenly did a u-turn and, while still covering itself with the rather false argument that it was protecting Albert's and the monarchy's interests, began what would become a deluge of criticism for the Exhibition project.

The situation was exacerbated by the Royal Commission's failure to choose a winning design from its competition for the exhibition building, simply giving 'honourable mentions' to the more worthy. Instead it extracted ideas from a cross-section of them to publish its own design.[20] When this turned out to be a heavy brick-built structure, with a dome twice the size of St Paul's Cathedral, that positively radiated permanence, the leader writer of *The Times* led the attack:

> The case against the appropriation of Hyde Park as the site of the buildings for the intended Exhibition becomes stronger as the plans of the projectors are developed. We are not to have a 'booth', nor a mere timber shed, but a solid, substantial edifice of brick, and iron, and stone, calculated to endure the wear and tear of the next hundred years ... By the stroke of a pen our pleasant Park – nearly the only spot where Londoners can get a breath of fresh air – is to be turned into something between Wolverhampton and Greenwich Fair.[21]

The Illustrated London News, an enthusiastic supporter of the exhibition project to the point of appearing a mouthpiece for the organisers, mounted a spirited riposte:

> much nonsensical correspondence has lately been in some of the daily journals respecting the injury which will be done to this portion of the Park by the erection of the building, the enormous amount of traffic which will be hereabouts, the withholding from the public so large a slice of the Park, and great complaints have been made that some of the trees must be removed.

The author dismissed these arguments and alluded to the only trees earmarked for removal as being 'some half-dozen small ones'.[22] A fevered correspondence ensued as *The Times* leader writers weighed into the argument and correspondents made renewed suggestions for possible exhibition sites in Battersea Park and the Isle of Dogs.[23] The *Illustrated London News* produced its counterblast, pointing to the amounts of subscription money already raised, noting that the 'whole civilised world' had been told about the exhibition and that the building only occupied 20 out of 387 of Hyde Park's acres. People, the writer argued, 'still had 1568 acres of alternative space in the other Royal Parks if they felt deprived'.[24]

In the event, the opposition melted away. Parliamentary votes in early

July went heavily in favour of the exhibition, with the Attorney-General refusing to intervene on the protestors' behalf.[25] In addition, the chosen design for the exhibition hall was withdrawn. Quite apart from any aesthetic shortcomings, the committee's proposal for a brick-built hall was not feasible, since it was impossible to procure and put to use the estimated nineteen million bricks necessary for construction by the planned opening date in May 1851 (Conrads and Sperlich, 1963, 160). Instead the commission turned to a late alternative proposal submitted by Joseph Paxton.[26] Paxton proposed a translucent iron and glass structure, with an internal area of 19 acres (eight hectares). This allowed sufficient floor space for the proposed exhibition, with a domed transept that provided enough clearance where necessary to accommodate the retention of three remaining trees.

The underlying idea behind its construction originated in his previous work in greenhouse design. Paxton had earlier designed greenhouses at Chatsworth in Derbyshire on the Duke of Devonshire's estate; the largest being over 300 feet in length.[27] His design for Hyde Park was essentially a scaled-up version. It was popularly known as the 'Crystal Palace' – a term, coined by the writer Douglas Jerrold for the satirical magazine *Punch*,[28] that immediately became the pseudonym for both the building in Hyde Park and its later reconstruction at Sydenham (Pender-Gunn, 1999). The structure was 1848 feet long, 408 feet wide and 110 feet high, with 24 miles of guttering, 330 standardised iron columns, 250 000 sash bars and 293 655 panes of glass. On the north side, a 48-feet wide extension increased the maximum width to 456 feet – yet another measurement of the building that was either a multiple or dividend of the number 24.[29] Altogether the building roofed over 772 784 square feet of ground area, with an additional 217 100 square feet of galleries.

An essential part of the proposed Crystal Palace's attraction lay in the recommended building method. Its design featured a simple but effective structure of iron columns, glass panels and beams, which were prefabricated off-site before transport to Hyde Park for assembly. This offered prospects for rapid construction, with the contractors, Fox and Henderson, completing the job in just nine months (Benedict, 1983, 1). It also created opportunities for the structure to be dismantled and reused elsewhere once the exhibition was over, even though Paxton later argued that had not been in his thoughts and 'with care and attention', the building could last for 100 years.[30] At the same time, the design had drawbacks. Quite apart from the well-known episode of the nuisance from birds roosting in the building while under construction, the building, like any greenhouse, allowed enormous amounts of light into the interior. This eventually required special blinds and tented sections to protect light-sensitive artefacts and fabrics, such as the music and lace exhibits (Allwood, 1977, 27).

The exhibition organisers proceeded with their work of preparing the site, raising funds from nationwide subscriptions (£230 000)[31] and inviting exhibitors. Roughly half the interior floor space (400 000 square feet) was allocated to 7831 British and colonial exhibitors and half to the 6556 overseas participants.[32] Of the latter, French exhibitors received 50 000 square feet, the USA 40 000 (although they failed to fill it), Austria 22 000 and Belgium 15 000, with smaller allocations to other countries. Given that there was insufficient space for all who wished to participate, the organisers employed the French system of decentralisation as a means of allocating space. The commission determined the amount of space allocated to foreign countries, with their governments responsible for selecting and collecting goods to fill that space (Luckhurst, 1951, 111). For British goods, local committees compiled lists of recommendations with a central committee making the final choice. Understandably, therefore, the resolution of issues about inclusion and exclusion rested with a socially restricted group of decision-makers. Problems, however, remained with the classification system. The original tripartite taxonomy (see above) was too vague and ambiguous to provide an inadequate basis for categorising exhibits for purposes of display or for the award of medals. These problems were only lessened when Lyon Playfair, a professional administrator who came to prominence during the exhibition, provided a revised system (Edwards, 2001, 37). He added a fourth category, machinery, to the classification and subdivided the four resulting categories into thirty classes. This gave greater flexibility when judging objects against one another.

Yet even as this work proceeded, the support from the host city remained patchy. With the recent European revolutions and the British Chartist demonstrations still firmly in mind, sections of the London elite harboured considerable doubts about the wisdom of holding the exhibition almost until the time that it closed. Although the business and retail communities lent their support (Auerbach, 1999, 55), subscription income varied according to dominant economic interests of the area. Parishes that had an interest in shipping and free trade gave more generously than those like Spitalfields and Bethnal Green, where weavers were strongly opposed to free trade and predisposed against the exhibition (Auerbach, 1999, 81). The so-called 'Kensington lobby', which objected to development in the park, voiced significant local opposition over possible traffic nuisance and law and order. Support for the exhibition also reflected deep-seated rivalries between different localities, such as that between the City of London and Westminster. The two had formed separate subscription committees and were not inclined to work together. A report in December 1850 found the two groups needing arbitration to find neutral territory before they would sit down together:

> Some disinclination having appeared among the Westminster committee to attend the general meetings of the metropolitan committee in the city, and an objection having been urged by the London committee against sitting at Westminster, the matter has been settled by the handsome offer of the Society in the loan of its rooms in John Adam-street, Adelphi for committee meetings.[33]

The squabbling between different factional interests drew exasperated comment from other parts of the country, which saw the prospects of a project of national importance foundering over local disputes. Yet, in truth, there was comparatively little in any of the contemporary debate that saw the Great Exhibition as promoting the specific interests of London. The exhibition was seen primarily as redounding to the credit of Great Britain and all that it stood for. London entered the frame as the exhibition's natural home because it was the British capital and not through any burning aspirations on the part of the city's authorities to hold the festival.

The Unique Assemblage

The Great Exhibition was opened, as planned, by Queen Victoria on 1 May 1851, although the precise nature of the opening ceremony remained uncertain until the last moments. Victoria's coronation in 1837 had been a relatively low-key and bumbling affair; there were doubts about the wisdom of exposing the royal party to possible attack from political revolutionaries.[34] During the last two weeks of April, the organisers decided to embark on a spectacular and scripted opening ceremony that combined pageantry with religious solemnity. The royal party dressed as if for a state occasion and arrived in procession. Prince Albert gave a speech that reflected on the ideology of peace and harmony through industrial progress and strongly underlined Victoria's role as patron of the exhibition. The Archbishop of Canterbury, prelate of the Anglican Church, offered prayers for the success of the exhibition and for the well-being of the monarch and her realm – an activity repeated by ministers and preachers throughout the land.[35] Two organs and massed choirs performed the 'Hallelujah Chorus' from Handel's *Messiah*. The occasion was nothing if not quintessentially Victorian in asserting the link between material creativity and spirituality.

The queen toured the building in procession with key dignitaries, before returning to the podium and declaring the exhibition officially open. The exhibition itself, as most contemporary observers confirm,[36] provided a bewildering compilation. The 'unique assemblage'[37] in the Crystal Palace, with more than 100 000 exhibits from 28 different nations, made it difficult to make sense of what was on display. In particular, the arrangement did not accord with the thirty-part classification system devised by the organisers. Machinery was placed along the north side because the power source was located in the north-west corner. Structural considerations dictated that lighter exhibits were placed in the galleries. Raw materials were located in the south and the manufactured goods in the centre. Overseas exhibits were grouped by country rather than by category, giving them a more random appearance than the British display (Leapman, 2001, 165). The central spaces were occupied by displays from exhibitors from India, Australasia and other parts of the British Empire; symbolically asserting the imperial power of Britain as well as emphasising the centrality of manufacturing to the exhibition.

With so many competing considerations, it was understandably difficult to envisage exhibits as part of a pedagogic sequence from raw material to finished item, as that would have meant repeatedly criss-crossing the building. Moreover, as Auerbach (1999, 91) adds:

> the arrangement of the exhibits emphasised the fact that the Great Exhibition was not just an exhibition of the works of industry, it was a spectacle. The layout made little sense from the perspective of educating people about the *process* of industrialisation, but made perfect sense for a nation that wanted to educate its citizens about the products of industrialisation.

To some extent, this educational element was emergent rather than consciously planned from the outset since the idea of social inclusiveness did not spring readily to the minds of the elite in mid-nineteenth century England. As noted earlier, fear of the mob was endemic. There had been concern that, on days when the admittance price was cheap enough to attract the general public, they might turn up drunk and possibly steal or vandalise exhibits. Instead, as the writer Henry Mayhew (1851; quoted in Harvie et al., 1970, 248) affirmed, the working classes' behaviour at the Crystal Palace exceeded:

> the hopes of their well-wishers. The fact is, the Great Exhibition is to them more of a school than a show. ... If we really desire the improvement of our social state, (and surely we are far from perfection yet), we must address ourselves to the elevation of the people; and it is because the Great Exhibition is fitted to become a special instrument towards this end, that it forms one of the most remarkable and hopeful characteristics of our time.

The extent of their interest clearly surprised and delighted the organisers of the Great Exhibition. The general public's sense of curiosity about the world need not have signified anything more than might earlier visits to London's dioramas and panorama shows, but contemporary reports suggested that the exhibition engendered a qualitatively different experience. Its exhibits showed the wonders of the wider world as well as familiar elements of everyday life. They offered glimpses of luxuries that were far beyond the reach of working people, yet there were also many examples of ordinary household products and machinery serving functions that were a regular part of their working lives (Leapman, 2001). Many of those machines emphasised a sense of modernity by showing how to remove some of the drudgery out of everyday lives. This combination of the exotic and commonplace allowed people of all classes to engage with and learn from the Great Exhibition, regardless of whether or not they could interpret the broader conceptual organisation of the exhibits. In turn, the working classes' enthusiasm for the exhibition had a profound impact on the thinking of liberal and progressive intellectuals keen to develop the didactic possibilities of such events. They were impressed by what 'rational recreation', activities with direct links to self-improvement, might offer in terms of social improvement.[38] Henceforth no international exposition would be complete without its explicit pedagogic dimension.

   The Great Exhibition addressed significant social and cultural goals. First, although its exhibits included agricultural machinery and artefacts, the exhibition firmly asserted the role of British manufacturing industry in the mid-nineteenth century and further symbolised the inescapable shift of power away from the landed aristocracy. Secondly, there was concern for the state of working-class housing, as expressed by a set of model cottages for four working-class families built for Prince Albert in the grounds of the Cavalry Barracks opposite the Exhibition.[39] By 1851, working-class housing was seen as a problem, primarily due to the issues concerned with sanitation and disease. The idea of providing visitors with practical demonstrations of how matters might be improved presaged later interest in housing reform (Gaskell, 1986, 11), as well as hinting at a theme taken up by later expositions. Finally, the exhibition greatly reinforced the prestige of Empire and monarchy. The contents of the Crystal Palace powerfully emphasised the extent and wealth of Britain's colonial 'possessions' – a significant word used extensively in the catalogues. The centrally placed Indian courts in particular substantiated powerful narratives of oriental splendour and imperial conquest (Kriegel, 2001). The royal family bathed in reflected glory. A popular ballad sheet of the day, for example, praised not only the exhibition, but also the Prince Consort's part in designing it (quoted in Newburg, 1973, 205). A verse proclaimed:

Great praise is due to Albert,
For the good that he has done,
May others follow in his steps
The work he has begun,
Then let us all, with one accord,
His name give with three cheers,
Shout huzza for the Crystal Palace,
And the World's great National Fair!!

The idea that the exhibition offered a valid forecast that technological progress might act as the engine of improvements in which all might share gained credence from the weight of visitors that attended (Gay, 1998, 22). The Great Exhibition drew more than six million visitors during the 141 days that it was open (see Table 3.1). These included an estimated one million visitors from London alone which, notwithstanding people making multiple visits, was a remarkable total for a city of just 2.5 million inhabitants. This figure included many from the lower-middle and working classes, who took advantage of the so-called 'shilling days' when the admission price was much lower than the one pound charge of the opening days and the standard five shillings admission thereafter.

Table 3.1   Statistics for the Great Exhibition, London 1851

Dates	1 May–11 October 1851
Site	Hyde Park
Area of showground	26 acres
Exhibition buildings	Single multinave basilica covering 19 acres
Preparation time	June 1849–April 1851
Visitor numbers	6 039 195
Profit/(loss)	£186 000
Post-exhibition conversion time	October 1851–June 1854
Post-exhibition changes	Landscaping in Hyde Park.
	Dismantling Crystal Palace and re-erection in enlarged form at Sydenham Hill.
	Use of funds to develop South Kensington museum quarter.

Their presence led many commentators to see the exhibition as a point of social contact and reconciliation between the classes. To elaborate, until 1851, it was rare for all sections of society to share a common recreational focus, yet here was an opportunity for all classes to meet away from the socially segmented environment of the city. The frequent visits by Queen Victoria and the enthusiastic participation of a wide cross-section of the population, many encouraged to attend by their employers or by working men's associations and mechanics' institutes, caused great satisfaction to those who had supported the cause of the exhibition project. Henry Cole, for example, noted: 'I need not dwell on the advantages conferred by friendly intercourse, how mutual prejudices are dispelled, and friendly confidences established' (Cole, 1853, 437). Whether, of course, being admitted to the same exhibition and seeing the same sights provided any evidence for real social intermingling is debatable. It was fully open to the wealthier classes to avoid 'shilling days' and, in any case, the trains that conveyed travellers to London were rigidly divided into first, second and third-class compartments (Behagg, 1991, quoted Edwards, 2001, 29). Nevertheless, the ideological significance of the exposition as a melting pot, an island of social understanding set in a sea of discord, proved pervasive.

London, of course, gained materially from staging the event, regardless of local sentiments towards it. The five million visitors who travelled from elsewhere in the British Isles or from overseas saw London as an additional attraction. Most stayed between three days and one week in the metropolis and freely visited the other sites, which extended their opening hours and increased their accessibility. The city's economy benefited greatly. An enormous number of official and semi-official gatherings were arranged for distinguished visitors. Banquets, public feasts, balls and other paid entertainments were organised. The shops in the West End and City quickly exploited the exhibition themes in their retail promotions, with some taking the previously inconceivable step of putting up signs in foreign languages to welcome overseas customers. Theatres and music halls put on special performances and the pleasure gardens added to their repertoire of entertainments and re-enactments. Even the British Museum opened five days a week and it, like the National Gallery, postponed its summer vacation (Davis, 1999, 172). Guidebooks, souvenirs and memorabilia were produced in large numbers and eagerly purchased (Ogata, 2002).

Accommodation posed logistic problems. The upper classes maintained their town houses and acted as hosts for 'country cousins'. Recently built hotels at the rail termini supplemented the stock of hotels in the West End, particularly in Mayfair, as sources of higher-quality accommodation. Traditional inns and taverns retained their position in the market, alongside a huge sector of boarding houses and private residences that supplied lodgings. Recognising the additional strains likely from a huge influx of visitors, the Royal Commission had inquired into the possibility of creating official listings of lodgings. Few landlords, however, were willing to commit themselves to setting prices in advance. There was thus no comprehensive plan either from the organisers or civic authorities to ensure a sufficient supply of accommodation, allowing a shortage to develop and permitting hoteliers and boarding-house proprietors to charge premium rates for the season. Hotel and guest houses, especially those near the major rail termini, often filled beyond their capacity.[40]

Agents arranging block bookings for their clients exacerbated this shortage of accommodation. Thomas Cook and Son actively publicised their excursions in Yorkshire and the East Midlands in collaboration with the Midland Railway. Altogether an estimated 165 000 people travelled to the exhibition with Cook's newly founded firm, which also arranged accommodation. This ranged from bed and a substantial breakfast at the Ranelagh Club, a converted furniture depository in Pimlico, for two shillings a night to barrack-like dormitories at a shilling a night on board an emigrant ship moored on the Thames at Vauxhall Bridge (Brendon, 1991, 63). *The Circulator*, a periodical publication, listed a selection of private homes, dormitories and hotels offering accommodation to exhibition visitors at prices ranging from 1s 3d a night to £6 a week (Leapman, 2001, 69).

Over 58 000 visitors came from further afield, including France (27 000), the German states (12 000), the USA (5000) and Belgium (3800). The exhibition's popularity in western Europe led, for the first time, to a coordinated approach between railway and steamship companies on both sides of the English Channel, with commercial benefit accruing directly and indirectly (through associated hotels and catering). Many arrived on package deals, including transport and accommodation – usually in hotels and private lodgings at the upper end of the market. Mivart's Hotel and the Clarendon in Mayfair attracted a broad cross-section of foreign visitors; Americans favoured Morley's Hotel in Trafalgar Square; three multilingual French-owned hotels on Leicester Square acted as a base for many French visitors (Thorold, 1999, 257).

Predictably not all were happy. Quite apart from the isolationist lobby that had opposed the project from the outset, parts of the retailing and entertainments sectors felt themselves disadvantaged by the exhibition. As one correspondent laconically noted:

> But the Great Exhibition has its unpopular as well as popular side.

> City merchants and their correspondents say that it has 'killed business' for the season and they grumble accordingly. The caterers for public amusement are still louder in their complaints. The theatres do not fill; panoramas – of which the name is legion, and which succeed each other more rapidly than memory can keep pace with them – are losing speculations, and people are so busy with the one Great Exhibition that they cannot encourage any minor ones, or find time for them even if they would. Business cannot be 'killed' when so much money is spent and spending; and it is certain that it will awake in due season. As for the public amusements, we believe that there is a chance even for the panoramas.[41]

In the event, the fears of the shopkeepers and other proprietors proved unfounded. There would also be significant long-term advantages for the city that flowed from the exhibition's largely unplanned aftermath.

Sydenham and South Kensington

The Great Exhibition closed on 15 October 1851, but its organisers had made no firm decisions about the future of its major remaining assets, namely, the empty exhibition hall and its considerable surplus revenues (£186 437). Disposal of the Crystal Palace, which still belonged to Fox and Henderson, was the first priority. One proposal, actively canvassed by the newly knighted Paxton, was that the building should remain permanently *in situ* to serve as 'a winter park and garden under glass – for the use and enjoyment of London and its two-and-a-half millions of inhabitants'.[42] Paxton wanted admission charges to the Crystal Palace to cover the annual maintenance costs, which he estimated as £12 000 (although other estimates placed the cost at £14 200). This suggestion gained support from Cole and influential magazines such as *Punch* and *The Economist*, which argued that it would be foolish to destroy a building that was now a national symbol. A fete was held in the palace on 3 April 1852, where thousands put their names to a petition in favour of its retention. Nevertheless, local opposition to any possible reneging on the commitment that the pavilion was only a temporary building was upheld by a parliamentary inquiry, which found that the commissioners had a binding contractual obligation to restore land to the park (Leapman, 2001, 274).

The prefabricated construction of the Crystal Palace, however, meant that removal need not mean destruction. The building, as James Buzard (1999, 441) notes, was scarcely 'site-specific'. Its glass panes and iron supports could be dismantled, stored and removed to a new site if one was found. Paxton, keen to preserve his undertaking, took the lead by raising £500 000 by a rights issue and forming the Crystal Palace

Company.[43] This company purchased both the building and 200 acres of wooded parkland at Sydenham Hill in South London to serve as its new home (Gurney, 2001, 122). The dismantling and rebuilding process began almost immediately, although the new structure incorporated the original into a larger building rather than replicated the exhibition hall in Hyde Park.

The Sydenham version (see Figure 3.1) was taller and broader than its predecessor, with new transepts and wings added at the north and south ends, plus a basement to cope with the sloping ground. Three-hundred feet high towers at each end provided sufficient head of water to power the network of fountains in the extensive landscaped gardens. The interior was also modified to introduce new attractions, particularly from the fine arts. Pugin's medieval court from the Great Exhibition was joined by others displaying Assyrian, Grecian, Roman, Byzantine, Romanesque, Pompeiian, Chinese, Moorish, Renaissance and Egyptian art. These were intended to provide insight into the art of great civilisations, as well as their progress and eventual decline. If the Great Exhibition was a microcosm of Victorian industry, then the Sydenham Crystal Palace was one of Victorian leisure (Beaver, 1970, 99). Its grounds, always a central feature of its attraction, far surpassed those of London's existing pleasure grounds, with extensive areas of landscaped

Figure 3.1　The Crystal Palace in its Sydenham incarnation

gardens, a maze, replica dinosaurs towering over the woodlands, an underground grotto, a boating lake and children's playgrounds.

The official inauguration ceremony on 10 June 1854 was attended by 40 000 people. The promoting company's commitment to the 'cultivation of a refined taste amongst all classes of the community' was echoed by Queen Victoria's speech (Gurney, 2001, 123). In declaring the Crystal Palace open, she stated that:

> It is my earnest wish and hope that the bright anticipations which have been formed as to the future destiny of the Crystal Palace may, under the blessing of Divine Providence, be completely realised; and that this wonderful structure, and the treasures of art and knowledge which it contains, may long continue to celebrate and interest as well as delight and amuse the minds of all classes of people.

During the first 30 years, it attracted around two million visitors a year, drawn by the permanent displays and a diet of musical extravaganzas, temperance meetings, firework displays and festivals. Its contents also marked a further reinforcement of the commercial orientation that remained implicit at the Great Exhibition. Exhibitors in Hyde Park had displayed rather than sold their goods, even if their underlying aim remained trade (Benedict, 1983, 3). The Sydenham building now included sections in which manufacturers offered items directly for sale, partly turning the Crystal Palace into a department store (Gurney, 2001, 123). There was again to be a large-scale exhibition in the Crystal Palace, when it hosted the 1911 Festival of Empire but, by that stage, the Crystal Palace Company was in serious financial difficulties. After serving as a naval supply depot during the First World War and later containing the Imperial War Museum, it returned to popular entertainments but continually operated at a deficit. By the time that it was destroyed by fire in 1936, it had probably outlived its usefulness.

Decisions about how to use the funds left over from the Great Exhibition were more complicated than those concerning the fate of the Crystal Palace. After dismissing the claims of local committees and other subscribers for reimbursement of contributions, projects suggested for support included a museum of Aboriginal products, a free hospital for all nations, a fund for the alleviation of Irish and Scottish Highland destitution, and the purchase of an Irish estate for Prince Albert (Leapman, 2001, 262). The final decision followed the lines of a tentative memorandum of 10 August 1851, in which Prince Albert proposed buying a Kensington estate to accommodate institutions fostering science and the practical arts. The commissioners adopted this plan, with the purchase of Gore House and 70 acres of land on the south side of Knightsbridge directly south of the site of the Crystal Palace. The site cost £336 000, with nearly half contributed by the Government (Hobhouse, 2002).

The first buildings put on the site were arcades and a conservatory for the Horticultural Society, which leased part of the ground. This was followed in 1857 by the relocation from Marlborough House of the South Kensington Museum, which, in 1909, became the Victoria and Albert Museum. Established in 1852 and first known as the Museum of Manufactures, the South Kensington museum's collection originated in exhibits left over as free gifts from the Great Exhibition. In 1873, the British Museum's collection of natural history exhibits moved to new premises at a site on the other side of Exhibition Road from the South Kensington museum.[44] The Science and Geological Museums, both spin-offs from other collections, gained their own adjacent buildings in 1928 and 1935 respectively. The Albert Hall, a major concert venue built to honour the Prince Consort's memory, was constructed between 1867–71 by a private company. Educational institutions and learned societies also moved to sites in the area, including the Royal Geographical Society and the Royal Colleges of Art and Music (Summerson, 1978, 327). In 1887, the Imperial Institute (now the Imperial College of Science and Technology) was founded, using profits from the 1886 Indian and Colonial Exhibition. Although far from being the only source of funding, therefore, the Great Exhibition was the essential stimulus behind the creation of London's first significant museum and cultural quarter. Besides supplying the precedent for future expositions, the Great Exhibition illustrated an important avenue by which host cities could exploit showcase events to create new social and cultural infrastructure. It was a lesson that other cities readily absorbed.

London's interest in major exhibition projects did not end with the Great Exhibition. Initially, the Royal Society of Arts wanted to hold international exhibitions at decennial intervals to maintain the momentum initiated by the 1851 event. The emerging South Kensington cultural and museum quarter, sometimes referred to affectionately as 'Albertopolis', hosted nine major exhibitions in its own right. These began with the International Exhibition of 1862, a reprise of the Hyde Park event that, despite its low-key treatment from historians for not showing major innovations in organisation, actually drew a larger audience than the Great Exhibition. A series of eight other events were held, culminating in the 1886 Indian and Colonial Exhibition.[45] Thereafter, as the estate continued to fill, exhibition organisers developed venues elsewhere, notably at Earl's Court, Olympia, White City and the Sydenham Crystal Palace. Many were large-scale events, requiring the construction of temporary or permanent structures, which attracted huge audiences. For example, the 1908 Franco-British

Exhibition at the White City and the British Empire Exhibition at Wembley (1924–5) drew 10.5 and 27 million visitors respectively.[46] These exhibitions shared many features with international expositions, but their gradual adoption of a more specialised focus and shedding of the pedagogic focus (for example, see Greenhalgh, 1989, 79–82) distinguished them from the strands of thought and practice that are the subject of the next two chapters.

Notes

1   The Exeter Change Royal Menagerie closed in 1829; the Tower Menagerie in 1835.
2   *Illustrated London News* (henceforth *ILN*), 18, 7 June 1851, 511.
3   Discussion of the origins of museums and art galleries lies beyond the scope of this text. For more information, see Bennett, 1995, and Prior, 2002.
4   Richard Crary (1990, 14 et seq.; see Marsh, 1999, 276) argues that the explosion of interest in the visual was underpinned by a philosophical 'reorganisation' of human vision between 1810 and 1840. Whether or not one accepts that position, there is no doubt that the crazes for visual technologies lasted throughout the century including, for example, microphotography, cinema and x-rays. See Altick (1978), Benjamin (1996) and Pamboukian (2001).
5   The society had organised an annual prizegiving since 1756, which brought together exhibits. In 1761, it bought the exhibits and put them on display (Allwood, 1977, 9).
6   Its design was influenced by an exhibition held in 1797 at the uninhabited and unfurnished Chateau of St Cloud near Paris. Organised by the Marquis d'Avèze, an industrialist from the ancien régime who had successfully survived the Terror, this exhibition symbolically linked the modernising tendencies of pre- and post-revolutionary France.
7   Apart from the 1806 exhibition, which were held on the Esplanade des Invalides.
8   *ILN*, 7 July 1849, 5.
9   Ibid.
10 See Kusamitsu, 1980, and Greenhalgh, 1988, 6.
11 Exhibition activities might be regarded as an extension of the mini-museums that many Mechanics Institutes kept as part of their educational commitment. It is worth pointing out in passing, however, that an exhibition by the Leeds branch in 1839 attracted 200 000 visitors (Auerbach, 1999, 11).
12 *ILN*, 1 December 1849, 357.
13 The population of Greater London for 1851, as defined by the Metropolitan Police District, was 2 685 000 (Hall, 1998, 657).
14 The Metropolitan Police was established in 1829. Specific bodies were also set up to oversee building regulations and provide sewers and sanitation in 1844 and 1847 respectively (Davis, 1988).

15 *ILN*, 18, 15 March 1851, 208.
16 For more information, see in particular Luckhurst (1951), Allwood (1977), Gibbs-Smith (1981), Auerbach (1999, 9–90) and Davis (1999, 1–120).
17 Davis (1999, 16) notes that the Society of Arts had proposed Hyde Park as a location for the exhibition and mooted that a building should be constructed for the purpose.
18 Henry VIII acquired Hyde Park in 1536 from the Benedictine monks of St Peter, Westminster, to serve as a hunting ground for deer and wild boar (Whitehead, 1989, 8).
19 Opposition to the exhibition proposal came from many quarters. Supporters of protectionism deplored its free trade bias. Xenophobic sections of the press disapproved of greater contacts with foreigners and, at their shrillest, warned of a 'coming invasion of aliens who would foment revolution, commit robbery, perpetrate murder and bequeath Britain a piebald generation' (Harvie et al., 1970, 250). Provincial businessmen were hostile to centralisation of such an undertaking in London. In addition, a wide swathe of opinion was hostile to government interference in the business sphere (Fay, 1951, 5).
20 *ILN*, 22 June 1850, 445.
21 'Great Exhibition: Note on the Building', *The Times*, 27 June 1850, 8.
22 *ILN*, 16, 27 June 1850, 446.
23 For example, see *The Times*, 1 July 1850, 4; 3 July 1850, 4, 8; 4 July 1850, 5; and 6 July 1850, 7.
24 *ILN*, 17, 20 July 1850, 53.
25 *ILN*, 17, 27 July 1850, 88.
26 *ILN*, 6 July 1850, 13.
27 The measurements in this section are only given in imperial scales, since they have numerological significance in this form that the metric versions lack.
28 *Punch*, 2 November 1850.
29 The precise reason is obscure, but seems to have had numerological significance.
30 *ILN*, 19 July 1851, 86.
31 Auerbach (1999, 54–88) provides a detailed account of the fund-raising process.
32 Their goods would be exempt from import duties as the government agreed to treat the exhibition building in the manner of a bonded warehouse.
33 *ILN*, 17, 14 December 1850, 454.
34 Fear of revolutionaries joining the crowds in London had led the Royal Commission to suggest that foreign police be sent over to work with their British counterparts in preventing revolutionary activities in London. As a result, 36 police from several foreign states were present during the exhibition (Davis, 1999, 114).
35 When the Reverend Thomas Aveling (1851) preached a sermon to his congregation at the Kingsland Chapel on the Sunday evening before the opening of the exhibition, he readily invoked scriptural reference to endorse

the 'Great Sights' on view. These included: 'I will now turn aside, and see this great sight' (Exodus 3.3); 'Thou shalt see greater things than these' (John 1.50); 'That sight' (Luke 23.48).

36 Davis (1999, 183–203) and Auerbach (1999, 91–97) offer overviews of a range of responses from writers including Dickens, Thackeray, Carlyle and Ruskin.

37 The phrase is Charlotte Bronte's and found in a letter to her father, quoted in Gay, 1998, 22.

38 Cunningham (1980) goes so far as to argue that the Crystal Palace was a manifestation of the elite's desire to control and direct the recreation of the masses.

39 These were later removed to Kennington Park in South London, where they still remain.

40 'London Lodgings during Great Exhibition', *The Times*, 4 August 1851, 5.

41 *ILN*, 18, 17 May 1851, 424.

42 *ILN*, 19, 5 July 1851, 2.

43 Although its personnel overlapped with that of the Royal Commission, the Crystal Palace Company was entirely separate from the 1851 commissioners. Indeed its chairman was Samuel Laing, chairman of the London, Brighton and South Coast Railway Company (Leapman, 2001, 276).

44 This was first entitled the British Museum of Natural History and subsequently the Natural History Museum.

45 Greenhalgh (1989) lists 31 major exhibitions that took place in Britain between 1871–1914, 23 of which were held in London. He also argues against omitting the major post-1851 British exhibitions from the narrative about the development of international expositions.

46 In passing, it is worth noting that both of these exhibitions left behind extensive redundant exhibition buildings, at Shepherd's Bush and Wembley respectively, that to this day have served uneasily as commercial structures.

CHAPTER FOUR

New York's World's Fair, 1939

> We left via the Helicline, a ramp leading from the
> Perisphere to the ground. From this close both
> structures could be seen in their texture, the sunlight
> illuminating the gypsum board of their siding. The
> rough siding made dimples of shadow on the
> Perisphere. At one point the whiteness turned silver
> and I could imagine it as the flank of a great airship.
> Then I could see where the paint was peeling, which
> was discouraging. But then as we neared the ground
> the two structures loomed in their geometry, gradually
> becoming more and more monumental and revealing
> more of their familiar form, until everything was all
> right again.
>
> E.L. Doctorow (1985, 269)

From the Great Exhibition to the outbreak of the Second World War, roughly 35 cultural festivals merited the description 'international exposition'. As Table 4.1 shows,[1] there was a remarkable degree of concentration in the places staging these events; a phenomenon that, in turn, had a marked impact on the purposes that they served. Nine western nations staged all the expositions up to the Second World War: the United States of America (ten), France and Belgium (eight each), Italy (three), and Australia (two), and the Netherlands, Austria, Spain and the United Kingdom (one each).[2] Given this dominance, it was not surprising that western thinking exerted a powerful hold over exposition design and presentation of content that challenged any assertion about their claims for true universality. Expositions may well have been efficient ways of communicating the wonders of science and technology to the public in a pre-televisual age, but they primarily responded to the western world's interwoven priorities of trade, promotion, city rivalries, and imperialism.

This chapter proceeds against this background. Its main focus is on the 1939 New York World's Fair, an event that occurred at a time of the utmost tension in world politics. The New York show saw the transformation of a huge municipal rubbish dump into a carefully planned celebration of scientific advance and consumerism. Although it lost money heavily, the city corporation had successfully insulated itself from significant loss and gained much from the prestige of the event. We

Table 4.1   International expositions, 1853–1939

1853	New York *World's Fair of the Works of Industry of All Nations*
1855	Paris *Exposition Universelle*
1862	London *International Exhibition*
1867	Paris *Exposition Universelle*
1873	Vienna *Weltausstellung*
1876	Philadelphia *Centennial Exposition*
1878	Paris *Exposition Universelle*
1879	Sydney *International Exhibition*
1880	Melbourne *International Exhibition*
1883	Amsterdam *Internationale Koloniale en Uitvoerhandelstentoonstelling*
1885	Antwerp *Exposition Universelle d'Anvers*
1889	Paris *Exposition Universelle*
1893	Chicago *World's Columbian Exposition*
1894	Antwerp *Exposition Universelle d'Anvers*
1897	Brussels *Exposition Internationale*
1900	Paris *Exposition Universelle*
1901	Buffalo *Pan-American Exposition*
1902	Turin *Esposizione d'Arte Decorativa Moderna*
1904	St Louis *Louisiana Purchase International Exposition*
1905	Liège *Exposition Universelle*
1906	Milan *Exposizione Internationale*
1907	Hampton Roads *Jamestown Tercentennial Exhibition*
1909	Seattle *Alaska-Yukon Pacific Exhibition*
1910	Brussels *Exposition Universelle et Internationale*
1911	Turin *Exposizione Internationale d'Industria e de Laboro*
1913	Ghent *Exposition Universelle et Industrielle*
1915	San Francisco *Panama-Pacific International Exposition*
1925	Paris *Exposition Internationale des Arts Décoratifs et Industriels Modernes*
1929	Barcelona *Exposición General d'España* and Seville *Exposición Ibero-Americana* (joint centres)
1930	Antwerp and Liège *Exposition International* (joint centres for Belgian international exhibitions)
1931	Paris *Exposition Coloniale Internationale*
1933	Chicago *Century of Progress International Exposition*
1935	Brussels *Exposition Universelle et Internationale de Bruxelles*
1937	Paris *Exposition Internationale des Arts et des Techniques Appliqueés à la Vie Moderne*
1939	New York *World's Fair*

follow the production cycle of this event from the inception of planning in 1934–5, identifying the degree that the city itself was an active investor in the project. We describe the hopes invested in the project for the improvement of open space and infrastructure, the process by which the exhibition site was reclaimed and prepared, through to clearing the exhibition site in 1941–2. It is important, however, to understand its context. The initial sections therefore examine the general background to staging and regulating international expositions. We then specifically examine the American world's fairs that were its predecessors, drawing particular attention to their role in the continuing business of inter-city rivalry.

Progress and Order

The act of inviting the world's art and industry to one place allowed comparisons to be made; an enterprise that the host nation could manipulate for its benefit by shrewd positioning of domestic exhibits or pavilions compared with those of foreign rivals. Expositions asserted the benefits of free trade. By bringing together commodities and artefacts in what was often legally a bonded warehouse, the exposition declared what could be available under circumstances of unfettered trading. The accompanying rhetoric of opportunity and prosperity was often coded language designed to support the major western trading nations' wish to create a world in which they were free to exert their economic might. Indeed, the campaign for free trade usually lay at the heart of the early international expositions.

Expositions also provided opportunities for conspicuous displays of wealth and power. Host nations could show off the magnitude of their colonial possessions, with careful attention to cultural ascendancy and associated representations of precedence, deference and loyalty. The British, French and Belgians, in particular, vied with one another to show off their imperial splendour alongside their aspirations at industrial leadership. Japan and America, relative newcomers to the scramble for colonies, were equally eager to show off the bounty of their conquests when the time arrived. Developments in display of empire went hand-in-hand with more general assertions of cultural superiority. Despite commonly being regarded as 'milestones along the highway of human progress' (Peabody, 1902), exposition organisers were habitually selective in their conceptions of what comprised civilised human society.

Possession of 'culture', as noted in Chapter 1, often signified comparison. The inclusion of the so-called 'ethnographic' exhibits, for instance, turned displays of how others lived into spectacle, equating difference with primitiveness. Between 1867 and 1939, expositions routinely featured halls of static 'anthropological' exhibits and fanciful 'native' villages in which inappropriately clothed Kalahari bushmen, Inuits, Patagonian giants, native Americans or Gaelic-speaking Scottish Highlanders performed folk dances or sat around disconsolately demonstrating handicrafts.[3] Pygmies were in particular demand. The executive committee of the 1893 World's Columbian Exposition in Chicago (1893), for example, dispatched an expedition to Zanzibar to locate a recently discovered tribe and to bring to the fair 'a family of twelve or fourteen of the fierce little midgets'.[4] The Congo, then treated as a private treasury for the Belgian throne, was another source of this human cargo.

These activities aroused little controversy at the time, with few intellectualising the exploitative nature of what they saw (Greenhalgh, 1988, 84). Expositions were compendia of the world and viewing how other peoples lived seemed a natural part of that endeavour. Yet while capitalising on genuine popular curiosity about foreign lands, the dominant representations of the inhabitants of the ethnographic villages undoubtedly supported narratives about the superior worth of mainstream Euro-American civilisations over all others. Displays of differences in cranial capacity and manual dexterity, for instance, rarely appeared without accompanying notes about the greater evolutionary progress of the Caucasians. Sometimes organisers sought to use ethnographic exhibits to provide direct justifications for imperial conquest. The organisers of St Louis's Louisiana Purchase International Exposition (1904), for example, commissioned prominent anthropologists to curate exhibits that might give scientific substance to views about the supremacy of the white race. Among the aboriginal peoples brought as living exhibits were members of the Igorrot tribe from the Philippines. The Philippine Reservation, constructed with the support of the federal government, presented them implicitly as both characteristic inhabitants of the Philippines and as savages in need of the civilising presence of the white race. The civilising force in question was the United States of America, which had just assumed control over the country after the Philippine-American War of 1899–1902.[5]

A further recurrent feature of international expositions was the increasing size of their showgrounds. Paris, the 'Queen City of Expositions' (Chandler, 1990, 283), staged no fewer than eight expositions between 1855–1937. The first in 1855 occupied 34 acres (14 hectares) just off the Champs Elysées. The 1867 Exposition, occupying 165 acres (67 hectares), switched to the much larger space of the Champs de Mars. In 1878 the exposition occupied sites measuring 192 acres (78 hectares) in the Champs de Mars and the Trocadéro (on the other bank of the Seine). By 1889, the organisers used the Champs de Mars, the Trocadéro, the quai d'Orsay and the Esplanade des Invalides, totalling 237 acres (96 hectares). The 543 acres (219 hectares) required for the 1900 Exposition Universelle meant adding new sites in the Avenue Alexandre III and the Bois de Vincennes, as well as demolishing the Palais de l'Industrie to make way for new buildings. Visitor numbers swelled as if in direct relationship to the size of the showground. Paris in 1855 received just over five million visitors, in 1867 nine million, 1878 sixteen million, and 1889 32.3 million. The 1900 figure of 50.8 million visitors remained the single season record until Montreal's Expo 67 in 1967.

The Parisian authorities, therefore, drew their Expositions Universelles into the very fabric of the city, with their permanent features becoming added cultural attractions for the French capital. Other cities found it more difficult to assimilate expositions into their central areas. Most used adjacent estates or parkland. London's 1862 International Exhibition took place in the South Kensington estate purchased with Great Exhibition funds. Vienna's Weltausstellung (1873) took place in the Prater, a parkland area beside the Danube. Philadelphia's Centennial Exposition (1876) was held in the city's Fairmount Park. As expositions grew in size and aspiration, it became common to seek larger, more marginal sites that could be treated as a tabula rasa. Land reclamation along the shores of Lake Michigan provided sites for the 1893 and 1933 Chicago expositions.

This increasing scale might seemingly have exposed the city to greater financial risk for events that seldom made a profit, but municipal city authorities were rarely major risk-takers for the events shown in Table 4.1. The 1851 Great Exhibition had established a pattern whereby initial funding primarily came from public subscription and state-appointed commissioners handled the organisation and management. Although few other exhibitions followed that exemplar closely, subscriptions and sponsorship remained the prime sources of funds, with varying involvement of the public purse. In the USA, federal support largely consisted of conferring cities with the right to hold an exposition rather than directly financing it. Cities might accept greater involvement when an exposition's future depended on it, if their exposure to risk was contained. Losses, which frequently accrued, tended to fall on private consortia. The European model, however, saw greater commitment of public money – a characteristic that perhaps made the Europeans more sympathetic than their American counterparts to efforts aimed at regulating international expositions.

The idea of regulating expositions to improve their chances of success was first mooted at the Paris Exposition Universelle of 1867 where an unofficial memorandum signed by Henry Cole and five of the other foreign commissioners recommended introducing measures to control the scope, duration and location of expositions (Allwood, 1977, 179). Nothing came of these proposals, but fears persisted that the standing of expositions would be devalued by overuse or indifferent execution. In 1908, a group of national representatives met to form a permanent alliance, the Féderation des Comités Permanents des Expositions, but this remained inadequate without cooperation at the diplomatic level (Allan, 1990, 372). In 1912, ministers representing Japan and fifteen European countries signed the International Convention of Berlin to establish a basis for a convention to regulate expositions. Noticeably, however, the American government chose not to attend this meeting and, indeed, took exception to the agreement (Galopin, 1997, 42).

The outbreak of hostilities in 1914 prevented ratification of this convention. Although European governments took up the matter again in 1920, it was not until 1928 that a conference of 40 countries met in Paris at the invitation of the French government to discuss the question of regulation. On 22 November 1928, the conference produced a 'Convention Relating to International Exhibitions'. This defined international exhibitions, or 'general exhibitions' as events of a non-commercial nature (other than fine art exhibitions), with a duration of more than three weeks, which were officially organised by a nation and to which other nations were invited through diplomatic channels (BIE, 2002). Any exhibition that included the products of more than one branch of human activity or showed the progress achieved in the whole of a given sphere of activity (such as hygiene, applied arts, modern comfort or colonial development) was deemed a general exhibition. These would not last longer than six months. General exhibitions comprised two categories: one, events in which the participating countries built their pavilions; and two, where they were not so obliged. Another variant, 'special exhibitions', covered smaller events lasting no more than three months, with a specialised theme and showgrounds no larger than 25 hectares. Host countries might hold a category one event no more than once every fifteen years, but there should be no category one event anywhere within six years of another. Equally, there should be no category two exhibition anywhere more than once every two years.[6]

The conference also advocated forming a permanent body, called the Bureau International des Expositions (BIE). The BIE would have a president and secretariat. Member countries would fund these posts and their holders, along with the members of the organisation's various committees. These were collectively responsible to six-monthly general assemblies attended by member states and observers from international agencies. The BIE's main function lay at the planning stage for future expositions. The BIE would examine an initial proposal from an organising body, make recommendations and then seek a detailed proposal. Once scrutinised, the secretariat would make recommendations to the general assembly. The assembly would then be asked to vote on reserving a particular year for an applicant, if necessary voting on rival proposals. The final stage would see the registration of the exposition as an official BIE event.

By creating these simple restrictions and a body to enforce them, the signatories hoped to spread expositions more evenly over time and make them less prone to manipulation for national gain. Regulating the number of expositions might give an individual event a better chance of being profitable and having lasting impact. Participants in expositions might also benefit from the BIE's assistance in bringing down excessively high charges if set by organisers. The convention came into force in 1931 when sufficient nations had ratified it. The BIE was established at its Paris headquarters at the same time. Their net impact, however, was limited. The agreement lacked the sanction of international law and some signatory nations ignored it, despite having committed themselves under the convention to withhold state patronage, subsidies and other privileges from expositions that failed to comply with the rules. In addition, while most European and many Latin American nations joined, the USA – initially unwilling to grant an international agency authority over events organised on its sovereign territory – remained a prominent absentee from the signatory group.[7] This proved a weakness, since on several subsequent occasions cities in the USA went ahead with expositions that the BIE did not support.

Staging American World's Fairs

It is difficult nowadays to realise how much significance expositions once had in the USA. The 1893 Exposition in Chicago, for example, was contemporaneously equated with the War of Independence and the Civil War as key events in the nation's history. At one level, it was seen as the moment when the USA turned back the wilderness and fully took control over its continental interior (Macy and Bonnemaison, 2003, 14–15). At another level, it was taken to uphold the creative imagination of America against the best that Europe could offer (Larson, 2003). More prosaically perhaps, the ten expositions held in the USA between 1853–1939 do effectively chart America's changing place on the world stage and the development of its industrial culture.

That period began somewhat inauspiciously with the New York World's Fair 1853 (see next section), which singularly failed to transplant the exposition ideals of the Great Exhibition. The Civil War temporarily ended further thoughts of such ventures, but the approach of the centenary of the American Republic in 1876 brought the possibility of using an exposition as a symbol of national reconciliation. The first suggestion to hold such an exposition was made in 1866, but no further steps were taken until August 1869. After protracted negotiations, the Philadelphia Centennial Exposition took place in the city's Fairmount Park in August 1876. Its plan followed the recent pattern of European expositions, which broke with the early schema of classifying exhibits functionally in displays contained within a single building. Vienna's Weltausstellung (1873), for example, had a main hall, with a standard rectangular floor plan partitioned off by seventeen transept halls, but also had machinery, fine art and agricultural halls. With the change to multiple buildings on an enclosed showground, organisers actively rethought their basic approaches to exposition design. Greater size and greater complexity of exhibits demanded new principles of organisation and ways of creating thematic order that might support those principles. The Philadelphia show took this trend to its logical conclusion, with five main pavilions: the main building, machinery hall, agricultural hall, horticultural hall and a permanent memorial hall (intended as a museum after the fair's closure). Clustered around, and often in the shadows of these pavilions were a further 250 buildings, providing smaller pavilions for states and foreign countries, and incidental buildings for catering, commercial and support services. It was planned with integral transport including an elevated railway, a foretaste of what inevitably occurred as showgrounds became ever larger. The exposition drew in 9.9 million visitors and earned a small profit.[8] Significantly, too, it acted as an effective showcase for American industry.

The switch from a single giant enclosure to separate pavilions did not alter the categorisation of exhibits radically, but it did remove the constraints on size. Whereas space in the Crystal Palace was rationed, providing more pavilions could now accommodate all exhibitors. Size, spectacle and grandeur were now firmly established as abiding elements in American world's fairs over the next 65 years. Staging imposing expositions became a powerful gambit in the game of place promotion played by American cities. Given the potential risk of running up a substantial deficit, the decision to hold an event made a statement about a city's significance and the depth of its pockets. The scale and spectacle also indicated something of the weight of its ambition. Yet the nature of the competition between American cities was different from that between the cities that staged Europe's expositions. The latter displayed their place within imperial orders, drawing attention to their traditions and cultural pre-eminence. Leaving aside cities like New York and Philadelphia that had substantial historic cores, aspirant American cities were experiencing explosive growth and actively creating their pecking orders. Expositions were a valuable tool in staking a claim.

This was certainly the case at the next three US world's fairs: Chicago (1893), Buffalo (1901) and St Louis (1904). Holding an exposition to commemorate the four-hundredth anniversary of Columbus's landing in the New World in 1492 had been discussed since 1882. The idea rapidly gained support nationwide, with local and civic groups in New York, Philadelphia, St Louis, Cincinnati, Washington DC, Baltimore and Chicago promoting the claims of their respective cities. The battle between the favourites, New York and Chicago, was particularly acrimonious. Groups in each had formed private corporations to promote the fair and had started fund-raising. In early 1890, Congress voted in Chicago's favour, subject to the fair's corporation agreeing to underwrite the exposition by $10 million. The enabling bill was signed in April 1890 for an event during the spring and summer of 1893, rather than 1892, to allow an additional year for preparation (Badger, 1990, 123).

The organisers of the ensuing World's Columbian Exposition struggled to find an exhibition site within the city, finally selecting Jackson Park, which bordered Lake Michigan eight miles (13 kilometres) to the south. The choice of Jackson Park initiated the trend towards selecting areas for fairgrounds that needed extensive and costly reclamation. The logic was simple but unavoidable. Good quality, level sites were unlikely to be found close to large cities since they would otherwise have been swallowed up by urban expansion. If larger and more spectacular showgrounds were required to house expositions, then suitable sites were only likely to be found at a considerable distance from a host city or in places previously shunned for their hostile environments. Jackson Park, parkland in name alone, fitted the latter category. It comprised:

> one square mile of desolation, mostly treeless, save for pockets of various kinds of oak – burr, pin, black, and scarlet – rising from a tangled undergrowth of elder, wild plum, and willow. In the most exposed portions there was only sand tufted with marine and prairie grasses. ... It was ugly, a landscape of last resort (Larson, 2003, 95).

Within 22 months, however, the organisers transformed the 600-acre (243-hectare) site. It was drained and graded, with a system of ornamental canals and lakes dividing the site into component areas. Surprisingly for a city that had become a crucible for architectural innovation after the Great Fire of 1871,[9] the organisers decided on a pronounced neo-classicism. The buildings, known as the White City, were in a Florentine style, and laid out with Beaux-Arts formalism. Following the French rather than the English model, the organisers included a formal amusement park on the narrow strip of land (the 'Midway') situated between Jackson and Washington Parks. Situated where it would not significantly detract from the aesthetics and serious-mindedness of the White City, the so-called Midway Plaisance featured ethnographic displays, international food, wild animal shows, and balloon rides. It also offered the 250-feet (76-metre) diameter Ferris wheel.

This echoed the precedent set by European expositions. Paris in 1867 had offered a 150-feet (45-metre) high lighthouse with a beam capable of reaching the clouds and surpassed it in 1889 with the 984-feet (300-metre) Eiffel Tower, undoubtedly the most enduring signature feature of any exposition.[10] Chicago itself had toyed with building an even larger tower as a response,[11] but settled for the Ferris wheel. This supplied panoramic views over the showground and continued the theme of vertical features that were regarded as a prerequisite for succeeding shows. The 1901 Pan-American Exposition at Buffalo offered the Electric Tower, a 389-feet (118-metre) high structure studded with 40 000 lights, intended to show off the abundant power from Niagara's hydro-electric plant. San Francisco's Panama-Pacific International Exposition (1915) featured a 435-feet (132-metre) high Tower of Jewels. Built in Italian Renaissance style with Byzantine features, the tower was encrusted with 100 000 hand-cut crystals called Nova-gems, which refracted the powerful spotlights in a shimmering rainbow of colour (Nye, 1990, 35).

American cities also pioneered techniques of lobbying and persuasion in their efforts to gain world's fairs. When Congress decided in favour of Chicago in the contest for the 1893 exposition, St Louis's civic leaders continued to press for their own exposition at another suitable date. This was partly an effort to reassert the city's credentials against Chicago as gateway to the west, but also an attempt to improve St Louis's image and aid its ailing economy.[12] At the end of the 1890s, a group that included a former governor, the sitting congressman and local business representatives grasped the forthcoming centenary in 1903 of the Louisiana Purchase as a suitable pretext for an exposition – although, as at Chicago, that anniversary was missed by a year. Achieving their goal required a well-oiled publicity machine. Like many towns in the American West, St Louis had developed efficient mechanisms for selling the supposedly unbridled bounty of the frontier lands to potential settlers. This was now steadily expanded until, when the show opened, its press bureau comprised two divisions, one devoted to domestic and the other to foreign promotion. The former alone employed 76 people, including 26 full-time reporters and editors, six stenographers and many clerks (Rydell, 1993, 23).

The lesson that publicity counted was not lost on other aspirants. Local groups in Virginia campaigning for an exposition to celebrate the three-hundredth anniversary of the colony at Jamestown, for example, used the evidence from St Louis to proclaim that: 'Facts and Figures Prove that Business Benefits Have Been Immense.'[13] In a similar vein New Orleans and San Francisco, the two main competitors for the 1915 Panama-Pacific Exposition, waged a fierce propaganda war to secure the nomination. New Orleans mounted a strident case for the fair by claiming that it was more centrally located, lining up many congressional supporters. San Francisco replied with a massive postcard campaign, urging people to write to their congressmen to support its bid for the fair. In the event, San Francisco won the battle less because of promotional activity than because, unlike New Orleans, it was prepared to accept federal recognition without demanding federal funds (Benedict, 1990, 219).

As in Europe,[14] international expositions revived only slowly after the First World War. During the 1920s, the smaller Sesqui-Centennial International Exposition (Philadelphia, 1926) attempted to capture the same ground as its 1876 predecessor but suffered heavy losses due to low visitor figures. Only in 1933 was the genre fully relaunched with Chicago's Century of Progress International Exposition (1933); an event that stressed the role of science as the key to a bright new future after the severe shock of the Great Depression. The exhibition subject was developed thematically through a central Hall of Science (see Figure 4.1), enclosing eight acres (3.2 hectares), which expounded the basic sciences. Other buildings were devoted to applications of science, such as radio and communications, electricity, and food and agriculture, and the social sciences. Exhibits that directly addressed everyday life augmented the sense of science as the key to the future. The Home and Industrial Arts Exhibit, for instance, displayed a variety of low-cost, prefabricated homes with the notion of building 'houses like Fords'.

Judged a cultural and financial success, the Chicago fair employed 22 000 people during the construction phase, drew over 48 million visitors, boosted retail sales in the city by 19 per cent, and returned a profit of $141 000. It reinforced the idea, inherent in much New Deal thinking, that targeted spending could bring more than proportionate benefits to the economy of an area. The organisers of the Century of Progress Exposition also showed a ready pragmatism, expressed in their decision to open the exposition for a second year to allow it an opportunity to recover its costs. Its aesthetics, design and the themes of

Figure 4.1   A postcard artist's impression of the Hall of Science, Chicago World's Fair (1933)

science and of the world of tomorrow proved popular with the public and with critics. This positive message was quickly absorbed by groups of civic and business leaders promoting other expositions, particularly New York's World's Fair (1939).

The 1939 World's Fair

The 1939 World's Fair, as noted above, was not New York's first foray into the field of international expositions. The 1853 World's Fair of the Works of Industry of All Nations, as the name clearly suggests, was a direct derivative of the Crystal Palace and clearly connected with the aims and spirit of the Great Exhibition. It built on a core of established interest. There had already been attempts to hold industrial exhibitions, notably in 1828 with the national industrial exhibition in New York (see Chapter 3). An article in the *New York Tribune* by Horace Greeley reported on London's Crystal Palace in May 1851, proposing a similar structure for New York.[15] Later that year, a group of New Yorkers who had enthusiastically attended the Great Exhibition formed a private company to organise an American equivalent. Although failing to obtain federal government support, they gained sufficient backing from the local business community to initiate the project.

Their first choice of location was a central city location at Madison Square, but this encountered opposition from local residents. In January 1852, they obtained a five-year lease from the city corporation on an alternative, if peripheral, site at Reservoir Square, Manhattan (now Bryant Square).[16] As landlord, the city only charged a peppercorn rent but specified, through lease conditions, that the building should comprise iron-and-glass and that no entrance charge should exceed 50 cents (Allwood, 1977, 27). The winning entry from the international competition to design the exhibition hall produced a building with a similar structure to the Crystal Palace, although in a cruciform shape with central dome to fit the square site. The organisers succeeded in gaining extensive foreign participation, with the US Government similarly treating the exhibition hall as a bonded warehouse. By contrast, funding proved consistently difficult, especially with the growing problems of interstate rivalry in ante-bellum America.

Building delays caused the fair to open three months late on 14 July 1853. The exhibition hall contained around 60 000 exhibits from 4000 exhibitors. Most came from the USA but there were also substantial numbers from Canada, the West Indies and European nations. The organisers classified exhibits in a similar manner to that used at Hyde Park, but also included an art gallery. From the start, there were difficulties in attracting enough visitors and losses mounted. Despite its novelty in a country without museums or academies of any kind (Greenhalgh, 1988, 38), the public were insufficiently enthused by its content or message to attend. In a move that unwittingly presaged the future, the organisers succeeded in involving the circus proprietor and showman, P.T. Barnum, to try to stem the losses.[17] Though bringing in a range of new attractions, he too failed to turn the tide of debt around. Only 1.25 million visitors had come to the World's Fair when it closed on 31 October 1854, leaving a large deficit of $340 000 (see Table 4.2).

After closure, the building staged concerts, charity balls, banquets, and various festive gatherings. Ownership eventually reverted, via the Official Receiver, to the City of New York. This Crystal Palace, in a forerunner of the fate that befell its more illustrious predecessor, showed the problems of glass-and-iron-framed buildings. It caught fire during the American Institute's fair on 5 October 1858 and was reduced to a 'shapeless mass of incandescent ruins' within twenty minutes (Stokes, 1939, 44). Few mourned its passing. As one local critic observed: 'So bursts a bubble rather noteworthy in the annals of New York. To be accurate, the bubble burst some years ago, and this catastrophe merely annihilates the apparatus that generated it' (quoted in Rydell et al., 2000, 17).

This experience soured further forays by New York into this field for some years, but interest picked up again in the last decades of the nineteenth century. The city had obtained the federal government's approval to hold an exposition in 1883 to celebrate the centenary of the peace treaty that ended the revolutionary war. The project foundered on

Table 4.2   Statistics for the New York World's Fairs, 1853 and 1939

	1853	1939
Dates	14 July 1853– 1 November 1854	30 April–31 October 1939 and 11 May– 26 October 1940
Site	Reservoir Square, Manhattan	Flushing Meadows, Queens
Area of showground	5 acres (2 hectares)	1216 acres (492 hectares)
Preparation time	2 years	4 years
Visitor numbers	1 250 000	44 932 978
Profit/(loss)	(£70 013)	(£4 680 850)
Post-exhibition changes	Exhibition building destroyed by fire, 18 October 1858	Site clearing but no longer-term developments to Flushing Meadows Corona Park

financial problems and lack of local support (Allwood, 1977, 176). Like St Louis, it tried to capture the 1893 World's Columbian Exposition but, although a favourite, its bid was weakened by factional squabbling amongst the city's Republican leadership (Rydell et al., 2000, 31). Nevertheless, the city gained considerable skill and international reputation for putting on pageants and large-scale events. The funeral of Ulysses S. Grant in 1885, the centennial of George Washington's inauguration as president in 1889 and the celebration of Admiral Dewey's triumphal return from the war against the Spanish (1899) attracted large numbers of sightseers. A three-day celebration of Columbus's voyage in October 1892 drew two million people.

Further proposals then followed in the twentieth century. In early 1910, the New York Advancement Company, a local ginger group, proposed holding an exposition in 1913 to celebrate the three-hundredth anniversary of the settlement of Manhattan. Although discussed by a feasibility committee established by the mayor, the consensus was that there were too many expositions taking place. The city could not afford an event to match the St Louis exposition and doubted in any case that another fair would bring permanent benefits to the city (Findling and Pelle, 1990, 403). In 1918, the showman Harry F. Mcgarvie initiated a permanent exposition site in the shape of the Bronx International Exhibition. Although this reached the construction phase, the war and general economic problems meant that this produced little more than the creation of Starlight Park, an amusement area (Roth, 1990). In 1927, another proposal suggested holding an exposition to commemorate the two-hundredth anniversary of George Washington's birth in 1932. This foundered on opposition from Chicago, concerned about upstaging their Century of Progress exposition, and the Merchants Association of New York, which claimed that expositions were obsolete in an age of movies, radios and cars (Findling and Pelle, 1990, 404).

Gestation

After these various near misses and abortive projects, it was always likely that New York would wish to underline its credentials as a centre for such festivities if it ever did make a successful bid. New York in the late 1930s was a far different proposition from the city of 1853. Its population had spiralled, more than doubling between 1870–1900 and again between 1900–40. Demographically, it was the world's third largest city in 1875, second in 1900 and first by 1925. New York dominated the American economy in almost every area of commerce, trade and culture (Hall, 1998, 746–7). Yet, for all its pre-eminence in many areas of American life, New York had long been missing from the roll call of cities that entertained world's fairs despite having initiated the process in 1853.

The chance to rectify matters came in the mid-1930s, although exactly when the idea for staging the 1939 World's Fair was first mooted is disputed, with different versions placing the event in either late 1934 or early 1935.[18] Whichever is correct, the pretext remained the sesquicentenary of the inauguration in New York of George Washington as president in April 1789 and the real motive remained economic. The New York financial community had noted the beneficial impact that Chicago's Century of Progress International Exposition had on that city's economy. They believed that a similar event in New York would boost confidence, still battered by the Wall Street Crash and its aftermath. It would also invigorate the city's retail and service sectors, with estimates that visitors to the fair might inject as much as one billion dollars into the local economy. However, where Chicago's Century of Progress International Exposition had looked back over a century of scientific advance, it was agreed that New York's equivalent should look forward. This, after considerable deliberations (see below), would eventually lead to the theme of 'Building the World of Tomorrow'.

A steering committee was formed, led by Grover A. Whalen (chairman), whose career as a former New York police commissioner and president of Shenley Distilleries spanned the public and private sectors;[19] Percy Strauss, the head of Macy's stores; and George McAneny, president of the Title Guarantee and Trust Company and head of the Regional Planning Association. The press carried announcements of the project on 23 September 1935, with the establishment of a non-profit corporation in October 1935. The corporation included the head of 23 banking and trust companies, 30 commercial corporations, 15 Wall Street law firms, eight insurance companies and retail firms, and eight business associations. By contrast, there were only 15 representatives from city, state and national politics, eight representing the arts and education, and one trade unionist (Cusker, 1980, 3). In 1936, the Fair Corporation established its offices on five floors of the newly built Empire State Building.

The site chosen for the exposition was in many ways key to the widespread support that the exposition enjoyed. Previous exposition organisers had selected blighted sites for their fairgrounds when there was no adequate alternative. The Chicago Exposition of 1893 had taken place on the barren and polluted Jackson Park. The sprawling 1272-acre (514-hectare) site for the succeeding Louisiana Purchase International Exposition (1904) surpassed that by picking the heavily wooded Forest Park, bisected by the heavily polluted and flood-prone Des Peres River.

The derelict and pestilential Corona Dumps in north central Queens, however, far exceeded its predecessors in these respects. Extending south from Flushing Bay in a wedge-shaped strip roughly 3.5 miles (5.6 kilometres) long and 1.25 miles (2 kilometres) wide centred on Flushing Creek, the Corona Dumps were a paradigm of industrial dereliction. The area was split into unequal segments by railways, trolley lines and the metropolitan parkway system. The construction of the Long Island Railroad saw landfill deposited in the tidal wetland to the north and the blocking of a river from Flushing Bay. The resulting backwater became a notorious breeding ground for mosquitoes. Much of the area was used for waste tipping, particularly dumping of ash by the Brooklyn Ash Removal Company. One mound of ash reached a height of almost 100 feet (30 metres) and was known locally as Mount Corona (Kuhn, 1995, 420). These activities had turned the Corona Dumps into heavily polluted marshland interspersed with mounds of spoil and pools of stagnant, sometimes toxic water.

Yet despite requiring the largest land reclamation project ever attempted in the eastern USA to turn the area into an exposition showground, it was immediately attractive to the general public and city authorities alike. It was close to the geographical centre of the city, within easy reach of major transport routes and with ample room to hold a lavish event.[20] The large central portion of the site would house the main exhibit area and the narrower southern end, when developed around an artificial lake, offered good prospects for the amusement area (Santomasso, 1980, 30). Clearance and redevelopment had few implications for existing private housing or property. Development also met the strategic planning objectives of the city's corporation. One of the fair's most important supporters within New York's civic authority, for example, was the redoubtable Robert Moses, whose power base in the city far exceeded his official title of Parks Commissioner. Moses had long cherished the idea of a park in northern Queens to rival Manhattan's Central Park.[21] The world's fair project offered an opportunity to achieve this or, at the very least, boost the amount of public open space available in this area if the city gained control of the site when the exposition finished. Under its agreement with the fair corporation, brokered by Moses, the city of New York agreed to fund the reclamation work in return for receiving the site as municipal open space once the world's fair was over. It would then be renamed Flushing Meadow Park (although was most often called Flushing Meadows).

The formal planning process began in January 1936. Grover Whalen and the city's mayor, Fiorello La Guardia, performed the groundbreaking ceremony on 19 June 1936. The contractors levelled mounds of refuse and ash, installed water mains and sewers, and drained the marshes. Difficult waterlogged or marshy areas were landscaped as lakes or water features. A series of associated infrastructural projects were undertaken to provide visitor access to the fair, including constructing the Bronx-Whitestone Bridge and the Whitestone Expressway. Connections were needed to the recently built Grand Central Parkway, which ran alongside the showground.[22] Other improvements included subway and railway extensions, new rail stations, a sewage plant for Bowery Bay, and La Guardia Airport (Kroessler, 1995, 1275). Dredging made Flushing Bay accessible by sea, with moorings for ocean-going vessels.

Finance for these developments and the construction of pavilions came from various sources. New York City donated $26.7 million to the fair, most of which was allocated to land reclamation and building its own permanent pavilion. The federal government and New York state contributed $3 million and $6.2 million respectively. Foreign governments subscribed $30 million, an amount materially assisted by the Bureau International des Expositions being persuaded to give the fair their seal of approval as *the* international exposition for 1939 (Applebaum, 1977, xi). Working capital was raised through redeemable bonds, with the fair corporation issuing over $27 million in bonds, repayable in 1941. These paid 4 per cent interest and were backed by the prospective receipts from concessions, rents and admissions. Any profits from the show would help to convert the site to its post-exposition state (Applebaum, 1977, x–xi; Kroessler, 1995, 1275).

Deciding the show's main theme taxed New York's intellectuals, with battles between those who wanted a more traditional fair and those who wanted a showcase for progress and modernity. In part, this concerned architecture: the fight of the progressives against the neo-classicists who dominated American practice and whose success at the 1893 Chicago Exposition remained fresh in the memory. Yet the dispute was also about philosophy, with the progressives wanting to impart a clear message, rooted in the American experience, about the implications of science for future life. For example, Lewis Mumford, whose contemporary writings talked of the metropolis as 'a World's Fair in continuous operation' (Mumford, 1938, 265), relished the pedagogic possibilities that the New York World's Fair might bring:

> The story we have to tell ... and which will bring people from all
> over the world to New York, not merely from the United States, is
> the story of this planned environment, this planned industry, this
> planned civilization. If we can inject that notion as a basic notion of
> the Fair, if we can point it toward the future, toward something that
> is progressing and growing in every department of life and
> throughout civilization, not merely in the United States, not merely

in New York City, but if we allow ourselves in a central position, as members of a great metropolis, to think for the world at large, we may lay the foundation for a pattern of life which would have an enormous impact in times to come.[23]

From an architectural standpoint, the result was a compromise between the neo-classical and modern (see below) but the progressives gained the upper hand regarding the show's message. The approach chosen for the New York World's Fair extended what was attempted at Chicago in 1933. When Chicago's exposition planners showed the future, they represented it as science fiction. The New York planners conceived of it as 'an attainable goal, presented on a grand scale in the tangible form of elements from commerce and industry, expanded via architecture and art. Design and daily life were conceived as one. The visitor to the Fair was to be thrust into the full-blown Age of Consumerism and the Age of the Machine' (Santomasso, 1980, 29).

Translation of these ideas into practice was assigned to a theme committee. It was headed by Walter Teague, an industrial designer who had worked at both the Chicago and Dallas expositions, and Robert Kohn, a New York-based architect with a deep appreciation of the significance of planning.[24] They, in turn, were able to call on the services of a growing body of exhibition designers and consultants. The frequency with which US cities had organised expositions meant that, by the 1930s, exhibition design had become a professional activity. Alongside the press and public relations specialists were now many individuals and firms skilled in planning, realising, laying out, managing and publicising expositions.

The theme committee's final report emphasised the need for the fair to propagate a central message and recommended the theme of 'Building the World of Tomorrow'. This started by analysing the role of the machine in all aspects of human activity and ended with a vision of how new communities might be constituted (Cusker, 1980, 5).[25] The showground would be divided into seven sectors, intended to coincide with the major functional divisions of modern living: communications and business systems, medicine and public health, science and education, community interests, food, production and distribution, and transportation. Each zone would feature the exhibits of participating firms, groups or countries, but also had a 'focal exhibit' provided by the organisers designed to provide 'a graphic summary and panoramic index' (Monaghan, 1939, n.p.). In addition, and in light of the sesquicentenary that the fair commemorated, the organisers would construct a central exhibit to show how the new community would appear in a society dedicated to democratic ideas. A board of design led by Stephen A. Voorlees prescribed standards for buildings, murals and statuary to harmonise the aesthetics of the showground. This comprised a mixed vision: a combination of Beaux-Arts principles, particularly in layout, and a version of the primary stylistic vocabulary of the Streamline Moderne (Art Deco) design that many interwar expositions favoured. This version, known as 'Streamform', saw objects smoothed down into aerodynamic shapes reminiscent of aircraft regardless of whether their function warranted it.

Various factional interests caused problems during the creation of the exposition. Following the example set by Chicago in 1933, industrial corporations built and furnished their own pavilions. Design briefs were given, but inevitable tensions arose over medium and message. From a political standpoint, the sensitivity of the 1930s meant that care was needed in presenting the theme of democracy to prevent a swathe of potential contributors from Fascist and authoritarian countries boycotting the show. In the event, Nazi Germany decided not to participate, but there were pavilions from Italy, Japan and the Soviet Union. There were also disputes with the scientific community that, at times, threatened to undermine the credibility of the world's fair. The New York plan bore similarities to that adopted for Chicago in 1933, but at Chicago, scientists had participated as full partners in planning the show. By contrast, as Rydell (1993, 106–7) notes, their counterparts at the New York World's Fair found their position less favourable: 'Scientists suddenly found themselves facing instead a corporate takeover of the cultural prerogatives that they had asserted at the earlier fair. ... it became increasingly clear that science, but not necessarily scientists, would determine the shape of the 1939 fair ...'. Tensions eased after the organisers made the conciliatory gesture of establishing an advisory committee on science to guide the scientific content and later by providing a hall for joint displays of science and education. The director of the department of science at the New York World's Fair, Gerald Wendt, explained the basic approach taken in *Science for the World of Tomorrow* (Wendt, 1939, 14–15), a book published for the fair:

> we shall examine the various aspects of life today as social phenomena brought to their present state by the progress of science and subject to further change from the same source. Behind the social picture is a story of economics and industrial organisation, and behind that is the story of technology and science. The world of tomorrow will inevitably develop from this background. ... The Fair offers no programme, no panacea for society, nor does this book. Yet both look toward tomorrow with the confidence that comes of understanding today.

'The World of Tomorrow'

President Franklin D. Roosevelt opened the world's fair on 30 April 1939. Costing more than $155 million, it drew record participation from 33 US states and 60 nations and international organisations, along with 44 million visitors over two seasons. Besides using private cars, for which 35 000 parking spaces were provided, visitors primarily travelled to the fair from New York City by public transport. Ferries from Manhattan docked at the fairground. The Long Island Railroad ran a train service from Pennsylvania station on Seventh Avenue to a specially constructed world's fair station at Flushing. The journey took ten minutes. Special city buses, coach routes and the subway departed from the city for the fair (Gelernter, 1995, 13). Packaged holidays including city attractions and fair passes proved popular. Guidebooks counselled the need for careful planning and organisation if the visitor was to get the best from the city and the fair. For example, after twelve chapters of explaining where to find accommodation and recounting the delights of New York City to the single woman traveller, Hillis (1939, 187) finally turned her attention to the event that was 'so stupendous, gigantic, super-magnificent a greatest-show-on-earth that people could write a whole book about it'. Her particular advice for the first-time visitor was to take a specially conducted bus tour of the fair from New York City for $3.50, including gate entry, with the possibility of taking a return bus later back to Fifth Avenue. The information so gained would help lessen the weariness that would come from selectively trudging 'sixty miles of asphalt roads and I don't know how many miles of walks' (ibid., 189).

The showground itself was essentially divided into two areas, the exhibit area and the amusement area. The exhibit area contained the seven functional zones, plus the government area. These were kept spatially distinct within the plan, which adopted geometric Beaux-Arts principles. Tree-lined avenues converged on focal points and divided the showground into fan-like sectors. Constitution Mall, the central axis, ran from the Theme Centre through the Lagoon of Nations (around which were clustered many national pavilions), to the US federal government's building. Two bridges across the Grand Central Parkway gave access from the main showground to the transportation zone. The amusement area was clustered around the Fountain Lake at the southeast end of the fairground, deemed a safe enough distance to prevent its frivolity impinging on the main exposition site.

The Beaux-Arts principles underpinning the plan were characteristic of the appeal that geometric design has always had for sections of the architectural profession. Quite apart from creating pleasing spectacle, ideal geometric forms were felt to impart the basis for order and harmony. It was said, for example, that geometric formalism in the ground plan provided greater clarity of organisation, allowed the different zones to be clearly recognised by visitors, and eased the circulation of people. Whatever theoretical validity these points may have, masses of multicoloured flags, pylons, booths and statues blocked the vistas and interfered with direction finding (Allwood, 1977, 146). What the plan undeniably did, however, was to create a symbolic central point, an *étoile* situated on slightly higher ground, at which the organisers could place the fair's bluntly ideological Theme Centre with its paean to American democracy.

The Theme Centre contained three elements: the Trylon, Perisphere and Helicline (see Figure 4.2). The Trylon, a 728-feet (222-metre) high, triangular tapering obelisk, provided the vertical feature. This was connected to the Perisphere, an eighteen-storey high globe with a 180-feet (55-metre) diameter. On entering the Perisphere, visitors were carried up a 50-feet (15-metre) escalator and deposited on circular balconies. From this point, they looked down on the main 'World of Tomorrow' exhibit, a diorama of the city of the future entitled 'Democracity' designed by Henry Dreyfuss. Spectacular light shows played overhead. These two buildings had steel frameworks clad with white-painted gypsum board. The Helicline was a spiral ramp, 950 feet in length, that encircled the other two buildings and gave fairgoers panoramic views of the fair as they moved up to enter the Perisphere. Although their precise symbolism was not wholly clear, the strength of their visual image made the outline shapes of the Trylon and Perisphere the fair's signature feature. Besides appearing on the fair's logo, they were reproduced on postage stamps, bumper stickers, lapel badges and magazine covers, with replicas even sold as salt and pepper shakers.

As an expression of the fair's commitment to planning, as an illustration of scientific rationality, at all scales, the fair – its surroundings, grounds, buildings, landscaping, sculpture and murals – represented a microcosm of how planning should proceed.[26] Different zones were colour-coded, with colours graded in progressively darker hues, from very pale pastel tints near the theme structures to basic rich hues for buildings on the outside perimeter of the fair (Allwood, 1977, 146). Here again practice obfuscated the underlying theory. A mass of banners, murals, kiosks and applied decoration obscured the exteriors of many pavilions and reduced any possible benefits from a unified colour scheme.

The exhibits, many of which articulated the future through spectacular displays of sleek buildings, mobility and automated domesticity, also embraced the planning ideal. The Consolidated Edison

Figure 4.2   The Trylon, Perisphere and Helicline, New York's World's Fair (1939)

building had Walter Teague's 'City of Light' diorama. A 'Town of Tomorrow' showed fifteen low-cost model houses made from different materials and arranged in a suburban setting. The transportation zone, containing exhibits by nine industrial corporations, enthusiastically embraced the futuristic theme. The Ford Motor Company, for example, addressed the 'Road of Tomorrow'. Visitors rose in facsimiles of Ford's latest models on a tight, triple-tiered spiral ramp around the outer edge of the Industrial Hall. The exhibit blended the commercial, didactic and spectacular. It promoted Ford cars and gave panoramic views over the fair, but the ramp's specially coated surface was intended to show advances in road technology. The same company's turntable-based 'Ford Cycle of Production' display illustrated the processes of car production with carefully constructed special effects. The accompanying promotional brochure summarised the exhibitor's chosen theme: 'It shows how the Ford Motor Company, pioneering the idea of a low-priced car that millions could afford to buy, has stimulated employment in every corner of the globe' (quoted in Gelernter, 1995, 159).

The adjacent General Motors pavilion showed a similar blend. At its heart was a multilevel road intersection of the future. Within its pavilion was a display of the latest General Motors cars and an auditorium containing Futurama, the fair's most popular attraction. Futurama comprised a 36 000 square feet scale model forecasting the America of 1960. Designed by Norman Bel Geddes, a leading industrial designer of the 1930s, Futurama provided a complete landscape of futuristic homes, urban complexes, bridges, dams, surrounding landscape, and an advanced highway system that permitted speeds of 100 miles (160 kilometres) per hour. Visitors viewed the exhibit from moving chairs with individual loudspeakers, seeing the view as if from an aircraft flying at low altitude from coast to coast. Not surprisingly, given the exhibit's sponsors, the world of tomorrow was car-centred, with urban design remade to cope with the needs of the internal combustion engine (Hauss-Fitton, 1994). Pedagogy was inseparable from consumerism in these visions of the future.

The End of Illusion

The publicity machine rolled on relentlessly. The wire services sold pre-packaged telegrams to visitors, with the most popular being: 'Fair wonderful, climate gorgeous, having a swell time, wish you were here' (quoted in Gelernter, 1995, 349). The fair corporation's publicity department actively fed the press and news agencies. Over 305 000 photographs were distributed to the media, 181 newsreels were sent to theatres in the USA and Canada, and an endless stream of press releases was distributed. Some measure of their success is that during the first season 160 magazines had run special issues devoted to the world's fair, 731 programmes relating to it were broadcast on radio, and over 12 million column inches appeared in newspapers across America (Mullen, 1990, 298). Special campaigns with pageantry were organised to help sell tickets (Susman, 1980, 19). Yet despite the optimism expressed, the mood quickly changed. The high cost of building the fair required 50 million visitors even to make a small profit. The 25.8 million visitors attending in the first season, far below expectations, led to mounting losses. Away from the fair, Manhattan shopkeepers and hoteliers expressed their disappointment with their profits from visitors (Applebaum, 1977, xvii).

As the end of the fair approached on 31 October 1939, it was decided to follow Chicago's lead and reopen for a second season in 1940 to recover costs. Changes were also made to enhance the fair's appeal. Admission prices were lowered and rents to exhibitors reduced. The organisers brought in many new concessions to the Amusement Area, now renamed the Great White Way. The guide book was revised with exhibits listed in alphabetical order, omitting all mentions of zones. The earnestness with which the scientific message was conveyed was toned down. Most importantly, the changing political environment completely altered the presentation necessary for a *world's* fair. Whatever the pretensions as to the fair being an island of tranquillity in a tempestuous world, the vision of a future illuminated by American science and democracy seemed hollow given the outbreak of the Second World War. The theme was changed, therefore, from 'Building the World of Tomorrow' to 'For Peace and Freedom'.

Even before the end of the fair, the exhibits had become increasingly dilapidated. The flags outside the French and Polish exhibits were draped in black to symbolise the fall of their countries. The Czechoslovakian Pavilion, completed with American funds after invasion by Germany, remained as a symbol of resistance. Combatant nations carefully maintained their pavilions in the hope of directing favourable propaganda at the American public and, in turn, the US government. The British added new elements to emphasise the justice of their cause in the fight for democracy and liberty. Despite German occupation, Norway remained represented by local concessions; Denmark pulled out and was replaced by Iraq. The deteriorating world situation resonated throughout the fair. The Soviet Union declined to attend for the second season. After the Non-Aggression Pact between Stalin and Hitler, the Soviet pavilion was dismantled and returned to Russia at the exhibitor's request. In its place came an open air amphitheatre called the 'American Common' – an area devoted to the perpetuation of democracy. A bomb exploded at the British Empire exhibit. After the fair closed, arsonists destroyed the Japanese pavilion in protest at the attack on Pearl Harbor. Figuratively rather than actually, the Trylon and Perisphere's 'four thousand tons of steel were scrapped during World War II to make bombs and military equipment' (Rock and Moore, 2001, 278). The war also caused the cancellation of two fairs planned by Axis powers to promote their regimes – the 1940

Tokyo World Exposition, linked with the twelfth Summer Olympiad, and the BIE-backed 1942 Rome World Exposition or E42, intended to celebrate the twentieth anniversary of the Fascist march on the city (see also Chapter 7). An age of wilful innocence had ended.

Having said this, the balance sheet for the city of New York was far from negative. Admittedly the fair itself accumulated formidable debts. Attendance forecasts proved wildly overconfident. Visitor figures were 44 931 631 – well short of the anticipated 100 million – and debts of £4.6 million were incurred. The fair corporation was forced to declare bankruptcy, with only some 40 per cent of money invested being repaid (Kroessler, 1995, 1276). Most of this went to New York city, which enforced its contractual right to the first slice of receipts from admissions, rents and concessions. The city, therefore, did not incur significant loss, took pride in being host to an event held in the most difficult circumstances, and rebuilt its Depression-tarnished prestige. Indeed, the fair was an iconic event of the decade, 'mesmerising New York the way New York mesmerised the nation' (ibid.). More prosaically, the city benefited from the fair's associated infrastructural projects. There were major improvements to transport, the metamorphosis of a giant rubbish dump into public open space, and conversion of the few permanent buildings to new uses. The amphitheatre, for instance, became the entrance and service area of a paid bathing establishment on Meadow Lake. The New York city building was converted to an ice-rink and, after serving as the temporary home of the United Nations from 1946 to 1950, became the Queens Museum of Art. Lack of funds prevented Flushing Meadows becoming the equivalent of Central Park, but work to make it acceptable as public open space intensified in the years after the end of the war. Certainly, as the next chapter notes, it provided a readily available space where another world's fair could be mounted in 1964.

Notes

1   The list shown in this table represents our judgments as to the key events. It differs from inventories produced by other scholars, just as their lists each differ from one another (for example, see Luckhurst, 1951; Allwood, 1977; Mattie, 1998) and, indeed, at times we make allusion to other, smaller events that do not appear in Table 4.1. Quite simply, there is no precise agreement about what makes an exposition truly international. Even the establishment of the Bureau International des Expositions in 1928 (see later in this chapter) did little to resolve the prevailing confusion.

2   It would be unfair to leave this point without noting that there were large

industrial exhibitions staged in African, Asian or South American countries within this period. In the 1890s, for example, there was an International Exhibition at Kingston (Jamaica) in 1891, the South Africa and International Exhibition at Kimberley (South Africa) in 1893, and the Exposición Centro-Americana at Guatemala City (Guatemala) in 1897 (Allwood, 1977, 182). None, however, contained the range of participants or international scope that typify the expositions considered here.

3 Benedict (1994, 59–60) provides a listing of the peoples most often so depicted for international expositions from 1867 to 1986.

4 *Chicago Tribune*, 20 February 1891, quoted in Larson (2003, 121).

5 Expositions also reflected prevailing attitudes towards race and ethnicity by their organisation and their policies towards employment. Exposition sites were far from being islands of harmony in a sea of social exclusion. The Jamestown Tercentennial Exhibition (1907), for instance, accommodated the prevailing segregation policies in Virginia. Less overt policies also worked in the same manner. The policies of management and labour unions at the 1933 Century of Progress International Exposition in Chicago (see below) meant that few black Americans were employed in building or operating the fairgrounds. For the first time, however, representatives of the black community and their white supporters directed sustained criticism at the overt racism that stalked this, like many previous expositions (Rydell, 1993, 170–1). In the process, attention was directed at what, in later years, became an increasingly bitter struggle over modes of representation and the underlying hegemony of cultural elites.

6 The basic principles of the 1928 convention still apply, but they were updated by a 1972 protocol. Changes particularly concern the length of time required between events. In addition, the two categories of event are no longer officially used, although commonly used informally.

7 There were 88 member countries in 2002.

8 Although this was more than absorbed by the federal government demanding repayment of its loan.

9 The regeneration of Chicago had seen the city become the world leader in experimental use of iron-framed buildings. These were then springing up throughout the city centre.

10 Gustave Eiffel's design was the winner of a competition that included entries such as a giant guillotine and a 960-feet (350-metre) stone pyramid bearing sculptures of the heroes and main events of the Revolution (Hall, 1990, 109).

11 Plans ranged from a log-built tower 500 feet higher than the Eiffel Tower and a hydraulic telescoping tower to a proposal in August 1891 from Gustave Eiffel himself to design a scaled-up version of the Paris tower (see Jay, 1987; Larson, 2003, 135).

12 The local economy had been badly affected by the depression of the mid-1890s; the city's image had been tarnished by labour unrest during a violent transit workers' strike and a reputation for political corruption. In passing, it may be noted that its reputation for violence would long outlive its 1904 incarnation as festival city (for example, see McLaughlin, 2002).

13 *Virginia Pilot*, 7 July 1905, 1.
14 Understandably because of the political climate of the time and their normal lengthy gestation period, European expositions did not restart until the mid-1920s with the British Empire Exhibition at Wembley, London (1924–5) and the Paris Exposition Internationale des Arts Décoratifs et Industriels Modernes (1925).
15 Quoted in Findling and Pelle, 1990, 13; commentary in *The Times*, 21 May 1851, 4. Greeley's writings are reproduced in collected form in Greeley, 1851.
16 The site is located next to the present-day New York Public Library.
17 Barnum had been originally approached at the planning stage in 1851, but had declined.
18 Grover Whelan, the fair corporation's eventual president, attributed the event to a meeting between himself and other business leaders in 1934 (Gelernter, 1995, 339–40). By contrast, Applebaum (1977, xi) states that Joseph Shagden, an engineer and a distant relation of Eleanor Roosevelt, first presented the idea of the fair to a group of potential supporters from the business world in May 1935. Accuracy here depended on standpoint, for Shagden brought a law suit against the fair corporation for firing him on the grounds of 'not fitting in'. As the case was settled out of court, no verdict was published.
19 Whalen was also chairman of the mayor of New York's reception committee (1919–53) and, as such, oversaw many of the city's famous ticker-tape parades. Events like the reception for Charles Lindbergh in 1927 were reminiscent of the city entries of the classical era.
20 Indeed at 1216 acres (568 hectares), the showground was second only to St Louis in the history of international expositions.
21 For an analysis of the way in which provision of public open space fitted into Moses' broader analysis, see Gandy, 2002, 115–52.
22 In the final plan a small section of the showground, devoted to the transportation zone, lay on the other side of the parkway.
23 Quoted in Cusker, 1980, 4.
24 Kohn, for example, was a co-founder of the Regional Plan Association of America.
25 Few sources summarise the connection between this philosophy and the vision of the future community more succinctly than the film *The City* (1939, Civic Films/American Institute of Planners). *The City* was directed by Ralph Steiner and Willard van Dyke and was made for screening at the New York World's Fair. It traces the evolution of the small town into the great metropolis, highlighting the desire to escape from the city, and suggesting an alternative 'green city', produced by benign application of technology that re-established society's harmony with its living environment.
26 Not all buildings could be brought into the overall design remit. Classical designs, for example, were allowed in the government zone, where it was recognised to be politic to allow that foreign governments building their own pavilions choose the style they preferred.

CHAPTER FIVE

Expo 67

> There can be no better standpoint for an
> intelligent survey of modern progress than that
> afforded by an international exhibition. This
> must be viewed, however, not merely as an
> extensive bazaar with attached places of
> amusement, but as a central museum of
> industry; too vast and costly for permanence,
> but all the more fully illustrative of production,
> and of social progress in every respect. ... Nor is
> an exhibition a landmark of progress merely, but
> a starting point as well; it is filled not only with
> the flower of present industry but with the seed
> of that of future years.
>
> Patrick Geddes (1887, 1)

Any type of international festival capable of surviving in recognisable form from 1851 to the present is clearly resilient. Despite the profound social and economic changes that had occurred in the two decades between the 1939 New York World's Fair and its successor, the 1958 Brussels Exposition Universelle et Internationale, the old pattern soon returned. The list of host cities and nations shown in Table 5.1, for instance, contains few surprises. Brussels, Seattle and New York, which staged the first three expositions after the Second World War, had all previously done so and each persevered with the science-as-progress theme. Brussels and New York even reused parts of their previous fairgrounds. Two of the three new host countries found in Table 5.1 – Canada and Portugal – were entirely within the established mould. The third, Japan, differed by being the first Asian country to stage an exposition, but the Japanese had enthusiastically participated in such events since the Exposition Universelle in Paris in 1867. They themselves had planned to hold expositions in Tokyo in 1917 and 1940, but were twice thwarted by the outbreak of war. Any suggestion that the entry of Japan represented much departure from the norm is, therefore, debatable.

Yet the resumption of expositions after the Second World War was not simply business as usual. Prewar ideological conflicts had given way

Table 5.1   International expositions, 1958–98

1958	Brussels *Exposition Universelle et Internationale de Bruxelles (Expo 58)*
1962	Seattle *World's Fair (Century 21 Exposition)*
1964–5	New York *World's Fair*
1967	Montreal *Expo 67: Universal and International Exhibition of 1967*
1968	San Antonio *Hemisfair 68: a Confluence of Cultures of the Americas*
1970	Osaka *Japan World Exposition (Expo 70)*
1974	Spokane *Expo 74: the International Exposition of the Environment*
1975	Okinawa *International Ocean Exposition (Expo 75)*
1982	Knoxville *International Energy Exposition*
1984	New Orleans *Louisiana World Exposition*
1985	Tsukuba *Expo 85*
1986	Vancouver *Expo 86: the 1986 World Exposition*
1988	Brisbane *World Expo 88*
1992	Seville *Universal Exposition*
1998	Lisbon *Expo 98*

---

to Cold War rivalries, which had reconfigured the world into two mutually antagonistic power blocs, each led by a nuclear superpower, and a 'third world' of emerging nations. Statements of imperial pride and 'civilising mission' still abounded, but were soon eclipsed by new issues of economic development and client-state dependencies. In time, even the key notion of science-as-progress was found wanting, with expositions increasingly addressing questions connected with the environment, and human relations. Indeed, towards the close of the twentieth century, issues concerning the *abuses* of science and technology gained almost as much prominence as the traditional celebration of their potential benefits.

It would be some years, however, before the full significance of these points became apparent. Indeed, as measured by visitor figures, the zenith of the exposition's appeal had still to arrive. The three shows between 1964–70 attracted the highest attendances on record, with the 54.9 million who visited Expo 67 and 64.2 million at Expo 70 finally beating the single season record of 48.1 million set by Paris (1900). In this chapter, we take a case study of Montreal's Expo 67, the first North American exposition held outside the USA, which effectively represented the highwater mark of the international exposition movement. As in the two previous chapters, we again examine the progress of this exposition through the span of its production cycle, but before doing so, it is important to examine the revival of the international exposition movement after the Second World War.

Revival

The delay in resuming expositions was not for want of potential candidates. St Louis announced plans in 1948 to hold an exposition commemorating the sesquicentenary of the Louisiana Purchase, but met objections that such a fair would aggravate the city's housing shortage and deprive citizens of their parkland. Plans for world's fairs in Houston and San Francisco, both scheduled for 1956, not only failed to attract sufficient support but also encountered criticisms that world's fairs *per se* were outmoded (Findling and Pelle, 1990, 406). European rivals repeatedly cancelled their plans in light of austerity and severe material shortages. In May 1950, the French announced plans for an event in 1955 to commemorate the centenary of the first Parisian Exposition Universelle. These were shelved in November 1950, when the French delegation informed the BIE that it was postponing its exposition until 1961 because funds were needed for rearmament and economic modernisation (Schroeder-Gudehus and Cloutier, 1994, 157). The British wanted to mount an event in London to mark the centenary of the Great Exhibition, with a government committee of inquiry (the Ramsden Committee) arguing that if the exhibition went ahead: 'it should surpass the New York World's Fair in size and technical achievement' (quoted in Luckhurst, 1951, 166). That was never a realistic option and scaled-down plans produced the more modest national exhibition, the Festival of Britain, held in the summer of 1951.

The first full postwar exposition, the 1958 Brussels Exposition Universelle, was originally proposed in 1947 and received BIE endorsement in November 1953 (Schroeder-Gudehus and Cloutier, 1994, 157). Entirely government-funded, it was intended to stimulate Belgian economic growth and the development of the nation's African colonies. Expo 58 occupied the spot where the city had staged its 1935 exposition, although the need for 50 per cent more space saw it spill over into the adjacent Royal Park of Laeken. The resulting 494 acres (205 hectares) of undulating parkland offered pavilions in an eclectic range of modernist styles. Cold War rivalries found expression in the cultural politics of design. Expositions had seen ideological rivals build competing pavilions before, as with the sight of the broodingly symbolic neo-classical Soviet and German pavilions facing one another across the

Champs de Mars at the 1937 Paris Exposition Internationale. Now the USA and the Soviet Union squared up to one another, with the USA's pavilion, featuring the bounty of life in everyday America, judged to be outclassed by the Russian display of space technology.

Although making a considerable loss of 3 billion Belgian francs, the informal balance sheet recognised the significant local economic impact of the exposition. The construction phase employed around 15 000 workers. Many of the 41 million visitors stayed at least a weekend and spent money on food, hotels and transport in Brussels. More lastingly, the city gained 30 miles (48 kilometres) of new roads, five miles (eight kilometres) of tunnels, a large area of attractive parkland and a new skyline feature in the Atomium (see Figure 5.1) – a scaled-up model of the iron atom that symbolised Belgium's past, made connection with the atomic age, and signified Belgium's position within the European Community (Brussels was the home of the European Atomic Energy Community).

The two ensuing expositions took place in the USA. Seattle's Century 21 Exposition (1962) attracted 9.6 million visitors. It was held on a downtown site of just 74 acres (30 hectares) that was so small by contrast with other expositions that Reyner Banham (1962, 134) called it the first 'country fair of the space age'. The fair grew directly out of Cold War rivalries. The American scientific community promoted it after witnessing the Soviet Union beating the Americans into space in 1957. Concerned at this affront from what had previously been regarded as a 'bellicose but scientifically backward nation' (Ashdown, 1990, 319), a meeting of defence and astronautical scientists in Washington DC proposed holding a fair to show that the USA remained pre-eminent in space research. At much the same time, city planners in Seattle were canvassing support for a fiftieth anniversary reprise of the 1909 Alaska-Yukon Pacific Exhibition. Although scarcely the geographical heart of the American space effort, a meeting between the two parties saw Seattle designated as the host city for an international exposition celebrating scientific achievement and imagination.

The resulting fair was arranged into zones dealing with commerce and industry, art and entertainment, the World of Science (dominated by the US pavilion) and an eleven-storey high 'World of Tomorrow' display. The 'World of Tomorrow' had eight major sections including 'Man's Past Futures', 'Your Future Today' and 'Century 21 City' – a celebration of mass car ownership. Shops, bazaars and restaurants lined the Boulevards of the World (Ashdown, 1990, 320). Other attractions that became permanent additions to the cityscape included 'the Space Needle', a vertical feature that served as an observation tower (see Figure 5.2), and a high-speed monorail link with the central city. After

Figure 5.1   The Atomium, Expo 58 (Brussels 1958)

the fair closed the showground was converted to the Seattle Centre, complete with museums, exhibition space, shops, an opera house and a sports arena. Besides earning a profit, the fair left an extensive area of new infrastructure[1] and supplied an example that other smaller American cities tried to emulate in the 1970s and 1980s.

The 1964–5 New York World's Fair was on a wholly different scale. Ostensibly celebrating the three-hundredth anniversary of British forces

Figure 5.2   The Space Needle, Seattle World's Fair (Century 21
              Exposition, 1962)

gaining control of the Dutch city of New Amsterdam in 1664, it occupied 646 acres (268 hectares) of the area occupied earlier by the 1939–40 World's Fair. Unlike its predecessor, however, it was denied BIE approval. This was partly because the bureau had already recognised Century 21 as a 'special exposition', but probably owed more to the New York delegation antagonising the BIE by making it clear that the exposition would not run under its rules. In response, the BIE requested member states not to support New York World's Fair. This deterred the Soviet bloc and most western European countries, apart from Spain, although there was significant support from the Middle East, Asia and Latin America. Of the 140 pavilions, 36 were taken by foreign countries and 21 by US states. American commercial corporations constructed most of the rest, with firms such as Ford, General Motors, Chrysler, General Electric, Pepsi Cola, Kodak, IBM and Westinghouse investing more than $1 billion in pavilions designed to present the advance of science as corporate public relations. Their contents largely invited the spectator to see the sponsoring company as midwife of the bright new world of tomorrow. These implicit corporate advertisements only served to bolster the already close association between expositions and the goals of western market capitalism.

Adopting the theme of 'Man in a Shrinking Globe in an Expanding Universe', the fair ran for two seasons: from 22 April to 18 October 1964 and from 21 April to 17 October 1965. Against the advice of the initial architectural panel, who resigned in protest, the fair's organisers returned to a modified version of the 1939 Beaux-Arts ground plan. The organisers divided the site into five thematic areas – federal and state, international, industrial, transportation, and amusement – with the last two occupying the same locations as in 1939–40. They aligned new avenues with loop and radiating avenues to simplify the earlier layout and tie its elements together, using plantings, lighting, and focal points to bring clarity to the fair's underlying schema (Lawrence, 1990, 328; Stern et al., 1995). The AMF monorail system supplied internal transport as well as synoptic views over the show (see Figure 5.3). Replacing the 1939 fair's Theme Centre was the Unisphere, a 120-feet (36-metre) diameter model of the earth cast in stainless steel and set in a circular fountain lake.[2] There was, however, more than a little symbolism in visitors now being presented with the spectacle of a hollow globe as a signature feature rather than, as in 1939, being invited into an imposing dome to witness a display depicting the potential of the city and technology in a progressive democracy.

The 1964–5 world's fair received a mixed reception. The two-season attendance of 51 million was a record, but losses amounted to over $7 million. Investors received back only 62 cents in the dollar and the fair

Figure 5.3 The AMF monorail system, New York World's Fair (1964–5)

again failed to generate the funds necessary to finish Flushing Meadows Park in the ambitious manner that Robert Moses had hoped. Critically, too, reviews were disappointing despite the relentless operations of the publicity machine. Although intended as a showpiece for the American way of life, the emphasis on manufacturers' products and the attention given to the amusement park emphasised the extent to which the pendulum had swung from the moral internationalism and rational recreation of the Crystal Palace. Perhaps damaged by the lack of full international participation, the 1964–5 New York World's Fair proffered a rampant and inescapable commercialism. As Allwood (1977, 162) remarked: 'The wheel had come full circle and the showmanship of the medieval salesmen had arrived back having spent some time banished to the trade and funfair areas.' It was certainly an issue that would tax the thinking of Expo 67's planners as they consciously tried to reconnect their exhibition with the universalism of the international exposition movement.

Montreal 1967

That, of course, was not the only issue on the minds of Expo 67's organisers. If the 1964 world's fair testified to New York's confident claims to global status, Expo 67 (see Table 5.2) expressed Montreal's hopes of setting aside its long history of frustrated international aspirations. With a population in 1967 of 2.49 million, Montreal remained Canada's largest city and the seventh largest in North America. Nevertheless, it had experienced steady decline since the early twentieth century when it was the country's leading manufacturing centre, a major nucleus for the arts and culture, and a transport hub with strong ties to European and American capitals (for example, see Germain and Rose, 2000, 2; also Lewis, 2000). As the centre of Francophone and Catholic Canada, Montreal's standing had suffered relative to the emerging Anglo-Protestant core. The development of Ontario and particularly Toronto, 340 miles (550 kilometres) to the southwest, had eroded Montreal's hold over the resources of the vast St Lawrence-Great Lakes hinterland, especially through its better location relative to major US economic centres. Toronto's industrial growth outstripped that of Montreal, with industrial headquarters, financial institutions, and ancillary business and professional services increasingly concentrated there. Shipping tonnage switched to west coast ports.

Montreal's standing, therefore, threatened to dwindle to little more than that of a regional city serving North America's primary Francophone area. A 'regional city' identity, however, did not sit well with Montreal's ruling elite. Quite apart from loss of prestige, the city's leaders feared that this reduced status would irrevocably damage

Table 5.2   Statistics for Expo 67 (Montreal, 1967)

Dates	28 April–27 October 1967
Site	St Lawrence Islands and former dockyards (MacKay Pier)
Area of showground	988 acres (410 hectares)
Preparation time	$4^1/_2$ years
Visitor numbers	54 992 000 (50 306 648 paying)
Profit/(loss)	(C$233 million)
Post-exhibition changes	Establishment of reduced permanent exposition site. Subsequently piecemeal conversion of buildings and downgrading to general public park. Lakes redesigned for competitive sports for 1976 Olympics. Construction of Formula 1 motor racing circuit.

Montreal's chances of competing for mobile commercial investment and employment. As a result, they looked for high profile opportunities to reassert Montreal's place on the world stage (Germain and Rose, 2000, 3). The strategy of acting as hosts for international festivals offered a chance to do so, as Montreal's determined pursuit of the nominations for both Expo 67 and the 1976 Olympic Games shows (see also Chapter 7).

Gestation

Expo 67 was not the first large-scale exhibition held in Montreal. Between 1850–97, the city acted as host for more than twenty national exhibitions, ranging from agricultural fairs to the 1868 Military and Industrial Exhibition and the 1891 International Electrical Exhibition (Cooper, 1969, 110, 194). Larger international expositions were planned in 1917 and 1942 to commemorate, respectively, the fiftieth anniversary of the 1867 British North America Act and the three-hundredth anniversary of the founding of Montreal. Similar to the experience of Japan (see above), both proposals were abandoned on the outbreak of war. In the late 1950s, these ambitions were revived. While representing Canada at the 1958 Brussels Exposition Universelle, the Quebec senator Mark Drouin put forward the idea that Canada might emulate the example set by the USA and celebrate its centenary by holding an exposition. Montreal took up the proposal after it had first been rejected by Toronto. Backed by the mayoral regime of Sarto Fournier, the city's authorities persuaded the federal government to apply to the BIE for recognition of the exposition as a category one event. Drouin and Fournier duly presented Montreal's case at the BIE's 1960 meeting. Montreal, however, faced a rival bid from Moscow, which wanted to hold an exposition in 1967 to celebrate the fiftieth anniversary of the Bolshevik Revolution. Despite initial optimism,[3] the General Assembly nominated the Soviet Union by 16 votes to 14, leaving the Montreal party to ruminate on Moscow's alleged sharp practices in winning the vote.[4]

The Soviet Union's concern about spiralling costs of the project, however, led Moscow to relinquish its nomination in April 1962. Jean Drapeau, who became mayor of Montreal in October 1960,[5] lobbied the federal government to renew Canada's exposition bid, obtaining somewhat reluctant support from John Diefenbaker's federal government in September 1962.[6] The bid for the exposition, intended at first to be a year-long celebration, was hastily resubmitted to the BIE and accepted on 13 November 1962. Its theme of 'Man and His World' stemmed from the title of Antoine de Saint-Exupéry's book *Terre des*

Hommes (1939)[7] and was designed to meet the BIE's condition that an exposition must cover the full range of activities of contemporary society. Adopting this focus inevitably meant that celebrations of Canadian national identity were perforce set against a prescribed international agenda.

Enabling legislation, passed in late 1962, established the Canadian Corporation for the 1967 World Exhibition as a crown company to run the exposition. Its funding came from the public purse, with 50 per cent from the federal government, 37.5 per cent from the province of Quebec, and 12.5 per cent from the city of Montreal. Its first task was to decide the precise location for the event – a matter of some urgency given the loss of two years' preparation time while Moscow held the nomination. The city offered few spaces capable of containing a large-scale exposition without recourse to wholesale clearance. Initial ideas comprised having a single showground at Parc Mont-Royal in the heart of the city or a combination of separate sites: Porte St-Charles, Ville Lasalle and Parc Maisonneuve. After eliminating Parc Mont-Royal, feasibility studies were carried out on six candidates in February 1963. These included the three initial suggestions of Porte St-Charles, Ville Lasalle and Parc Maisonneuve, and three new proposals: St Leonard-Anjou, Mercier, and the Islands in the St Lawrence River to the east of the city centre.[8] The planners made inventories of each site's relative advantages and drawbacks and sketched layout plans for the two more serious contenders, Parc Maisonneuve, located to the northeast of the city centre, and the St Lawrence Islands.

After analysis it was decided in March 1963 to proceed with the latter option. The islands had long been canvassed as a suitable place for holding expositions. In 1895, for example, A.S. Brodeur had published drawings in the journal *Le Monde Illustré* showing how the main island, Ile Ste-Hélène (St Helen's Island), could become a first-rate location for future exhibitions (Allwood, 1977, 166).[9] Seventy years later, the site still clearly posed constructional difficulties, but seemed to offer real advantages for the forthcoming exposition. First, the burdens of sequestration and compensation were less than at other locations, falling primarily on Goose Village, a poor neighbourhood near the Victoria Bridge (Pont Victoria) that was already scheduled for slum clearance. Second, there was less active opposition to development than at other locations, mainly coming from wildlife groups over the loss of avian habitats and from residents of the adjacent suburb of St Lambert, who did not want the project on their doorstep. Thirdly, the site fitted the city's linguistic geography, being situated strategically between French- and English-speaking areas of the city. Fourth, the islands met the Drapeau administration's preference for a location that was close to downtown Montreal and easily connected into the city's transport systems. Finally, the islands enjoyed the advantage of their spectacular setting. In the middle of the wide and ever-changing St Lawrence, and offering sweeping vistas of the city's downtown skyline, they supplied exciting opportunities for imaginative exhibition design.

Initial assessments, however, showed that the Ile Ste-Hélène was too small by itself for an exposition of modern proportions, particularly given that it was necessary to retain its popular wooded area, the Parc Hélène de Champlain, for public recreation. The diminutive neighbouring islands – the Ile de Ronde, Ile de Vert and Moffatt Islands – offered little else that could be incorporated into an exposition plan. Moreover, the site was awkwardly split into four areas by the channels of the St Lawrence River. It would therefore require reshaping and enlargement to provide a satisfactory space for the showground. Montreal's harbour master, Guy Beaudet, suggested adding reclaimed land to both ends of the Ile Ste-Hélène and creating a new adjacent island, later called the Ile Notre-Dame (Safdie, 1970, 65–6). The fill needed for reclamation would partly be obtained by quarrying small islands or rocky outcrops not needed for the showground and by dredging the river. The rest would come from spoil produced by construction projects elsewhere in the city, notably those associated with the new metro system.[10]

Given the shortage of time, Edouard Fiset, the chief architect, invited a distinguished French academic planner, Professor Paul Beaudoin, to draft a master plan for the exposition. Beaudoin's plan, submitted in April 1963, had an important bearing on the final scheme. He suggested, for example, adding an extra exposition centre across the river in land then part of Montreal's dockyards. This area, known as the MacKay Pier, was later renamed the Cité du Havre. Beaudoin also proposed adding a new bridge from the Ile Ste-Hélène to the Ile Notre-Dame (although not quite in the present alignment) and supplied a statement of general principles about where to place the national pavilions.[11] Reception of Beaudoin's plan, however, was hindered by the nature of its rendition, especially the Beaux-Arts traditions that it embraced. Although the same design principles were employed at both New York and Chicago in the 1930s, Gilles Gagnon, the architect chiefly responsible for the exposition's layout, argued that by this time the visual language of his plan was unacceptable: 'Beaudoin produced this very Beaux Arts Master Plan with avenues and a Champs Elysées approach. The rendition was not acceptable to the North American architect's approach and the Modern Movement, but the planning was first class, excellent.'[12]

Another consultant's report, prepared by Massachusetts Institute of

Technology's dean of humanities John E. Burchard, recommended calling a high-level symposium to flesh out the organising principles for the exposition. The administration of Expo 67 adopted his suggestion, arranging an invited symposium at Montebello in western Quebec in May 1963, under the chairmanship of Dr Davidson Dunton, vice-chancellor of Carleton University. It brought together the corporation's planning staff and a group of external advisers that included academics and prominent figures from the arts. The initial agenda revolved around Beaudoin's plan but, perhaps surprisingly given the constraints of time, the group decided on a more radical approach. Reacting strongly against the commercialism apparent in the strategy being taken at the imminent world's fair in New York, the symposium proposed a scheme that would have broken decisively with the established pattern. Its conceptual background lay in Saint-Exupéry's dictum: 'To be a man is to feel that through one's own contribution one helps to build the world.'[13] The theme of Expo 67 was not simply to be carried by a signature feature or central exhibit but by the exposition as a whole. Telling the story of the work, problems and aspirations of human society should be a shared endeavour as opposed to the work of nations or corporations (Baker, 1967, 151). Hence instead of building individual pavilions that expressed national self-esteem, countries should exhibit cooperatively within theme pavilions, and thus provide a consensual international coverage on a specified topic. The theme pavilions would be clusters of structures that could expand and contract to meet the needs of participants.

The mechanism chosen to address this ambitious outcome was to build a megastructure, an idealised urban form that had enormous appeal in the 1960s. Megastructures were large grids or networks, capable of considerable extension, to which modular units (whether buildings, facilities or services) could be attached almost at will (Banham, 1976, 8). The theme pavilions in this arrangement would be linear structures attached to the primary circulation system, which connected up the various elements of the fair. Smaller pavilions developing sub-themes would cluster around the theme pavilions. Story threads would run horizontally through buildings, but where nations or industry wanted to explore themes further, it would be possible to use space in levels above or below. Several vertical levels might give continuity to this associated story thread. Secondary and tertiary systems of movement were integrated into the general scheme, each having a specific role at a particular scale. The secondary systems would serve transport and sightseeing functions, moving at slower speeds through and around structures to provide greater contact and exposure for visitors. These would link to tertiary systems, comprising moving

pavements and pedestrian paths, that would allow onlookers to examine
parts of the whole in more detail (Miller, 1967, 45–6).

Such an architectural arrangement would have reinstated the ethos of
the Crystal Palace, bringing exhibits back into an exhibition structure
that functioned like a single entity, while also using modern technology
as a vehicle for promoting international harmony. Perhaps inevitably, as
happened with megastructural ideas generally,[14] the overarching concept
was soon abandoned. Although ideologically oriented accounts of the
planning phases insisted that 'hesitant conservatism' was to blame
(Anon., 1967, 123), in reality this idealistic scheme made little
connection with the pragmatic business of funding and organising an
exposition. The short amount of time available made it impractical to
undertake radical experiments in the design of built structures and
transport systems for a showground that had yet to be reclaimed from
the St Lawrence. The proposed flexibility of the megastructural grid
would also have been sorely tested by the constant changes in the lists
of participants and their degree of participation.[15] Moreover, it ignored
political realities. As we have seen, large nations and commercial
corporations participate in such events because they supply the
opportunity to build prestigious pavilions that serve as advertisements
for the occupants. They would not necessarily be prepared to make the
same commitment for a development that fused their separate national
identities into the common cause of humankind.

Yet even if the megastructural concept was rejected, aspects of the
philosophy of the Montebello symposium remained. The planning and
management team adopted the recommendation of employing the
technique of critical path analysis[16] as their operational framework when
constructing and, later, administering the exposition. Five theme
pavilions and four associated buildings retained something of the
proposed internationalism. Aspects of the circulation design were
retained, as was the decision that there would be uniformity in signage,
street furniture and graphics – a move that paralleled the practices of the
1964 Tokyo Olympics (see Chapter 7). The landscape design would
ensure there were no fences or boundary markers to create visible
demarcations between the plots, but the original idea of imposing design
control over the built structures at the fair was reversed. As a result,
individual nations, charities or commercial corporations were again free
to design their pavilions in the manner of their choosing.

The final scheme, with the proposals on content, was submitted to
the Canadian parliament and approved. Various complications emerged
at the implementation stage. Internal wrangles and personality clashes
led to the replacement of the original planning team led by Daniel
('Sandy') van Ginkel at the end of 1963. Potential transport

arrangements were redesigned to respect the linguistic geography of Montreal rather than necessarily selecting the most functional routes and interchanges. For example, the preferred routing of rail connections from the city centre to the Cité du Havre would have linked the exposition to the English-speaking section of the city. In the event, the organisers felt obliged to serve the exposition through metro connections under the St Lawrence from the eastern Francophone part of the city. Construction costs soared from C$10 million to C$40 million. Part of the reason lay in the severe difficulties that arose over the poor match between the need for fill for land reclamation and the amount of spoil available to achieve it. In August 1963, the operation began to raise 26 970 feet (8220 metres) of external walls for the islands and 21 150 feet (6446 metres) of internal protection walls (Stanton, 1997). Almost immediately, it was clear that the geologists had overestimated the amount of alluvium forthcoming from dredging the riverbed, since the bedrock occurred much closer to the surface than originally expected. Nine million out of the 15 million tons required for land reclamation then had to be brought by dumper trucks, working a 24-hour shuttle service from locations where the metro was being excavated. Yet a considerable shortfall persisted. Leaving areas as water, suitably landscaped into lakes, canals and water panes, eventually solved this problem. Although perhaps enhancing the visual quality of the showground, this strategy meant making fundamental changes to the exposition layout, since the water features occupied space originally intended for other purposes.

The reclamation work added 297 acres (123 hectares) of land, with the site turned over to the Canadian Corporation for the 1967 World Exhibition on 1 July 1964. The two bridges were completed by the middle of 1965. The Concordia Bridge (Pont de la Concorde) linked the city of Montreal directly to the Ile Ste-Hélène. The Bridge of the Islands, which resulted from Beaudoin's plan (see above), supplied access from the Ile Ste-Hélène to the Ile Notre-Dame. These crossing points eased the flow of fill and raw materials, reducing congestion at the previous single point of entry. The continuing absence of a comprehensive master plan, however, created problems. In the early stages, the planning team worked purely from a statement of design intent, comprising ideas derived from Beaudoin's plan with the principles supplied by the Montebello symposium. There was no indication yet of the precise layout or topography of the fairground, much less any indication of the relative locations of the pavilions.[17]

These matters awaited the publication of the master plan in December 1964. The plan divided the 988-acre (410-hectare) site into four main areas. The first, the Cité du Havre, contained the main entrance, the Place d'Accueil. From here visitors would cross, via the Concordia Bridge, to the second exhibition area on the western section of the Ile Ste-Hélène. The third exposition area occupied the Ile Notre-Dame. La Ronde, the 135-acre (56-hectare) amusement park on the eastern side of the Ile Ste-Hélène, comprised the fourth area. As intended, there was no encroachment on the Parc Hélène de Champlain.

With these broad areas demarcated, contractors started laying the foundations for the buildings in the summer of 1965. In line with the requirements of a category one event, participating nations built their own pavilions but could combine with other nations in regional pavilions. Ideological conflicts and economic problems, however, continually required the alteration of the plans. Some participating nations belatedly withdrew freeing up plots; others made late applications to participate, creating demands for new spaces. Each type of decision about space allocation in turn created 'ripple effects' that affected a wider area than simply that on which a specific pavilion would stand.

As implemented, buildings covered a total of 121 acres (50 hectares) of the site (see Figure 5.4). To encourage people to circulate through the fairground, the organisers placed the large pavilions at either end of the site so that the crowds would pass through the full length of the exposition. The medium- and small-sized pavilions were placed in the centre to gain the benefit of passing crowds. The planners located the theme buildings strategically around the fairground as 'points of polarisation' that symbolised their importance. Promenades and open spaces at the margins permitted vistas of the river. The decision to exclude use of hedges, fences or other plot markers, as noted above, allowed the landscaping to flow throughout.[18] After completion of the pavilions in June–July 1966, participants had roughly nine months in which to install their exhibits.

Exposition by the St Lawrence

On 28 April 1967 the Universal and International Exposition, better known as Expo 67, formally opened against a background of pealing church bells, fireworks, water fountains from tugs on the St Lawrence and strikes by security personnel.[19] In careful recognition of the country's colonial history and the province's linguistic sensitivities, Roland Michener, Governor-General of Canada, inaugurated the fair first in French and then in English. The president of the exposition company, Pierre Dupuy, and Mayor Drapeau added their respective interpretations of the exposition's aspirations. The Canadian Prime Minister, Lester Pearson, lit the exposition torch in imitation of the

Figure 5.4 Expo 67 fairground, under construction

Olympic opening ceremonies (see Chapter 6). Antoine de Saint-Exupéry's widow was one of the 5000 guests at the inaugural ceremony in the Place des Nations, the main ceremonial space. At the final count, there were 60 854 participants, including 120 foreign governments that built or shared space in 60 pavilions. Commercial corporations or charitable groups occupied a further 53 pavilions. When the exposition closed 183 days later on 27 October 1967, an event somewhat overshadowed by the Arab–Israeli (Yom Kippur) War, 50.3 million paying visitors had passed through its gates. An estimated additional five million visitors had also gained admission on free passes (O'Leary, 1988, 738–9).[20] Expo 70 in Japan comfortably surpassed this total (see below), yet distance and cost meant that an overwhelming proportion of those visitors were Japanese nationals, rather than significant numbers of foreign visitors. In many ways, Expo 67 would represent the high water mark for such events as foci for international tourism.

Visitors could arrive at the Place d'Accueil by ferry, bus or car connections, although underground passengers disembarked at the new Ile Ste-Hélène station on the Longueil branch of the metro. On arrival, they could walk or switch to the exposition's own rail transport network, with its two separate levels. The primary level was the Expo-Express, a mass transit system running eight full-sized computer-controlled electric trains similar to those used on the Toronto underground. This ran on an elevated track from the entrance gate down to La Ronde, with an interchange station connecting to the city's metro. The secondary system comprised approximately six miles (9.6 kilometres) of mini-rail systems, with tracks passing around and through some pavilions (Warner, 1990, 329). This used track and rolling stock purchased secondhand from the 1964 Swiss national exposition in Lausanne, supplemented by new trains purchased from the same manufacturers. For the first time, an exposition also offered access by private yacht, with moorings available at the marina at La Ronde.

Expo 67 engaged with its host city more decisively than any exposition since Chicago in 1893. Montreal's downtown was undergoing active reconstruction in 1967, especially with the construction of a multilevel city where business and commerce might function more easily in winter (Richards, 1967). This activity resonated with a showground that bubbled with radical ideas for architecture in an exposition 'almost programmed into making a serious contribution to city design' (Baker, 1967, 151). Despite the original wishes of the organisers and their limited attempts to exert some aesthetic control,[21] architectural spectacle abounded at Expo 67, with a riotous profusion of architectural styles. The spectacle of the buildings, of course, had been part of the experience of attending expositions since the Crystal

Palace, but for many the quality of the containers dwarfed the exhibits. As an observer remarked:

> I can't remember much about what was in the pavilions apart from the wonderful film shows ... But I do remember walking round and round looking at the buildings from all the different angles. It was a really exciting display.[22]

Architecture itself was closely associated with progressive credentials in the mid-1960s. Many national and corporate exhibitors tried to show those credentials through the design of pavilions that embraced the possibilities of modern materials and suggested their potential for future built environments. Space-frame buildings, which employed advanced engineering techniques to create an outer shell within which exhibitors could arrange the interiors in whatever manner they wished, were particularly popular. Otto Frei and Rolf Gutbroad's West German pavilion, for example, comprised a tent-structure in which eight 120-feet (38-metre) high masts and cable-nets supported a suspended translucent membrane. It was completely prefabricated in Germany and simply assembled in situ. The Dutch pavilion featured similar principles. Designed by Walter Eijkelenboom, it consisted of a building suspended in a cage of aluminium tubing. The American pavilion, designed by Buckminster Fuller, comprised a geodesic dome. Two hundred and fifty feet in diameter (80 metres) and tall enough to enclose a twenty-storey building, Fuller's dome comprised an inner hexagonal steel skeleton, an outer triangular steel exoskeleton and an acrylic membrane to keep out the elements (see Figure 5.5). Its size and translucent qualities, especially when seen at night, made it one of Expo 67's major attractions.

Yet perhaps the most striking structure in this respect was Habitat 67, an experimental housing project related to the exposition's theme buildings. Habitat resulted directly from the Montebello symposium's wish to follow the lead of previous expositions and make a significant statement about the design of housing and settlements (for example, see Chapter 3). It was designed by a young Israeli architect, Moshe Safdie, who had studied at Montreal's McGill University. Habitat presented a radically new approach to the provision of apartments. Instead of stacking them in conventional manner by interior partitioning of a rectangular box structure, Habitat 67 had sets of prefabricated apartments attached to a megastructure of A-frames to create a three-dimensional structure that gave an individual identity to each dwelling unit (Safdie and Kohn, 1997, 81). External walkways connected the apartments rather than interior corridors. The whole edifice was mass-produced as prefabricated units in a factory, with the dwelling units taken out and manoeuvred into place by tracked cranes (see Figure 5.6).

Figure 5.5   The US pavilion, Expo 67

As originally conceived, Habitat 67 would have comprised 1000 flats with retail facilities, rising to 22 storeys and stretching down the spine of the Cité du Havre. Limited finance, however, meant this was never likely to occur. Habitat 67 was gradually reduced to a pilot project of just 158 dwellings rising to 12 storeys. It was never even remotely able to generate the economies of scale desired by its creators and, in turn, to show its viability for providing low-cost, high-quality social housing. It also drew widely divergent opinions from visitors. As one commentator noted:

> This show piece for Expo has been ... hailed as a good place to live in. It has been dismissed as a highly priced conventional living space. Some see it as a visual delight, a sculptural *tour de force*.

Figure 5.6   Constructing Habitat 67, Montreal 1966

> Others see it as a grey, inhuman exercise in building blocks. Optimists see it as a sparkling solution to housing the masses of India and Ghana. Realists ... say it has all been done before.

As with previous expositions, buildings also served as ideological statements, well exemplified by the French and British pavilions. Given the history of the province of Quebec, it was not wholly surprising that French and British would compete with one another when they found out that they had been allocated adjacent plots. The French pavilion, designed by Jean Faugeron, parodied a chateau with its array of aluminium fins, panels, balconies and masts. Great Britain's castle-like pavilion had walls rendered to look like stone, with a 200-feet (61-metre) broken-off tower topped by a three-dimensional version of the Union Jack. Concerning the eventual size of Sir Basil Spence's British pavilion, Gilles Gagnon noted:

> They (the British) wanted to have the biggest pavilion on the site, because Canada was a former colony ... and because of the Commonwealth. France next door had a pavilion that was getting bigger, adding more floors, it was getting higher than the British one. The British decided to do this truncated tower so that it would be higher than the neighbour's. And they kept detrunking the thing to make it higher and higher and higher. It was a kind of folly.[23]

The 'Theme Buildings', however, did remain to remind the onlooker what Expo 67 might have been. Reduced in size from those suggested by the Montebello symposium and increasingly Canadian rather than international, they nevertheless offered a wider perspective that was not specifically tied either to host nation or commercial corporations. The theme buildings were mostly scattered at strategic points within the showground apart from Man the Creator, which had sculpture exhibits on the Ile Ste-Hélène but had its fine arts, photography and industrial design displays in a permanent building in Montreal. The Ile Ste-Hélène also housed the Man the Producer and Man the Explorer buildings, both steel-framed spaces of truncated tetrahedrons that created 'totally flexible and spectacular spaces for the theme exhibits' (Warner, 1990, 331). Man the Provider was on the Ile Notre-Dame, with Man in the Community on the Cité du Havre.

Away from the main pavilions, the popularity of La Ronde stressed the importance of amusement areas as part of expositions. Although built with fairgoers in mind, it was open to the public without them first having to pay admission to the exposition. Once inside, La Ronde offered an enormous aquarium, an open-air concert venue and a range of attractions and rides now more typical of theme parks. The specially built triodetic structured Gyrotron, for example, offered a trip into space followed by an encounter with a mechanical monster rising from a sea of molten lava. Although lacking the funds to develop the concept fully, it was symptomatic of things to come (Allwood, 1977, 169). La Ronde also provided the only significant vertical feature of the exposition in the shape of a small tower.[24]

Annual Expositions

The balance sheet for Expo 67, as ever with such events, was many faceted. The federal government credited the exposition with helping to produce a national trade surplus in 1967, reversing Canada's normal deficit on tourism and presaging a federal investment drive to try to retain some of the gains. The province of Quebec experienced the greatest immediate impact of Expo 67, seeing a rise of 134 per cent in the number of cars arriving from the USA between January–August 1967. Although the supply of temporary accommodation created problems, Montreal's newly expanded hotel sector filled its rooms for the season and profited from being allowed to increase charges by 10–25 per cent for the duration of the exposition.[25] The food and drink sector, catering and ancillary industries also benefited enormously. More generally, Canada received an additional C$200 million in foreign investment through Expo 67, with the city itself gaining important infrastructure.

Montreal had gambled heavily to gain the exposition. The loss of two years while Moscow held the nomination meant that the Drapeau administration had raised C$140 million in loans to hasten and complete the metro before the exposition started. When adding in construction costs for the fair, highways, bridges, hotels, a permanent exhibition and convention centre, the bill totalled C$2 billion. It is likely that much of this construction work would have occurred without the exposition, but would have spread itself out over 10–15 years. Here it was compressed into five years, as a city administration noted for its laissez-faire policies took an unusually pro-active stance (Anon., 1967, 131). Admittedly the short-term debt of C$233 million arising directly from the exposition was large, with one-eighth (C$29.2 million) falling on the city itself, but this could be partly offset by disposal of assets that perhaps totalled C$70 million.[26]

This calculation, however, was thrown off course by the announcement on 9 October 1967, three weeks before the end of the show, that the city authorities intended to turn the exposition into a permanent exhibition of 'Man and His World'. This development lay outside the normal frame of reference for international expositions, conceived as short-lived gathering places for high-intensity spectacle. It was always envisaged that the city would gain additional recreational and cultural facilities with local or perhaps regional value, but this proposal suggested retaining the exposition as a focus for national and international tourism. Not surprisingly, the announcement resulted in heated negotiations. The BIE's rules stated that exhibitors had to clear their site within a certain period; a rule intended to protect the host city from facing complete financial responsibility for clearance. The Drapeau regime's plan contravened this arrangement. It also rested on the agreement of the other parties, notably the provincial and federal governments as fellow funding agencies, and the willingness of exhibitors to donate their pavilions and their contents to the exposition company free of charge.

The exhibitors were mostly willing to oblige, but fellow funding agencies were less forthcoming. Toronto, the home of the Canadian National Exhibition, demanded C$180 million in compensation if the federal government was simply to turn its investment over to Montreal. Equally the province of Quebec, which estimated the cost to itself of C$50 million over three years for converting the exposition, stated that other parts of Quebec now had prior claims on its funds.[27] While avoiding commitment of extra resources, the federal government offered Montreal a two-year moratorium on its indebtedness while it sorted out the future of the exposition and its showground. Subsequently, and despite considerable scepticism about the plans for a continuing fair, Toronto withdrew its financial claims provided that Montreal received no further federal contributions.[28]

Initially, it seemed that this plan might work. The city received the gift of assets worth C$225 million, including 78 pavilions, all the theme buildings, and the fair's minirail system. The profits from an annual exhibition, estimated at C$6 million on summer attendances of 20 million, would have been enough to service the interest on the debt, without taking into account the indirect benefits from increased tourism. Under the agreement reached between the parties that established the original Crown Company, the Canadian Corporation for the 1967 World Exhibition was freed from its obligation to return the site to its original condition. The city took over Expo 67's assets on the Iles Ste-Hélène and Notre-Dame. The federal government received the assets of land at the Cité du Havre owned by the National Harbours Board. This included Habitat 67, the Labyrinth and the administration building. The Expo-Express would be sold through public tender.[29]

On 29 January, Jean Drapeau announced that the 1968 Man and His World exhibition would open between 17 May–14 October. It would definitely feature 40 pavilions, with decisions pending on six more, in what was described as the 'greatest permanent cultural exhibition ever mounted'.[30] Drapeau estimated that the exposition would break even with 15 million visitors, but predicted between 20–30 million. In the event, the first of the permanent exhibitions received only 12 million visitors. Despite initial statements from Drapeau that the exhibition still 'broke even', in reality it accumulated a further deficit of C$5.28 million caused mainly by charges on capital improvements. At a meeting on 28 January 1969 the city's executive committee heard that no further funding was forthcoming, despite appeals to province and government. It therefore decided not to reopen the exhibition for another season, although the amusement area at La Ronde would continue to function.[31] Although supporting the decision, Drapeau announced that he would have to consider his future as mayor. Partly in response and partly because the city soon reached a three-year funding agreement with the province, the full council reversed its executive committee's decision on 28 February. The exposition could then open again for a restricted season in 1969, lasting from 12 June to 7 September.[32]

The energy, however, had ebbed away from the project. The annual fairs continued to lose money, for example, with the province agreeing to meet the likely C$5 million deficit in 1972.[33] Although the exhibitions continued in reduced form until September 1978, they had lost the original sense of exhilaration as a meeting place for the world. Their eventual cessation, therefore, had an aura of inevitability. The showground became valuable public open space that is occasionally used to stage large-scale events. The rowing events at the 1976 Olympics (see Chapter 7) were staged on the Ile Notre-Dame, as was the 1980 Floralies Exposition. The Gilles Villeneuve circuit, the Formula 1 grand prix motor-racing track laid out around the Ile Ste-Hélène, provided an annual boost to the Montreal economy until a ban on cigarette advertising cost Canada its grand prix in 2003. Most of the pavilions were gradually removed or converted. The French pavilion now serves as Montreal's casino. The Christian pavilion stands empty. Habitat 67 remains in its isolated location on the Cité du Havre, but is now simply private housing – an unusual and still avant-garde place to live that, to the resigned annoyance of its occupants, is also a place of pilgrimage for students of the built environment. The dome that had housed the American pavilion remains as a shell, a spectacular piece of festival architecture that now houses buildings containing Montreal's Biocentre (Environmental Interpretation Centre).[34]

The long and disappointingly attended continuation of Expo 67, however, did not seriously dispel the general success and positive impact of the original festival. With the eventual federal decision to write off the debts of Expo 67,[35] the city could look back on an event that had brought Montreal international acclaim. Expo 67 had won considerable critical approval for its spectacle and as the meeting place of nations that the 1964–5 New York World's Fair failed to be. The experience gained from staging Expo 67 whetted the appetite for staging other international festivals. The Drapeau regime had grasped the extent to which culture was a multimillion dollar business, holding out the opportunity to make significant gains.[36] The Olympic Games became another target. Montreal had earlier bid for the 1972 games, which were awarded to Munich. It was chosen on 7 September 1968, with Vancouver, as one of the two Canadian cities that could bid for the subsequent games in 1976. Involvement in that project (see Chapter 7) made up for any immediate disappointments over the failure of the permanent exhibitions to carve a new future for the traditional exposition.

International Expositions, 1968–92

After Expo 67, there were only two further expositions during the twentieth century that met the BIE's former category one status – at Osaka (1970) and Seville (1992) – along with nine smaller events. Starting with the latter type of exposition, two – in Okinawa (1972) and Tsukuba (1985) – were used to support Japanese regional development initiatives. World Expo 88, timed to coincide within the Australian Bicentennial in 1988, attracted 18.5 million people to Brisbane for an exposition on the theme of 'Leisure in the Age of Technology'.[37] Another two – at Vancouver (1986) and Lisbon (1998) – combined an increasingly prevalent theme park-style element with ambitious waterfront regeneration. Vancouver regenerated areas along False Creek. Lisbon used its Expo 98 to regenerate three miles (five kilometres) of centrally situated, but heavily derelict land alongside the Tagus River previously occupied by a refinery, an arsenal, a waste disposal plant and polluted mud-flats (Alden and da Rosa Pires, 1996, 32; see also Chapter 8). It succeeded in running up a deficit of around $300 million.

American cities staged the remaining four smaller expositions, which effectively charted the ending of the USA's love affair with the world's fair. All started well enough with Hemisfair 68, held in San Antonio (Texas) between 6 April and 6 October 1968 and the first of a sequence of events inspired by the example of Seattle. Although incurring a $5.5 million deficit and failing in its attempt to convert the showground into a permanent cultural area (Eoff, 1990, 337), Hemisfair 68 provided a major boost to San Antonio's hotel and retailing sectors, and was considered to have improved the city's competitive standing. Spokane's Expo 74 (1974), recognised by the BIE as a category two event and by the United Nations as a centre for World Environment Day activities, seemed to repair something of the fair's image. Expo 74 recorded a surplus of more than $47 million, helped central city regeneration, and brought an estimated $699 million over a decade in revitalised commerce and increased tourism for an outlay of $78 million (Migliazzo, 1990, 348).

Other indications, however, were less positive. The abandonment of plans to mount a large-scale event in Philadelphia in 1976 as the centrepiece of American bicentennial celebrations pointed to growing indifference to world's fairs within the USA (Findling and Pelle, 1990, 406–7). The two subsequent US world's fairs of the early 1980s, Knoxville (1982) and New Orleans (1984), encountered financial problems. Knoxville (Tennessee) attempted an exposition around the theme of 'International Energy', but provided few innovations in energy technology compared with more general scientific exhibits or displays of historic artefacts – the exposition's most popular exhibits. Despite attracting 11.1 million visitors, it made a substantial loss and gained few of the expected benefits from urban regeneration, employment or increased tax revenues (Doak, 1990, 353–4). New Orleans' Louisiana World Exposition (1984), beset by severe underfunding and administrative confusion, culminated in the Fair Corporation declaring bankruptcy in November 1984 with the planned central city regeneration largely failing to occur. Even the grant of the BIE's category one status for an exposition in Chicago in 1992 was insufficient to save that project from collapse (Hardy, 1990; see also below).

Major Expositions

The respective experiences of Expos 70 and 92 strongly hinted at the decline of the exposition as a focus for international interest. The Japan World Exhibition (Expo 70), which occupied 865 acres (358 hectares) in the Senri Hills of Osaka, consciously continued the work of previous expositions. Before selection by the BIE in September 1965, the Japanese had sent observers to the 1964–5 New York's World's Fair to study organisation and administration. An even larger contingent attended Expo 67.[38] Their affinity with the Montreal exposition in particular was shown in the proposed design of the exhibition buildings for 1970. The organisers of Expo 70 also proposed housing exhibits within one megastructure but, again, the idea foundered under pressure from exhibitors who were unwilling to cede their identities by being cast under one all-encompassing roof (Mattie, 1998, 236). Despite this the aesthetics and functional principles of the Metabolist movement, Japan's leading proponents of megastructures, infused much of the exposition (see Figure 5.7).[39]

Figure 5.7 The Takara pavilion, an example of Metabolist architecture, Expo 70

The integrated internal transportation system featured a computerised monorail that travelled the 2.7 miles (4.3 kilometres) circuit of the fair in 15 minutes; battery powered cars able to seat six people; and a system of moving walkways (Manning, 1990, 340). The central theme area known as the 'Symbol Zone' carried the explication of Expo 70, 'Progress and Harmony for Mankind'. Designed by the fair's chief architect Kenzo Tange, himself a leading member of the Metabolist group, the Symbol Zone straddled the main gate with its specially built bus and underground railway stations beneath. Its main feature, the Festival Plaza, had a transparent saucer-shaped roof held up by six enormous pillars, and covered an area of 7.8 acres (3.2 hectares). Within this enclosure, a series of moveable units made it possible to devise performance spaces suitable for events from intimate theatre to full arena (Allwood, 1977, 173). Clustered around the Festival Plaza were a series of other focal points, including the Expo headquarters and a series of vertical features – the Communications Tower, the Tower of Motherhood and the Central Tower of the Sun.

Expo 70 was organised and financed by the Japanese government in consultation with the prefecture and city of Osaka. The profits raised by the exposition ($146 million) and the number of visitors (64.2 million) were both comfortably the highest in the history of the international expositions. Expo 70, like other expositions, also delivered a solid package of lasting benefits. After the exhibition closed, the showground, which had previously been bamboo groves and rice paddies, became a national culture park. The monorail was demolished as planned, but stimulated the development of a system of monorails connecting the airports in the Osaka region. Road and associated developments contributed major infrastructural improvements to the Osaka–Kobe region. Although 62 million of the visitors had come from Japan, a significant number of affluent foreign tourists had visited, more than half of them from the USA. Japan's visibility in world affairs, already improved by the 1964 Tokyo Olympics (see Chapter 7) had received another significant boost.

Yet despite this positive picture, doubts were surfacing about the event itself. Critics suggested that the organisers 'had been so careful not to make the mistakes of New York and Montreal that they had little time for innovation' (Allwood, 1977, 171). Others felt that, with so many buildings in concrete, the fair had a grey appearance, leavened only by the colour on some of the commercial pavilions (Mattie, 1998, 237). What was readily apparent was that, despite conscious efforts at creating structures of architectural distinction, the exposition lacked signature features. The growing exhaustion of the lexicon of towers, globes and monorails created problems for the organisers of each succeeding event.

The final category one event of the twentieth century, the Seville Universal Exposition (Expo 92) saw these doubts amplified. Seville had previously co-hosted an exposition in 1929, a smaller event that celebrated Spain's ex-colonial and cultural links with Latin America and served as 'a catalyst for growth and modernisation' in the city (Palmer, 1990, 256). The 1992 exposition, on the theme of 'The Era of Discoveries', returned to the New World connection. It commemorated the quincentenary of Columbus's voyage to the New World, a nomination originally awarded jointly to Seville and Chicago at the BIE's 1983 meeting. Chicago, however, had withdrawn in 1985 over problems with funding, leaving Spain free to exploit the joint visitor potential of Seville's exposition, the 1992 Olympics at Barcelona (see Chapter 7) and Madrid as European City of Culture (see Chapter 8). The Spanish authorities again saw an exposition in Seville as a catalyst for an ambitious scheme for improvements to regional transport systems, including a new road network, airport and high-speed rail links to Madrid. Partial funding came from the European Community, with Spain qualifying for grants under provisions for disadvantaged areas.

Besides sailing from Seville on his first trip to the New World, Columbus also frequently visited the Carthusian monastery of Santa Maria de las Cuevas, situated on La Cartuja, an island in the Guadalquivir River. The island, now much enlarged through flood defence-related land reclamation, was chosen for the exposition.[40] When designated, La Cartuja contained little besides the monastery other than parched soil and scrub. The 415 acres (193 hectares) site was extensively landscaped with widespread tree planting. The showground comprised three zones: one containing Spanish regional pavilions; another the international pavilions; and a third with the obligatory vertical feature (the Trian Tower) and the Pavilion of Discoveries. The arrangement of the national pavilions was, as ever, imbued with considerable symbolism. Spain, like other host nations, took the opportunity to arrange the world in a manner of their choosing. Although the arrangement of buildings was described as cramped (Mattie, 1998, 247), Penelope Harvey (1998, 142, 144) commented:

> One of the standard features in which visitors were obliged to participate was the redrawn map of the world. Spain dominated this new ideal world with its commanding focal site at the head of the Avenue of Europe on the edge of the newly constructed Lake of Spain. The space it occupied was doubled by the display of its disaggregated parts, the 17 autonomous regions, ranged around the far shores of the lake.

Critics, however, castigated many features of the plan for lacking inspiration, being cramped and, in particular, failing to make connection with Seville (Mattie, 1998, 247). Indeed notwithstanding the carefully contrived appeal of the pavilion architecture for the visitor's attention, on this occasion the signature features of the exposition were two bridges across the Guadalquivir by Santiago Calatrava. In principle this suggested the symbolic links between the exposition and the historic city, but in practice the connection was limited. Although promenades were constructed on the riverbanks, the physical layout of the fairground encouraged visitors to remain within the showground rather than visit Seville's historic core. The feeling of a city within, and apart from, a city was prevalent, to the disgruntlement of those who questioned the morality of spending an estimated £9 billion on an exposition when Seville's impoverished squatter settlements remained untouched (Hopkinson, 1992). This feeling hardened over time. The exposition finished with a loss of Pts60 billion (£285 million) against an initial forecast of a profit of Pts18 billion (£85 million). The hopes of integrating the regenerated island into Seville life had come to nothing. The pavilions steadily rotted. Cartuja was 'little more than an offshore ghost town',[41] with a 'limp, melancholy air that could not be more alien to Seville's vibrant personality'.[42] As a last throw of the dice, a 'magic island' adventure theme park was built at a cost of £68 million. Its impact, as an idea borne of desperation rather than sustained market analysis, has not been impressive. Taken overall, the outcome could scarcely have been bleaker. As Spanish environmental activist Pepe Garcia Rey noted:

> Unemployment was unaffected, except during the building works. Many of the hotels and offices remain empty and are being sold off. Few permanent homes were built and the city's slums remain as bad as ever. We've just come out of a four-year drought. Water gushed during the Expo, but the minute it ended, the authorities rationed the water. They hadn't given a thought to investing in new pipes or reservoirs.[43]

Conclusion

Like so many previous expositions, however, the legacy of Seville remains contentious. 1992 saw Spain making a sustained effort to re-establish itself in the European cultural field after the isolation of the Franco years. Spain's feat in holding an international exposition, an Olympics and a City of Culture festival in the same year represented a major step towards reaching out to the wider world and, in turn, being accepted back into the European fold after the years of Fascism. Expo 92 had its successes. The total of 43 million visitors at Seville in 1992 was comfortably the largest total since Montreal and Osaka, with the arrival of large numbers of cultural tourists helping to counter the image of Spain as the favoured destination of the downmarket cheap package holiday. The participation of 105 nations shows that expositions retain credibility as an adjunct to diplomacy, as a relatively parsimonious way for those countries to present a positive image of their ingenuity, resources, tourist destinations, or progressive outlook to a global audience for six months or so. Yet Expo 92 also represented, in many respects, the antithesis of the real progress made by its counterpart that summer – the 26th Summer Olympic Games held in Barcelona. Against the real success of Barcelona, particularly concerning urban reconstruction (see Chapter 7), the Seville authorities needed to try to ameliorate the damage left by ill-conceived and over-ambitious plans. Inevitably, too, questions remained as to whether, after almost 150 years, the international expositions retained their appeal. In light of events, for example, the USA decided that it would no longer sponsor official pavilions at international expositions after Seville. This, coupled with the effective withdrawal of US cities from competing for world's fairs, certainly suggested an erosion of the exposition's role as a meeting place for the world. Moreover, the exposition's traditional function as a medium for celebrating technological achievement and social progress had fallen foul of the changing political climate of the late-twentieth century. These questions would inevitably resurface at the next universal exposition in 2000 at Hanover, to which we return in Chapter 9.

Notes

1   Ashdown (1990, 320) reports that the city may not see this entirely positively as the buildings and their grounds, designed in the early 1960s, are deteriorating and imposing increasing costs on the city's budget.
2   Observers noted the similarities with the spectacular structures offered at the Paris 1900 exposition. See 'Fair comparisons', *The Times*, 4 February 1964.
3   Wilson, L. 'Our World's Fair chances looking lots better now', *Financial Post*, 26 March 1960, 8.
4   'How Russia pulled fast move and Montreal lost World [sic] Fair', *Financial Post*, 14 May 1960, 3.
5   For more background on the local government of Montreal at this time, see Kaplan, 1982, 406–66. For literature specifically on Mayor Drapeau and his strategy of using international festivals and sporting gatherings as part of urban boosterism, see Roy, 1982.
6   The federal government was concerned that two years out of the seven normally required for preparation had already gone by and that there were

two other world's fairs at Seattle and New York already taking place in North America in the first half of the 1960s. See 'Ottawa Will Back Drapeau Bid', *Montreal Daily Star*, 7 September 1962.

7   Stanton (1997) states that this theme emerged in 1962 at a high-level government meeting in Montreal. Pierre Sevingy, the Associate Defence Minister is said to have suggested the title 'Terres des Hommes' ('Man and his World'), as an appropriate theme given that Saint-Exupery's writings explored human society's place in the universe.

8   'Evolution of the Master Plan of Expo 67', frames 1–24, ref. no. 100–70b, microfilm 11, Gilles Gagnon archive, Canadian Centre for Architecture. (This is miscatalogued as microfilm 6.) The Islands had been trailed in the press as the most likely site since mid-February: for example, 'Montreal's World Fair likely on waterfront site', *Financial Post*, 16 February 1963, 4.

9   In keeping with the materials in the official archives, the French versions of place names are normally used here except where the English names are far better known, for example, retaining the name St Lawrence River rather than its French equivalent (Fleuve Saint-Laurent) and using the unaccented form of Montreal.

10 There were precedents for this linkage between staging an exposition and infrastructural improvement, for example, both Chicago (1893) and Paris (1900) had constructed metro (subway) systems in conjunction with expositions.

11 The main difference was that La Ronde would have had the commercial pavilions with the amusement centre at the far end of the Ile Notre-Dame. 'Project of Professor Beaudoin', frames 1–30, ref. no. 100–70f, microfilm 11, Gilles Gagnon archive, Canadian Centre for Architecture.

12 Interview between G. Gagnon and J.R. Gold, Shaughnessy House, Canadian Centre for Architecture, 5 October 1998.

13 Translation, quoted in Anon. (1967, 123).

14 See, for example, Banham (1976).

15 This is a feature of all expositions. Participants are notorious for the late arrival of their exhibits and delay in building pavilions, while changing economic and political circumstances in the outside world often lead countries to make last-minute decisions to participate or withdraw. In this instance, the truncated preparation time made the negotiations even more difficult.

16 'Critical path analysis' is a technique for controlling and coordinating the various activities necessary in completing a major project.

17 For an informative but not wholly chronologically reliable account of developments, see Safdie, 1970, 65–71.

18 As outlined by Gilles Gagnon; interview with J.R. Gold, Shaughnessy House, Canadian Centre for Architecture, 5 October 1998.

19 Anon., 'Expo '67 security men on strike', *The Times*, 28 April 1987, 1.

20 It is estimated that as many as an extra five million visitors may have been lost by a transport strike in Montreal during the last 30 days of Expo 67.

21 Some small measure of aesthetic control, for example, stemmed from the

organisers providing lists of specified materials for buildings and requiring foreign architects to work in partnership with a Canadian counterpart. Information in this paragraph from Safdie, 1970, 65–6; Baker, 1967, 151; and interview between G. Gagnon and J.R. Gold, Shaughnessy House, Canadian Centre for Architecture, 5 October 1998.

22   Personal communication with Anthony Ferguson, August 2001.

23   Gilles Gagnon, interview with J.R. Gold, Shaughnessy House, Canadian Centre for Architecture, 5 October 1998.

24   There had been various ideas for spectacular centrepieces for Expo 67, including a giant communication tower, a huge spinning wheel complete with three equally large Indian peace pipes, and an arch bridge with a span of 1830 feet (600 metres) and a height of 457 feet (150 metres) (Anon., 1963, 5, 7). In the end, the organisers decided that there should be no symbolic vertical feature of the type that had become a cliché of previous expositions, other than that which was clearly in the amusement area of Expo 67.

25   *Canadian News Facts* (henceforth *CNF*), 1, 16 January 1967, 6. Initially, the Quebec assembly had proposed freezing hotel rates at existing levels: see Crane, D. 'Quebec's bill drafted to freeze hotel rates', *Financial Post*, 8 October 1966, 1–2. Other information from *CNF*, 1, 18 December 1967, 186, and *CNF*, 2, 19 April 1968.

26   *CFC*, 1, 6 November 1967, 161. The debt figure, then estimated as C$250 million was later amended to C$295 and finally to C$233 588 537: see *CFC*, 2, 19 March 1968, 39; and 2, 19 October 1968, 152.

27   *CNF*, 1, 20, 23 October 1967, 158–9.

28   *CNF*, 1, 21, 6 November 1967, 161.

29   *CNF*, 1, 31 December 1967, 197.

30   *CNF*, 2, 22 January 1968, 13.

31   *CNF*, 2, 19 January 1969, 207.

32   *CNF*, 3, 4 March 1969, 224.

33   *CNF*, 6, 11 June 1972, 2.

34   'Houses' is perhaps a euphemistic word. Fire destroyed the interior acrylic membrane in 1976, which means that the buildings within the dome remain open to the weather since it is neither economically or practically feasible to replace the membrane.

35   *CNF*, 3, 4 December 1969, 359.

36   Anon. 'Drapeau: man with a billion dollar dream', *Maclean's Magazine*, September 1967, 3; Thompson, S. 'Corporate strategy: business is part of culture and Expo proves it', *Monetary Times*, 135, August 1967, 33–4.

37   This event was notable for featuring what turned out to be the last USSR pavilion.

38   'Expo a training ground for next show in Japan', *Financial Post*, 1 July 1967, J18.

39   The Metabolists worked on utopian urban plans that blended an emphasis on mechanisms with the modularity adopted in the construction of space vehicles. For a brief introduction, see Donat, 1964.

40 The 1929 exposition took place in the Parque de Maria Luisa, one of the city's major parks.

41 Savage, C. 'Expo 98 will profit from Seville's pain', *The European*, 24–30 April 1997.

42 Nash, E. 'Seeking substance after a show', *Independent on Sunday*, 22 September 1996.

43 Ibid.

CHAPTER SIX

The Making of the Modern Olympics

> Coubertin was by inclination and by influence very
> much more swayed by the idealistic optimism and
> purposive certainty of the nineteenth century than he
> was by the contrary sentiment that governs the
> current epoch. ... Olympism is trapped in the
> conjunction between the 19th and 20th centuries.
> Robert Osterhoudt (quoted in Daly, 1996, xviii)

In 2001, eleven US cities submitted bids to the United States Olympic Committee (USOC) to become the American candidate city for the 2012 Olympic Games. Their candidacy smacked of unbridled optimism given that Atlanta (Georgia) had entertained the Summer Games as recently as 1996 and that Salt Lake City (Utah) would stage the Winter Games in 2002. Nevertheless, it showed how much American cities now recognise the benefits that even bidding for the Olympics brings. Rivalry to stage festivals, already manifested by the contests to hold international expositions (for example, see Chapter 4), has reached unprecedented heights with the Olympics. Cities often mount expensive campaigns to vanquish *domestic* rivals before facing the ensuing battle to persuade the International Olympic Committee (IOC) to favour their bid against foreign rivals. For example, New York, the chosen American candidate for 2012, committed around $13 million in private funding to back its domestic campaign ('NYC2012: Bringing the Olympic Games back to the World's Second Home'). The city then raised further amounts to campaign against the likes of London, Paris and Madrid for the IOC nomination in September 2005.[1] Quite simply, the prize is felt to merit the effort and expense involved. Just as winning the Olympic gold medal represents the pinnacle of achievement for an athlete so, by extension, gaining the nomination to stage the Olympics is the highest accolade that a city can now attain in the game of place promotion.

These priorities, however, are a recent phenomenon. The modern games restarted at Athens in 1896 with competitors from just 14 nations. As indicated in Table 6.1, the IOC selected future host cities with little controversy in the early years, choosing between a few polite bids. The number of bids increased dramatically after the Second World

Table 6.1 Cities bidding for the Olympic Games, 1896–1944

Games	Year awarded	Host city	Other candidates
1896	1894	Athens	London
1900	1894	Paris	
1904	1901	St Louis*	Chicago
1908	1904	London**	Berlin, Milan, Rome
1912	1909	Stockholm	
1916	1912		Berlin, Alexandria (Egypt), Budapest, Cleveland, Brussels
1920	1914	Antwerp	Amsterdam, Atlanta, Brussels, Budapest, Cleveland, Lyon, Havana, Philadelphia
1924	1921	Paris	Los Angeles, Atlantic City, Chicago, Pasadena, Rome, Barcelona, Amsterdam, Lyons, Paris
1928	1921	Amsterdam	Los Angeles
1932	1923	Los Angeles	
1936	1931	Berlin	Barcelona, Buenos Aires, Rome
1940	1936		Tokyo, Helsinki, Rome
1944	1939		London, Athens, Budapest, Lausanne, Helsinki, Rome, Detroit

* The nomination was originally to Chicago
** The nomination was originally to Rome

Source: Based on Buchanan and Mallon, 2001.

War, leading the IOC to impose the rule that only a single bid from any one state was allowed. In the USA, this meant that USOC had to establish an internal bidding procedure to determine the single candidate to be put forward to the IOC. The demand, however, fluctuated. As recently as the late 1970s, holding the Olympics appeared to be an open invitation to achieve municipal bankruptcy, especially following Montreal's experience in 1976. Only two candidates bid for the 1980 and one for the 1984 games – the ideologically charged sequence of Moscow followed by Los Angeles – but the outstanding commercial success of the latter transformed the outlook for all subsequent hosts. There were still only two candidates worldwide for the 1988 games, since their candidacy was decided before the Los Angeles games. By contrast, six cities competed for the nomination for the 1992 games, six again for 1996, eight for 2000 and 11 for 2004. Many more fell by the wayside before getting even that far.

With the new commercialism reducing the financial risks, the unrivalled status of the Olympics as an international festival shone through. No sporting event receives the media attention or has the prestige of the Olympics, especially the summer games. The Olympics provide a stage for host cities and nations to project themselves to the world, with their impact made more memorable by the powerful spectacle integral to the event. That spectacle stems primarily from the sheer scale of the Olympics, from the grandeur and drama of their setting, and from the colourful ceremonies, rituals and symbols embedded in the modern games. No other international festival *demands* that the host nation stages such lavish spectacle; no other festival approaches the Olympics in the extent to which sporting stadia become the setting for pure theatre. From the outset, the IOC designed the opening ceremony to appeal to artistic as well as sporting sensitivities, with an equally imposing closing ceremony taking shape from 1920 onwards. While ancillary to the sporting contests, these ceremonies nevertheless consistently draw the largest televisual audiences of the entire games. Moreover, although certain elements of their ritual content are fixed, the organisers of each games can otherwise interpret and embellish the occasion as they see fit, provided they gain the overall approval of the IOC. The thought in organisers' minds is invariably how they can create ceremonies and settings that surpass what went before.

In this and the ensuing chapter, we trace the intricate history of cities staging the summer games from Athens in 1896 to the present. Here we concentrate on the first part of that task, charting their development through the initial eleven Olympiads (see Table 6.1). The early games revealed tensions between the wishes of the organisers, who frequently attached them to other events, and the wishes of the nascent Olympic movement. Nevertheless, strategies for staging the games gradually emerged. By the time of the 1936 Berlin games, the subject of the final part of this chapter, the Olympics were a coherent event with ingredients broadly replicated by each succeeding festival, although one that still gave the home nation scope to mould the associated spectacle according to its own needs.

Revival

The idea of reviving the Olympic Games after 1500 years came from various sources. In itself the term 'Olympic' had never been lost, since organisers of sporting tournaments readily appropriated it for their events (Redmond, 1988; Buchanan and Mallon, 2001; Toohey and Veal, 2000, 26–32). Robert Dover founded an 'Olympick Games' on his Cotswold estate in the early seventeenth century (Mandell, 1976, 29), largely as a protest against Puritan proscriptions against games and other frivolities (see Chapter 2). Hampton Court Palace, by contrast, witnessed an Olympics, largely devoted to dog racing, in the time of King Charles II.[2] A Scandinavian Olympics took place in 1834 and 1836. The Anglophone community in Montreal formed an Olympic club in 1842, with their own 'Montreal Olympics' in 1844. In 1850 Dr William Penny Brookes founded the Shropshire Olympics at Much Wenlock. Still in existence as an annual event, the Wenlock Olympian Society's Games includes track and field events, cricket matches, jousting, as well as literary and artistic competitions.[3] John Astley Cooper proposed an Olympian 'Pan Britannic' or 'Pan Anglican Contest and Festival' of science, sport and culture in 1891 to promote goodwill and understanding in the British Empire. Although the idea drew considerable interest and eventually contributed to the founding of the Commonwealth Games (see Chapter 1), Cooper failed to supply significant detail about how to stage such an event. Elsewhere the Greeks had revived a version of the Olympic Games in 1859 to celebrate their re-emerging nationhood. In 1870, for example, 30 000 spectators watched Greek athletes compete in the specially excavated and renovated Panathenian Stadium in Athens. The games opened with a hymn and King George crowned the victors with olive wreaths (Young, 1987, 276).

Official versions of Olympic history, however, typically ignore these 'pseudo-Olympics' (Redmond, 1988); an approach that, in particular, wilfully diminishes the significance of Greece's role in the revival of the Olympics. In part, this is a by-product of historiography. Given that knowledge of classics was a privileged part of the educational curriculum, western intellectuals had long assimilated the cultural legacy of ancient Greece into the history of their nations – to which they deemed the mantle of civilisation had passed. Hence when reports were published between 1890–6 outlining the results of archaeological excavations at Olympia, the home of the ancient games, they appropriated the results to corroborate the noble origins of sport in western society.[4] By contrast any games held in modern Greece were considered, at best, merely of local interest. Yet other, more overtly ideological, factors were also at work in downgrading the Greek contribution to Olympics' revival. In the first place, accepting the Greeks' proprietorial claims to the Olympics and their wish to provide a permanent home for the event meant ceding control. This, in turn, would have interfered with the prospects of establishing the Olympics as an ambulatory global event. Secondly, and perhaps most important, admitting the existence of precursor events contradicted the narratives told about the modern games by the nascent Olympic movement. These centred around the seminal contribution made by the French aristocrat, Baron Pierre de Coubertin, who essentially established that movement's claims for 'ownership' of the event.

Historians following this narrative trace, not without some justification, Coubertin's role in campaigning for the revival of the Olympics and, subsequently, as a visionary who exerted a formative influence on the games' early development. They trace his contribution as the 'renovateur' of the modern games (Mandell, 1976; MacAloon, 1981) to a series of initiatives undertaken in the 1880s. To elaborate, France's defeat in the Franco-Prussian war (1870–1) and consequent loss of territory to Germany had led to a mood of national soul-searching. One strand of debate centred on the role of sport in education and its possible long-term role in national revival. American and English educators had already fostered the idea that education, sport and national character were interlinked, with sports helping to build the qualities needed for military prowess. Influenced by those ideas, activists like Coubertin similarly argued that sports should play greater role in French schools. In July 1888, Coubertin became founding secretary-general of the Committee for the Propagation of Physical Exercise in Education, a pressure group campaigning for reform of sports education. In 1889, he organised the First Congress of Physical Exercises and School Competitions at the Paris Exposition Universelle, subsequently publishing monographs on Anglo-American pedagogic practice (for example, Coubertin, 1889, 1890).

These beginnings established Coubertin's credentials as an educational reformer and provided a platform from which he expanded his purview to the potential role of sport in world affairs. Reflecting on the need to recognise the 'democratic and international' dimension of sport, he made a speech at the Sorbonne (Paris) on 25 November 1892 that called on the audience to aid 'this grandiose and salutary task, the restoration of the Olympic Games' (quoted in Müller, 2000, 297).[5] Although the audience was then sceptical, Coubertin enjoyed greater success with an international Sports Congress that he organised at the Sorbonne in 1894. This meeting supported the re-establishment of the Olympic Games and laid down key principles for organising them. Stated briefly, the congress proposed that the games would be staged every four years, like the ancient Olympiad cycle, but ambulatory rather than at a permanent site. They would be open to amateur sportsmen and should comprise modern, rather than classical, sports. The IOC would be the governing body, with an international membership. It would select the host city, but a local organising committee would plan the games. The congress decided that the first two locations for the modern games would be Athens (1896) and Paris (1900).

Coubertin also played a key role in turning the idea for the modern games into reality – a task fully comparable with that undertaken by the commissioners for the exhibition of 1851, who went beyond the scope of national industrial exhibitions to create the first international exposition (see Chapter 3). With a small group of supporters, Coubertin gathered representatives and administrators to oversee progress towards organising the modern Olympics. He also played an important role in crafting and supporting a durable, shared agenda, underpinned by the notion of 'Olympism', around which this sporting festival crystallised. Notions of Olympism found initial expression in the Olympic Charter[6] and were then further articulated and embellished by the practices of subsequent games. The central philosophy of 'Olympism' reflected Coubertin's interpretations of the ancient Greek festival, defined initially in the Olympic Charter (1908; revised 2002) as:

> a philosophy of life, exalting and combining in a balanced whole the qualities of body, will and mind. Blending sport with culture and education, Olympism seeks to create a way of life based on the joy found in effort, the educational value of good example and respect for universal fundamental ethical principles.

Subsequent refinements of the term sought to capture the essence of Hellenism and the ancient games and translate them into a modern context and idiom. Coubertin recognised that reviving the outward form of the games was comparatively easy, since it only involved restarting the four-year cycle of Olympiads with their schedule of sporting competitions. Restoring their deeper meanings was much more difficult

(Müller, 2000, 569). For the ancient Greeks, these meanings centred on the power of religious observance and athleticism to honour the gods (ibid., 566). Coubertin believed in the importance of athleticism,[7] but recognised that giving the modern games a spiritual component was difficult in a world of competing religions:

> The primary, fundamental characteristic of ancient Olympism, and of modern Olympism as well, is that it is a *religion*. By chiselling his body through exercise as a sculptor does a statue, the ancient athlete honoured the gods. In doing likewise, the modern athlete honours his country, his race, and his flag. Therefore, I believe that I was right to explore, from the very beginning of modern Olympism, a religious sentiment transformed and expanded by the internationalism and democracy that are distinguishing features of our day. Yet this is the same religious sentiment that led the young Hellenes, eager for the victory of their muscles, to the foot of the altars of Zeus.
>
> From this sentiment derive all the cultural expressions that constitute the ceremonies of the modern Games. I had to impose them one after another on a public that was opposed to them for a long time, seeing them merely as theatrical displays, useless spectacles incompatible with the seriousness and dignity of international athletic competitions.
>
> (quoted in Müller, 2000, 550)[8]

Central to those ceremonies was the idea of 'modern patriotism', symbolised by the national flag 'being raised on the pole of victory to honour the winning athlete – that was what would keep the faith alive at the newly rekindled hearth' (ibid., 573). Athletes swearing an oath to honour their country at the outset of the games would echo the practice of the ancient games where their counterparts swore an oath to Zeus.

Olympism would also imbue the nascent games with notions of harmony. Coubertin used the word 'eurhythmy' to describe the harmonious marriage of sport and culture, athletics and art, muscle and mind. He believed that the fusion of art and sport lay at the heart of the classical games and no revival would be complete without reuniting them. This would be difficult since 'the masses', as he disparagingly called them, had lost all sense of eurhythmy and would need re-educating before they might properly appreciate the relationship between sport, sculpture, music and architecture. Only then would they be capable of recognising and experiencing the harmony and beauty in performance and setting intrinsic to his vision for Olympism (ibid., 612).

Coubertin highlighted three areas in which art and culture could help to achieve this goal. The first was the introduction of artistic competitions as an integral part of the Olympics, taking their place alongside the sporting events. The second was to devise ceremonies to lend dignity to the games, making use of stirring music, colourfully dressed athletes and participants, and conscious use of symbolism and ritual. Of particular significance were distribution of awards to the victors, administration of the athletic oath, and the proclamation that the games were open (usually performed by the head of state of the host nation).[9] The third was to instigate significant programmes of arts and cultural activities to accompany the games and provide entertainment for participants, officials, visiting spectators and the local population. Some suggested activities – for example, drama, choreography, concerts and oratory – were distinctly highbrow. Others, such as processions, parades, street decorations and night festivals (including fireworks), would have a more popular appeal. To these would be added formal banquets and receptions, exhibitions, artistic performances and less formal gatherings that might enhance the impact of the Olympic festival.

Table 6.2 shows the variety of symbols, rituals, emblems, flags and mottoes developed as part of the protocol, rituals and ceremonies that surround the staging of the games. Some, like the hymn or anthem, were

Table 6.2   Key aspects of Olympic protocol

Item	Introduced
Opening ceremony Motto: 'Citius, Altius, Fortius' Pigeons (doves) Hymn (anthem)	1896
March of nations	1906
Competitors' oath Olympic flag Closing ceremony	1920
Olympic flame	1928
Olympic creed	1932
Olympic torch relay and flame lighting	1936
Informal entry of athletes in closing ceremony	1956
Adoption of the 1896 Olympic hymn as the official hymn	1960
Judges' oath	1972

written specifically for the Olympics. Others, such as the creed or competition motto, were assimilated from elsewhere.[10] Certain elements, like the release of pigeons or doves, were elements of the ceremonial from the outset; others such as the judges' oath, did not appear until 1972. As noted above, the opening ceremony dates from 1896, but did not assume its present pattern until 1908 and witnessed incremental additions in the name of spectacle with each passing Olympics. The current pattern of holding medal ceremonies primarily dates from 1932, with earlier games having copied the classical Greek practice of handing out the medals in a 'prizegiving' ceremony after the sporting contests finished. Ceremonial use of the Olympic flag similarly took time to reach its contemporary form. Designed by Coubertin, the flag, with its characteristic symbol of five intertwined rings, was first exhibited in the IOC's display at the San Francisco Panama–Pacific International Exhibition in 1915 (see Chapter 4). Its use in the opening ceremony dates from 1920 and the transfer of the flag from one Olympic city to its successor became the subject of elaborate ritual in the closing ceremony.[11]

Probably the most evocative aspect of the opening ceremony – the physical relaying of the torch to the host stadium and the lighting of the flame – only slowly entered Olympic practice. In classical times, a flame burned at Olympia for the duration of the games, but the 'Olympic flame' was revived initially as a figure of speech. Metaphoric allusions to the Olympic spirit as a flame passed from nation to nation first appeared in speeches in 1912,[12] with references to the idea that the flame needed to be kept alive occurring from 1922 onwards (Müller, 2000, 209, 448). Only later did Olympic ceremonial see the appearance of a physical torch and the kindling of the Olympic flame at the games' principal stadium. The idea of a flame that burned throughout the games was introduced at Amsterdam in 1928 and continued at Los Angeles in 1932. The notion of lighting a torch at Olympia, the birthplace of the Olympics, and carrying it in relay to the Olympic stadium is attributed to Carl Diem, General Secretary of the German Olympic Committee, who introduced the ceremony at Berlin in 1936.[13]

Yet, again, the Greek contribution needs stressing. The inaugural modern games in Athens successfully launched the modern Olympics, even if they were not widely reported at the time. They were followed by two disastrous games where the 'Olympic' element was all but invisible. As we show later, the Paris games (1900) completely subsumed the Olympics within the Exposition Universelle. The St Louis games of 1904 repeated that experience and added overtones of racist supremacy in the guise of 'anthropological experiment'. That the games survived as an international festival at all after this inauspicious start owed as much to Greek efforts at the unacknowledged 1906 intercalated games as to Coubertin's energy and sustained commitment.

Recreating the Modern Games

From the outset, the Olympics have been a collaborative exercise. The current pattern sees the IOC, as the body controlling the Olympic events, working with the International Sports Federations, which control the conduct of specific sports, and the National Olympic Committees, which organise teams and forward bids from selected host cities. However, this pattern, like the IOC itself, developed over time. The IOC was initially a small, conservative and entirely male-dominated body, heavily under the sway of Coubertin. Its members were primarily prominent sportsmen and titled individuals whose social status might lend weight to the embryonic organisation. The first committee comprised 15 members from 12 countries. By 1904, this had increased to 32 members, of whom 17 had aristocratic or civil titles (eight counts, three barons, two princes, a knight, a professor, a general and a bishop). To Coubertin, that social standing seemed to suggest people whose impeccable background and private means would ensure their impartiality. To later commentators, it would provide the recipe for cronyism and an unrepresentative self-perpetuating oligarchy (for example, Simson and Jennings, 1992; Lenskyj, 2000).

Initially, the IOC's selection of cities to stage the games revolved more around the internal goals of the Olympic movement than active competition between host cities. Early requests to stage the games mostly came from IOC members enthusiastic to encourage sport in their countries rather than to promote wider social or economic goals. Such expressions of enthusiasm were particularly valued. The IOC wanted to reward contributions to the Olympic movement and to spread the staging of the games geographically. The principles of Olympism, in Coubertin's view, were best understood by participating in the games either as competitor or spectator. This partly underpinned the logic of making the games ambulatory and staged in cities outside Europe when possible to prove their international character and mission. Having said that, there was a level of pragmatism involved in early locational decisions (Young, 1987, 271). Even though the IOC had already decided that Athens, with its symbolic associations, was the only city that could launch the modern Olympic movement, serious consideration was given to London as a site for the 1896 games given its advantages regarding access and venues.

Athens (1896)

The first modern games proceeded against a background of profound political and economic difficulties, which made preparations difficult. In the face of huge foreign debt, bad harvests and declining export prices, Greece could neither afford to finance the games nor be seen by creditors to be spending money on such a project (MacAloon, 1981, 182). Controversy raged within the country. For example, the Prime Minister, Charilaos Tricoupis, opposed the games for economic reasons, while the opposition leader Theodorus Delyannis sympathised with the games as a prestigious project that might reflect well on Greek identity and international standing. With support from the monarchy – manifested in Crown Prince Constantine assuming the presidency of the organising committee (ibid., 186–7) – the games' supporters won the day. Finance, as with many of the early international expositions, was raised through a mixture of private and public sources, including appeals for subscriptions, donations from wealthy sponsors,[14] and a special issue of postage stamps (ibid., 196).

More specifically, the games capitalised on Athens already having suitable facilities that could be pressed into service, such as the Zappeion Building on the Piraeus beachfront and the ancient Panathenian stadium of Herodes Atticus. The latter, already excavated and restored for the 1870 games, posed problems through its shape and layout. It comprised an elongated horseshoe enclosing a running track measuring one-third of a kilometre (360 yards) in length. Despite the symbolic value of running in the footsteps of the ancients, the accentuated curves at each end clearly hindered athletic performance. Little could be done about the constricted nature of the track, but plans by the architect Anastas Metaxas aimed to create a modern running surface as well as redesign the stadium with tiers of marble seating. In the event, the organisers only completed the lower sections of the stadium in time, with wooden seating provided in the upper sections – although the stadium still held crowds of more than 50 000. A new velodrome, a shooting gallery and seating for the swimming events were also constructed (Davenport, 1996, 4–5; Gordon, 1983).

Despite problems, the Athens meeting successfully relaunched the Olympics. The games, which opened on Greek Independence Day (6 April), attracted 245 athletes from 14 countries to compete in 45 events. The opening ceremony filled the stadium to capacity, with onlookers occupying the hillsides and streets surrounding the stadium. Estimates of the total crowd varied between 80 000 to 120 000 – an impressive total given that the Athenian population was only 130 000 and that tourist participation remained limited (MacAloon, 1981, 212). The opening ceremony took place in the presence of IOC officials, Greek and visiting royalty, politicians and the diplomatic corps. Crown Prince Constantine's speech charted the challenges overcome in the staging of the Olympics, the king declared the games open, cannons fired and pigeons were released. A choir of 150 with orchestral accompaniment sang the Olympic hymn, composed by Spyros Samaras with words by Kostis Palamas. This was followed by the first sporting competitions.

There was a short ceremony after each event when the victor's flag was raised but, as noted earlier, presentation of medals occurred in a prizegiving at the close of the games. At this time, winners received an olive branch from Olympia, a diploma, and a silver, rather than gold, medal. The athletes then processed around the stadium led by the marathon winner, Spiridon Louis, who carried the Greek flag. George Robertson, an Oxford University student and competitor, recited a 'Pindaric' ode that he had composed in ancient Greek. The king pronounced the games over and left the stadium. The band played the Greek national anthem to end proceedings.

The event took over the entire city. The authorities decorated the streets and illuminated the Acropolis. The programme included torchlight processions, parades, fireworks, an orchestral concert by the Athens Philharmonic Orchestra and a performance of Sophocles's 'Antigone' (Mallon and Widlund, 1998). There were banquets and receptions for the athletes, organisers and IOC members, culminating in a luncheon given by the king in the palace ballroom. The scale of the event, the size of the crowds and the engagement of what seemed the entire population overwhelmed many foreign visitors and competitors, who pronounced themselves left speechless by the 'indescribable' sight of the first modern games (MacAloon, 1981).

The marathon race, a key element in the new spectacle, also played an important symbolic role in uniting city and games. Despite its classical associations – marking the Greek victory over the Persians at Marathon – the race had no counterpart in ancient Greece, where distance races rarely exceeded three miles (five kilometres).[15] The idea for a race over what was then 25 miles (42 kilometres)[16] came from Michel Bréal, a member of the French Institute and a classical philologist, who offered a silver trophy for the winner. In 1894, Bréal suggested that a marathon race would stimulate interest in the games and that, as its final event, would provide a spectacular finale. His innovation proved enormously successful. Despite the unprecedented nature of the event, 25 athletes participated in the marathon. Spectators lined the route through Athens and filled the Olympic stadium. Its impact was enhanced by the victory of Spiridon Louis. Besides stirring patriotic fervour amongst the crowd, the romance of a Greek shepherd winning such a race fitted the notion of the natural athlete, of humble origins who, with little practice, could vanquish foreign competitors from privileged backgrounds.[17]

The Athens games were broadly judged a success. Admittedly, they were only small-scale and participants were not members of national teams by modern standards. The British team of ten athletes included two employees from the embassy in Athens, an expatriate resident in Athens, and an Australian national then living in London (MacAloon, 1981, 210). As noted, there were few foreign visitors. Coubertin had engaged Thomas Cook and Son to organise travel to the games, with John Cook himself travelling to Athens to oversee arrangements,[18] but Greece had a poor reputation as a tourist destination (Brendon, 1991, 238). Specifically, there were complaints that visitors were discouraged by the steep accommodation prices (Mallon and Widlund, 1998, 61). Yet, having said that, the Greeks emerged from the games with their reputation for organisation and hospitality much improved. The British envoy to Athens reported to the Foreign Office that 'nothing could have been better managed, the Greeks appearing in the best possible light as competitors, spectators, organisers and hosts' (cited in Polley, 1996, 98). Moreover, the Athens games showed the potential of the Olympics as a coherent framework for a new international festival. For some, this immediately suggested that the games should remain in Greece permanently, an idea quickly taken up by various Greek officials. The twelve members of the American team, for example, endorsed this view, writing a joint letter to the *New York Times* declaring that 'these Games should never be removed from their native soil' (cited Mallon, 1999b, 2).

Coubertin moved quickly to counteract the threat that this suggestion posed to the ambulatory basis of the games. At pains to stress the 'brilliant success of *our* undertaking'[19] against those who focused only on the Greek contribution, Coubertin prompted the IOC to offer a compromise to Prince Constantine. This confirmed that the original plan of rotating the games remained in place but Greece, in non-Olympic years, might hold a series of intercalated games at four-yearly intervals. A meeting of the IOC at Le Havre in 1897, which the Greek representatives failed to attend, ratified this scheme. Meanwhile Greece's defeat in the war against Turkey left the country bankrupt and without any imminent prospect of staging such a games (Davenport, 1996, 10).

The Early Games

The Athens games restarted the familiar four-year cycle of Olympiads.

With hindsight, there seems a natural and inevitable progression at four-yearly intervals from 1896 to the present – an unbroken line save for the outbreaks of two world wars. Yet the reality is very different. The games of 1900 and 1904, as already mentioned, fell far short of the grand vision of the Olympics derived from history. The Greeks still harboured their intention to host regular Olympic Games and there were rival Olympics from groups such as workers and women, who felt excluded from the bourgeois and gentlemanly circles of the IOC (for example, Riordan, 1984).

The potential vulnerability of the Olympics was shown by the second games held in Paris in 1900. The choice of Paris was a project close to the heart of Coubertin who, at the 1894 congress, had initially suggested the first games should be part of the Paris Exposition Universelle of 1900. Although accepting the inaugural modern games in Athens, he retained his view that the Exposition Universelle was a prestigious event that would attract many visitors and supply a festive backdrop to the games. Coubertin wanted to build a replica of Olympia, with temples, stadia, gymnasium and statues and an archaeological display.[20] The organisers, however, were disinterested in this idea and disputes over the control of the sporting element resulted in the Olympic movement effectively withdrawing from the games.

The result was that a new committee was formed to plan the sporting element (Mallon, 1998, 6) and that the games held at the 1900 Paris Exposition became an international games rather than a true Olympics. There was no stadium or running track. The track and field events were staged at the Racing Club of France's grounds in the Bois du Boulogne, but the owners refused permission to remove any trees. As a result, discus and javelin throws often landed in wooded areas. The 500-metre (546-yard) grass running track sloped and undulated. Rigid former telegraph poles were used as hurdles. The organisers hastily constructed a grandstand, but a row of trees obscured the track from spectators (Howell and Howell, 1996).

The Exposition Universelle opened on 14 April 1900, but it is difficult to identify precisely the dates of the 'Olympic' component since there were no opening or closing ceremonies. At best, its opening seems to have coincided with the national holiday of Bastille Day on 14 July 1900. Some competitors had entered tournaments connected with the exposition, without realising that they had entered Olympic competitions. Various events did not conform to Olympic standards. The greatest confusion occurred with the marathon, where spectators and cyclists obstructed the competitors with no officials on hand to indicate the route. No medals were awarded to the victors of the athletic competitions. Michel Theato, the marathon winner, was only informed in 1912 that he was the 'gold medallist' at the 1900 games (Mallon, 1998, 9).

The sheer weight of problems encountered might well have proved fatal for the Olympic movement. Eclipsed by the exposition rather than the two events being mutually supportive, the movement that had shown 'so much promise in 1896 seemed to have collapsed by 1900' (Howell and Howell, 1996, 17). Matters did not improve with the 1904 Olympics in St Louis. Coubertin keenly endorsed the idea of the games taking place outside Europe and favoured the USA as an early location. Five cities were considered as possible hosts: New York (the initial favourite), Philadelphia, Chicago, Buffalo and St Louis. Buffalo wanted to stage the games in 1901 rather than 1904 as part of its Pan-American Exposition. The Philadelphia delegation was only interested in track and field. By contrast, Chicago actively welcomed the games *in toto* and soon emerged as the leading candidate, receiving the IOC's approval in May 1901.

At this point, St Louis challenged the decision. Its Louisiana Purchase International Exposition was timetabled for 1904 and the organisers had already planned to include 'athletic Games of all descriptions' (Sullivan, 1905, 157). They then announced that they wanted these games to be 'Olympic'. Simmering in the background to this dispute was St Louis's resentment at having lost to Chicago a decade earlier in the contest for the World's Columbian Exposition. The St Louis promoters saw no reason to give way a second time. Forced to adjudicate, the IOC recognised that it was clearly impossible for America to host two major international events concurrently without one damaging the other. The St Louis organising committee held their ground, threatening to stage their games regardless of whether Chicago's invitation stood. Faced with their intransigence, the IOC decided that St Louis was the less harmful choice even if it was inevitable that the Olympics 'would only be a sideshow attraction to the much larger international exposition' (Barnett, 1996, 19).

Understandably, St Louis was a difficult location for participants to reach on grounds of cost and distance, but was made more problematic for the Olympic movement by the attitudes of the organisers. The 1904 games commenced with 'something approaching' an opening ceremony on 14 May 1904 (Mallon, 1999a, 11), but sporting competitions continued at irregular intervals through to November. Little distinction was made between sports that were truly Olympic and those that were not. The Department of Physical Culture, under whose jurisdiction the games were placed, considered that 'all sports that were to be given under the auspices of the Louisiana Purchase Exposition must bear the name "Olympic"' (Sullivan, 1905, 157). If so, then the Olympic programme included college football (gridiron), local cross-country championships, professional events, the national championships of the American Athletic Union of the United States, and 'automobiling' – speed trials, hill climbing and other contests to show the 'worth of the machine and the skill of the operators' (Anon., 1904, 3, 48).

The Olympic stadium held 10 000 spectators and had a one-third mile (536-metre) track instead of the standard quarter-mile circuit of the time. All events were held out-of-doors in the infield of the stadium apart from two basketball games (staged in Washington University's gymnasium due to rain). The stadium witnessed perhaps the most infamous aspects of the 1904 Olympic Games programme in the shape of the Anthropology Days held on 12–13 August 1904. An extension of the organisers' white supremacist and pseudo-scientific interests in the physical prowess of different races, the Anthropology Days saw African, Asian and indigenous Americans competing in a range of athletic contests including 100 yards, 440 yards, the mile, shot putt, long jump, baseball throwing, javelin, tug of war, high jump and pole climbing. Terms such as 'savage tribes', 'cannibal', 'crude' and 'barbarian' littered the official and newspaper reports of this event (Goksyr, 1989). The photographs in the official report, in which semi-naked competitors were juxtaposed with the well-dressed officials, reinforced this impression.

The results of the competitions were used to denigrate the standing of indigenous peoples further in western eyes. The standard in the Patagonian shot-putting competition, for example, was regarded as 'ridiculously poor' and was compared unfavourably with results for American schoolchildren: 'it is doubtful if there is a high school championship that is not won with a better performance' (Sullivan, 1905, 251). The official report of the competitions pointed out that the results 'disproved' assumptions concerning 'the natural all round ability of the savage in athletic feats' and went on to call for lecturers and authors to omit reference to the 'natural athletic ability' of such peoples in future (ibid., 249, 259). Only slight mention was made of the lack of training received by the competitors or the absence of interpreters to explain the rules of the competition. Following hard on the heels of the debacle of the 1900 Olympiad, the St Louis games threatened the future of the revived Olympics. Few Europeans travelled to St Louis, with Americans the only competitors in many events. With his expressed misgivings about the St Louis games, Coubertin, like most of the IOC, stayed away. The Anthropology Days and the discredited marathon race, in which the apparent winner had ridden part of the way in a car and the actual winner had taken stimulants en route, further reduced the value of the competition (Barnett, 1996, 23).

In the event, the future of the games was secured by a sporting festival often not reckoned as part of Olympic history – the 1906 Intercalated Games held in Athens (Young, 1996, 166; Mallon, 1999b, 5). The 1906 games were the first, and only, product of Coubertin's 1897 tactical compromise over Greece's claim to act as permanent hosts for the Olympics (see above). Although still reluctant to support anything that appeared to recognise Greece's proprietorial claims, Coubertin's position was severely weakened by the St Louis games. He therefore felt obliged to consent to Greece's requests to hold an additional, Intercalated Games in Athens with IOC approval.

The 1906 games returned to the Panathenian stadium where the now complete marble construction raised the capacity to 70 000. The largest sports gathering so far, the Intercalated Games revived and advanced the ceremonial content of the Olympics and re-established the idea of a free-standing sports festival after their damaging linkage with international expositions. The Intercalated Games were also the first in which competitors attended as part of nationally organised teams. The British sent 52 athletes and the USA selected its team based on their athletic records (Mallon, 1999b, 6). Sixty thousand spectators watched the opening ceremony. This contained the first March of Nations, as uniformed teams paraded in the stadium behind their flag-bearers. The Greeks brought up the rear as hosts (a custom that has continued). Four massed choirs sang the hymn composed for the 1896 Olympic Games. Each event had its own victory ceremony, with the flags of the first-, second- and third-placed competitors being raised (although the prizes themselves continued to be handed out at the closing ceremony). Ten days later, the King of Greece officially closed the games, with the festivities rounded off by a reception for athletes and officials.

The accompanying festivities were more extensive and eye-catching than those staged in 1896. The Athens authorities reconnected the games with the host city, in a way that contrasted with the experience of Paris and St Louis. The streets and buildings of Athens were again decorated, the Acropolis illuminated, evening concerts were commissioned for the city's squares. There was a sustained programme of plays, concerts, receptions, official luncheons and dinners, lectures, archaeological visits and conferences, as well as a Venetian festival in Piraeus. The international press was more in evidence than at previous games, although the eruption of Mount Vesuvius (4 April) and the San Francisco earthquake (18 April) detracted from the coverage that the games received (Mallon, 1999b, 6).

The Athens games of 1906, like those of 1896, set standards for the celebration of the Olympics and production of spectacle. The active participation of the head of state in the opening and closing ceremonies, the rituals, the scale and the sporting festival spilling over into the city were all vital ingredients that subsequent games tried to emulate. The Greeks, however, were not destined to be the beneficiaries. Despite intending to hold further Intercalated Games in 1910 and 1914, political crises in the Balkans meant that the 1906 games were the only event of its type. Moreover, true to its ideological stance, the IOC subsequently refused to acknowledge the 1906 games as an official Olympics in spite of conforming to the ideals of the movement far better than either the 1900 and 1904 games. The standard narrative of Coubertin's unassisted guiding hand in reviving the games remained intact.

London and Stockholm

Two more Olympiads would be held before the First World War: London (1908) and Stockholm (1912). Rome held the original designation for the 1908 games – an award designed to reinforce the movement's cherished classical credentials. The same eruption of Vesuvius in April 1906 that had detracted from the coverage of the Athens games, however, also put paid to its successor as the severe strains that recovery from the devastation placed on the Italian economy led to Rome abandoning its attempt to hold the games.[21] Lord Desborough, the chairman of the British Olympic Committee, formally offered London as replacement for the 1908 Olympics during the Athens games. The IOC formally confirmed the transfer in November 1906 (Mallon and Buchanan, 2000, 3).

The problem was that the games would again be linked to an exposition – in this case the Franco-British Exhibition of Science, Arts, and Industry. Held between 14 May and 31 October 1908 on a 140-acre (56-hectare) plot of agricultural land at Shepherd's Bush (west London), the Franco-British exhibition was a major expositionary event despite not now being regarded as a part of the sequence of international expositions discussed in Chapters 3–5. Called as part of the process of consolidating political alliances – the exhibition celebrated the entente cordiale – it displayed the power of Britain, France and their colonies in the face of growing mistrust of Germany.

At first glance, the extent and expanse of the exhibition – with its pavilions, waterways, amusement area ('Merryland') and parklands – threatened to pose precisely the same danger of eclipsing the games as was seen at Paris and St Louis. That this did not happen was due largely to the exhibition organising committee agreeing to construct a purpose-built stadium. The foundation stone of the White City stadium was laid in August 1907 and the stadium was inaugurated on 14 May 1908 on the opening day of the exhibition. It held 93 000 spectators, of whom

63 000 were seated. Its infield was large enough to contain not just the athletics and cycling tracks but also a 100-metre swimming pool, platforms for wrestling and gymnastics and even archery.[22] Dressing rooms, restaurants and emergency services were located under the stands. This separate facility effectively gave the games a distinct and self-contained identity that overcame any association with the exhibition. By supplying the basis for 'a compact and independent Olympic festival' (Wimmer, 1976, 22), London 1908 was a milestone in the history of the games, even if the self-contained nature of the event somewhat reduced the interaction between festival and city.

The Stockholm games of 1912 restored that link. The Swedes constructed their stadium in the grounds of the royal Djirgaden (zoological gardens) on the archaic U-shaped pattern with corner towers. Able to seat 22 000 people and containing a quarter-mile (383-metre) running track, the stadium was financed by a lottery organised by the Swedish National Gymnastic and Sporting Association and the Central Association for the Promotion of Athletics. It was deliberately designed to be multipurpose rather than only devised for sport, a decision that helped to promote a new and more helpful relationship between the games and host city. In Coubertin's words (quoted in Wimmer, 1976, 27):

> The Gothic Stadium ... seemed to be a model of its kind. You could see it turned into a banquet hall, a concert hall, or a dance hall, and yet on the following morning always ready once again for carrying on with the contests. You could see how in a single night it got covered with ready-made squares of lawn, how hurdles were being put up, and how it decked itself with blossoming brushwood for the riding tournaments. All this was achieved without any ado, any delay, any blunder. While in London it had proved impossible for the life of the great city to be in any way affected by the proximity of the Olympic Games, Stockholm turned out to be thoroughly imbued with them. The entire city participated in its efforts to honour its foreign guests, and one had something like a vision of what the atmosphere must have been like in Olympia in the ancient days ...

The stadium, therefore, provided the focal point of the festival, with daily sporting events and evening entertainments that included a military concert, displays of popular sports and Icelandic Glima (wrestling), gymnastics, folk dancing, choral festivals, fireworks and illuminations. The Olympics also overflowed into the city. The Artists Club took responsibility for supervising arrangements by which streets and squares were decked out with flags. The authorities encouraged householders to put more flowers on their balconies and decorate their homes with flags (SOC, 1913, 825–6). Opera, theatre, and a two-day aquatic festival accompanied the usual round of receptions, banquets and garden parties. The city also played somewhat reluctant host to the artistic competitions that were a cherished part of Coubertin's vision of encompassing the Olympics in a modern panegyris. Run in this instance by the IOC rather than the city's organisers,[23] the winning entries nevertheless went on display in Stockholm as an extra attraction for visitors.

For the first time, too, Stockholm saw the games promoted internationally in a co-ordinated manner. The organisers sent information not simply to national Olympic committees but to representatives of the Swedish Tourist Association in 21 overseas countries as well as Swedish consuls, legations, newspapers and Swedish clubs abroad (SOC, 1913, 259). Advertising was also taken in the continental edition of the London-based *Daily Mail* newspaper in 1911 and 1912, using the by-line 'Stockholm the Venice of the North' (ibid., 278). The makings of the promotional activity that typified later Olympic Games had clearly started to emerge.

Consolidation

The Stockholm games were the first celebration of an Olympiad where the event was freestanding and planned without interruption over a three-year period. With the stadium in Berlin built and inaugurated in June 1913[24] in readiness for the sixth Olympiad, the Olympic movement appeared to have established both a routine for staging the festival and an international identity. The outbreak of the First World War in 1914, however, disrupted any such thinking. With the impossibility of holding the 1916 games in Berlin, six US cities (Chicago, Cleveland, Newark, New York, Philadelphia and San Francisco) offered to host the games to avoid disrupting the series. The German Olympic Committee, however, remained adamant that Berlin held the nomination. They received the tacit support of the IOC, which clung to the view that it had no right to withdraw a city's nomination without consulting that country (Durick, 1996, 52). The sixth Olympiad, therefore, was never held and the games resumed their four-year cycle with the seventh Olympiad in a war-damaged Antwerp in 1920.

Selected at an IOC meeting in Lausanne in April 1919, the choice of Antwerp was as much a political act of moral support to Belgium as a sporting event. No other games were put together at such short notice. The organisers used the quickly renovated Beerschot stadium, although shortage of resources and materials meant that the standard of facilities was much poorer than at Stockholm. The games made first use of the now standard 400-metre running track, but constant rain left its surface pitted and rutted. The rowing contests were held in the industrial setting of the canal at Willebroek near Brussels: a setting so ugly that Coubertin called it 'anti-Olympic' (Renson, 1996, 57).

As such, the games' main significance lay in restarting the series, its role in rekindling the perennial complaints from previous Olympiads about bias amongst officials, in its development of Olympic ritual, and in bringing home the growing cost of the event. The question of cost was a minor concern for the early Olympics, given that they used existing facilities, were small-scale, and had budgets that were hard to differentiate from the expositions of which they were part. Although the London Olympics, for example, had suffered from lack of funding and poor attendance, the organisers of the Franco-British Exhibition met the costs of the stadium facilities. The economic success or otherwise of the 1908 Olympics 'was of little concern for the Games organisers' (Coates, 1996, 39). By contrast, the Antwerp games recorded a deficit of 626 million Belgian francs, prompted accusations of acute financial mismanagement and left the organisers open to the charge of treating the event as 'a symbol of conspicuous consumption' (Renson, 1996, 59).

The two ensuing games at Paris (1924) and Amsterdam (1928) may be paired together, partly because they represented a phase of consolidation for the Olympics and partly because they were designated as hosts at the same meeting. The 1924 games marked the first occasion on which growing prestige of the Olympics led to serious international competition among cities to act as hosts. Four US cities (Los Angeles, Atlantic City, Chicago and Pasadena) and five European cities (Rome, Barcelona, Amsterdam, Lyons and Paris) expressed interest in staging the Olympics (Welch, 1996, 61). The return of the games to Paris for the thirtieth anniversary of the Olympic movement reflected complex negotiations. The lingering economic aftermath of the First World War made the IOC unwilling to choose an American location, given the extra travelling costs such a location would have imposed on European competitors and officials. The Dutch delegation withdrew its bid a month before the IOC meeting in June 1921 on the understanding that the French would support Amsterdam's candidacy for the 1928 games. The French, for their part, gave assurances that the Olympics would be treated as an important international event, unlike the previous 1900 games.

The French initially intended to use the Pershing stadium that had housed the 1919 Inter-Allied Games, but decided in June 1922 to construct a purpose-built stadium with seating for 20 000 spectators and standing room for an additional 40 000 (Welch, 1996, 64). Unlike the Exposition Universelle, which had been absorbed into the fabric of the city, the organisers scattered the Olympic facilities around the Parisian city-region. The stadium was at Colombes in the suburbs, with some of the athletes housed in the first Olympic village some distance away at Rocquencourt. The swimming pool at the Porte de Lilas required bus rides lasting anything up to two hours. The exception related to the associated arts competitions, which made full use of central city venues. Paris in 1924 saw the first wholehearted attempt to include the arts competitions. The Marquis de Polignac, in addition, organised the Eighth Olympiad Season of Art at the Champs Elysées Theatre, which included a performance of Beethoven's Ninth Symphony by a Dutch orchestra and choir as representatives of the next hosts. The Dutch Ambassador also gave a speech where he talked about carrying the torch forward.

The symbolic involvement of the Dutch effectively marked the completion of the process by which the Olympic protocol gradually emerged. In Coubertin's words: 'I had constructed it little by little and in stages, so as not to take by surprise spectators and actors who might be ill-prepared or unreceptive' (quoted in Müller, 2000). Growing maturity, however, also meant looking hard at the size and complexity of the games. The logistic problems created by their steadily increasing scale, coupled with a full women's programme and continual addition of new sports, spurred efforts to eliminate other, less popular events to reduce the burden on future host cities. Rugby (union) football, for example, made its last Olympic appearance at the 1924 games.

The 1928 Amsterdam games employed the 'Cité Olympique' idea of rebuilding the stadium and replanning the surrounding area to create a sporting complex. This, in turn, was integrated into the broader city plan. Dutch cities saw notable early attempts to carry out large-scale urban planning projects that aimed to bring about environmental improvement for the working-class population (Gold, 1997, 49). South Amsterdam, where the stadium was sited, had already seen extensive areas of model worker housing constructed between 1902–20. The new track-and-field stadium,[25] built on reclaimed marshlands, could hold a seated audience of 40 000 people, with the surrounding facilities housing a further 30 000 spectators. The open-air swimming pool was located next to the main stadium, with adjacent gymnasiums for the boxing, wrestling and fencing competitions. The athletes were housed on ships in the harbour rather than in a specially constructed village (Goldstein, 1996). Again there was concern about the growing size of the games, although this time the target was the associated activities. The official report of the 1928 games suggests that the IOC was concerned about 'excessive festivities' being organised during the games and that there should be reforms to allow only those that 'the reception of authorities and officials demanded' (Organising Committee, 1928, 957).

Increasing Scale, Widening Agendas

The two final interwar games stand out for the broader role that the games were perceived to have had, in one case, for the city and, in the other, for the state. Los Angeles (1932) was an Olympiad conceived in the American boosterist tradition, resolutely advancing the city's economic and cultural interests against rivals. The 1936 Berlin Olympics presented Germany's Third Reich with an opportunity to advance both its internal and external political goals. Echoes of both these approaches to the games would be seen more overtly in the games that took place after the Second World War (see Chapter 7).

Los Angeles (1932)

Place promotion has always occupied an important place in the history of Los Angeles. Its modern history dates from the last quarter of the nineteenth century, when aggressive local leaders and entrepreneurs secured the South Pacific Railroad for the city in 1876 and the Santa Fe Railroad in 1886. The population of just 11 183 in 1880 rose to 576 673 in 1920 (Johnson, 2003, 152), with the city experiencing explosive centrifugal growth. Civic leaders expressed concern at the city's lack of industrial diversity and the apparent severance of its links with its Hispanic past. In 1919, the California Fiestas Association (CFA) was formed 'at the instance of the publishers of the daily newspapers of that city', with the ostensible object of reviving the old Spanish fiestas typical of the 'history and atmosphere of our State and city' (TOC, 1933, 33). Discussion immediately centred on the need for a stadium to host such celebrations and soon the possibility grew of linking this to a larger enterprise, the Olympic Games. Getting the games would provide opportunities to promote Los Angeles globally, as well as nationally, and attract tourists. It might also allow Los Angeles to show the East Coast financial establishment that Southern California was a thriving commercial and cultural centre (Gruneau and Cantelon, 1988, 353).

These diverse considerations jointly underpinned a formal proposal to the CFA in November 1919 that Los Angeles should apply to stage the Olympic Games. The president of the CFA, William May Garland, had planned to go to Europe in the summer of 1920 and agreed to visit Antwerp and to contact 'the proper Olympic body' with an invitation to stage the games in Los Angeles in 1924. Garland, a real estate magnate and prominent civic booster, was ideally suited to this task. He carried with him letters of support from the city, county and leading civic organisations, plans for the proposed athletics stadium and an outline of the advantages that Los Angeles offered. Garland presented these to the IOC and 'orally urged an award to Los Angeles' (TOC, 1933, 37). Coubertin enthusiastically supported the bid, but indicated that the 1924 games had already been awarded to Paris and the 1928 games tentatively to Amsterdam. The setback, however, proved temporary. Garland gained a seat on the IOC and successfully proposed Los Angeles for the 1932 games at the IOC meeting in Rome in 1923 (TOC, 1933, 33–37).

Work soon began on renovating the coliseum in the city's Exposition Park into an Olympic stadium (Pieroth, 1996, 75). With further enlargement in 1930, the Los Angeles Memorial Stadium had a seated capacity for the games of 105 000. Further buildings followed as private enterprise and sporting clubs developed facilities that would contain the games and enhance the sporting community's infrastructure. In 1927 the Community Development Association (CDA),[26] the successor to the CFA, sponsored the California Olympiad Bond Act to raise $1 million for the staging of the games. This Act required an amendment to the state constitution, which in turn required approval at the ensuing elections of November 1928. The city of Los Angeles in 1928 voted a $1.5 million supporting bond issue. The CDA set up the California Olympiad Commission to administer the fund allocated to the organising committee, a limited company called the Tenth Olympiad Committee of the Games of Los Angeles USA 1932.

The steady progress made over a production cycle lasting no less than nine years was nearly derailed by the financial crash of 1929. The ensuing economic depression created problems both for competing countries and spectators. It also led to local difficulties. With record unemployment and soup kitchens established in California, sentiment ran against the 'frivolity' of the games. Pickets at Sacramento called for their cancellation. The federal administration refused to help, leading in due course to President Hoover declining the conventional invitation to open the games (Pieroth, 1996, 75).

Their continuance owed much to the organisers' determined efforts to ease the cost of attending and competing. They produced certificates entitling participants to reduced overland fares and the Transatlantic Steamship Conference granted official Olympic personnel a 20 per cent reduction below off-season steamship rates. The American railways offered a special round trip rate of $100 for the return trip to Los Angeles from New York (TOC, 1933, 228). The Hollywood film studios, with their global reach, mobilised to support the games.

Filmmakers created short feature films around Olympic subjects, and stars such as Mary Pickford and Douglas Fairbanks broadcast invitations to come to the Olympics. To make the offer economically feasible for competitors and maximise participation, the Los Angeles organising committee constructed the first true Olympic village.

From the outset, this innovation was intended to combine economy with Olympic ideology. Planned in 1930 as a prefabricated village to house the male athletes,[27] it had the added aim of epitomising the spirit of Olympism. The official report of the games (TOC, 1933, 235, 237) waxed lyrical about the symbolism of the village, stating that it was built:

> in the fervent belief and faith that the children of the nations, unscathed by maturity and assumed nationalism, would find in each other brothers in the flesh, regardless of colour, race or creed, and react accordingly ... Where else could you find a wealthy nobleman sharing a cottage with a humble blacksmith ... [with] the nations of earth sleeping quietly together and peacefully together, like infants in the lap of some material goddess of Olympia.

Yet for all the rhetoric of fraternity – with the organising committee being mentioned for the Nobel Peace Prize for the brotherhood of the games and Olympic village (Stump, 1988, 199) – it was the availability of heavy subsidy that essentially saved the games. The organisers offered concessionary rates by which athletes were housed, fed, entertained and transported locally for two dollars a day. By these means, the entire trip of one-month duration need work out at no more than $500 per capita. The result was that 1500 athletes representing 34 nations found their way to Los Angeles in the spring of 1932. Apart from the auditorium for the indoor competitions, most of the stadia were at Olympic Park (the renamed Exposition Park). The main facility was the recently enlarged and renamed Memorial Stadium, the last Olympic arena to use the old-fashioned modified U-shape (Wimmer, 1976, 39). The swimming stadium and the state armoury, which staged the fencing competitions, were nearby. The Olympic Park also housed the Los Angeles Museum of History, Science and Art, which held more than 1100 exhibits from 32 countries that were entries to the Olympic art competition. The exhibition drew 384 000 visitors during the duration of the games – a figure that might well have been higher if the opening hours of the museum could have been better co-ordinated with the Olympic programme.

The organisers decorated the Olympic venues with streamers and bunting in the official colours of blue, yellow, black, green and red. They also extended these decorations to the city of Los Angeles, using funds allocated by the city council. National flags of the competing nations,

Olympic flags and large insignia hung across the main streets. The organisers encouraged the owners of buildings and businesses to buy specially manufactured materials to embellish their buildings. A programme of formal receptions and less formal gatherings provided hospitality for athletes, dignitaries and visitors. Some, like the ceremonial dinner on the eve of the games, were a standard part of Olympic festivities, but others were uniquely Hollywood events. Metro-Goldwyn-Mayer Motion Picture Studios, for example, provided a studio tour for members of the official Olympic committees and their wives with opportunities to watch filming with the stars (TOC, 1933, 329). Mary Pickford and Douglas Fairbanks threw the grandest of the private parties at their mansion, Pickfair, where guests dined in a marquee transformed into a Norman castle.[28] The Hollywood Bowl, an open-air amphitheatre on the classical model, offered a series of symphony concerts and other programmes.

The two-hour opening ceremony combined Olympic ceremonial with a scale that deeply impressed visitors. A 1200-voice chorus and a 350-piece orchestra supplied the music. The giant scoreboard emblazoned Coubertin's words: 'The important thing in the Olympic Games is not winning, but taking part. The essential thing is not conquering, but fighting well.' More spectacle followed with the March of Nations, fanfares, cannon fire, the kindling of a flame to burn throughout the games, a new Olympic hymn by Bradley Keeler, the unfurling of the Olympic flag and the release of doves. The president of the University of California delivered an address, after which the Olympic oath was administered. After the chorus sang 'Lord of Hosts be with us yet', the athletes left the stadium.

The medal ceremonies also gained new elements. The victory stand appeared for the first time, with the orchestra playing the national anthem of the gold medal winner's country while the victorious athletes stood on the podium. By contrast, the closing ceremony was staged as a melancholy affair, lamenting the passing of the games, with appropriate speeches, choruses, trumpets, further cannon fire and lowering of flags. The official report commented: 'the stadium, the music, the flags, the banners, all were there – the nations on parade but the pulsating life-blood of the Games, the athletes, was gone' (TOC, 1933, 773). The chorus and crowd sang 'Aloha: Farewell to thee' and the Olympic flame was finally extinguished.

The climate, the festivities and the glamour of the Hollywood film industry supplied opportunities on which the city readily capitalised. Tourist agencies put together packages featuring the Olympics and the scenic attractions of southern California.[29] The All-Year Club of Southern California, a tourism promotional organisation, marketed the games in the USA with the slogan 'Southern California and the Olympic Games ... means your greatest vacation' (TOC, 1933, 215). A visiting journalists' programme dealt with several hundred reporters from around the world in the three years leading up to the games (ibid., 211). Another area of success lay in attracting associated conferences. Sixty-two conventions were attracted to Los Angeles during the games, enabling their delegates to enjoy the games and further boosting the local economy at a time of continuing economic depression (ibid., 220). Finally, the games themselves ran at a profit, with 1.25 million people having paid $1.5 million to watch events over the 16 days of the games.

The city remained keen to repeat the exercise. Mayor Tom Bradley rated the 1932 games as 'an important municipal turning point' and led the movement for the games to return to Los Angeles. William May Garland, in his resignation speech to the IOC in 1948, suggested that Los Angeles would be a good place for the 1956 games and even declaring that 'we could be fully prepared with all facilities to again celebrate the Games with one year's notice or even less'. When the games eventually returned in 1984, it would create another landmark in the history of staging the Olympics (see Chapter 7).

Berlin (1936)

The Olympic Games of 1936 stand out as one of the twentieth century's most important sporting festivals and, indeed, a landmark in interwar European history well beyond the realm of sport. Berlin had bid unsuccessfully for both the 1908 and 1912 games, seen the cancellation of the 1916 games, and saw further ambitions placed in abeyance by Germany's exclusion from the Olympic movement. The readmittance of Germany in time for the 1928 games in Amsterdam saw the renewal of Berlin's candidacy by the German IOC members. In May 1931, the IOC awarded the 1936 games to Berlin as an act of reconciliation,[30] but the choice proved problematic. Initially, this centred on concern about Europe's economies, residual discontent within the IOC about the choice of Germany, and the political situation in the country. The National Socialist Party, then steadily growing in support, expressed open hostility over the financial burden of the games and the Olympic movement's avowed internationalism and pacifism. Hitler himself denounced the games as an 'invention of Jews and Freemasons' (Hart Davis, 1986, 45). When he assumed the chancellorship in January 1933, many believed that this inheritance from the Weimar Republic era would quickly be dropped but, in the event, the reverse occurred. Within weeks, Hitler informed Dr Theodore Lewald, president of the German Olympic Committee, that the games would proceed with state finance (Mackenzie, 2003, 302).

The Nazis quickly appreciated the value of the political stage and propaganda possibilities that the Olympics afforded. After reappraising the classical origins of the games and how they fitted National Socialist ideas of German origins,[31] they realised that the Olympics would allow the regime to present their conceptions of German nationhood wrapped in the excitement, enjoyment and pride associated with the Olympics. The mobilisation of public support started in earnest in January 1934 when the Publicity Commission for the Olympic Games was set up within the Ministry of Propaganda and Popular Enlightenment under the slogan: 'The Olympics, a national task'. Despite Germany's increasingly aggressive foreign policy stance, the Olympics were also a vehicle for showing off the new Germany to the wider world as a 'decent, friendly, peace-loving state' (Mackenzie, 2003, 302–3). Moreover, the games provided a seemingly apolitical event through which to address domestic political goals, for example, an ideal vehicle for legitimising the ideology of the regime concerning national identity and physical training.

Yet the racial underpinnings of the Third Reich's sports policy inevitably created difficulties for the continuance of the games. Sport, according to the Minister of Propaganda Joseph Goebbels, was a means of strengthening the character of the German people, 'imbuing it with the fighting spirit and steadfast camaraderie necessary in the struggle for its existence' (USHMM, 2003). That only applied, however, to those who fell into the regime's definition of nationhood. In 1933, the Aryanization of sport banned Jews from the use of public sports facilities or membership of German sports organisations. Such racial and religious discrimination in sports policy breached Olympic rules and prompted calls for the removal of the games from Germany.

This applied particularly to the USA. The American IOC member Ernest Lee Jahncke, for example, implacably opposed the games saying that participation meant acquiescing 'in the contempt of the Nazis for fair play and their sordid exploitation of the Games' (USHMM, 2003). Avery Brundage, president of the American Olympic Committee and later IOC president, toured Germany in 1934 on a fact-finding mission organised by Karl Ritter von Halt (a German IOC member and already a National Socialist Party member). Persuaded by what he saw, Brundage announced that Jewish athletes would be treated fairly and threw his considerable weight behind American participation. A visit in September 1935 by General Charles E. Sherrill, member of the American Olympic Committee and the IOC, produced the same result. The Amateur Athletic Union defeated a proposal to boycott the games in December 1935. For his continued opposition, in July 1936 Jahncke became the first person to be expelled from IOC membership, being replaced by Brundage. Some Jewish athletes did refuse to attend the games, with alternative games being organised in Barcelona (but abandoned due to the outbreak of the Spanish Civil War), and Prague. Yet, finally, opposition remained muted. For their part, the Germans only included two token non-Aryan athletes in their Olympic team – Rudi Ball in the ice-hockey team for the winter Olympics and Helene Mayer who won a silver medal in the individual foil in the summer games.[32]

From the outset, scale suffused the Berlin Olympics. Hitler personally vetoed the plans for the simple expansion of the 1913 stadium, already approved by the IOC, in which Werner March proposed a glass and concrete design. Instead he favoured a proposal for a 110 000-seater stadium with a steel- and stone-clad structure. Problems over land ownership and pre-existing planning restrictions on the nature of the development were set aside, making way for the world's largest sports complex. Besides the new stadium, the complex contained swimming and diving pools with seating for 18 000, facilities for lawn tennis, hockey, equestrian sports, the House of German Sports (Deutschland Halle) for boxing, fencing, weightlifting, wrestling, the Reich Academy of Physical Education, accommodation for female competitors and the Maifeld Parade Ground. The Langenmarch Hall on the far side of the Maifeld, for example, was named after German students who voluntarily sacrificed their lives at Langenmarch in 1914, effectively linking political to athletic struggle (Rürup, 1996, 69). The Dietrich-Eckhart Theatre, an open-air amphitheatre seating 20 000, contained echoes of ancient Greece, as did the statues and reliefs glorifying Aryan athletic youth scattered liberally around the site (Gordon, 1983). Taken together, the whole complex could hold 400 000 people (Rürup, 1996) and was specifically intended for later use in Nazi Party celebrations and festivals. A great festival avenue – the Via Triumphalis – ran from City Hall and Lustgarten in the east to the stadium in the west, and beyond to the Olympic village at Döberitz, intended to house roughly 4000 male athletes. Railway and tram connections capable of moving the large number of expected spectators linked the sports complex to the city.

The lengthy production cycle necessary to create the Olympic complex ensured that propaganda about the games reached into every corner of Germany. Posters, brochures, booklets and a monthly magazine, *The Olympic Games* were published. In February 1935 two mobile exhibitions – one for cities and one for smaller rural settlements – were launched. Carl Diem assembled a display illustrating the origin of the ancient games, its revival, and models of the facilities for the 1936 games. This opened in Berlin for six weeks and then toured German cities. For the rural population, an 'Olympic Train' – in reality three lorries that could be converted into exhibition rooms and auditoria – toured Germany. They were seen by over 600 000 visitors (Rürup, 1996, 80).

The regime carefully stage managed the appearance of town and country to create a good impression for foreign visitors and the international press. The authorities lavishly decorated Berlin for the event. Householders on procession routes were encouraged to repair and decorate their homes, building sites were disguised, streets and public buildings were covered in banners, flags and garlands of greenery. Offensive literature was removed from stalls and street displays, in particular the newspaper *Der Sturmer* (although it did not cease publication during the games). Anti-Semitic slogans and posters were removed. Berliners were advised about their behaviour. Publications in disfavour and foreign papers appeared on sale and jazz was allowed in dance-halls (Hart Davis 1986, 139). Advice included showing civility to strangers including instructions for men to give up seats to women 'even if the woman looks like a Jewess'. There was to be no discussion of 'Jewish matters' between 30 June and 1 September and no inquiries about the origin of 'exotic-looking strangers' (Hart Davis, 1986, 126). Dissidents, known confidence-tricksters and trouble-makers were quietly arrested (Mandell, 1976, 140).[33]

The games' intrinsic spectacle was the element that undoubtedly most excited the Nazi regime, since spectacle was also a major part of the way in which the Nazi party machine operated. Indeed, Olympic ceremony was treated as a natural extension of that experience. For example, two innovations – the Olympic bell and torch relay – appeared in the months leading up to the games. The Olympic bell, nine feet in diameter and over fourteen feet high, was decorated with the Olympic motto 'Citius, Altius, Fortius', the German eagle, and the legend 'Ich rufe die Jugend der Welt' ('I summon the youth of the world'). It was cast in Bochum, leaving on 16 January 1936 for its journey to Berlin by trailer. As it passed through the countryside, it provided a focus for orchestrated celebrations, with the proceedings broadcast on national radio as part of the promotion of the games (Organising Committee, 1936, 113–14). The bell was hung in a specially constructed tower on the Maifeld, featuring in the opening and closing ceremonies and some of the pageants held in the stadium during the Olympic festival.

While the Olympic bell was essentially a project for domestic consumption, the torch relay was of wider and more enduring significance. Devised by Carl Diem, as noted above, it married together the idea of distance running with the torch ceremony.[34] He suggested that the stadium flame would be lit by a torch brought to Berlin from the site of the original Greek games at Olympia[35] rather than simply being lit at the stadium as at the 1932 games. The torch would then be timed to enter the stadium during the opening ceremony. The IOC approved the plan in May 1934. Just over 3000 relay runners carried the torch on a route passing through Bulgaria, Yugoslavia, Hungary, Austria, Czechoslovakia and finally Germany. This lengthy journey provided opportunity for official ceremonies in anticipation of the games. Each major town received an outline programme for an appropriate ceremony. This typically consisted of the runner's arrival, lighting the Olympic fire, singing of the hymn 'Burn, Olympic flame', an address by the mayor, general singing, gymnastic exercises, sporting demonstrations, singing the Olympic hymn, a festive address dealing with the Olympic Games, folk dancing, folk songs, preparation for the departure of the next runner, words of consecration, singing of the national anthem, departure of the runner and the pealing of bells (Organising Committee, 1936, 515). The organisers sent the words for the Olympic address in the local languages.

As with the Olympics generally, the Third Reich contrived to gain the maximum propaganda advantage from the relay run. While the IOC saw it as making a connection between the modern games and their origin, the Nazis envisaged it making symbolic linkage between the cultural legacy of ancient Greece and modern Germany. In his speech at the opening ceremony, for example, Theodore Lewald claimed that the relay created 'a real and spiritual bond of fire between our German fatherland and the sacred places of Greece founded 4000 years ago by our Nordic immigrants' (cited in Graham, 1986, 76). German radio, therefore, accompanied the torch relay and a team directed by Leni Riefenstahl shot footage for the official film of the games.[36] Unofficial pro-Nazi demonstrations took place along the route, particularly in Vienna where sympathisers disrupted the official welcome (Hart Davis, 1986, 136). Huge crowds lined the route of the relay through Germany culminating in a rally of 25 000 Hitler Youth and 40 000 storm troopers in the Lustgarten before the opening ceremony. Here amongst the decorations designed by Albert Speer, a gathering including Goebbels, von Shirach (the Hitler Youth leader), Goering and IOC members witnessed the arrival of the flame and the lighting of an altar flame, guarded by Hitler Youth until it would be carried to the Olympic stadium (Graham, 1986, 75). Yet despite the domestic agenda of the torch relay, it fitted within the philosophy and spirit of Olympism. It was repeated at the next Olympics, the 1948 London games and then at subsequent summer games, being also added to the itinerary of the winter games at Oslo in 1952.[37]

The opening ceremony developed Olympic protocol incrementally rather than introducing radical departures, with the more overtly militaristic and ideological ceremonies kept elsewhere in Berlin. The Olympic bell tolled to summon the youth of the world. There was the parade of nations, a message from Coubertin played to the crowd, speeches, flag raising, the release of pigeons and the performance of a new Olympic hymn composed by Richard Strauss, who also conducted the orchestra and choir of 3000 voices. This was followed by trumpets, a gun salute for the entry of the Olympic torch, lighting of the flame, the swearing of the Olympic oath, the singing of the 'Hallelujah' chorus from Handel's *Messiah*, Spiridon Louis presenting Hitler with an olive branch from Olympia, and proclamation of the opening of the games. The closing ceremony was held at night to permit the spectacle of the cathedral of light, where searchlights surrounding the stadium created a dome above the heads of the crowd.

The cultural programme, easily the most ambitious so far, again allowed the regime scope to address its wider goals. Seventy thousand visitors saw the exhibition of entries to the Olympic art competition (15 July–23 August 1936), containing over 700 contributions from 23 countries. Other exhibitions included 'Sport in Hellenic times' at the Pergamon Museum, 'Great Germans in contemporary portraits', and 'Masterpieces of nineteenth and twentieth century German art'. The largest was the 'Deutschland' exhibition, a propaganda exercise aimed primarily at the 1.3 million German visitors who attended. This, in the words of Goebbels, was intended to show 'a reawakened, reborn nation, pulsating with the desire to create ... the eternal Germany'. It contained items such as the Gutenberg Bible, the manuscript of *Mein Kampf* and a television phone.

There was an extensive season of musical, operatic and dance performances. The international dance competition had entries from 14 countries. The German opera house offered a Wagner festival, with regular concerts at the Schloss Niederschönhausen, Concerts Philharmonie, Berlin Schloss, Monbijou Palace and Charlottenberg Palace. The Dietrich-Eckhart theatre staged performances of Handel's *Heracles*, with 2500 performers, and *Das Frankenburger Wurfelspiel*, a choral dance play by Wolfgang Eberhard Möller. An epic-scale performance of *Hamlet* saw the Prince of Denmark accorded 'a first class Party funeral', with marching soldiers, trumpets and displays of weapons (Rürup, 1996). The winning entries from the music competition were also performed in the Dietrich-Eckhart theatre. The Olympic stadium staged spectacular performances during the period of the games, including the Kraft durch Freude (Strength through Joy) movement presenting 'Music and dance of the peoples' (10 August), a military concert involving over 2000 musicians (13 August), and the showpiece festival play *Olympic Youth* organised by Carl Diem.

Performed in the stadium after the opening ceremony and again two days later as a para-Olympic event, *Olympic Youth* presaged the cultural content of contemporary opening ceremonies. It was conceived as 'an artistically constructed echo of the opening ceremony ... a spiritual happening that [the onlooker] would have to explain to himself' (Organising Committee, 1936, 577). Diem used massed performers, international celebrities, light, sound, and a musical score written by Carl Orff and Werner Egk to create an imposing spectacle. It involved around 10 000 performers, each of whom had signed a declaration claiming their Aryan descent, and presented a series of tableaux weaving Olympic, medieval and modern themes: 'Children at play', 'Maidenly grace', 'Youth at play in a serious mood' and 'Heroic struggle and death lament'. The last of these contained a celebration of sacrificial death for the fatherland, ending with the 'Ode to Joy' from Beethoven's Ninth Symphony, at which point searchlights created a dome of light above the arena and flames of fire leapt up around the edge of the stadium.[38]

Although often remembered for the performances of the black US athlete Jesse Owens in the capital of Nazi Germany, the regime drew great satisfaction from the games. While not dominant in the track and field events, Germany won a total of 89 medals against 56 for the USA, its nearest competitor. Fewer foreign visitors than expected came to the games, but those that did attend were influential. A series of official receptions and themed parties provided extensive hospitality for competitors, officials and visiting dignitaries. These allowed the Nazis to project their chosen image of a peaceful, contented and progressive society to the world.

That process was helped by the presence of the largest press corps so far at an Olympics, comprising over 2000 journalists, reporters and photographers from 59 countries. The authorities were unable to control what journalists wrote, but ensured that what they saw had been carefully prepared. In addition 41 foreign radio broadcasting companies covered the games, as well as newsreel teams whose footage would relay impressions of the games to a world-wide cinema audience. Television made its first appearance. It provided a short-distance relay of events to the Olympic village, to halls and theatres in Berlin, and to overflow spectators in the Dietrich-Eckhart theatre in the Olympic complex. It daily catered for an additional estimated audience of 160 000 viewers. Leni Riefenstahl's official film *Olympia* eventually appeared after a two-year delay for editing and recreating scenes where necessary.[39] Still regarded by critics as one of the best sports films ever made, Riefenstahl provided a powerful and lasting visual record of the Olympics that skilfully understated the ideological context of the games while still making the connection between modern Germany and ancient Greece.

The international response to the Berlin Olympics also delighted the Nazi regime. Potential protests and alternative events melted away. Pierre de Coubertin, ill and frail in Lausanne, thought the Berlin Olympics to be the culmination of his work and, on his death, his papers went to the new International Olympic Institute set up in Berlin. The British Olympic Association official report (BOA, 1936, 38) stated that 'what was surely one of the greatest Sports Festivals of all time came to an end, having made its magnificent contribution towards a fitter youth and more peaceful international relationships'. The American Olympic Committee (AOC, 1936, 31) wrote that the games were 'unquestionably the largest and most magnificent yet held'. The *New York Times* declared that the Germans were now 'back in the fold of nations' (USHMM, 2003).

These impressions in official reports outweighed any stated misgivings about the level of military activity. The German government had presented themselves as exemplary Olympians and continued to win plaudits and awards through 1937–38. The IOC awarded the Olympic Cup to the Kraft durch Freude movement in 1938 for its work in furthering the Olympic idea and developing pathbreaking pedagogical concepts. As late as June 1939, the IOC's approval of Germany was such that it invited Germany to host the 1940 winter Olympics, after the original plans to hold the games in St Moritz (Switzerland) fell through. Riefenstahl's film was released to international acclaim in 1938 and she was awarded an Olympic Diploma in 1939. The IOC also praised the German intention of excavating Olympia as a 'monument to the Third Reich outside its borders that will last for all time' (cited by Rürup, 1996, 51).

The games, therefore, achieved most of what the authorities intended. The state also gained the infrastructural legacy of a sports complex and parade ground that could be used for National Socialist celebrations in the future that would 'speak to every German of his racial community and remind him that he was part of a revitalised state with empire as its destiny' (quoted Gordon, 1983, 27). Hitler's conversion to the Olympics was so complete that in 1937 he was thinking of Germany as a permanent home for the games. While looking at Speer's model of the Nuremberg parade grounds with its stadium capable of seating 400 000, Speer commented that the ground did not conform to the proportions prescribed by the IOC. Hitler replied that after the Tokyo games of 1940 they would return to Germany 'for all time to come' and that then 'it is we who will prescribe the necessary dimensions' (Sereny, 1995, 154). It was an extraordinary affirmation of the significance that the Olympics had assumed just 40 years after their revival; an importance that, as we shall see, ebbed and flowed during the second half of the twentieth century.

Notes

1 *New York Times*, 29 August 2002.
2 The event was mentioned in a letter dated 30 April 1679, written by Colonel Edward Cooke in London and addressed to the Duke of Ormond, Viceroy of Ireland, in Dublin. Source: *Notes and Queries*, Tenth Series, X (22 August 1908), 147.
3 The Shropshire Olympics indeed contributed directly to the Olympics' revival, since there were direct links between the ideas of Coubertin and Brookes. The two had corresponded and Brookes staged a games in Coubertin's honour when he visited England in October 1890. Moreover, Brookes wanted a more international dimension to sporting competition and had made overtures to the Greeks on precisely this matter in the 1850s. He was rebuffed because the Greeks then, as later, regarded the games as part of their national heritage rather than the common property of the international community. Undaunted, Brookes sent £10 as a prize for the Greek games of 1859 (Toohey and Veal, 2000, 29). The Wenlock Olympian Society celebrates its annual games in July, with 2004 being the 118th event (WOS, 2003).
4 The site of Olympia had been discovered in 1766. German archaeologist Ernst Curtius had conducted the latest series of excavations, the third since rediscovery of the site, between 1875–81 (Mandell, 1976).
5 This came at the end of a speech made at a jubilee event to celebrate the fifth anniversary of the founding of the Union of French Sports Associations.
6 See the quotation at the start of this chapter. The Olympic Charter is the 'constitution' of the Olympic movement. Coubertin first set out its rules in 1908. These were added to over the years and finally became known as the Olympic Charter in 1978 (Buchanan and Mallon, 2001, 119).
7 One of Coubertin's earliest surviving writings on the subject, dating from 1908 (cited in Müller, 2000, 543), talks about an ideal world where sport is so embedded within society that all young men practise physical exercise to perfect their health and increase their strength.
8 Quotations from Coubertin are invariably translations and these vary in rendition from one version to another. Those used here are taken from Müller (2000), which was published by the International Olympic Committee and can essentially be regarded as an 'official version'. This particular quotation comes from a radio broadcast recorded in Geneva in 1935.
9 The only failures in this respect were in 1900 and 1904. In a number of cases, vice-presidents opened the games, as in 1932, or the Duke of Edinburgh rather than Queen Elizabeth II (1956).
10 This dates back to the 1908 London Olympics where Coubertin was inspired by the sermon in St Paul's Cathedral delivered by Ethelbert Talbot (Bishop of Central Pennsylvania) to participants in the games: 'In these Olympiads, the important thing is not winning, but taking part.'

11 The 1920 'Antwerp Flag' was used in subsequent games until Los Angeles in 1984. Seoul presented the IOC with the flag used since 1988. A flag for the winter Olympics was donated to the IOC by Oslo in 1952 and this second primary flag is passed between hosts of the winter games (Buchanan and Mallon, 2001, 124).

12 Coubertin's words at the closing banquet of the Stockholm Olympics 1912 referring to the games passing on to Germany for the 1916 games were as follows: 'a great people has received the torch of the Olympiads from your hands, and has thereby undertaken to preserve and if possible to quicken its precious flame' (quoted in Müller, 2000, 448).

13 Some confusion still arises in the literature between Mount Olympus, the home of the gods in northern Greece, and Olympia, the home of the Olympic Games in the Peloponnese. Indeed, a considerable number of authors assume the torch is lit on Mount Olympus.

14 In particular, the donation by Georges Averof, a wealthy Greek living in Alexandria who donated one million drachmas to the campaign.

15 The mythology surrounding the original marathon run became somewhat confused. It conflates Pheidippides's 125-mile run to Sparta to enlist their aid against the Persians with a runner covering 25 miles to give Athens the news of victory with the message 'Rejoice we conquer' – after which he expired (Lovett, 1997).

16 The final exact distance for the marathon race was fixed at the 1908 London games at 26 miles, 385 yards – the exact distance between Windsor Castle and the White City stadium.

17 Athletes returning from the Athens games established the Boston marathon the following year (Lovett, 1997, xii).

18 For developing 'the facilities of international communication', the Greeks made him an officer of the National and Royal Order of the Saviour (Brendon, 1991, 238).

19 Letter to the editor of *New York Times*, 30 April 1896, 12, cited in Müller, 2000, 363. Emphasis added.

20 Mallon, 1998, 5, points out that Coubertin had previously suggested a re-creation of Olympia for the 1889 Universal Exposition in Paris, with some sporting events.

21 There may well have been an element of pretext here: it is now suggested that the Italians were preparing to withdraw from the games before the eruption occurred (Mallon and Buchanan, 2000, xxxvii).

22 Although by virtue of its size, spectators were not always able to see properly.

23 See note 10, above.

24 This was also the date of the silver jubilee celebrations of Kaiser Wilhelm II.

25 For the last time, this also included a cycle track.

26 The CDA was a non-profit association of 21 members representing the great and the good among Los Angeles society, including the growing film industry.

27 The female athletes were housed in the Chapman Park Hotel as it was thought they required a rather more permanent type of residence (TOC, 1933, 292).

28 After dinner guests were shown Fairbanks' own preview version of his classic 1922 movie *Robin Hood*. Bobby Tisdall, the 400-metre hurdles champion at the games remembers sitting next to Amelia Earhart at the Fairbanks' party and opposite Norma Shearer at an open-air breakfast party (Tisdall, 1956, 32).

29 Promotional literature, such as *Olympic Games Official Pictorial Souvenir* produced, despite its name, before the games showed idyllic scenes of LA and California (TOC, 1933).

30 The German delegates were Duke Adolf Friedrich von Mecklenburg-Schwerin, Dr Theodore Lewald, Dr Karl Ritter von Halt and Dr Carl Diem. It is interesting that Conrad Adenauer, later West German Chancellor, complained that the Berlin lobby was so strong in Germany that other cities interested in hosting the games did not 'stand a chance'. These other cities included Cologne, Frankfurt and Nuremberg (Rürup, 1996, 49).

31 It was suggested, for example, that ancient Greece was partly settled by early Germanic migrations during the Neolithic period (Arnold, 1992, 32).

32 The team dropped Gretel Bergman, the German high-jump record-holder, only weeks before the start of the games.

33 The countryside also received attention, with everything done to create the appearance of a happy, tolerant, stable and peaceful Germany in contrast to the discord and internal conflict experienced before 1933 (Hart Davis, 1986, 125).

34 Diem had a close association with distance races, having been instrumental in inaugurating the Potsdam to Berlin race in 1908.

35 See note 13 above. In 1928 and 1932 the flame simply burned during the games. From 1936 the actual lighting of the flame became an important part of the opening ceremony.

36 Although much of the footage of the lighting of the torch and the relay was re-shot at Delphi (Graham, 1986, 64–5).

37 Although the flame here was not brought from Olympia, but kindled at the home where legendary Norwegian skier Sondre Nordheim was born.

38 This glorification of sacrificial death was echoed in the final months of the war when Diem addressed the Hitler Youth in March 1945. He lectured them on the men of Sparta and appealed to them not to shrink from sacrifice for the fatherland, even if they were conscious of possible defeat (Rürup, 1996, 219). Just over a month later many of these boys, and the Peoples Reserve Battalions troops fighting with them were killed trying to regain control of the Reich Sports Field from Russian troops.

39 The original intention was to screen *Olympia* as two separate films: *Fest der Völker* ('Festival of the Nations') and *Fest der Schönheit* ('Festival of Beauty'). The film is today normally viewed as a single epic (Downing, 1992, 70).

CHAPTER SEVEN

The World's Games

> When you clear your head of the Olympic quasi-religious mumbo jumbo, and stop caring for a minute about just how badly Mastercard and IBM and Coca-Cola want you to *desire* the Olympic spectacle, you can find ample reason to oppose the Olympics – or at least to question the whole damnable racket. But the simplest criticisms are usually the best: there are too many social problems in the cities and countries that host the Olympics to waste money on an international party, complete with athletic entertainment. As for the unfortunate *billions* for whom the Olympic spectacle is callous mockery of their plight, they'd certainly be uplifted by the 'spirit of Olympism,' if only they could get better television reception, or if they could just get ahead of starvation long enough to enjoy the merits of the hammer throw or Greco-Roman wrestling.
>
> Kendall Clark (2000)

By the outbreak of the Second World War, the Olympic Games had developed into a truly international sports festival while still framed within the philosophy, ceremonial and ritual developed by Coubertin and watchfully protected by the IOC. Yet, like the international expositions, their organisation and spectacle intimately reflected their global political context. By the end of the war, for example, what had seemed the triumph of the Berlin Olympics now cast a dark shadow over the games through its association with the Third Reich's propaganda. From 1948 onwards, the Olympic movement struggled first to throw off this shadow and then to come to terms with the challenges of a rapidly changing world. These included decolonisation, ideological conflicts, globalisation, terrorism, political boycotts, wavering support, overt commercialism, the professionalisation of sport, cronyism and corruption. Although it is impossible to deal with these issues *per se* in detail here,[1] they form an important background that underpins the discussion of city experiences in this chapter.

Restarting the Olympics

The bidding process after 1945 revived the pattern set in the interwar period (see Table 7.1). American cities, with their ingrained city rivalries and boosterist agendas, featured prominently, with formal bids from Baltimore, Los Angeles, Minneapolis and Philadelphia and informal interest from several other potential US contenders. There was a feeling, however, that the USA was too far away for affordable travel in these austere years (Voeltz, 1996, 103). After conducting a postal ballot, therefore, the IOC officially awarded the fourteenth summer Olympics to London.[2] The British Olympic Association had already approached the Foreign Secretary Ernest Bevin in January 1947 to discuss staging the games, since postwar shortages, controls and rationing meant nothing could be done without government backing. Bevin gave them his wholehearted support. He recognised the potential of the Olympics as a source of much needed foreign exchange and believed that by 1948 London would be equipped to receive large numbers of visitors. That point, coupled with arguments about the honour and prestige of staging the games, swayed the Cabinet.

The next two years proved far more difficult economically than Bevin anticipated, with few surplus resources for staging the games (Holt and Mason, 2000, 27–9). The organisers had to abandon any idea of providing custom-built facilities and laying on stunning spectacle. They employed existing sports facilities, with the Empire Stadium (Wembley) serving as the centrepiece and the athletes housed in Royal Air Force accommodation at Uxbridge, a convalescents' camp in Richmond Park, Southlands College in Wimbledon, and convenient school premises (Organising Committee, 1948). The organisers borrowed sports equipment from the armed forces or from manufacturers on a lend and return basis. The Board of Trade adjusted rationing regulations for participants and new tourist voucher books made it easier for foreign visitors to spend money in British shops.

In line with the practices of previous festivals, such as the 1851 Great Exhibition and the 1908 Olympics, London's opening ceremony on 29 July 1948 embraced a 'traditional solemnity' (Organising Committee, 1948, 199). Besides the official Olympic rituals, it featured displays by military marching bands, the parade of nations, fanfares, gun salutes, the release of pigeons and sacred choral pieces. The Archbishop of York gave a five-minute address referring to a world 'largely hag-ridden by hate and fear', in which this 'peaceable and friendly rivalry of sport' was a 'happy omen for the future'. After lengthy deliberations, the organisers included the torch relay from Olympia. Although anxious about the likely cost and the uncertain political situation in Greece, the relay's symbol value in lighting 'the path to a brighter future for the youth of the world' ensured that the ceremony was preserved (Organising Committee, 1948, 220).

Table 7.1 Cities bidding for the Olympic Games, 1948–2008

Games	Year awarded	Host city	Other candidates
1948	1946	London	Baltimore, Lausanne, Los Angeles, Minneapolis, Philadelphia
1952	1947	Helsinki	Amsterdam, Chicago, Detroit, Los Angeles, Minneapolis, Philadelphia
1956	1949	Melbourne	Buenos Aires, Chicago, Detroit, Los Angeles, Mexico City, Minneapolis, Montreal, Philadelphia
1960	1955	Rome	Budapest, Brussels, Detroit, Lausanne, Mexico City, Tokyo
1964	1959	Tokyo	Brussels, Detroit, Vienna
1968	1963	Mexico City	Buenos Aires, Lyon, Detroit
1972	1966	Munich	Detroit, Madrid, Montreal
1976	1970	Montreal	Los Angeles, Moscow
1980	1974	Moscow	Los Angeles
1984	1978	Los Angeles	Teheran
1988	1981	Seoul	Nagoya (Japan)
1992	1986	Barcelona	Amsterdam, Belgrade, Birmingham, Brisbane, Paris
1996	1990	Atlanta	Athens, Belgrade, Manchester, Melbourne, Toronto
2000	1993	Sydney	Berlin, Beijing, Manchester, Istanbul (Brasilia, Milan, Tashkent withdrew)

Table 7.1 *concluded*

Games	Year awarded	Host city	Other candidates
2004	1997	Athens	Buenos Aires, Cape Town, Istanbul, Lille, Rio de Janeiro, Rome, San Juan, St Petersburg, Seville, Stockholm
2008	2001	Beijing	Bangkok, Cairo, Havana, Istanbul, Kuala Lumpur, Osaka, Paris, Seville, Toronto

The games helped to lift the mood of postwar Britain and recorded a profit of £30 000. Visitor numbers in 1948 were a postwar record, with hotels enjoying a bumper season (Holt and Mason, 2000, 31), but London was not *en fete* as Berlin or Los Angeles had been. Few cultural events materialised that were not directly related to the games and the Olympic art competition was deemed unsuccessful. Held at the Victoria and Albert Museum on the theme of 'Sport in Art', it attracted participation from just 27 countries with no entrants from the USA, Australia, New Zealand or South America. Some contributions failed to meet the entry requirements, with the jury strongly criticising the process involved. Largely as a result, subsequent Olympics discontinued arts competitions in favour of *exhibitions* (Organising Committee, 1948, 198).

The succeeding games followed London's low-key example. Helsinki (1952) had held the nomination for the twelfth summer Olympics (1940) after the Japanese withdrew, and built a stadium, swimming and diving arena, and a competitors' village in anticipation of that event. These facilities were renovated and expanded for the 1952 games with the aid of a $1.25 million grant from the Finnish government.[3] The Olympic village posed greater problems, since the one originally constructed at Käpylä had been converted to public housing. The increased size of the games required new accommodation not just at Käpylä, but also at Otaniemi and Töölö. The situation was further complicated by the Soviet Union's demands for a separate village for the socialist bloc's athletes (Hornbuckle, 1996, 117). In response, the organisers allocated the Otaniemi site to the USSR and its allies, placing competitors literally as well as figuratively into two ideological camps.

This intense rivalry between the USA and the 'Soviet bloc', which saw sport as a surrogate competitive arena for global political conflict, persisted for almost 40 years.

Melbourne was the last summer Olympics developed under conditions of postwar financial stringency. The Melbourne contingent lobbied hard for the 1956 games. In their submission to IOC members in 1948, bound in Merino sheep's fleece (MIC, 1948), the Melbourne Invitation Committee had issued a photographic guide to their city's finer points. It projected an image of a prosperous, developed and well-equipped 'city of culture and civic consciousness', its 'people noted for enthusiasm for sport', located in 'a country of unique birds and beasts'. Addressing the city's most serious disadvantages – the distance and expense for European and North American teams to travel to Australia – the submission reassuringly countered by saying: 'Melbourne is only hours away by air ... a pleasant cruise by sea ... 93 hours from London, 3–4 days from Europe or North America'. The writers stressed that choosing Melbourne would move the games into a new global arena (southern hemisphere) and that Australia had displayed outstanding commitment to the Olympic movement, having sent athletes to every games since 1896. The brochure ended with plans for a new Olympic stadium complex on the banks of the Yarra River east of the Melbourne Cricket Ground (MCG).

Economic considerations compromised the grand vision. After repeatedly vacillating over whether or not to build a new Olympic stadium, the organisers finally decided to use the MCG. In order not to overburden the state of Victoria's budget, the Australian government agreed to meet half the costs of modifying the MCG, of providing new buildings for the swimming pool and velodrome, and of administering the games. Available display spaces at the local university, museum, art school and public library housed the four associated art exhibitions – on architecture, painting, graphics and literature. The Olympic village was built as a cheap housing project in the suburb of Heidelberg, thereby using the existing structure of government loans. These buildings, however, presented so many subsequent constructional and social problems that the games might well have been 'a force for urban degeneration rather than regeneration' (Essex and Chalkley, 1998, 194).

Perhaps the Melbourne games' most telling contribution to the Olympic movement was to inject greater informality into the closing ceremony. The games took place against a background of heightened international tension arising from the Suez crisis, the Budapest uprising against Soviet rule, and political boycotts. On the penultimate day of the competition, the IOC approved a suggestion to allow athletes to mingle 'as one nation' rather than march into the stadium country by country.

Although now seeming a mild gesture, it represented a major departure from the jealously guarded protocol, for while Olympism embraced the rhetoric of peace and harmony, the IOC based its ceremonial on national groupings (Jobbing, 1996, 123–4). This subsequently became the model for closing ceremonies and was carried further when the games returned to Australia in 2000 (see Chapter 9).

The Modern Era

The 1960 games propelled the Olympics into the modern era. Although important for their host nations, the financially straitened 1948–56 games scarcely altered the pattern set by the Los Angeles or Berlin Games (Mandell, 1976, 246).

Rome (1960)

Rome 1960 was the first Olympic meeting able to throw off the pall of austerity and create a setting and scale that could be described as 'lavish', 'romantic' and a 'delight' (Pilling, 1960, 16). The city's Olympian aspirations stretched back many years. Rome's stature as a crucible of classical civilisation appealed to Coubertin, who regarded it as a natural setting for an Olympics. Its withdrawal from staging the 1908 games (see Chapter 6) set back this ambition, but the Italians retained their interest in acting as hosts. Indeed, the 1960 Olympics effectively capitalised on two sites developed by Mussolini's regime with international festivals in mind. One, the Foro Italico in the north of the city, offered an imposing sports arena built in 1931 that could be converted into an Olympic stadium (Bondanella, 1987, 192). The other was EUR, a district founded in 1936 in the south of the city to create a spectacular setting for the 1942 Esposizione Universale di Roma or E42 (see Chapter 4).[4] Its monumental and spacious qualities made it an ideal place for the core of the Olympic facilities, including the Palazzo dello Sport (Sport Palace), the velodrome, the Piscana delle Rose (swimming pool) and the Fontane Sports Zone training area.

Ten other venues were scattered throughout the Rome city region. The rowing, for instance, was held at Lake Albano, close to the papal summer residence at Castel Gandolfo (Davies, 1996, 129). The organisers placed the Olympic village across the river Tiber from the stadium at Campo Paroli. Designed as a self-contained residential area with service and recreational facilities, it comprised 33 buildings from two to five storeys high that provided over 1 300 apartments for competitors (Organising Committee, 1960, 89, 225). To offset costs, the entire neighbourhood was sold after the games as private housing. New roads and bridges connected the village to the main Olympic sites. In addition, the authorities modernised the airport and central railway station, improved the telephone, telegraph and radio networks, and encouraged expansion of the stock of hotel accommodation (ibid., 53, 55).

The Organising Committee emphasised the relationship between the modern games and Rome's imperial past. The route of the torch relay from Olympia, for instance, symbolically connected the 'two apexes of classical civilisation, Athens and Rome, and would pass through the sites of Magna Grecia' arriving on Italian soil at Syracuse, the first Greek colony in Sicily. The planned route also linked cities that had participated in the ancient games (Organising Committee, 1960, 199). Two ancient monuments served as competition venues to lend the games 'a more particular Roman character'. The vaults of the Basilica of Maxentius, built in AD 303, housed the Greco-Roman and free wrestling contests. The Caracalla Baths, built in AD 217, staged the gymnastics (ibid., 76). By holding events in the evening and manipulating the lighting, the organisers achieved 'stunning theatrical effect ... in ways that wrung every ounce of drama from the competitions and their historic surroundings' (Gordon, 1983, 60). Similarly, they adjusted the timing of the marathon so that the runners approached the finishing line at the Arch of Constantine at dusk, with soldiers at 10-metre intervals holding flaming torches to light the competitors' path along the Appian Way. At other times, significant heritage sites acted as venues for illuminations and firework displays.

The cultural programme also linked classical and modern Rome through exhibitions, theatrical performances, ballet and folklore festivals. The organisers, for example, staged a three-week season of re-enacted traditional pageants from central and northern Italy in the Circus Maximus and the Piazza di Sienna. The 'Sport in History and Art' exhibition in the Palazzo delle Scienze (the Palace of Science) brought together more than 3000 exhibits from across Italy in tracing issues such as competition, prizegiving ceremonies, and the history of sports buildings from Etruscan times to the nineteenth century. An exhibition of sports photography invited entries from Italian photographers and entries from national Olympic committees, although the response was considered disappointing (Organising Committee, 1960, 313–15).

The Italian football pools, the Totocalcio, provided funding for the games. This was supplemented for the first time by sales of television rights. Broadcasters had refused to pay for rights at Melbourne, arguing that covering the games was akin to televising news and should be similarly free to the broadcaster. The organisers of the Rome Olympics, however, managed to convince the major television networks that the games were a proprietorial commodity for which payment was necessary. The American Columbia Broadcasting System (CBS) paid $600 000 for US television rights, with the Eurovision television syndicate subscribing another $540 000. It marked another significant step towards realising the economic potential of the games and, arguably, towards commodifying the 'Olympic brand' (Davies, 1996, 132). Certainly, when leaving aside wider infrastructural improvements, the Rome Olympics ran at a profit.

Tokyo (1964)

The 1964 games resembled the Rome games in many respects. Like their predecessors, Tokyo's planners embarked on major urban development projects before the games, merging the specific proposals for the Olympics into the city's ten-year development plan. Aiming to cater for Tokyo's infrastructural needs up to the year 2000, the combined works cost $2.7 billion and included housing, hotel developments, harbour improvements, a monorail system, water supply, sewage disposal and a public health programme (Essex and Chalkley, 1998, 195). The city had 30 Olympic sites, with thirteen major facilities concentrated into three districts: the Meiji Olympic Park, which contained the Olympic stadium; the Yoyogi Sports Centre, which housed the swimming competitions; and the Komazawa Sports Park. Accommodating participants in six Olympic villages ensured, at least in principle, that competitors and officials had no more than a 40-minute journey to reach their venues (Organising Committee, 1964, 114). Hoteliers received grants to remodel their premises for western tourists, with a further 1600 visitors lodged on ships in Tokyo harbour. On a more mundane level, preparations for the games included a campaign to transform public behaviour. Construction of public toilets and hiring portaloos accompanied an advertising campaign taking the slogan: 'the Olympics are coming – don't piss in the streets' (Sheil, 1998, 38).

In a move that preceded and paralleled Montreal's innovations at Expo 67, the Tokyo Organising Committee ran a competition to select a designer who would provide visually consistent designs, or a common 'look', for all the ephemeral elements of the games – symbols, signs, pamphlets, posters, tickets, decorations and even the colour scheme used for the city and at Olympic venues (Yew, 1996, 176). The winner, Yusaku Kamekura, wanted to create a 'seamless festive atmosphere' and a 'single visual landscape' that would be apparent even where venues were spatially separated. In particular, 'the look' was intended to create an impression of intimacy for the television lens while bringing out the character of the host city and giving the games a distinctive identity. This assignment, now a standard feature of preparation for the Olympics, remains coveted by graphic designers as one of the premier showcases for creativity on offer in the modern world.

With the games taking place in Asia for the first time, the organisers wanted to put their cultural stamp on the opening and closing ceremonies. This initiated the opening ceremony's gradual evolution away from the established western military, choral and symphonic tradition. Although not yet deviating radically from the standard pattern, the Organising Committee wanted to 'make use of sound, colour, and light in the technical arrangement of these ceremonies' (Organising Committee, 1964, 221). The result was what one observer[5] described as 'a modern pageant', featuring electronic campanology, jet planes tracing Olympic rings over the stadium, daytime fireworks, and a lighter touch – exemplified by a marching band of tiny tots leading the Olympic flag into the stadium. Yoshinori Sakai, born on the day of the Hiroshima atomic blast 19 years earlier, lit the Olympic flame. The growing global television audience witnessed vivid images of 'colour and excitement'.[6]

The cultural programme diverged from previous occasions in that the organisers no longer felt it necessary to link art to sport or even to seek overseas contributions. They arranged a six-week festival of traditional and modern Japanese culture, attracting over 400 000 visitors to an exhibition of ancient art treasures in the Tokyo National Museum and sizeable audiences for supporting exhibitions of modern fine art, photography and sports philately. In the performing arts Kabuki drama, Imperial court music, Noh drama, Bunraki Puppet shows, traditional dance, music and folklore entertainment ran throughout the games (Organising Committee, 1964, 269, 270). The programme attempted to convey an image of Japan as a peaceful nation with a deep and rich culture. As such, it complemented the peaceful-but-progressive approach adopted at the international expositions held in Japan between 1970 and 1985 (see Chapter 5).

Mexico City (1968)

The final games of the 1960s saw Latin America, and more specifically a developing nation, host the Olympics for the first time. Set against a background of political tension and sports boycotts, the Olympics initially stretched Mexico's resources and contributed to domestic unrest in the months leading up to the games. The organisers responded by using many existing buildings and blending them with new structures by means of a common 'look', in the manner pioneered by Tokyo, to supply a sense of visual unity.[7] The existing structures included the former University City Stadium suitably renovated as the main games venue, the Insurgentes theatre for the weightlifting, the National Auditorium in Chapultepec for gymnastics, the National University pool for water polo, and a military base for target shooting. The major new buildings included a 22 000-seater Sports Palace to the northeast of the main Olympic village, an adjacent velodrome, an aquatic centre for swimming and diving, a rowing and canoeing facility to the south east at Xochimilco, and a prefabricated fencing arena (Arbena, 1996, 142). The Olympic football tournament took place at the privately financed Aztec Stadium (subsequently used for football's World Cup Finals in 1970 and 1986).

The opening ceremony introduced new elements, including traditional Mexican music and a set of Olympic rings composed of helium-filled balloons that were released before the athletes marched into the stadium. The torch relay followed the route of Christopher Columbus's journey to the New World and culminated in the 'New Fire' ritual at the ancient Aztec site of Teotihuacan. This juxtaposed New World myths and legends with the ancient Greek symbolism and ritual that accompanied the start of the torch's journey.[8] The closing ceremony ended with a 15-minute firework display, Beethoven's Ninth Symphony – making a connection with the next games in Munich – and traditional Mexican songs ending with 'Las Golondrinas' ('Song of Farewell') (Organising Committee, 1969, 503). As at Tokyo, however, the ceremonies remained dominated by the formal martial pattern, with the main input of Mexico's distinctive culture appearing in the year-long cultural programme that accompanied the summer games.

The organisers called this programme a 'cultural Olympiad' since, like the sports competitions, it was an international festival that would promote 'mutual understanding and respect, brotherhood and friendship between nations and genuine international accord'.[9] Invitations to participate were dispatched with the entry forms for the games. The programme laid out 20 activities organised into five themes, mixing performance with participative and creative activities (see Table 7.2). The 'international meeting of sculptors', for example, invited 21 sculptors from 16 countries to contribute works of art for display in the city during the games. The 'ballet of the five continents' was a year-long programme of dance with companies from 11 countries. The 'world folklore festival' involved 24 Mexican and 30 foreign groups. Performances took place throughout Mexico to maximise public participation and stimulate greater interest in the games. Ninety-seven nations participated, with as many as 552 cultural events taking place outside Mexico City.

Table 7.2   Cultural programme, Mexico City, January–December 1968

Theme	Contents
I	*The Olympic Games and Youth* Reception by Mexico's youth to the youth of the world Festival of short films on the mission of youth Mexican Olympic camp for world youth
II	*The Olympic Games and Art* Exhibition of selected works of world art International festival of the arts International meeting of sculptors International reunion of poets Festival of children's painting
III	*The Olympic Games and Popular Artistic Expression* World folklore festival Ballet of the five continents International exhibition of folk art
IV	*The Olympic Games in Mexico* Arrival of the Olympic flame at Teotihuacan . International Olympic philatelic exhibition Exhibition of the history of art of the Olympic Games
V	*The Olympic Games and the Contemporary World* Exhibition of the application of nuclear energy for the welfare of mankind Exhibition of space research The programme on human genetics and biology, comprising two international seminars studying Olympic athletes Exhibition of sites for sports and cultural activities and the international meeting of young architects Advertising at the service of peace Projection of the games

Source: Organising Committee, 1969, 272–5.

Despite their troubled beginnings, the Mexico City games finished with a positive balance sheet. Costing $175 million, much of which was expended on facilities with a life and cost-frame that extended well beyond the festival, the Olympics were considered to have covered their costs. For some observers, the 1968 games represented an important moment of achievement and harmony for the Mexican nation that fully justified the cost. Arbena (1996, 145–6), for example, remarked that:

> For this price Mexicans received not just the pleasure and profit of the Games themselves. In theory they indirectly benefited from the increased spending by visiting teams and tourists and an increase in tax collections. They also inherited a technologically superior television and communications system, a few pre-Hispanic archaeological ruins exposed during construction, housing units in the two Olympic Villages, many works of art created especially for the occasion and left for public enjoyment, an improved athletic infrastructure, vast experience in organising and conducting an elaborate global festival,[10] and a sense of national achievement and pride.

Other commentators were more sanguine, arguing that the spectacle had been bought at too high a price. Money diverted into the Olympics had exacerbated the divide between Mexico City's rich and poor. Before the games, for example, the city chose to transfer $200 million from the social services budget to city improvement projects in an elaborate urban and national re-imaging campaign. Not only did this have a detrimental long-term impact on the city's provision for the poor, it also prompted protest demonstrations that left no less than 325 dead (Lenskyj, 2000, 109–10). The ability of the Olympics to polarise opinion would escalate steadily over the next decade.

A Troubled Decade

The games of 1972 and 1976, in their ways, created dilemmas for the Olympic movement. Both traded on the increasingly upbeat view of the Olympics that emphasised its apparently risk-free character, guaranteeing host cities advantageous international attention and endless prospects for undertaking urban regeneration. Partly as a result of this growing confidence, Munich and Montreal were lavish affairs, with huge expenditure on iconic Olympic facilities that created distinctive urban quarters. Each also took place against a tense international political climate that profoundly affected participation in the sporting competitions. Montreal was particularly severely hit by political boycotts. Black September's hostage-taking at Munich in 1972 and the subsequent loss of life represented the nadir for the Olympic spirit.

This stood in stark contrast to the mood when Munich prepared for the 1972 Olympics. The organisers deliberately tried to counter the lingering memories of 1936. The Munich organisers consciously set out to stage the 'Carefree Games' (Organising Committee, 1972, 28) as powerful militaristic and nationalist imageries were still associated with the Berlin games. Munich's bid to the IOC had emphasised the importance of embracing international and modern cultures, as well as the social and architectural heritage of the host city. Munich was presented as a rich hearth of 'the arts and Muses' with four orchestras, 23 museums, 17 theatres, and an artistic tradition that embraced global as well as local and national scales (ibid., 24, 28).

As elsewhere, the games integrated preparations for the Olympics into the host city's broader objectives. Munich in the early 1970s was in the throes of rapid economic and demographic growth, with severe pressures on services and physical infrastructure. The city's administration saw the games as a historic opportunity to tackle a broad range of planning goals, fitting Olympic developments alongside schemes to restore and pedestrianise Munich's historic centre, to improve and extend public transport, construct 145 miles of expressways, provide underground parking, and build new retail and hotel accommodation (Essex and Chalkley, 1998, 195). The location for the new Olympic park in the north of the city was a derelict area long earmarked for redevelopment. Originally flat, its surface was bulldozed into a gently rolling landscape, with a hill created from wartime rubble and a small lake formed by damming up the Nymphenburg Canal. The organisers then placed the athletes' warm-up facilities, the swimming pool, many smaller sports venues, restaurants, a theatre, the Olympic village, press centre and stadium around the lake. The 80 000-seater Olympic stadium was an innovative tent-roofed structure designed by Gunter Behnisch and Frei Otto (whose West German pavilion featured at Expo 67, see Chapter 5). The Olympic village, which housed 10 000 athletes, was designed for conversion into a 'self-sustaining' community for single people and middle- and lower-income families – groups who found it difficult to find accommodation in the city (Essex and Chalkley, 1998, 195; Organising Committee, 1972, 125). Trams, an underground rail line and a rapid transit provided links between the complex and the city centre.

The rhetoric of the 'Carefree Games' evoked images of an Olympics where the athlete and visitor felt at home, in a city that retained the spectacle of cultural heritage with first-class modern facilities. This sense of feeling at home again partly rested on 'the look' for the games, which was intended to lend familiarity to unfamiliar surroundings. The organisers commissioned Otl Aichers, a graphic designer from Ulm, to take charge of this task (Organising Committee, 1972, 268). His remit was wider than that given to his counterparts at Tokyo and Mexico City, because it included also designing the decorations for the city, venues and orientation of visitors. Aichers applied a holistic approach to the colour and design of the uniforms of staff and volunteers, typeface, pictograms, posters, tickets, invitations, city brochures, maps, calendar of events and Olympic newsletter. He intended the chosen colour scheme – light- and middle-intensive blue, middle-intensive green, with white and silver as supporting colours – to foster a 'positive psychological climate on the level of high holiday spirits'. The dominant colour of blue symbolised peace, with the 'aggressive' colour red deliberately avoided (Organising Committee, 1972, 269; Yew, 1996, 213).

In line with the 'carefree' theme, the opening and closing ceremonies reaffirmed the trajectory away from martial or overtly nationalistic practices in favour of emphasising 'universal understanding, social justice and joie de vivre' (Organising Committee, 1972, 81). The Olympic flag would be carried into the stadium by the 1968 gold medal rowing eight and the torch brought in by a schoolboy, as a 'representative of the future', escorted by athletes from Africa, Asia, America and Oceania. Folk songs rather than traditional marches would accompany the March of Nations (ibid., 81–82). The Organising Committee also wanted to 'enliven' the traditional ceremonial by having children welcome the athletes and Bavarian and Mexican folk dancers 'enhance the somewhat dreary transfer of the flags' (ibid., 82). The wish for greater spontaneity sometimes brought the organisers into conflict with the conservative IOC. The latter approved some suggestions, such as removing one rendition of the German national anthem and using alphorns rather than a brass fanfare to greet the arrival of the German president,[11] but blanched at the idea of replacing the flight of pigeons with a technical effect employing 'electronic age symbolism'. Plans for the closing ceremony were similarly overlain with symbolic intent, emphasising peace and the 'unity of all nations' (ibid., 87). The national flags would enter the stadium as a group without any placards bearing the countries' names or marching in military formation. The ceremony would have included folk dancing, but plans for a laser light show were abandoned due to technical difficulties and cost. Instead a giant balloon would rise to 400 feet (130 metres) over the stadium.

The associated cultural festival would last three months and finished when the games closed. The programme subsumed Munich's normal summer festivals and brought in foreign companies including Teatro della Scala (Milan), Sadler's Wells Opera (London), the New York City

Ballet, the Royal Shakespeare Company, the Vienna Symphony and Philharmonic Orchestras, the Moscow Philharmonic and the Leipzig Gewandhaus. An international folklore festival, planned since 1966, was officially supported as an opportunity for countries that lacked a history of winning gold medals to show their high level of culture (ibid., 28). Other events included an avant-garde music festival entitled 'Music of our Time', international jazz and film festivals, and major exhibitions, comprising 'World Cultures and Modern Art', '100 years of German Excavation in Olympia', the sport-oriented 'Olympia and Technology', and 'Olympic Philately'. A series of events highlighted regional culture. 'Vita Bavarica' mixed film with Bavarian folk dance, a series of concerts explored the roots of chamber music in the folk tradition, and the 'Bavarian Art and Culture' exhibition traced Bavarian cultural achievements from the Roman era to the present. Visitors to the Olympic park could enjoy the 'Avenue of Entertainment' along the southern shore of the lake. Intended to connect art and sport through 'total theatre' (ibid., 247), 50 temporary stages were constructed for performances from 10 am until 10.30 pm. The programme would culminate in a great festival to mark the end of the games.

These plans, like many other aspects of the Munich games, were thrown off course by events. The twentieth summer games were critically regarded as being impressively organised and for generating a working profit, with marketing and television rights producing over $12 million for the IOC and international federations. Munich and Bavaria gained lasting publicity benefit (Brichford, 1996, 151). Nevertheless, the massacre of the Israeli athletes and officials on 5 September effectively destroyed the Organising Committee's attempts to stage a light-hearted, non-nationalistic Olympics. The IOC controversially decided to continue with the games but curtailed ceremonial aspects in line with the executive board's statement: 'The Olympic Games are proceeding for the sake of sport and sport only. All official receptions are cancelled. All ceremonies will be kept as simple as possible' (Killanin, 1983, 97). The organisers cancelled the Avenue of Entertainment and the cultural programme. They removed any parts of the closing ceremony intended to give it a 'joyous and colourful touch'. The folk dancers, for example, stood solemnly on the track rather than dancing the star polka as originally proposed (ibid., 95). Few events in Olympic history ever inverted the intended meaning of spectacle more poignantly.

Montreal (1976)

Like Moscow, Montreal presented a 'kaleidoscope of contradictory narratives and outcomes' (Kidd, 1996, 153). Although popular with spectators and competitors, the 1976 summer Olympics became a byword for uncontrolled expenditure and unchecked ambition, despite the stated intention that they should be 'modest' and 'self-financing' (ibid., 153). Mindful of the recent experience of writing off the outstanding debts of Expo 67 (see Chapter 5), the Canadian federal government required written assurances from the city of Montreal and province of Quebec that they would not request federal aid if the games produced a deficit. By the end, however, costs had increased five-fold so that a maximum expenditure of $310 million had become $1.5 billion (Organising Committee, 1976, 15). The final shortfall of $1.2 billion, primarily caused by cost overruns on the buildings, effectively crippled the city's budget for almost two decades.

There were many contributing reasons. Second thoughts about designing an orthodox open-air Olympic stadium were ditched in favour of a design that might be used all-year round. As the Olympic movement would not countenance a fully enclosed stadium for athletics, it was decided to build a new stadium with a retractable roof – understandably at a much greater cost (Killanin, 1983, 123). The games took place at a time of severe world recession and inflation profoundly affected costings. Problems with subsoil meant the velodrome needed new foundations to support its roof (Organising Committee, 1976, 16–17). Labour problems caused the loss of 155 working days in the 18 months leading up to the games. Lack of proper operational planning in sequencing the construction process led to delays and bottlenecks.[12] Round-the-clock working was introduced at great expense to meet the games' deadline, but it still proved impossible to complete all the facilities. In May 1976, emergency work began to erect temporary installations for several sports rather than continue with the intended venues. The revolutionary designs for the stadium, pool and velodrome added enormous complexities, which the construction industry struggled to overcome. Indeed the main stadium remained incomplete when the games opened in July 1976, with the infamous roof not completed until 1987.

The history of the Montreal Olympics shared certain similarities with Expo 67. Both were part of Montreal's fight to assert itself on the international stage in the face of its domestic rivalry with Canada's Anglophone core (see Chapter 5). The city had shown interest in staging the 1932 Olympics and bid unsuccessfully for both the 1956 and 1972 games. The latter stemmed from Mayor Jean Drapeau's somewhat apocryphal visit to the Swiss National Exhibition in Lausanne during 1964, which led directly to the Crown Company buying the internal rail system for use secondhand at Expo 67 (see Chapter 5). During this visit Drapeau toured the Olympic museum. Enthused by what he saw, he met later that year with the IOC, finally announcing in November 1965 that Montreal would bid for the 1972 Olympics. The next month, the IOC President Avery Brundage told Drapeau that the preparations for Expo 67 'would help to give the city an advantage over its competitors' in bidding for the 1972 games (Organising Committee, 1976, 12–15). While that prediction proved inaccurate in the short term, Montreal persisted in its campaign and in 1970 was nominated to stage the 1976 games against competing bids from Moscow and Los Angeles.

The new Olympic park occupied a quadrilateral site near the St Lawrence river three miles (five kilometres) downstream from the Expo 67 fairground. It housed the stadium, pool, velodrome, the Maurice Richard arena and the refurbished sports centre renamed as the Pierre Charbonneuve centre. The adjacent Olympic village lodged participants in four ziggurat structures that were some 19 storeys high at their tallest points, widely regarded as architecturally innovative but difficult to service. The rowing basin came from converting the lake at the Expo 67 site on the Ile Notre-Dame to the required dimensions. Investment in Olympic facilities was more than matched by infrastructure improvements, including the metro extension out to Honoré-Beaugrand, building new roads, hotels and constructing a remote and largely redundant international airport at Mirabel. From the outset, the designs for the stadia embraced an unmistakable monumentality. The Olympic stadium was a conscious spectacle in its own right. Designed by the French architect Roger Taillibert, who designed Paris' Parc des Princes, its 575-feet (190-metre) tower, inclined at 45 degrees, supported the retractable roof on 26 steel cables. The radical technology plagued the construction phase and merely led, in the fullness of time, to a stadium with an impressive observation tower and a non-retractable roof.

The opening and closing ceremonies navigated a cautious path between the sensitivities of the various interested parties: the mannered internationalism of the IOC, the mandatory bilingualism of the Canadian national identity, and the distinctive Quebecois culture. Recognising that these ceremonies would be televised to global audiences of 1.5 billion people, many watching in colour for the first time, the organisers appointed directors with television experience to take charge of proceedings. One resulting innovation was to create a single musical score that would act as a storyboard for the event, synchronising and choreographing events in the stadium. The music chosen was compiled and arranged from original works by the recently deceased composer André Mathieu, himself a Montrealer. Combining orchestral music with 1970s disco funk, it provided the music for the entry of the national teams ('The March of the Athletes'), the arrival of the torch and the lighting of the flame ('Olympic Cantata') and the tribute of Canadian youth to the world's athletes ('Quebec Concerto').[13]

The opening ceremony introduced performance elements to augment the formal rituals. Folk dancers from Munich and Montreal celebrated the transfer of the Olympic flag between the two cities. After performing separate routines, they came together to perform a programme of Bavarian and Quebecois music. Before the swearing of the Olympic oath, 1380 school children and 12 international gymnasts performed a seven-minute ballet with flags, ribbons, and silk squares, choreographed by Hugo de Pot. The Olympic torch relay was given a modern twist in that the flame was kindled in the traditional way at Olympia and relayed by runners to a ceremony in Athens. From there it was transmitted 'electronically' to Ottawa and relayed by runners to the stadium in Montreal (ibid., 310). Two teenagers – one from Toronto and one from Montreal to represent the two founding communities of Canada – then brought the flame into the arena (ibid., 300).

The closing ceremony expanded the cultural content. In the initial dance sequence, 500 students formed five Olympic rings in the heart of the arena. Seventy-five native Canadians led the parade of flags and the athletes into the stadium to the accompaniment of Mathieu's 'Danse Sauvage' played on traditional instruments. They immediately built giant wigwams in the centre of the Olympic rings. After the ritual elements – speeches, the lowering of the Olympic flag and the extinguishing of the flame – screens relayed live television pictures from Moscow to invite the world to the 1980 games. The satellite-communicated pictures symbolically reinforced the sense of the Olympics as spectacle enacted for the virtual community of the global television audience. By contrast, the spectators and participants in the stadium increasingly seemed like the supporting players, at least as far as the opening and closing ceremonies were concerned.

Ideological Wars

The Olympics of 1980 and 1984 were essentially rival games, staged by two superpowers to show the superiority of their ideological systems. Moscow and Los Angeles were the only candidates for the 1980 games and, after the withdrawal of a half-hearted bid from Teheran, Los Angeles was the sole formal bidder for 1984. With an eye to the lessons of the Montreal games, both sets of organisers made virtues out of economy and pragmatism. The Organising Committee for the Moscow games righteously claimed that they had not tried to 'outdo' their predecessors by building huge structures. Rather they 'sought efficiency', building only 'essential' installations that would 'not remain monuments to vanity' but would be 'in constant use for the benefit of the Soviet People' (Organising Committee, 1980, 43). For Los Angeles, the commitment to fund the games without the public funds available in the USSR resulted in an event that added fine-tuned commercialism to cost-consciousness. Both games were hit by politically based boycotts inspired by their rivals.

Boycotts, of course, were nothing new at the Olympics. Montreal saw 25 African nations and Guyana withdraw their teams as a protest over the New Zealand rugby tour of South Africa, with Taiwan withdrawing over not being allowed to use the title 'Republic of China'. Fourteen socialist countries boycotted Los Angeles over concerns for their teams' security, which matched the American-led boycott of Moscow 1980 due to the Soviet invasion of Afghanistan in December 1979. Yet despite whether their arch rivals were present, the world's media and television audiences were there in force. The Moscow Olympics inaugurated a new era in the staging of the opening and closing ceremonies through the addition of long and spectacular entertainment segments. That innovation unquestionably threw down the gauntlet to Los Angeles to respond in kind.

The Soviet approach to the Olympics reflected the position of sport within the apparatus of the Soviet state, summarised by S. Pavlov, the chairman of the USSR Committee on Sports, as 'another sphere ... for evaluating the advantages of the Soviet political system' (quoted in Hazan, 1982, 39). Success in international competition would reveal the superiority of the Soviet system, especially to third-world states in regions where the two superpowers competed for influence (Riordan, 1996, 167). Staging major sporting events also provided an opportunity to allow visitors to glimpse the friendliness of socialism (Hazan, 1982, 48–9). The cultural programme offered foreign participants at the Moscow games a programme of visits that included factories and collective farms alongside exhibitions and trips to historical sites. Those opting to visit the Second Moscow Watch Factory, for example, could learn 'about the conditions of work and social welfare for the worker'; those taking the chance to visit the collective farms could learn about 'the working conditions of the collective farmers, their pensions and about achievements of sportsmen-farmers' (Organising Committee, 1980, 410).[14]

The USSR made much of rejecting the gigantism of previous games, leaving behind expensively maintained and underused sports facilities. Instead, the organisers planned to use Moscow's existing sports facilities wherever possible, employing temporary grandstands and ensuring that any new structures would be designed as multipurpose venues. Yet beneath the virtuous rhetoric was an undercurrent that wanted to proclaim Soviet technological expertise in designing large structures. Hence while the main ceremonies and the track and field competitions centred on the renovated Lenin Stadium (built originally in 1956), the organisers also commissioned the world's largest indoor arena in north Moscow for the basketball and boxing competitions. Capable of seating up to 45 000 spectators, it could be used either as a single space or divided into two separate auditoria, making it appropriate to serve as a multipurpose space for sports, political and cultural events after the games (Promyslov, 1980, 236–7).

Given the nature of the command economy, the authorities subsumed preparations for the Olympics into the city's planning strategy – the General Plan for the Development of Moscow 1971–1990 – and the state's tenth Five-Year Plan of Economic and Social Development. The former adopted decentralist principles, dividing Moscow into eight functional zones, each with a population of between 600 000 and 1.2 million and their 'town public centres' and subsidiary centres. The plan then allocated activities to these zones while simultaneously seeking to ensure that each zone would have a 'balance between labour resources and employment opportunities' (Lappo et al., 1976, 138–40). The Olympic Games provided the opportunity to improve access to sporting, cultural and entertainment facilities for those living within these zones by designing new venues for use once the games were over (Promyslov, 1980, 230). The games' main facilities were distributed into six main areas, with the Olympic village in a seventh. Located in the southwest of the city, the village comprised eighteen blocks, each 16 storeys high, arranged in groups of three with associated communal catering, social, facilities, entertainment, shopping and training facilities. After the games, the village would become a self-contained neighbourhood complete with cultural and sporting amenities (ibid., 245–6).

Moscow witnessed less infrastructural development than at many recent games. The dispersed nature of these sites may have posed logistic problems, but there was little need for new road construction given the low levels of private car ownership at this time. Increasing media presence, however, required the construction of new communications centres for press, radio and television. The city's three airports were also renovated, with a new passenger air terminal added to Sheremetyevo international airport. The authorities renovated historic buildings (especially churches), planted trees, expanded the hotel sector, and commissioned cafes and restaurants. In a distant echo of Berlin 1936, resident journalist Michael Binyon noted the absence of party slogans, posters and even propaganda from Intourist guides during the games.[15]

The idea of having an Olympic cultural programme again served the host nation's ideological needs, allowing the regime to acquaint visitors with 'the heritage and achievements of the Soviet multinational culture', as well as with the creative work of artists from all fifteen Soviet republics (Organising Committee, 1980, 402). The programme opened in 1979 with the Seventh Summer Spartakiad of the Republics of the USSR, a dress rehearsal of the 1980 games that featured more than 450 musical and theatrical performances and a sporting festival. The Olympic cultural programme incorporated some of Moscow's existing arts festivals, but catered for visitors rather than ordinary Russians. It covered theatre, opera, classical music, folk music and dance, circus, film, exhibitions and excursions, with special performances at the Olympic village for athletes and officials. The Organising Committee (1980, 404–6) recorded 144 opera and ballet performances, 455 plays, 1500 concerts and 350 circus performances. Although delegations from states wishing to express disapproval of Soviet policy in Afghanistan boycotted the cultural programme, an estimated 2.5 million visitors saw the exhibitions. These included a display of 100 masterpieces from the Hermitage Collection, an exhibition of Russian and Contemporary painting, and 'Sport, Ambassador of Peace'. A total of 103 400 foreign tourists visited the USSR's Exhibition of Economic Achievements during the games.

The games' opening and closing ceremonies in Moscow contained a full 'artistic programme', thereby setting the pattern for subsequent ceremonies. The organisers allocated 60 minutes of the opening ceremony and 32 minutes of the closing ceremony were allotted to elements intended to 'embody Olympic continuity ... the spirit of the times, and reflect the multi-faceted life and culture of the Soviet People' (Organising Committee, 1980, 280). The programme interwove classical Greek references with reminders of Soviet technology, athleticism, and folk art. The ceremony started with Shostakovich's 'Festive Overture' (the theme music of these games), and the entry of Greek chariots and maidens scattering rose petals as prelude to the March of Nations. After the raising of the Olympic flag and releasing of 22 white doves to symbolise the games of the twenty-second Olympiad, the stadium heard a message from two Soviet cosmonauts circling the Earth above Greece, welcoming the athletes to Moscow and calling for a 'durable and reliable world peace'. The torch bearer ascended a stairway that 'miraculously appeared before the eyes of the amazed spectators', as 4500 Red Army gymnasts sitting in the east stand held boards above their heads to create a human bridge leading to the Olympic bowl where the flame was lit (Organising Committee, 1980, 294; Booker, 1981, 80). They also created a giant picture screen or 'artistic background' to the ceremony. With television specifically in mind, each gymnast was equipped with five coloured flags, seven changeable shirtfronts, seven painted panels and five caps. By carefully orchestrating use of these props, they were able to create 174 images as the ceremony progressed including national flags, Olympic symbols and scenes of ancient Greece (Organising Committee, 1980, 297).

The closing ceremony continued in similar vein. The artistic programme involved 12 000 performers in Greek tableaux, 4000 flag bearers, fireworks, choreographed folk festivities, giant Matryoshka dolls, and inflatables. A 25-feet inflatable of the games' mascot Misha Bear, holding a bunch of balloons, floated up into the night sky; a final song 'Goodbye Moscow' was set against another, changing 'artistic backdrop' that showed Misha shedding a tear. The ceremony's content combined the conventional themes (the sorrow of parting and looking ahead to the next Olympiad), with careful projection of the host society as 'efficient, organised, contented, stable and hospitable'.[16] Much of this message was lost on the Olympic movement. Lord Killanin, speaking as President of the International Olympic Committee, pleaded: 'I implore the sportsmen of the world to unite in peace before the holocaust descends ...' (Killanin, 1983, 1). He later described the Moscow games as 'mutilated by politicians leaving torment, tears, anguish and remorse where there should have been friendship ...' (ibid.). The scale of the spectacle and the power of the ceremonial to convey messages about the host city and its society, however, were not lost on the representatives of Los Angeles. They clearly called for a more than equivalent response from the home of Hollywood four years later.

Los Angeles (1984)

The roots of the 1984 games, however, lay as much in the enduring place promotional rivalries of American cities as in the more fleeting arena of ideological rivalries. Just seven years after entertaining the 1932 summer games, local dignitaries formed the Southern California Committee for the Olympic Games (SCCOG) to raise funds for amateur athletics, contribute to the US Olympic Fund, and to 'maintain contacts with the IOC for the purpose of soliciting the IOC's approval of holding the Olympic Games in Los Angeles again' (Organising Committee, 1985, 6). The city had already bid in 1938 for the 1940 games after the withdrawal of Tokyo. This was followed by bids in 1948, 1952 and 1956. After no less than five US cities bid for the 1956 games (see Table 7.1), the USOC established a screening procedure to select a single US city to make a presentation to the IOC. Thus while Los Angeles continued to apply to the USOC for each succeeding games, Detroit succeeded in gaining the nomination for each of the four games between

1960–72 inclusive. Los Angeles then became the US candidate city for 1976, 1980 and 1984.

The prevailing assessment of the financial risks of staging the games had swung so drastically during the course of the 1970s that Los Angeles was the only candidate when the IOC voted in 1978. Public support for the bid rested upon the premise that the games would be privately financed. A poll conducted in 1977 at the insistence of USOC showed that 70 per cent of the public favoured Los Angeles' candidature, but that this figure dropped to 35 per cent if city or county funds were involved. The organisers' costings, based on private funding and the sales of the television rights, predicted a profit for the games. Yet despite the involvement of Los Angeles mayor Tom Bradley with the Olympic project, the city's authorities refused to assume the customary financial responsibility for the games. With little other option, the IOC exceptionally allowed the Los Angeles Olympic Organising Committee (LAOOC) and the USOC instead to assume joint financial responsibility.

In the words of John Argue, SCCOG President, these were to be 'spartan Games' (Organising Committee, 1985, 7). This meant using volunteers wherever possible and making maximum use of existing facilities. The Los Angeles Memorial Coliseum was refurbished as the Olympic stadium, with just four new venues required – for rowing, cycling, swimming and shooting. Each attracted high levels of sponsorship. The McDonald's Swim Stadium, for example, was built in Olympic Park for the University of Southern California. The Southland Corporation, parent company of the 7–11 chain of convenience stores, funded the velodrome on the California State University site. Fuji Film sponsored the shooting range. The three Olympic villages used sites on university campuses (University College at Los Angeles, University of Southern California and the University of California at Santa Barbara), with the accommodation later available for students (Burbank et al., 2001, 76–7).

This approach had two different, but equally important, implications for the 1984 Olympics. In the first place, the emphasis on named sponsorship and private finance introduced a degree of commercialism into organising the Olympics. The Olympic movement's unease about these being the 'commercial games' came to a head in opposition to a decision to sell participation in the torch relay at $3000 a kilometre as the flame toured the American states before its arrival at the stadium (Senn, 1999, 195).[17] Although the money was destined for charity, it offended the Greeks who saw this as a sacrilegious attack on their heritage. Secondly, the dispersal of Olympic sites around the sprawling, car-based Los Angeles city region made it harder to generate the greater intimacy of a games with a nucleated Olympic park. Part of the solution to creating a sense of place for the athletes, visitors and television audience again lay in the realm of design. The team of designers[18] appointed for the Los Angeles games aimed to create an 'ephemeral environment' that could be quite literally 'painted' on to the city. Called 'festive federalism', this 'look' would link the festival venues (Yew, 1996, 288). The designers intended their chosen colours – magenta, chrome, yellow, aqua, light blue, French (dark) blue, vermilion, green, lavender, vibrant yellow, pink and violet – to relate to the Mediterranean environment, making reference both to the Greek origins of the games and to the climate of California. The 'look' consisted of a 'kit of parts', comprising columns, tents, banners, spiral tubes, scaffolding, canopies and balloons, that could be assembled at venues and would mark out the key components of the games. Black and white columns marked the entrances to venues, magenta indicated the approach to a venue, high-peaked yellow tents were information points, a violet tent denoted souvenirs and an aqua tent refreshments. The 'look' was applied at the start of the arts festival on 1 June 1984 and dismantled at the end of the games, with many artefacts auctioned (Ueberroth, 1986, 322).

The organisers originally hired Walt Disney Productions to plan and execute the opening and closing ceremonies, but Disney pulled out in 1983 when unable to gain an increase on the allotted $5 million budget to execute an ambitious scheme for parades and street decorations.[19] In August 1983, the film-maker and SCCOG member David L. Wolper, took over as producer. Wolper wanted the Olympic ceremonies to be 'emotional, majestic and inspirational' in scale, making full use of the stadium space and actively engaging the audience. The opening ceremony's remit required it both to contain something strikingly original and showcase American culture. Watched by 92 655 spectators in the stadium and an estimated worldwide global television audience of 2.5 billion viewers (Wilson, 1996, 175), opinions differed about what followed. They ranged from a 'brilliant ... [and] emotional outpouring of friendship and the story of America set to music ... Hollywood at its best: glamorous but not glitzy; patriotic but not corny' (Ueberroth, 1986, 304) to 'patriotic to the point of crude ethnocentrism' (Tomlinson, 2000, 224).

What was not in doubt, however, was the extent of the spectacle (Wilson, 1996, 175). It opened with a 'welcome' sequence that included sky-writing, a man flying into the stadium with a jet pack strapped to his back, flowers being handed out to spectators and over 1200 dancers involved in a routine that created the Olympic rings, the word 'welcome' and ended with the release of 1200 white and gold balloons. The centrepiece of the entertainment segment was the 30-minute *Music of America*, which represented the musical development of the USA through six periods. This contained one of the ceremony's defining moments – the appearance of 85 grand pianos through the arches of the stadium's peristyle for a rendition of music by George Gershwin.[20] This was followed by a 'card stunt' to mark the entry of the athletes into the stadium. The version of this technique used in Moscow had involved the 4500 soldiers in months of practice to master the procedures necessary for complex picture changes. The Americans could not duplicate this training, so worked instead on scale. Spectators arriving at their seats found envelopes containing coloured plastic cards, which, when held aloft, formed the flags of the competing nations (Ueberroth, 1986, 301). The ceremony concluded with a children's choir singing the 'Ode to Joy' from Beethoven's Ninth Symphony – a staple of opening ceremonies – and the song 'Reach out and Touch' by Giorgio Moroder. Rewritten for the occasion and performed by Vicki McClure, a supermarket cashier, rather than by a celebrity, it involved a multi-ethnic group of 2000 Los Angelinos dressed in their national costumes lining the arena to encourage spectators and athletes to join hands in 'a moment of international brotherhood' (Organising Committee, 1985, 215).

The closing ceremony proceeded in a similar vein. Conceived as a show of 'fun and surprises' and a 'reward' for the athletes (Organising Committee, 1985, 215), it opened with performances by the Dance Theatre of Harlem and Seoul City Dance Theatre (in anticipation of the 1988 games in South Korea). At the end of the Olympic ritual elements and the extinguishing of the Olympic flame came a full-blooded entertainment section. Spectators were issued with light sticks, sponsored by Union Carbide, to signal to an 'alien spaceship' which 'landed' in the arena. This was followed by a 30-minute firework display celebrating the previous hosts of the games. The ceremony ended with a musical spectacular, culminating in Lionel Ritchie singing 'All Night Long' accompanied by break dancers against a backdrop of fountains, lasers and smoke effects (Organising Committee, 1985, 215). Literally and metaphorically, the ceremonies were worlds apart from London 36 years previously.

The ten-week Olympic arts festival took place between 1 June and 12 August 1984 under the direction of Robert Fitzpatrick, president of the California Institute of the Arts (Wilson, 1996, 175). The organisers wanted to create 'an atmosphere of festival and celebration' and be the year's major international arts festival (Organising Committee, 1985, 529). It was divided into two parts with different aims and different target audiences. The first, in the seven weeks leading up to the games, was for domestic consumption and offered an international programme of works not often seen in California. The second part ran during the games and was aimed at Olympic participants and visitors. It focused on the culture and artists of Los Angeles and the USA, covering dance, theatre, music, film and the visual arts. The festival offered nearly 900 performances drawing an aggregate audience of 1.3 million spectators (Wilson, 1996, 175). In keeping with the ethos of the games, the festival had its own sponsor, the Times Mirror Company, which subscribed $5 million of the $11.5 million necessary to run the event. A further $3 million from LAOOC and another $3m from ticket sales allowed this aspect of the Olympics to break even (Organising Committee, 1985, 539).

If Moscow and Los Angeles changed expectations for the opening and closing ceremonies, Los Angeles' commercial success dramatically altered the outlook for other prospective host cities. Against all expectations, it made a profit of $225 million, which was channelled into sports bodies and programmes in the USA. Local universities gained major new facilities. The event injected an estimated $2.4 billion into the southern Californian economy. The associated accusations of commercialism galvanised the IOC into taking control of sponsorship through TOP (The Olympic Programme). For all the disdain of commercialism, the IOC itself now invited corporations to pay tens of millions of dollars to become worldwide Olympic sponsors (Wilson, 1996, 176). After the events of the 1970s, the transformation was complete and the act of being host to the Olympics was fully restored as the pinnacle of ambition for cities with global aspirations.

Glittering Prizes?

The weight of that logic, however, had not yet emerged in 1981 when the IOC met at Baden-Baden to select the host city for the 1988 games. There were only two candidates – Seoul and the overwhelming favourite, Nagoya (Japan). Many factors weighed against Seoul: its lack of Olympic tradition, the nation's low standing in international sport, its lack of experience in staging sporting competitions, South Korea's internal political problems and the country's international standing (it was not recognised by the Soviet bloc and its selection might have triggered yet another boycott). Indeed, only two significant factors weighed in Seoul's favour – environmental protests against Nagoya and the desire of the IOC to spread the games more widely rather than return to Japan so soon after the 1964 summer games.[21] Nevertheless, against the odds and without feeling any need for explanation, the IOC chose Seoul.

Seoul (1988)

Seoul's decision to seek the games was undoubtedly inspired by the success of the 1964 games, which the Koreans believed had altered perceptions of the Japanese and helped Japan join the ranks of the developed world in the cultural, social, diplomatic and economic fields. The games would provide a positive context for international scrutiny, show the economic transformation and political progress within Korea, and establish dialogue with Communist and non-aligned nations.[22] It would also provide an opportunity to regenerate Seoul. The city faced serious problems caused by its recent turbulent history. The Korean War (1950–53) caused the destruction of 47 per cent of Seoul's buildings and resulted in an influx of displaced migrants. In the 1970s rising levels of car ownership, rapid expansion of the commercial sector, and annual population growth of around 30 000 per year left a legacy of squatter settlements, overcrowding, congestion, air and water pollution, urban decay and environmental degradation (Kim and Choe, 1997, 10, 11). The Olympics seemed to offer a means to short-circuit the process of replanning and reconstruction.

The methods chosen to improve the city's built environment and infrastructure, however, attracted international criticism for paying greater attention to urban form than social cost. Ideas of improvement centred on the removal of slums and the creation of modernistic, often high-rise, developments for high-income residential or commercial use. Traditional walking-scale urban forms (*hanoks*), built at high density with narrow streets and passageways, were bulldozed for commercial redevelopment. Laws covering preservation and conservation were not introduced until 1983 and, even then, only the oldest historical buildings with connections to the Yi dynasty benefited. Clearance continued in areas without that historic cachet (Kim and Choe, 1997, 209, 212). Less controversially, the authorities conducted a programme of repairing historical monuments, including palaces and shrines, tree planting, and improvements to streets, drainage and power supply. Two new urban motorways linked the airport to the Olympic sites and improved east–west traffic flows in the city. The authorities built new metro lines and expanded the airport. Seoul's planners instigated the Han River Development Project, which combined anti-flood measures, water treatment for the heavily polluted river, habitat regeneration and the creation of a series of recreational areas. Temporary measures that applied for the duration of the games included encouraging dust-producing firms along the marathon route and around Olympic venues to switch to shorter working hours or night-time operation, and advising smoke-producing bath houses to close on days of key events.

The organisers concentrated the Olympic facilities in the Seoul Sports Complex, built in the Chamshil area on the south bank of the Han river around eight miles (13 kilometres) south of central Seoul, with another six venues at the Olympic park, just over two miles (3.5 kilometres) to the east. The South Korean government had originally commissioned the Seoul Sports Complex in 1977, when the country lacked the facilities even to host the Asian games. The 146-acre (59-hectare) site contained a major stadium, which became the 100 000-seater Olympic stadium, as well as a 50 000-seater venue for the exhibition sport of baseball. The complex was linked to the Olympic expressway, which connected the airport with Seoul's downtown area. The Olympic park provided the venues for the cycling, weightlifting, fencing, tennis, gymnastics and swimming events. The Olympic village comprised blocks of flats over various heights (6–24 storeys) clustered in groups around common open spaces, thereby echoing the courtyard of the *hanok*. In total 5540 units were built, which were sold after the games as private housing for upper middle-income families (Kim and Choe, 1997, 197–8). During the construction of the park, the discovery of the earthen walls of a fortress from the Baekje Kingdom (18 BC–AD 660) led to the designation of a historic park within the masterplan (ibid., 208).

The Koreans emphasised the cultural festivals – an aspect of the Olympics sometimes regarded as a sideshow or even an unwanted chore by previous organisers. Dr Seh-Jik Park (1991, 103), president of the Seoul Olympic Organising Committee, argued that Korea wanted to establish a 'prototype' for subsequent games that would create a 'synthesis of sports, scholarship and arts of the world' to promote the Olympic ideal in a way not achieved at previous gatherings. This aim had its political underpinnings. The games provided an opportunity to create an artistic dialogue with nations that had refused South Korea political recognition. There were strenuous efforts, for example, to encourage the attendance of companies from eastern Europe, Russia and China.[23] The seven-week arts festival also featured the Seoul Metropolitan Opera, UNESCO International Theatre, Comédie Français of Paris, Kabuki dancers from Japan, the European Master Orchestra, Nana Mouskouri, choirs and singers, folk troupes, and even calligraphers (Park, 1991, 103).

This emphasis required a dramatic expansion of the city's arts institutions, including construction of the Seoul Arts Centre, the National Classical Music Institute, the National Museum of Contemporary Arts and Chongju Museum (Essex and Chalkley, 1998, 197). Exhibitions displayed art forms seldom seen in Seoul before the Olympics, with the aim of leaving an artistic legacy for the city once the games were over. The organisers created a sculpture area in the Olympic park by selecting five Korean sculptors who, in turn, would invite foreign sculptors to create, exhibit and donate work. In total, 155 sculptures from 66 countries were finally assembled on site and donated to South Korea. Similarly, they staged a modern art exhibition with 156 paintings from 62 countries, 40 per cent of which were donated to the Korean Museum of Modern Art.

The torch relay became a focus for cultural festivals throughout South Korea, starting with Korean dancers and musicians visiting Greece to celebrate the lighting of the flame. A large celebration involving 2978 performers convened at the international airport to welcome the flame to Korean soil. As the torch progressed around South Korea, the 19 cities where the torch rested overnight staged displays of folk music and dancing. Areas that traditionally held autumnal cultural festivals incorporated the torch celebrations into them to comprise 4–6 days of festivities. Foreign folk troupes frequently performed in these provincial celebrations before contributing to the main cultural events in Seoul (Organising Committee, 1989, 384, 386).

The crafting of the opening and closing ceremonies again assumed great significance as they were seen as setting the tone for the games or even in determining their success (Park, 1991, 41). The opening ceremony's theme of 'Heaven, Earth and Man' saw the organisers blend their desire for something truly Korean with an effort to emulate previous games. The organisers commissioned the theme song 'Hand in Hand' from Giorgio Moroder (who performed a similar role in 1984, see above) and his lyricist Thomas R. Whitlock. They involved the stadium's spectators in card stunts, as at Moscow and Los Angeles. Seventy-six sky-divers, echoing the rocket man from Los Angeles, formed themselves into the five Olympic rings before landing in the arena. Five jet planes traced lines in the Olympic colours across the sky as the Olympic flame was lit (evoking memories of Tokyo 1964). The Korean sequence began with a dragon drum procession,[24] followed by a taekwondo martial arts demonstration with 1000 special forces troops and 500 school pupils symbolising the breaking of barriers and progress of peace, children playing traditional games, and folk dance. The closing ceremony focused on light and colour in a display drawing on Korean culture. Using the arena as the stage, lines of dancers formed curved yin and yang lines that divided the space into two as a metaphor for world politics – with one side representing the east, the other the west. Dancers then created a bridge of understanding and reunion between them (ibid., 161).

Much about the Seoul games testified to their scale. They were the largest so far in size, technology and publicity (Palenski, 1996, 184), although not television audiences. Due to time zone differences, which meant either late night or early viewing times in North America, the 1.6 billion viewers for the opening ceremony were less than for Los Angeles (Larson and Park, 1993). That ceremony involved over 20 000 performers and so could be claimed the largest 'cast' in the history of the games (Organising Committee, 1989, 44). For once, size did translate into financial success as the games made a healthy profit. They also yielded some of the political gains that the South Koreans wanted. Although political clouds hung over the games at various points, the South Koreans gained diplomatic relations with China and most east European countries as a result of the Olympics (Palenski, 1996, 182).

Barcelona (1992)

The Barcelona games were the first since Tokyo in 1964 to be relatively untroubled by international politics. There were no boycotts and despite threats, there were no terrorism incidents at the games. The dissolution of the Soviet bloc also eliminated many familiar sources of tension. With these elements removed, the potential of the games to act as a vehicle for place promotion and urban regeneration could shine through. It was an opportunity that Barcelona fully grasped, providing a model for many other first-world cities in terms of the possible scale of urban improvement. Barcelona had suffered many years of under-investment during the Franco regime, failing to keep up with the impact of social and economic change. The city had many key buildings in a poor state of repair, general urban decay, severe traffic congestion in the central area, poor accessibility from access roads into Barcelona, lack of parking, a suburban railway system that stopped short of the central area, and the 'disarray' of the outlying districts developed since the 1950s (Martorell et al., 1992, 8). Telecommunications fell far short of modern standards. Waterways and beaches experienced heavy pollution, with inadequate sewerage and land drain systems. A semi-derelict industrial area and railway yards prevented public access to the sea. Plans drawn up in the early 1980s sought to tackle these problems, but the staging of the Olympics provided a means to accelerate the process.

This was not a new strategy, since Barcelona had used earlier international festivals to address urban planning goals. The 1888 Universal Exhibition in the Parc de la Ciutadella to the east of the old medieval centre and the International Exhibition of 1929 on Montjuic to the west both resulted in urban improvements and enhanced the city's cultural institutions, open space and transport (Hughes, 1992). The Olympics were seen in a similar light. Barcelona had previously bid to host the games for 1924, 1936 and 1972.[25] Selected at the IOC meeting in 1986 over Paris, the only other credible candidate, Barcelona undertook developments on such a radical scale that less than 20 per cent of the total expenditure (£2 billion) for the 1992 games went on sports facilities (Varley, 1992, 21). Indeed when bidding, the city boasted that 88 per cent of the necessary facilities for the games *per se* were already 'available'.[26] The Olympic stadium would be an updated and renovated version of that used for the 1929 International Exhibition. Ten more venues came from refurbishments to existing facilities, with 43 other facilities used very much in their existing state (Essex and Chalkley, 1998, 198). The promoters emphasised that only 15 new venues would be required.

The lion's share of the investment went instead on urban improvements. The Barcelona Economic and Social Plan 2000 identified three goals within the broader aim of consolidating Barcelona as 'an enterprising European metropolis, with influence over its macro-region and with a modern socially balanced quality of life, deeply rooted in Mediterranean culture' (Marshall, 1996, 153). These were: improving communications; improving the quality of life for people with reference to the environment, training, research, social opportunities for housing and cultural infrastructure; and supporting industry and advanced services to business with particular reference to telecommunications and technological innovation (ibid.). What began as a strategy to lever funds out of Madrid evolved into overt place marketing.

The planners concentrated the Olympic facilities in four areas located in a ring around the city, roughly where the outer limits of the nineteenth-century city met the less structured developments of the second half of the twentieth century. This type of location, it was asserted, would have a major impact on the urban structure and 'resolve a number of large scale problems' (Martorell et al., 1992, 8). The first area, the Vall d'Hebron in the north, was characterised by 'a great open space where existing housing and amenities have not as yet managed to create a genuine urban nucleus'. This housed the velodrome, archery range, and accommodation for journalists, which was subsequently turned into residential accommodation. Improvements to open space such as the Parc de la Crueta del Coll, created from a disused quarry, contained a boating lake and swimming pool, woodland paths and sculptures by Eduardo Chillida, Ellsworth Kelly and Roy Liechtenstein. The second area, around the City University, was described as lacking 'any clear urban structure' (ibid.), but had strategic importance in terms of communications to the rest of the metropolitan area. This became the location for the stadia for football, polo and tennis. The third area, the Montjuic, became the major Olympic site (Hughes, 1992, 39). The organisers gutted the 1929 stadium, lowered the floor to fit in another grandstand and 'refurbished' the remainder to hold 60 000 spectators.

The old Exposición General d'España buildings were restored, revitalising the Spanish village as a tourist attraction and adding night spots. The most significant new sports facilities were the Sant Jordi Sports Palace, designed by Arata Isozaki, and the swimming and diving pools. The latter supplied television viewers with the most dramatic images of the entire games, as divers performed against a backdrop of the city below. The fourth area was located on the coast to the east of the medieval city on land previously occupied by railways, warehousing and industry. This housed the Olympic village, lodging 15 000 participants in two tower blocks and associated low-rise developments. The tower blocks were later intended for conversion to a hotel and offices. Absorbing roughly 40 per cent of the total games' expenditure, this development also included shops, sculpture and a marina. A raised coastal promenade connected the area to the old port and improved protection against coastal erosion. Other works included cleaning and enhancing the existing beaches by bringing in fresh sand from the sea bed, removing an outfall sewer, and improving drainage to prevent flooding (Martorell et al., 1992, 14). While initially promising that the housing component of the scheme would provide over 2000 apartments at 'low competitive prices' (Mayor Pascual Maragall, cited in Hughes, 1992, 39), when they were constructed this was no longer the case. The poor had to be content with the open space and access to the sea.

Investment in the city's transport systems included the Cinturo de Ronda, a major ring road skirting the north of the city linking the outlying communities and two of the Olympic sites (Vall d'Hebron and the university area). Along the coast, the Cinturo del Litoral linked Montjuic with the Olympic village and on to the new ring road. This included tunnel sections beneath the old port and the Olympic village. The metro was extended, the coastal railway rerouted and the airport redesigned and expanded (El Prat del Llobregat). Norman Foster's telecommunications tower symbolised the modernisation of Barcelona's telecommunications systems. The old port was transformed into a leisure and recreational area. The medieval city centre was rehabilitated and prettified. A TV advertising campaign – 'Barcelona posa't guapa/ Barcelona puts on a pretty face', showing an attractive woman putting on her makeup – was devised to encourage householders to take advantage of the grants available to help with the beautification scheme.[27]

Barcelona's bid to stage the Olympic Games included a commitment to stage a four-year cultural Olympiad. This was conceived as an opportunity to show the city as a hearth of artistic and cultural innovation, combining a rich 2000-year heritage with a reputation for the avant-garde. Like many host cities, the Organising Committee wanted to tackle the problem of marrying art with sport in a meaningful way. The Olympiad opened in October 1988 with 'Gateway to the Olympiad'. This included 'La Festa', celebrations to welcome the Olympic flag to the city after the Seoul games, and 'La Nit', a rock and opera spectacular that included Freddie Mercury and Montserrat Caballe singing 'Barcelona'. An exhibition entitled 'Barcelona, the city and 92' showed the buildings and urban projects designed to stage the games. It attracted 350 000 visitors and later was shown in Rotterdam and provincial Spanish cities. An updated version staged in Barcelona between November 1990 to March 1991 received a further 100 000 visitors.

The next three years saw a sequence of exhibitions and three autumn cultural festivals of music theatre and dance, with existing festivals co-opted into the cultural Olympiad programme. The exhibition 'Planeta Esport' (May–July 1989), which attracted 250 000 visitors, showed exhibits, audio-visual presentations, sports demonstrations and interactive displays. In 1990, 550 000 visited an exhibition on 'Modernism' housed in Antonio Gaudi's Casa Mila. The exhibition also directed visitors out into the surrounding grid of streets to look at the buildings from the turn of the twentieth century – treating the streetscape as an 'outdoor museum' (Organising Committee, 1992, 351). From October 1990 to January 1991 another exhibition on 'Modernism' at the Museum of Modern Art covered painting, jewellery, sculpture, furniture, architecture and industrial crafts. The year 1992 started with 'Barcelona, 2000 years', 'Art and Sport' and finally the Olympic Festival of Arts itself, which ran over the summer period of the games.

Although the physical transformation of Barcelona was an indispensable part of the logic of staging the games, place promotion also figured heavily. Research showed that Spain generally and Barcelona in particular had serious image problems to overcome.[28] The games supplied an opportunity to put Barcelona on the world map as a centre for investment and tourism. Spain, as host country, wanted to portray itself as a mature, democratic state, a full member of the European Community (to which it acceded in 1986) and to counteract the stereotype of sun, sea and sand. The autonomous region of Catalonia saw the Olympics as an opportunity to gain government resources, stimulate economic development, emphasise its cultural distinctiveness and stress its political autonomy. The European Community wished to register its presence in the last games to be held in Europe in the twentieth century and convey a message pointing to the reinvigorated European project with the launch of the single market in January 1993 (Hargreaves, 2000, 58, 96, 121).[29] The advertising for the games emphasised the location and distinctiveness of Barcelona and Catalonia:

> Barcelona '92 Olympic Games
> In Catalonia, of course
> This is where Barcelona is, in Catalonia, a country in Spain with its own culture, language and identity ... A country with a population of only six million people ... A country in which many foreign enterprises – European, North American, Japanese – have invested ... A country which has understood and motivated the genius of Picasso, the force of Miro, the imagination of Dali ... A country which is visited every year by 16 million people from all over the world ... Now you know where Barcelona is. In Catalonia of course.[30]

The Olympics' opening and closing ceremonies were designated as arenas for reconciling the competing aims of nation, region, city and Europe. The Barcelona Olympic Organising Committee (BOOC) recommended in 1989 that the ceremonies 'display' Barcelona, Catalonia and Spain and that the city be portrayed as 'a Mediterranean, Spanish, European city, capital of Catalonia, open to the world, 2000 years of history, a city of contrasts, modernity and universality, and the balance between modernity and tradition' (Spa et al., 1995, 84). This was addressed through Olympic ritual and the cultural components of the ceremonies.

The traditional emphasis of Olympic ceremonial on the host nation's language, flag and anthem was problematic at Barcelona given the political history. For Catalonians recovering from a period of political suppression under Franco and with newly-won political autonomy, issues of language, flag and anthem were symbolically important. A skilful blending and overlapping of national and regional symbols and folklore created an opening ceremony that averted major nationalist opposition and was seen by foreign journalists as a product of Spanish maturity, cooperation and universal Olympic values. Threatened demonstrations, including plans to disrupt the television coverage of the opening ceremony, never occurred (Hargreaves, 2000, 78, 83). The king, symbol of Spain, opened the games in Catalan as well as Spanish; the Catalan flag appeared alongside the Spanish flag; the Catalan anthem preceded the Spanish anthem; and Catalan officials stood with Spanish politicians. Moreover, Catalan customs were used as vehicles of wider messages. Dancers performing the Sardana, a traditional circle dance banned under Franco, traced the Olympic rings. Following the local custom of building human pyramids, gymnasts constructed twelve such structures to symbolise the members of the European Community. A spectacular sequence 'The Mediterranean, Olympic Sea' wove sun, sea and classical myth together as Hercules sailed across a stadium transformed by billowing blue fabric into the Mediterranean Sea, and thereby making symbolic connection with Greece, Rome, the founding of Barcelona and the ancient games. The opening ceremony drew on opera, flamenco, high art and modern design, with Spanish, Catalan and international stars coming together to portray imagery of a Barcelona and Spain that oozed stability, modernity and tradition. Crowd participation, however, worked less effectively here than at equivalent ceremonies since Moscow. Spectators responded patchily to instructions. Card stunts failed to occur with the slickness necessary to make an impact. Gold and blue light wands distributed to spectators to create a European flag in the final 'Music and Europe' section were waved instead when the Olympic torch arrived in the stadium (Spa et al., 1995, 85).

On economic grounds, the tiny profit of $3.8 million made by the Barcelona games meant that the event scarcely broke even. Cost overruns ate into the projected $350 million surplus. The innovative design of the Sant Jordi Sports Palace, for example, contributed to costs of $89 million rather than $30 million. Construction costs on the ring road were 50 per cent more than the estimated $1 billion. The cultural Olympiad also spawned heavy losses, despite trading on Barcelona's rich heritage in the arts and architecture (Hargreaves, 2000, 106), partly through facing the competing attractions of Expo 92 in Seville and having Madrid as European 1992 City of Culture (see Chapters 5 and 8). Inflation and adverse movements in foreign currency rates also severely increased costs. Unemployment rose by 3 per cent in the city immediately after the Olympics, prices soared and business taxes rose 30 per cent (Maloney, 1996, 193).

On other grounds, critical opinion judged the games a success. Politically, there were no significant boycotts or other forms of disruption. The games successfully launched a challenging package of infrastructural reform and urban regeneration that countered years of neglect under the Franco regime (Maloney, 1996, 192). Place promotional advertising used the games to champion Barcelona as a centre for conventions, events, services and industry. The Barcelona Convention Bureau, for example, used the slogan 'Want to meet in Barcelona? From 10 to 10000, we can cope' with a picture of the Montjuic Stadium.[31] Their 1994 campaign advertised Barcelona as 'the new urban centre of southern Europe', claiming that 'in the future a lot of cities will be built like Barcelona'. The campaign featured portraits of leading architects who had contributed to Olympic projects, such as Oriol Bohigas (the Olympic village), Norman Foster (Collserola telecommunications tower), Santiago Calatrava (Montjuic telefonica tower), Arata Isozaki (Sant Jordi sports palace) and Rocardo Bofill (Barcelona airport). Press coverage remained dominantly positive, with the ceremonies giving exposure to Catalonia and Catalan identity.[32]

Transient Stadia, Prevalent Commercialism

Atlanta vanquished three other cities to gain the US candidature, with Minneapolis–St Paul offering the strongest national opposition (Burbank et al., 2001, 85). The IOC then awarded Atlanta the nomination for the 1996 games at its 1990 meeting against rival bids from Melbourne, Toronto, Manchester, Belgrade and Athens. While informed circles regarded Athens as favourite, given this was the centenary of the modern games' revival in Athens, the IOC was impressed with Atlanta's infrastructure, facilities, cultural associations and the general reputation of American organisational expertise. Four things made its bid particularly attractive. First, it was the home of CNN and IBM, with modern sporting facilities and a suitable metropolitan rapid transit system (MARTA) already in place. Secondly, the Atlanta team astutely proposed sharing profits with the IOC and national Olympic Committees. Thirdly, the city presented itself as a place of harmony and multiculturalism that celebrated its black culture and civil rights history – particularly through being the birthplace of Martin Luther King. It was a message, for example, that the black politician Andrew Young, a former mayor and UN ambassador, stressed when lobbying African IOC delegates (Maloney, 1996). Finally, Los Angeles had inspired general confidence in American organisational expertise and financial wizardry. As one correspondent extravagantly put it: 'the Olympic movement know they will get a superbly organised sporting extravaganza, delivered via the latest technology, and with the backing of some of the world's largest companies, to several billion homes around the globe'.[33]

Atlanta's bid was the latest phase of the city's place promotional activities. Founded at a railway junction with a name derived from the Western and Atlantic Railroad, Atlanta experienced 'waves of organised promotion' (Rutheiser, 1996, 4, 17). In the nineteenth century, its leaders arranged fairs to promote its economy and leadership in the south. These included the International Cotton Exposition (1881), the Piedmont Exposition (1887) celebrating Atlanta's recovery from the Civil War, and the Cotton States and International Exposition (1895), designed to emulate Chicago's Columbian Exposition and counteract the negative image of Atlanta and the south portrayed there (ibid., 27). By the 1940s, the city's leadership promoted Atlanta as the 'Capital of the South'. In the 1950s they touted its alleged tolerance in an era of provincial segregation as 'The city too busy to hate'. By the end of the 1960s they hailed it as the 'World's next great international city'.

The Olympic bid continued this process. The project was seemingly first discussed and shelved in the 1970s in view of the financial debacle at Montreal (Whitelegg, 2000, 805), but revived once Los Angeles had supplied a new financial model. Research had shown poor international awareness of Atlanta, with frequent confusion abroad between Atlanta and Atlantic City (ibid.). Part of the city's problem lay in the mismatch between its role as a highly successful economic hub and its less developed role as a social and cultural centre. A bid for an international festival that emphasised the city's credentials in the cultural sphere could help rectify that mismatch and place Atlanta on the global map. It could also help address the city's manifest social and economic problems. The map of Atlanta revealed sharp differentiation between poor, deprived and largely black inner-city neighbourhoods and wealthier, largely white suburbs, with their emerging business districts complete with office development and shopping malls.

The city's central areas also showed their own sharp disparities. On the one hand were neighbourhoods in which years of under-investment had led to derelict land, deteriorating properties, poor roads and a decaying infrastructure. Poverty was rampant, with 30 per cent of Atlanta's population below the poverty line in the late 1980s – half of whom lived in the central districts. With inadequate provision of homeless shelters, many of the estimated 22 000–28 000 homeless population lived on the streets (Lenskyj, 2000, 135). On the other hand, the central city also displayed abundant signs of new investment in corporate headquarters, hotels, shopping malls and renovation of old streets to create Underground Atlanta and particularly expansion of conference and sports industries. The establishment of the Georgia World Congress Centre (GWCC) had helped Atlanta become America's fourth convention city. The construction nearby of the Georgia Dome, home of the Atlanta Falcons football team, and the Omni Arena, used for basketball, were seen as important complements to the convention trade and a basis for attracting key sporting events in the future. As far back as 1961, building the Atlanta Fulton County Stadium as part of the redevelopment of the Summerhill district had been instrumental in attracting the Braves baseball team from Milwaukee. Nearly three decades later, there were threats that, without major investment in the stadium, the Braves would move out of central Atlanta.

The Olympic bid, therefore, rested on a consensus that saw the games as helpful to Atlanta's place promotional agenda, while offering opportunities for community revitalisation and urban regeneration

(Burbank et al., 2001, 82). Business leaders wanted the games to stimulate economic growth and to carry out urban improvement of a cosmetic nature, with an emphasis on beautification and removal of eyesores, rather than addressing fundamental social questions. The leaders of poorer communities anticipated benefits regarding job prospects, better roads and improved housing (Maloney, 1996, 196). The promoters stressed that these benefits would accrue without involving taxpayers' money, with Andrew Young, now joint chair of the Atlanta Committee for the Olympic Games (ACOG), stating that the games are 'not a welfare programme' but 'a business venture' (cited in Rutheiser, 1996, 238).

Unusually for the Olympics, a private consortium undertook the organisation. Georgia's constitution limited the role Atlanta could play and there was stiff resistance to the city raising funds from those means within its power (taxing tickets or increasing sales tax). Eventually the sale of two sets of bonds gave the city some resources – one to finance urban improvement and the other to upgrade the water system (Burbank et al., 2001, 91). What is certainly true is that Atlanta's business leaders set the agenda for the expenditure through ACOG, with the city exerting little influence. At the outset, this did not appear a significant problem since ACOG was remarkably successful in raising funds from sponsorship, broadcasting rights and merchandising. Combined with ticket sales, these sources raised $1.72 billion (Burbank et al., 2001, 94). The promoters established a two-tier sponsorship structure, with major partners (for example, AT&T, Anheuser-Busch, IBM and NationsBank) committing $40 million in cash and kind, and minor partners (for example, BMW, Holiday Inn and Nissan) each contributing between $20–25 million.[34] Nevertheless, the claim that the games were staged without taxpayers' money was not wholly accurate. The federal government expended nearly $1 billion on infrastructure, housing, safety and security, with smaller amounts expended by the state of Georgia and the city (Burbank et al., 2001, 116). Moreover, despite the rhetoric of hardheaded business, ACOG consciously attempted to smooth relations with the minority communities wherever possible when allocating contracts, recruiting labour and seeking volunteers.

Spending was concentrated into what was termed central Atlanta's Olympic ring – an area around three miles (five kilometres) in radius that would contain 16 of the 25 Olympic facilities and most of the urban improvements. Here the organisers made use of existing facilities such as the GWCC, Georgia Dome and Omni Arena, coupled with using and developing the facilities of Atlanta's universities. The Georgia Institute of Technology provided sites for the Olympic village, a new aquatic centre (swimming, diving, water polo) and boxing. Georgia State

University housed the badminton, Morris Brown College and Clark Atlanta University the hockey, and Moorehouse College the basketball. ACOG commissioned a new Olympic stadium in the south of the Olympic ring next to the Atlanta Fulton County Stadium, itself used for the baseball competition. Stone Mountain Park to the east of Atlanta provided venues for archery, cycling, pentathlon and tennis. Rowing, shooting and equestrian events were located elsewhere in the metropolitan area. Other locations in Georgia staged volleyball, rhythmic gymnastics and football (Athens), yachting (Savannah) and women's softball (Columbus). Part of the football competition, whitewater canoeing and kayaking took place outside Georgia. The pragmatism that underpinned these locational decisions was also expressed in the plans for the Olympic stadium. Built to house 85 000 spectators, it would be partly demolished after the games to create the new 47 000-seater stadium for the Atlanta Braves (Turner Field). The Fulton County Stadium would then be demolished to provide parking space for Turner Field (Larson and Staley, 1998, 281).

Besides areas directly affected by Olympic construction work, two further districts of central Atlanta received attention: the Techwood and Clark Howell public housing district to the immediate south of the Georgia Institute of Technology; and an area of car parks, derelict land, light manufacturing and marginal housing near the GWCC. Controversially, their problems were displaced rather than addressed by the Olympic strategy. The Techwood and Clark Howell district was demolished and replaced by a mixed gated community – bringing more affluent residents to the centre. Sixty per cent of the new properties were rented at market rates while subsidised housing imposed restrictions on tenants, namely, requiring that they were employed and had a clear credit rating. Consequently, the new scheme only rehoused 8 per cent of the original inhabitants (Burbank et al., 2001, 111, 118). The area near the GWCC was cleared to create Centennial Park as an area where visitors and spectators could congregate during the games and where entertainment could be provided. Similar schemes were carried out in nearby Woodruffe Park, where the homeless were designed out of the landscape by means of sleep-proof benches and intermittent sprinklers (ibid., 113). It is estimated that over 16 500 of Atlanta's poorest inhabitants were displaced by these and other Olympic-related investment, most notably in the Summerhill district where the stadium was built. The additional loss of a hostel and three homeless shelters effectively displaced around 10 per cent of Atlanta's homeless (ibid., 112).

The city organised further beautification projects through the Corporation for Olympic Development set up in 1992 by the mayor with the aim of revitalising neighbourhoods near Olympic sites (Lenskyj, 2000, 135). Limited resources meant concentrating work on improving central city streets and upgrading twelve pedestrian corridors that linked the venues. Projects included widening pavements, burying power-lines, installing new street furniture, tree planting, history panels, signage, and the redesign of five parks and plazas. The establishment of a public art programme included creating two folk art parks that featured the work of southern vernacular artists and 11 artworks within the Olympic ring (Bureau of Cultural Affairs, n.d.). The National Park Service gave $12m for renovation of the Martin Luther King Jnr Centre, including a new visitor centre.

The final method of 'improving' central Atlanta involved using city ordinances that criminalised anti-social behaviour. This included aggressive panhandling, loitering, camping, urinating, remaining in parking lots without a car, being in an abandoned building and washing windscreens. When the courts challenged the prohibition against lying on park benches in 1993, the measure was repealed and benches were redesigned with arms at three-feet (one-metre) intervals. Furthermore, the homeless were physically removed, first using the police and then through Project Homeward Bound, whereby the voluntary sector bussed the homeless out of town if they signed an undertaking not to return (Lenskyj, 2000, 138–9).

Atlanta's approach to the cultural programme comprised running a four-year cultural Olympiad culminating in an Olympic arts festival in the summer of 1996. The organisers boasted that this was the largest and 'most comprehensive' ever held, with over 2.6 million visitors (Organising Committee, 1996, 152). Thirty-seven out of the 41 venues employed by the arts festival were in the Olympic ring, with the free 'Southern Crossroads Festival' in Centennial Park running for 18 days and attracting two million visitors. Here, 1114 performers entertained the crowds on three stages from midday to midnight daily. A demonstration area also provided an opportunity for artisans from the South to show craftwork. Although the cultural budget was slashed from $40 million to $25 million, sponsorship was vital in staging key exhibitions. The centrepiece was the internationally-based 'Five Rings of Passion' exhibition at the Museum of Art, which concentrated on five emotions – love, anguish, awe, triumph and love. Another notable exhibition, 'African-American Culture: An American Experience', resulted in the allocation of funds to restore and rehouse the Clark Atlanta University collection of African-American art (Organising Committee, 1996, 160).

The organisers chose Don Mischer Productions of Los Angeles to produce the opening and closing ceremonies. The opening ceremony attempted to celebrate Georgia and the south, along with the themes of 'youth' and 'the centennial'. The first element came from Mischer attempting to tease out the 'spirit' of Atlanta and the south from contacts with residents, local historians, civic and business leaders, the arts community and civil rights activists. The result was an evocation of a peaceful, lush pastoral evening disturbed by a storm and followed by the rebirth of dawn. Youth was represented by an energetic welcome sequence and the 'Centenary of the Games' by tributes to ancient Greece, Pierre de Coubertin, past host cities and former champions. The organisers again requested audience participation, with spectators finding a 'giftbox' waiting for them on their seats containing a programme, scarves and flashlights. The result was described by one observer as 'an elongated event of tattiness and tawdriness' (Tomlinson, 2000, 69), which strove hard to weave the obligatory Olympic ritual into an incessant barrage of short-lived special effects.

Indeed Atlanta stands out for the criticism heaped upon it. Juan Antonio Samaranch, the IOC president, pointedly refused to follow convention in the closing ceremony and congratulate the city 'on staging the best games ever'. Concentrating so many facilities at the centre of the city placed pressure on the transport systems. Traffic congestion, slow journey times, and long queues to use the shuttle buses added to the difficulties for athletes, officials and spectators reaching Olympic venues (Larson and Staley, 1998, 278). Despite claims that venues were within walking distance, this was impractical in the very high summer temperatures. Besides this, the repeated systems failures of IBM's results service, the arrogance of officials, poor relations with the press, the large numbers of street vendors and aggressive sponsorship undermined Atlanta's desire to stage a modern, efficient games. Instead of the carefully designed 'look' developed for the Olympic Games from 1964 onwards, visitors saw squalor and overcommercialisation. Detonation of a pipe bomb in Centennial Park undermined the notion of a safe games (Burbank et al., 2001, 111). Tomlinson dubbed Atlanta 'a city of greed, ruthlessness and rapacious ambition' (2000, 181). For their part, the city's officials were so enraged by negative reporting that Mayor Campbell suggested that 'whining critics ... should be shot' (cited in Whitelegg, 2000, 811). Contrary, therefore, to initial hopes, Atlanta had become a byword for negativity. Even four years after the games, the very success of Sydney (see Chapter 9) again drew comparisons with Atlanta:

> Atlanta has become a password for all that is rotten in the Olympic history. The very mention of Atlanta stops conversations, ends arguments, silences Americans. Atlanta had no right to be chosen in the first place.[35]

Indeed, as a result of the Atlanta experience, the IOC stated that never again would the games be entrusted to an entirely privately run organisation (Whitelegg, 2000, 814).

Visiting Atlanta after the games, it is not difficult to agree with the observation that these games, 'the most transient ever', deserved to be remembered as 'the Disposable Games' (Rutheiser, 1996, 284). The central area was remodelled and Centennial Park stands as a memorial to the games, but there is no stadium, no museum, and no great urban projects associated with Olympic-led regeneration. Approximately 3100 jobs were directly created by schemes that attracted executives and their partners to Atlanta using the games as bait,[36] but this was much less than hoped. The Olympics certainly raised Atlanta's profile as a sporting venue, but failed to enhance its broader image as a cultural centre. Even a century after the revival of the modern Olympics, the formula for staging a successful event could remain downright elusive.

Notes

1   See Shaikin (1988), Hill (1992), Simson and Jennings (1992) and Lenskyj (2000).
2   The games of the twelfth and thirteenth Olympiads were not celebrated because of the war.
3   The IOC awarded Helsinki the Olympic Cup for its outstanding sports buildings.
4   It took its name from the Esposizione Universale di Roma or E42. The other aims for the project were to establish a new cultural quarter and assist Rome's future expansion towards the sea.
5   *The Times*, 12 October 1964.
6   Ibid. Doug Gardner (1965, 19), of the British Olympic Association, also noted the profound contrast between Tokyo and London, only 16 years earlier.
7   Lance Wyman and Peter Murdock won the competition for the games. Their choice of graphics combined Mexican folk art with kinetic typography, which Wyman believed 'powerfully expressed a sense of place and culture'. This was also a means of making over existing venues and creating something new without huge expenditure – the parallel lines could be painted on to the pavements and plazas (Yew, 1996, 196).
8   The 'New Fire' ceremony was part of a cosmology that saw humanity coming to an end after 52 years and in need of renewal in order to continue for a further 52 years. Over 1500 performers took part in the ceremony at the Teotihuacan pyramids, which was watched by 50 000 spectators.
9   The IOC congratulated Mexico City 'for expanding the cultural Programme ... in such a significant manner' (Organising Committee, 1969, 272). It subsequently incorporated these aims into the Olympic Charter Rule 44 (IOC, 2001, 70).

10 In passing, it is worth noting the value of that experience for the 1970 and 1986 football World Cups.

11 Although on the day the president arrived early and the alphorns were abandoned.

12 Interview between G. Gagnon and J.R. Gold, Shaughnessy House, Canadian Centre for Architecture, 5 October 1998.

13 Andre Mathieu (1929–68). The music 'Olympic Games: Music of the Official Ceremony' is available on Polydor (2424 124).

14 Ironically, one of the reasons western governments were so happy for Moscow to stage the games was that it would be a means of exposing Moscow to the liberalising influence of the world community (Riordan, 1996, 196).

15 M. Binyon, 'The way the Games were won', *The Times*, 4 August 1980.

16 Ibid.

17 See Wilson (1996, 174) for a description of the complex events surrounding this matter.

18 Jon Jerde, Deborah Sussman and Paul Prejza.

19 Part of the problem was also that Disney had appointed Bob Jani to plan the ceremonies. The chair of the LAOOC, Peter Ueberroth, had been present at the opening of Disney World's Epcot Centre produced by Jani and felt it was not well planned. He also felt Jani was incapable of capturing the imagination of 2.5 billion people (Ueberroth, 1986, 230).

20 *Music of America* comprised: 'Americana Suite' consisting of Sousa marches performed by an 800-member marching band; 'The Pioneer Spirit' celebrating the westward expansion of America; 'Dixieland Jamboree' featuring the birth of jazz in New Orleans; 'Urban Rhapsody' featuring the music of Gershwin; 'The World is a Stage' featuring American music from the 1940s Big Band era to the 1980s; and the 'Finale' in which the performers gathered in the arena to form an outline map of America (Organising Committee, 1984, 207–8).

21 There had also been a winter games in Sapporo in 1972.

22 The IOC materially assisted that process. Rather than the normal pattern of leaving it to the host city to issue invitations to the games, the IOC handled the task itself, thereby minimising the risk of offending those countries that did not recognise South Korea (Palenski, 1996, 182).

23 With some success. For example, the Bolshoi and Czechoslovakia's Crazy Mimes theatre came but there were no Chinese groups.

24 This is a huge drum 2.1 metres in diameter.

25 As noted in Chapter 6, the city was to host the Workers Olympics in 1936 as an alternative event to the Berlin games, but the outbreak of civil war on the eve of the games prevented it.

26 *Financial Times*, 15 October 1986.

27 'Fire in the Blood', BBC2 television, 5 March 1992.

28 Research carried out by Ovideo Bassat Sport (producers of the opening and closing ceremonies) suggested that Barcelona had few image associations outside Europe other than its designation as an Olympic city and there was

little recognition at all for Catalonia outside western Europe. Spain itself was associated with southern Europe, beautiful women, cheap wine, siestas, bullfights and flamenco (Spa et al., 1995, 165).

29 Funds were set aside in 1989 to promote the community's presence at both the 1992 winter Olympics in Albertville (France) and the summer games in Barcelona. Here, the community allocated funds used for street decorations, for promoting high-definition television technology in the international media centre, and for a 22-minute section in the opening ceremony. Entitled 'Music and Europe', it featured the building of 12 human towers, opera, the 'Ode to Joy' and fireworks (Spa et al., 1995, 180).

30 *Financial Times*, 25/26 July 1992.

31 *Financial Times*, 16 March 1993.

32 See *Financial Times*, 16 November 1993, and 27 September 1994, for contemporary commentary. As an illustration of the lasting positive impact of the games, see A. Bennett, 'How the Olympics gave Barcelona a boost', *The Times*, 8 March 2003.

33 Anon., 'A once-in-a-lifetime opportunity', *Financial Times*, 1 November 1994.

34 Anon., 'Atlanta counts its 1996 chickens', *Financial Times*, 3 November 1995.

35 *Independent on Sunday*, 1 October 2000.

36 Most notably Operation Legacy, a public-private partnership involving the Georgia Department of Industry, Trade and Tourism, the Georgia Governor's Development Council, Georgia Power and NationsBank that was designed to attract top companies to invest in Atlanta.

CHAPTER EIGHT

European Cities of Culture

Culture is everything you don't have to do.

Brian Eno[1]

The European City of Culture programme has become the highest profile European Union-sponsored cultural event and, more generally, an important part of the international artistic calendar. The original idea was that each of the member states of the European Community (as the grouping was known until 1992), would take it in turns to host an annual arts festival. It was then the responsibility of the state in question to nominate a city to stage the event. This chapter examines the origins and evolution of this idea from the first City of Culture festival in Athens in 1985 through to Weimar in 1999. We see how the festival has grown from a modest affair lasting a few months to a year-long event that is now embedded into the wider cultural schedule of the European Union. In doing so, we show how organising cities gradually began to recognise the festival's wider potential, in particular finding it amenable for use as part of urban planning strategies.

Origins

Intervention in the field of culture developed only slowly within the nascent European Community since the latter's roots were primarily economic. The 1957 Treaty of Rome made no specific provision for culture, widely regarded as a sensitive area best left to national, regional and local administrations. Nevertheless, thoughts turned to other dimensions of community life as the economic side of European integration advanced. In 1969, The Hague summit of heads of government declared that Europe was an 'exceptional seat of development, culture and progress' that needed preserving (McMahon, 1995, 122). In the short term, tensions between member states and frictions between the community's institutions impeded progress towards coherent action on cultural matters (see McMahon, 1995, 1999; Barnett, 2000; Delgado-Moreira, 2000; and Sandell, 2002). When considering culture, Europe's politicians and bureaucrats normally restricted their thinking to its role as an industry (McMahon,

1995, 129). It was only in the 1980s, when the community looked for ways to relaunch the European project after the stagnation of the 1970s, that member states renewed discussion about culture with any vigour.

The European City of Culture programme expressed the spirit of these times. Lastingly associated with the Greek Minister of Culture, Melina Mercouri, the proposal emerged from informal council meetings of culture ministers in September 1982 and November 1983 (McMahon, 1995, 134).[2] The European Commission had already mooted the possibilities of cultural exchanges, a European film festival, and a European music year in its 1982 position paper *Stronger Community Action in the Cultural Sector*. The culture ministers reviewed this document and agreed a programme that included establishing the European Music Year, a European youth orchestra, and a sculpture competition. Melina Mercouri, a former actress and the host at the November 1983 meeting, proposed an initiative that would address collectively current concerns about cultural cooperation, audience development and arts promotion. Her idea was for an annual arts festival that designated a European City of Culture to: 'improve communication amongst artists and the intelligentsia in Europe. It is time for our voice to be heard as loud as that of the technocrats. Culture, art and creativity are not less important than technology, commerce and economy' (quoted in Cogliandro, 2001, 12). Mercouri envisaged that the event would centre on the needs of Europe's 'cultural workers' (artists and arts managers), as well as audiences. It would open possibilities for collaborations across national boundaries, while vesting control of the event in the hands of the member states.

The initiative was well timed. The rise of culture on the political agenda resonated with the belief that closer European economic and political integration required associated measures to show the cultural affinities between the peoples of Europe. The solemn declaration of the heads of government, signed at Stuttgart in June 1983, expressed this as 'the awareness of a common cultural heritage as part of a European identity'. From now on, the intensity or otherwise of debate about culture was effectively a barometer of integration activity. The European Community approached culture in terms of 'the compatibility of contrasting identities'. This combined ideas of shared values and heritage, with history acting as the 'connective tissue' holding the European body together (Pantell, 1999, 46, 52). At the same time, the community recognised the need to celebrate and protect diversity in view of fears that economic integration, particularly through the advent of the single market (Pantell, 1999, 51), might generate cultural homogenisation.

The introduction of formal meetings of the Council of Culture

Ministers in June 1984 symbolised official recognition of the community's cultural role (European Community, 1992), with the European City of Culture initiative playing an important part in this new area. It had several redeeming virtues. First, it posed no threat to national sovereignty yet was capable of exciting even those states that felt the need to proceed with caution in the cultural field. Tactically it combined community-level cooperation with the participation of regional and local authorities, thereby involving ordinary people in a European project at a time when few such projects seemed to have relevance for the lives of the public. Secondly, the event could be adapted to changing political and economic circumstances; flexible enough to evolve into something that played a stronger promotional and regenerative role than the founders had envisaged. Finally, relative to the amounts of money expended on other areas of the community's activities, spending on the City of Culture initiative was remarkably low. As Table 8.1 shows, the total direct cost of the 15 festivals between 1985–99 was a mere 4.441 million.[3]

Greece played host to the first festival in the summer of 1985 with Athens as the City of Culture. In the same year, the Council of Culture Ministers passed resolutions setting out the objectives, selection criteria, organisation and finance for the event.[4] Its principal aim was to 'help bring the peoples of Europe closer together', displaying the host city, region and nation to Europe and, through cultural contributions from member states, to show Europe to the city. The ministers also stressed that the event should convey 'wider European cultural affinities' or 'common elements' as well as a 'richness born of diversity'. Responsibility for the organisation and financing of the City of Culture festival rested firmly with host nations, which would also take 'all possible steps' to publicise the event widely. The selection procedure stipulated that one city should be chosen each year and that member states would participate in alphabetical order, although states could alter that sequence by agreement. All existing members would host the event once before another round of festivals was agreed. Cities were to have at least two years' notice of designation to allow for proper planning. Recognising that European culture extended beyond the European Community's borders, it was agreed that other European and even non-European countries could be associated with the preparation of the event.

The initial phase saw each of the twelve member states[5] host the event between 1985–96. The early events made little impact on the European scene. Despite taking place in world-famous cultural centres such as Athens, Florence and Paris, the City of Culture festivals were primarily summer events staged for domestic audiences with little international marketing (Richards, 2001, 160–61). As the festival evolved it became

Table 8.1   European Cities of Culture, 1985–99, with levels of
European Union support

Year	City of Culture	
1985	Athens (Greece)	108 000
1986	Florence (Italy)	136 000
1987	Amsterdam (Netherlands)	137 000
1988	Berlin (Federal Republic of Germany)	200 000
1989	Paris (France)	120 000
1990	Glasgow (United Kingdom)	120 000
1991	Dublin (Ireland)	120 000
1992	Madrid (Spain)	200 000
1993	Antwerp (Belgium)	300 000
1994	Lisbon (Portugal)	400 000
1995	Luxembourg	400 000
1996	Copenhagen (Denmark)	600 000
1997	Thessaloniki (Greece)	400 000
1998	Stockholm (Sweden)	600 000
1999	Weimar (Germany)	600 000
	Total	4 441 000

longer, better planned, and more extensively marketed, particularly
through international tourist agencies. More sophisticated patterns of
financing developed, with a mixture of private and public sources
supplying the increasing funds required. In 1990 the culture ministers
concluded that, due to 'widespread interest' in the City of Culture event
both inside and outside the community, there was a need for an
additional cultural event. The new festival, entitled the 'European
Cultural Month', would be open to European cities outside the
community. This would have a separate identity, but the culture
ministers hoped that collaboration might take place between cities
entertaining the Month of Culture and the full City of Culture festivals.[6]
The first of these months was held in Cracow (Poland) in 1992, with the
title 'Europe in Cracow 1992'.

The second half of the 1980s saw the embryonic festival take shape. With little time to prepare, the Athens festival was handled by the Greek Ministry of Culture through an autonomous office. It concentrated on high culture, bringing in internationally known foreign artists to Greece, with less opportunity to mobilise local participation. That problem was resolved by Florence 1986, where the city authorities mounted a summer festival that highlighted Florentine history. Although running the festival for a longer period, Amsterdam in 1987 concentrated on projecting itself as an art city (Richards, 2001, 160). Berlin's City of Culture festival in 1988 lasted longer than those of its predecessors. Still beleaguered by Cold War divides, the authorities injected around £20 million into the festival to attract visitors, most notably by restoring the 80-year old Hebbel Theatre. Their approach to outreach would be a model for later hosts (most notably Glasgow, then gearing up for the 1990 event). By contrast, the Paris City of Culture festival of 1989, with its budget of under £0.5 million, reversed any progress made. Subsumed into the bicentennial celebrations of the French Revolution, it was 'hardly visible' as a distinct European event (ibid.). It was left to its successor, Glasgow (1990), to place the European City of Culture programme firmly on the map.

The Pivotal Festival

Glasgow 1990 had an impact both on the city and on the long-term development of the festival. There is scarcely a study of modern Glasgow that fails to represent this festival as a landmark in the city's modern history, whereas it passed largely unnoticed in the earlier host cities. Glasgow 1990 changed the scale of the event and showed what could be achieved by a city not usually associated with the arts. It allowed the municipal authorities to confront the city's established image, put Glasgow on the European map, and build venues that would enrich local cultural life when the festival was over. As such, the festival inspired other non-traditional cultural centres such as Antwerp, Thessaloniki, Bergen, Reykjavik, Rotterdam, Porto, Genoa and Lille when their turn came to host the event (Richards, 2001, 162). In particular, Glasgow 1990 shifted the agenda towards urban regeneration, thereby greatly increasing the interest in staging the event in the second round.

As Scotland's largest city and former industrial powerhouse, Glasgow had a different pedigree from earlier hosts. It had suffered severe and sustained deindustrialisation, with the decimation of its heavy industry, based on shipbuilding, locomotive construction and metalworking. It also had a deeply engrained reputation for social violence, bad housing, high unemployment and industrial strife. That image, epitomised by the 1930s novel *No Mean City* (McArthur and Kingsley Long, 1935; see also Gold and Gold, 1995), continued into the postwar period. The city became a byword for high-density working-class housing lacking basic amenities and high levels of social deprivation. Planning strategies that combined comprehensive redevelopment at the centre, where industry was declining, with overspill to peripheral districts or new towns resulted in an environment that was commonly described as 'spatially divisive', 'sterile' and 'soulless' (Booth and Boyle, 1993, 28).

Nevertheless, efforts were already underway in the early 1980s to improve matters. Glasgow pioneered the new era of place marketing in Britain (Ward, 1998, 191). The city's corporation launched a campaign under the slogan 'Glasgow's Miles Better' in 1983, mirroring the 1977 'I love New York' campaign (Gold and Revill, 2004). The campaign started locally in 1983, targeted London in 1984, and was followed by American and European campaigns, with the slogan translated into French, Spanish, Italian and German by 1986 (Ward, 1998, 192). The associated advertising drew attention to Glasgow's continental drinking hours, quality cuisine, weather, fashion, sport and newly cleaned buildings (ibid., 217–18). It also capitalised on the city's existing cultural sector. Although rarely attracting much attention, especially by comparison with Edinburgh, Glasgow was home, *among others*, to the Scottish Opera, the Scottish National Orchestra, the Scottish Ballet, the Scottish Early Music Consort, the Citizen's Theatre, the Hunterian Museum (Scotland's oldest public museum), and the Glasgow School of Art. The 1980s saw major additions to that sector in the shape of the Burrell Collection, which opened in 1983,[7] the Scottish Exhibition and Conference Centre (1985), and the Museum of Transport, which moved to a new building in Kelvingrove in 1988.

The idea of staging major festivals was not new. Glasgow launched its first International Exhibition in May 1888, with three further large-scale, open-air exhibitions in 1901, 1911 and 1938 (Kinchin and Kinchin, n.d.). In 1982, the city had inaugurated a three-week arts festival known as the Mayfest. In 1988 Glasgow staged the National Garden Festival, one of a series of events aimed at regenerating derelict areas in Britain's more depressed urban regions. The opportunity to bid for the European City of Culture event, therefore, fitted into this emerging strategy. As one observer noted (Myerscough, 1988, 177), the festival would:

> present a major opportunity for exploiting the specialist cultural tourism market. This will enable the city to bring itself to the attention of an international public and attract people who are

unfamiliar with the area, for a promotional period lasting a full 12 months.

In 1985, the then Conservative administration invited British cities to bid for the right to stage the City of Culture event in 1990 when it was the United Kingdom's turn to host the festival. Glasgow submitted its bid in April 1986, with eight other cities – Edinburgh, Cardiff, Swansea, Bath, Bristol, Cambridge, Leeds and Liverpool. The Office of Arts and Libraries visited the candidate cities over the summer with a view to announcing the nomination. Glasgow's submission emphasised the city's cultural facilities and institutions, organisational structures, and personalities. It stated four objectives in holding the event: to maintain the momentum of place promotional activities; to provide a 'corporate marketing platform' for the city's artistic activities; 'to utilise and build upon the existing organisational experience and cooperative effort within the city'; and 'to stimulate increased awareness, participation and cultural developments' (cited in Booth and Boyle, 1993, 33). The bid outlined a framework for the 1990 programme including one-off projects, participation by European cultural organisations, and an outreach programme taking Glasgow's culture into Europe.

The British government's Arts Minister, Richard Luce, announced that Glasgow was the winner in October 1986. In making the award, he praised the city for its 'impressive range of cultural activities and excellent facilities', 'an international outlook' and a 'keen desire to expand its European connections' (Glasgow City Council, 1992, 7). Once the culture ministers ratified the nomination in November 1986, the city council established a festival office to take charge of preparations and planning. At the outset, it was decided that the festival would run for a full year. It would start and end with a Hogmanay (New Year's Eve) party, using a definition of culture as 'everything that makes Glasgow what it is'. This included history, design, engineering, education, architecture, shipbuilding, religion and sport, music, dance, visual arts and theatre (Glasgow City Council, 1992, 8). That breadth of definition inevitably made the festival an ambitious undertaking. It incorporated three disparate goals. First, the festival had to meet goals familiar to arts administrators everywhere; namely, to provide an inclusive, relevant, exciting, high quality arts festival that would also, in the longer term, strengthen existing arts organisations and structures. Secondly, the festival had to serve as an effective focus for an exercise in culture-led regeneration. Thirdly, the festival had to meet a 'European' remit, furthering the spirit and purpose of the City of Culture idea while proving that Glasgow was a truly European city.

To complicate things further, the festival's participating funding agencies varied in the emphases that they laid upon these different objectives. Strathclyde Regional Council was keen to foster community-based arts, education and social work in the regional context. Glasgow City Council emphasised urban regeneration, placing the city on display in a positive manner, attracting cultural tourists, and recreating Glasgow as a cultural destination in the longer term. The Scottish Arts Council's interest centred on arts performers and performance while, not surprisingly, the European Community, wanted to promote European culture. These different constituencies guaranteed a wide funding base but, as the director of the festival Robert Palmer commented, it caused 'conflicts and incompatibilities' in organising the event (Jackson and Guest, 1991, 11).

Central government provided very little funding for the festival, with the bulk coming from local government and private investors. Glasgow City Council invested £19.34 million, Strathclyde Regional Council £12.83 million, central government £0.5 million and the European Community contribution a 'symbolic' £80 000. Sponsorship raised £6.46 million (Glasgow City Council, 1992, 31). Provision of new arts facilities, especially in those areas of activity in which Glasgow was traditionally weak, absorbed the largest share of resources (see Myerscough, 1988). The McLellan Galleries provided six interconnecting spaces for arts exhibitions. Refurbishment of the old Transport Museum created the Tramway, a new performance and exhibition space. A new 2500-seater international venue, the Royal Concert Hall, opened during the autumn of 1990. A Museum of Education was opened in the former Scotland Street School, originally designed by Charles Rennie Mackintosh. The Undercroft, comprising renovated spaces in the arches beneath Glasgow Central railway station, contributed exhibition space. The King's Theatre, Theatre Royal and the Citizen's Theatre were refurbished. The Glasgow Film Theatre gained a second auditorium, with improved disabled access. The People's Palace was extended, the Scottish Mask and Puppet Centre moved to new premises, and the Dome of Discovery on the National Garden Festival site was again pressed into service. Finally, 125 buildings were stone-cleaned and 80 buildings floodlit (Glasgow District Council, 1990, 7; Glasgow City Council, 1992, 33).

The promotional campaigns also made calls on resources. Glasgow 1990 differed from later festivals in the series by not having an overarching theme, mirrored perhaps by the strained slogan coined by the advertising agency Saatchi and Saatchi – 'There's a Lot Glasgowing On in 1990'. Replacing the previous 'Glasgow's Miles Better' promotion, the campaign was intended for consumption 'throughout the world' and locally, to raise awareness and encourage participation.

More generally, the campaign sought to underline what the festival could do to increase 'business and arts activity', 'to ensure that increased commercial investment and cultural activity continued beyond 1990', and 'to exploit the social and economic opportunities presented by the year' (Glasgow City Council, 1992, 23). The organisers published a special 'Highlights' brochure including selected events planned for the year, with two million copies distributed throughout the United Kingdom and at British Tourist Authority outlets worldwide. Quarterly information brochures were produced and distributed in the United Kingdom. Ancillary publicity media included advertising on buses and taxis, umbrellas, badges, T-shirts and posters. Particular efforts were made to promote the year's proceedings through the British Tourist Authority's New York office, which would also advertise direct flights to Glasgow airport. The British Travel Centre in London opened a 1990 information desk, a focal point for visitors seeking assistance with travel outside the capital (Glasgow City Council, 1992).

The scale of the event surpassed previous City of Culture festivals. It involved over 700 cultural organisations, 3439 public events, and performers and artists from 23 countries. The festival featured 40 major commissioned works in the performing and visual arts, 60 world premieres, 3979 performances of 656 theatrical productions, 3122 musical performances (2200 of them free), 1091 exhibitions and 157 sporting events (Glasgow City Council, 1992, 4). The festival attracted international participation from, *inter alia* the Bolshoi Opera, Leningrad Symphony Orchestra, Stuttgart Ballet, Cracow Philharmonic, Netherlands Dans Theater, the Moscow Festival Ballet, and theatre companies from Budapest, Leningrad, Japan, Indonesia and Stockholm. Exhibitions included the 'Age of Van Gogh', 'Pissarro', 'Art from Frontline States' featuring artists from southern Africa and central and eastern Europe, the British Art Show, French Contemporary Art and Italian Contemporary Art. 'Scotland Creates' celebrated 5000 years of Scottish art and design.

Yet two major events intended to commemorate Glasgow's history and heritage generated the most heated debate. The first, 'The Ship', celebrated the former importance and loss of shipbuilding on the Clyde through the re-enactment of the construction and launch of a ship. Although popular with the visiting public (it was fully booked and the run was extended), the press criticised the exhibition for being sentimental and superficial (Booth and Boyle, 1993, 39). The other exhibition 'Glasgow's Glasgow', held in the Undercroft, drew inspiration from a similar exhibition ('Berlin, Berlin') held at the 1988 City of Culture festival. Its purpose was to celebrate the people, history and intangible spirit of Glasgow using contemporary approaches towards exhibition design. As an advertisement proclaimed: 'This is not simply an exhibition you walk round and look at – you actually become a living part of it ... emigrate on a boat to Canada; explore a Glasgow tenement, use a periscope in the Great Western Road, meet Lord Kelvin, vote in the Act of Union, race the first ever bicycle' (Glasgow District Council, 1990, n.p.). The exhibition used live performance, audiovisual displays, and sound cones, with over 1500 objects on display. Its heavy costs and the correspondingly high cost of admission, however, drew much criticism. As the single most expensive event in the programme, costing £7 million to stage, its losses of £4.6 million severely dented the festival's profitability (Jackson and Guest, 1991, 83).

Perhaps not surprisingly in light of Glasgow's radical past, the European City of Culture event met with opposition that coalesced into a loosely formed group known as Workers' City. They argued that any celebration of culture in a city with a long industrial history had to tackle the working-class experience. Instead, the city had prioritised the marketing agenda and marginalised representation of Glasgow's working-class roots to cater for middle-class and tourist tastes. Some argued that any community involvement was no more than a token gesture (for example, Boyle and Hughes, 1994, 464–5). Others criticised the festival for misrepresenting the city's working-class heritage, repackaging it 'as some kind of anodyne and quaint survival instead of the result of two centuries struggle – first against the city's uncaring capitalists and then against the city's uncaring Corporation' (Damer, 1990, 211). Community groups resented the absence of press coverage of their events, which 'lacked the glamour of international ones'. Press coverage was interpreted as lending 'dignity and status' to an event, so, by extension, lack of coverage meant emphasising the culture of strangers 'imposed' from above (Glasgow City Council, 1992, 20, 21).

Notwithstanding these criticisms, the impact of the festival was largely positive when measured by the goals initially set (see above). It boosted attendance at theatres, concert halls, museums and galleries, with a total of 6.6 million visitors in 1990 compared to 4.7 million in 1989. Visitor numbers from London and the southeast rose particularly strongly. The organisational experience gained by holding the City of Culture festival contributed to the establishment of a series of new events since 1990, such as the International Jazz Festival, Choral Festival, and Festival of Folk Music and Dance. These have helped to diversify the city's arts base and spread the tourist season. Interpretations of the wider impact of the festival on Glasgow, however, are contested. MacDonald (2000), for example, identified three prevailing schools of thought. The first suggested that the gains from additional employment were short-term and that visitor numbers have subsequently dropped back. To this can be added the impact of devolution, which has attracted key players away from Glasgow to Edinburgh. The second view is that Glasgow 1990 sparked a renaissance in the city's service role, attracting call centres and media design companies, but this process is still not fully embedded. Finally, there is the view that Glasgow fully repositioned itself as a city of culture and has consolidated its approach to culture since 1990. Glasgow staged the 1996 International Design Festival and the 1999 City of Architecture and Design. Investment continues to flow into major projects, such as the opening of the Glasgow Science Centre on the National Garden Festival site, the refurbishment of Tramway, the opening of the Gallery of Modern Art, the rehabilitation of the Centre for Contemporary Art, and opening of the Lighthouse in the former Glasgow Herald Building to house the new Centre for Architecture, Design and the City.

The third view certainly lies closest to the city council's official line, namely, that Glasgow 1990 was part of 'an evolutionary process' and 'a well-managed campaign' by which the city moved from being characterised by having some of Europe's severest social and housing problems in Europe to becoming a City of Culture. The year 1990, therefore, was but one step in this 'line of development' (Glasgow City Council, 1992, 4). While this line may impart a greater seamlessness to policy than is perhaps justified, Glasgow certainly raised the reputation of the City of Culture festival and remains associated with it to a degree rarely matched by other host cities. Giles Havergal of the Citizens' Theatre believed the City of Culture event 'changed irrevocably the reputation of Glasgow as being a place of drunkenness and violence. Now, at the very least, it's a place of drunkenness, violence *and* culture' (quoted in McDonald and Schumacher, 1991, 4). Moreover while the event may well have been more about raising the city's profile than about Glasgow's culture per se, 'it could not have taken place without the indigenous culture of the city' (ibid., 2).

Completing the First Round

Glasgow 1990 was effectively the halfway point of the first round of the European City of Culture programme. The remaining six (see Table 8.1) proceeded in the light of the new agenda. Dublin broke with the pattern adopted before 1991 by which the festival was directly administered by staff within existing government structures.[8] Adopting the theme 'Bring Ireland to Europe and Europe to Ireland', the festival was run by an independent company that arranged the venues and programme.

Nevertheless, the occasion again showed the Irish government's adroitness in employing European funds for development purposes, in particular using Dublin 1991 as an opportunity to regenerate the city's rundown Temple Bar district. Temple Bar was a mixed area of housing and small businesses that was threatened with demolition to make way for a bus depot. Fierce opposition from local residents led to its reprieve and renovation as a cultural quarter in the 1990s. The physical regeneration began with work for the City of Culture festival in 1991, with the Irish government establishing Temple Bar Properties to oversee the renewal of the area (Avery, 2000, 39–40). The European Community funded this 'flagship' scheme as a pilot project. By contrast, the festival itself had much less visibility within the city's arts scene than was the case with Glasgow, a recurrent problem when the City of Culture festival took place in large cities with established traditions in the arts.

The next two festivals illustrated this point. Madrid 1992's budget of 57.9 million made it second only to Glasgow in the history of the festival (Richards, 2001, 163), but its impact was small. This was partly because the City of Culture events failed to stand out against Madrid's existing cultural attractions, but also because the festival was overshadowed by the higher profile events at Seville (Expo 92) and the Barcelona Olympics. Certainly compared with those cities, Madrid undertook little construction work or regeneration apart from renovations to the opera house and some of the museums.[9]

By contrast, Antwerp 1993 followed Glasgow's model more closely. Economic change had reshaped the port, leaving the centre of Antwerp with derelict wharves and warehouses. Regeneration of these and associated housing areas began in 1987 with the 'Stad aan de Stroom' ('City and the River') project, which aimed to give access to the waterfront, revitalise three districts of nineteenth-century housing along the river Scheldt, accommodate existing industry, and create a cultural quarter by making use of the flexible spaces of the redundant warehouses. The Museum of Contemporary Art (MuHKA), a photographic gallery and small galleries had already opened by 1990. Preparations for the City of Culture took this work further. The festival led to a major programme of streetscape improvements, including restoring building facades, redesigning the city's squares, and pedestrianisation projects. The Theatre Royal (the Bourla) and the Central Station were fully restored. It also stimulated the construction of a new Centre for Visual Culture and expansion of the open-air sculpture museum.

The City of Culture festival ran from March to December 1993 on the theme of 'Opting for Art'. This aimed, first, to reflect on the role of art in contemporary society by stimulating a dialogue between international artists and, second, to bring together cultural forms in nine categories – historical exhibitions, performing arts, contemporary visual art, music, architecture and urban planning, film, photography and media art, and literature and applied arts. The emphasis in this ambitious programme was less on the masterpieces that often featured in European City of Culture events, but on ideas and events that might challenge Antwerp's 'cosy provincialism'.[10] The programme, for example, staged two exhibitions that critically examined the city's past. One, 'Antwerp, Story of a Metropolis', confronted the 'myth' of the city through its relationship to art and culture during Antwerp's 'golden age' in the sixteenth and seventeenth centuries, examining particularly how foreigners viewed the city. The other, 'The Panoramic Dream: Antwerp and the World Exhibitions, 1885, 1894, 1930', recalled the atmosphere of the city's three international expositions (see Chapter 4), as well as confronting the social realities of Belgium's colonial activities in the Congo. An architecture and urban development programme, entitled 'Open City', aimed to convey Antwerp's past through a programme of city explorations on foot, bicycle or by minibus. Two major art exhibitions dealt, respectively, with Rubens and Jacob Jordeans. The performing arts and musical programmes, notable for the extent that they included ensembles from other European Union nations, celebrated the historical legacy of Flanders and the multicultural character of contemporary Europe. Various new works were commissioned and performed for the first time. Critical response to Antwerp 1993 suggested that the festival had a discernible impact on the European arts scene – an aspect in which earlier festivals had failed – as well as contributing to urban regeneration and consolidation of the cultural quarter.

Lisbon 1994 followed the increasingly strategic approach to the festival that had emerged in the 1990s. The European City of Culture festival was coupled with Expo 98 as opportunities to renovate and promote the city as a cultural and tourism centre. Both events aimed to deal with the effects on Lisbon of years of neglect under the Salazar regime. Rural–urban migration since the 1950s and the influx of migrants from Portugal's former African colonies in the 1970s had also stimulated the growth of squatter settlements. It was only as the City of Culture festival approached that the Portuguese government and the city authorities finally agreed on a plan to rehouse those living in these areas by the end of the century.[11] The 1992 strategic plan for Lisbon aimed to enhance its role as capital, as a competitive European city, and as an Atlantic city. This included the goals of improving its environment and cultural heritage in the face of loss of character and 'deculturisation' (Alden and da Rosa Pires, 1996, 32). Seen against this background, the

Expo 98 site involved large-scale clearance of land along the Tagus river on the eastern side of the city (see also Chapter 5). The more modest work for the European City of Culture festival comprised improving facilities in the central area, with refurbishment of the museums and the main concert hall (the Coliseum). Elsewhere, smaller projects sought to renovate the redundant port district and create a cultural quarter in the Seventh Hill.

Problems over finance hampered preparations for the City of Culture festival, particularly due to conflicts between Lisbon's socialist mayor and the conservative central government. Indeed, the delay in finalising the funding for the arts themselves led to the cancellation of two events.[12] Nevertheless, the festival opened in March as planned. The advance publicity for the festival promised that like the Celts, Romans, Visigoths and Moors who came in search of Portugal's treasures, so the visitor in 1994 would be met 'by the spectacle of exhibitions, shows and artistic events. They will be captivated by the ever changing architecture, classical, cheek-by-jowl with the post-modern ... But that's no surprise in a country with centuries of experience in entertaining the odd visitor.'[13]

The programme recognised this temporal dimension, beginning in March with traditional works and progressing to contemporary works as the festival proceeded. In May, an exhibition opened based around 'The Temptations of St Anthony', which fused old and new together by showing how Hieronymus Bosch's famous painting had influenced surrealist art. In September, 'The Day After Tomorrow' combined the work of contemporary Portuguese and international artists. The organisers showcased local culture, particularly the distinctive fado music, with concerts, books, recordings and an exhibition explaining its origins.[14] An exhibition of Angolan art, a pointed reminder of Portugal's colonial past, was one of the largest ever staged. The European dimension focused on film, opera and classical music. The one hundred-day film festival, not surprisingly showed Europe's hundred best films. Visiting European orchestras performed at major concerts, including the London Symphony Orchestra playing at the opening ceremony. While local critics claimed that this reliance on visiting virtuosi indicated the weakness of the city's cultural base, it did allow the festival to achieve something of the European Union's aims of introducing artists and works from around Europe to a new audience.[15]

Luxembourg 1995 broke new ground in two respects, largely through necessity. First, given that the Grand Duchy is wedged between two great cultures, had many resident non-nationals and was trilingual, the organisers wanted to assert the need for exchange and understanding as ways of countering the threat posed by rising tides of nationalism within

Europe. This fundamental concept of dialogue was mirrored in the wording of the festival's title 'Luxembourg European City of All Cultures' (Myerscough, 2003). Secondly, since Luxembourg had barely 400 000 inhabitants, the government decided to include other centres in the festival besides Luxembourg City. This too was reflected in the nomenclature, calling the festival the 'European Grand Duchy of Culture 1995'.

The festival had few wider regenerative objectives, but aimed to boost the role of Luxembourg as a cultural as well as a financial centre. This required expansion of available venues, particularly exhibition and gallery spaces. The Casino Luxembourg, for example, was converted from a club into a temporary exhibition centre for contemporary art. These developments, with booking and performance fees, made most calls on the budget of 875 million francs. This came partly from sponsorship (150 million) and receipts (100 million), with the government and the city of Luxembourg sharing the remaining 625 million francs equally (Dueppengiesser, 1995). Following Glasgow's model of a full-year festival, Luxembourg 1995 comprised around 500 performance events designed to 'reflect the cultural variety of Luxembourg', with a further 300 exhibitions organised throughout the year. Most were free, but the 19 paying exhibitions could be visited using a combined 'Euro-pass' ticket. Luxembourg also successfully linked the festival to the conference circuit, entertaining two conference cycles under the headline 'Sciences 95' (ibid.).

Perhaps the key long-term impact of the festival was its boost to the creation of cultural infrastructure. Coming hard on the heels of UNESCO's designation of the historic core of Luxembourg City as a World Heritage Site in December 1994, the festival directly stimulated the growth in museums and performance venues. While the opening of the Museum of the History of the City of Luxembourg, which occurred in 1996, was planned before the City of Culture festival took place, Luxembourg 1995 encouraged the inception of a new cluster of developments in the early twenty-first century. These included the National Museum of Natural History, Museum of the Fortress, and the Museum of Modern Art Grand-Duc (which opened in 2002), with the new Philharmonic Concert Hall opening in 2004. Each development was intended to capitalise on the linkage between the arts and cultural tourism. As Myerscough (2003) observed:

> Because of the small size of the city, the symbiosis of the historical aspect and the artistic aspect of culture will be near perfect: the new buildings set to accommodate manifestations of culture are erected on historic sites, whilst buildings that constitute an important part of the national cultural heritage will come to house new cultural

institutions. Cultural heritage and cultural life will be closely linked and continuously flow into one another. This new cultural dynamic will heighten the attractiveness of the city for its inhabitants as well as improve the 'international image of Luxembourg'. Ideally, the city will project an image of itself in the first place as cultural.

Image change, as much as urban regeneration, lay at the heart of the strategy for Copenhagen 1996, the last of the first round of festivals. For most commentators anticipating the event,[16] Copenhagen was a sleepy, 'provincial' capital, with quality, heavily subsidised cultural institutions that effectively served a mainly domestic audience. Few enjoyed international repute and most lacked the capacity to contain the visitor numbers that the festival would be expected to generate. Copenhagen's centre had experienced similar problems of physical and economic decline as those found in other European cities, although on a smaller scale. The loss of people living and working in the centre, partly encouraged by official policies, had increased the ratio of low-income groups in the city and weakening of the city's revenue base.[17] More specifically, the waterfront area of the old town and a redundant naval base in the south of the city needed regeneration. The election in 1989 of a council committed to addressing the city's problems actively paved the way for a new urban strategy.[18] Planners initiated three major projects: the regeneration of the waterfront area; the Oresund road and rail link connecting Copenhagen to Malmo (Sweden), begun in 1995 and completed in July 2000; and the new town of Orestad, a linear settlement that incorporated the redundant naval base. Orestad housed the Bella Centre conference and exhibition complex by 1996, with subsequent developments including Schools of Film, Architecture, Theatre, and Music.[19]

These developments contributed to the culture-based urban revitalisation programme that embraced the European City of Culture festival. The stated aim was to 'invigorate the city's innate qualities in the direction of an up-to-date and ideally balanced city culture that cares for the environment as well as for people' (cited in Engelstoft and Jorgesen, 1997, 232). Initial funding of £99.7 million was raised equally from central government, the city of Copenhagen and the 42 local authorities in the Greater Copenhagen area, with the residue from private sources and sponsorship. This was for capital projects (especially refurbishing important buildings and two of the city's central squares), establishing art activities, subsidising cultural events, and promoting Copenhagen 1996 through an international advertising campaign. Larger projects included construction of a new Museum of Modern Art (the Arken) in the south of the city and a new municipal concert hall on the waterfront, with extensions to the National Museum of Art and the Ny Carlsberg Glyptothel art gallery.

The City of Culture programme aimed to combine an international arts festival that would widen the experience of local audiences and attract foreign visitors, with events that involved and catered for local people. The programme comprised three 'seasons' each with its own theme. Spring concentrated on the historical city; summer on the global arts, featuring various series of international festivals, dialogues and environmental initiatives; and autumn on 'looking towards the future' with an emphasis on new technologies, contemporary music, experimental theatre and programmes for children.[20] It involved 50 000 residents, 700 organisations and almost 600 projects, with contributions from 500 contemporary visual artists and more than 200 international performing arts ensembles in the fields of theatre, opera, dance and ballet.[21] Its major exhibitions included 'Copenhagen: Gateway to Europe', which explored Copenhagen's dual role as centre for Danish identity and as a European city over the past 500 years, and 'Nordic Masterpieces' at the National Museum of Art. The Arken staged exhibitions by Emil Nolde, the Danish surrealist painter, and Per Kirkeby, a contemporary artist, that attracted 274 000 visitors in their first nine months.[22] Special events built on Copenhagen's reputation as a centre for dance, with a ballet season that featured the Kirov Ballet, the Royal Ballet from London, Ballet Nationale de Marseille-Roland Petit, Maurice Bejart Ballet Lausanne and the Royal Danish Ballet.

Copenhagen 1996 was one of the largest events attempted in the first round of European Cities of Culture festivals. Its size and complexity of programme was such that its director Trevor Davies admitted in advance that he and his staff did not have a complete picture of it. Nevertheless, the festival was credited with a positive impact on a variety of fronts.[23] It galvanised provision for the city's arts by giving a target date that injected a deadline into construction works. It led to works that enhanced the environment for tourists and the conference trade. It supplied an opportunity to promote Copenhagen to an international audience, after what was locally regarded as a long period of stagnation. Similarly, the Danish public's image of their capital city was thought to have improved, helping to encourage a slow increase in the population returning to the central city after years of decline.

Second Round

Copenhagen 1996 completed the first round of the European City of Culture programme. Discussions had taken place throughout the early 1990s as to what should happen next, given that much had changed within the European Community, now the European Union, following the Treaty of European Union of 1992 (the Maastricht Treaty). The treaty itself showed that culture had moved up the political agenda. Article 128, rewritten as Article 155 in the Treaty of Amsterdam (1997), articulated the thinking on cultural action as it had evolved since the mid-1980s. Three of its five paragraphs had particular relevance to the City of Culture programme. Paragraph 1 of article 128 (155) committed the community to contribute to 'the flowering of the cultures of Member States, while respecting their national and regional diversity and at the same time bringing the common cultural heritage to the fore'. Paragraph 2 encouraged cooperation between member states with the community 'supporting and supplementing' national action in four areas: 'the knowledge and dissemination of the culture and history of the European peoples'; heritage of European significance; non-commercial cultural exchanges; and artistic and literary creation. Paragraph 3 championed cooperation between the member states and third countries and international organisations such as the Council of Europe. This recognised that European culture did not stop at the borders of the European Union and that culture was increasingly important in relations with non-member states in western, central and eastern Europe.[24] The Maastricht Treaty firmly left member states with responsibility for cultural action. The procedure of co-decision-making between the European Parliament and the European Council applied in the area of culture, but the treaty specifically ruled out harmonisation of cultural laws between member states. It also required unanimity in the Council of Ministers on any proposed measures. Article 128 (155) therefore balanced the interests of those states wanting to allow wider community action in the cultural sphere with those wanting to set limits for cultural action (Forrest, 1994, 17).

The European City of Culture event fitted easily into the newly emerging cultural programmes of the European Union. In 1996 it was incorporated into the new Kaleidoscope programme for the support of artistic and cultural initiatives. This provided funding for the City of Culture programme until 1999. The means of designating the Cities of Culture, however, changed after 1996. Between 1990–92, the European Union agreed a new set of criteria and procedures. Unlike the first round, there was no longer a fixed order in which member states nominated cities for the festival. Instead, any European state could nominate a city, as long as it met with the basic requirements of democracy, pluralism and the rule of law. The Council of Ministers acting unanimously would now designate the City of Culture for a particular year from the list of cities submitted to it. The event would alternate between European Union and other European cities 'without this being a hard and fast rule'. As was already the custom with other international festivals, most notably the Olympic Games, host cities were not to be from the same geographical area in consecutive years. Nominations would balance capital cities and provincial cities. An important innovation comprised the possibility of designating a pair of cities for a particular year. Finally, cities should submit a dossier in support of their application so that the council could judge the state of preparedness and the plans of the city concerned.[25] The Council of Ministers designated the first city in 1992 for the 1997 festival. Their 1993 meeting dealt with applications and designations for the 1998 and 1999 events, with the cities for the years 2000 and 2001 designated in 1995.

The end-product of these deliberations saw the second round of festivals begin with Thessaloniki (Salonica) in 1997[26] and the festival returning to Greece. The contrasts with Athens twelve years previously were striking. Thessaloniki had four years to prepare for the event rather than a matter of months, with a budget of 295 million as opposed to Athens 7.7 million (Richards, 2001, 163). Its physical planning ambitions were also markedly different. The city already had a planning programme that aimed to control expansion of the metropolitan area, remodel the city, draw attention to its architectural heritage, and enhance the city's cultural facilities (Lebesque, 1997). The authorities instituted three architectural competitions for Thessaloniki 1997. These concerned, respectively, the ecological re-establishment and urban reintegration of the city's neglected suburbs, revitalisation of Thessaloniki's symbolic axis,[27] and revitalising the city's long seafront. This last project included 'provoking urban episodes on the coast', where eight international architects were invited to design a pier and pavilion that would punctuate the long waterfront extending eastward from the port and the old city to the airport.[28]

The goals for the festival perforce balanced the city's cultural heterogeneity. While seeking to place Thessaloniki on the national and international cultural map, the organisers also wanted to increase the local communities' engagement with the arts, emphasise the Orthodox faith, and make connections with the influence of Hellenism outside Greece, while making the event available to all through education. To help address these aims, the Greek Ministry for the Environment, Physical Planning and Public Works specifically allocated $25 million towards a programme of works related to the European City of Culture festival. This would provide for new and refurbished venues and museums and create an urban environment that might be attractive to visitors. Some key projects were completed in time, but there was a gap between the official rhetoric and what happened on the ground. As the journalist Clio Mirchell notes: 'Absent, though, are the dozens of gleaming new and renovated buildings and infrastructural projects which were announced as part of the cultural capital programme'.[29] Others reported buildings obscured by scaffolding,[30] but the incoming artistic director of the festival, the fourth to fill the post, was unfazed. Drawing comparisons with Glasgow, he argued that the project would last longer than a year. The festival would stimulate the construction of museums of photography, contemporary art, cinema and a new theatre that, he argued, would increase interest in culture and boost the city's image and self-confidence.[31]

The range and depth of the festival also contrasted with its Athenian predecessor. The exhibition programme included Caraveggio's paintings, Michelangelo drawings, and Goya engravings, with more contemporary art represented by Hans and Sophie Tauber Arp, Joseph Beuys, Loukas Samaras and Derek Jarman. The centrepiece was the 'Treasures of Mount Athos' held in the new Museum of Byzantine Culture (June–December), which displayed inaccessible items of international significance. Other exhibitions featured Alexander the Great's impact on European and oriental art, and 'From the Ends of the Earth', a programme of events and exhibitions exploring the world of diaspora Greeks – partly in the hope that Greek artists abroad would return to participate in the activities. The musical programme brought great European performers (Rostropovich, Yehudi Menuhin, Riccardo Mutti, La Scala Orchestra) to Thessaloniki 1997, as well as the St Petersburg Ballet. The theatre and opera season premiered a new opera, 'Antigone' by Mikis Theodorakis, as well as the first modern revival of a twelfth-century Byzantine play 'The Passion of Christ'.

Thessaloniki 1997 represented a major undertaking for a smaller European city. Despite not all the planned 311 projects being completed for the City of Culture event, the Committee of the Regions complimented it as an inspiring case of a provincial city 'flying the flag of European culture ... making it a benchmark for future events'.[32] Its successor, Stockholm 1998, represented another form of landmark in that when selected it was the first city from outside the community (given that Sweden did not join the European Union until 1995). The festival's main aim, at least as presented to Swedish politicians during the lobbying campaign, was to improve the long-term position and accessibility of culture in Stockholm and in Sweden generally, as well as to stimulate Stockholm's cultural contacts with the rest of Europe (Pipan and Porsander, 2000). By contrast, there were no major regeneration schemes or construction of new facilities necessary, given that the city already had 55 museums (including a new modern art museum) and 70 theatres, including the Royal Opera House. The festival itself offered more than 500 events, including an ice pavilion constructed in time for the opening ceremony. The event was organised by a committee, Stockholm '98, which was established in May 1994. At inception, it had seven staff, which grew to 100 as the project matured. It was, in turn, wound up at the completion of the production cycle in April 1999, once the post-festival arrangements were accomplished.

Weimar 1999 saw the festival return to Germany. Weimar in Thuringia, however, contrasted markedly with Berlin, its predecessor. Weimar's population of just over 60 000 made it the smallest city ever to mount the City of Culture festival, although few other European cities had stronger cultural resonances. Historically, the patronage of the Dukes of Saxe-Weimar had brought Goethe, Schiller, von Herder and Liszt to work in the city. Wagner stayed with Liszt during his troubles with the authorities and before fleeing to Switzerland. He premiered his opera 'Lohengrin' in Weimar. The historical legacy of the city's built environment and contribution to the arts had led to it being classified as a World Heritage Site by UNESCO in 1998. The commendation described it as 'the cultural centre of Europe of the day' (UNESCO, 2003). In the twentieth century the name of Weimar gained new associations. It lent its name to the failed democratic interlude between the collapse of the German Reich and the rise of Nazism, and was home to the Bauhaus. The infamous concentration camp of Buchenwald was built in the forest to the north of Weimar. Finally, as a town from the former German Democratic Republic (GDR), the selection of the city posed significant challenges as well as symbolic references.

In part war damage remained but, like many towns in the former GDR, lack of investment in the urban fabric and the economic impact of German unification, with the resultant factory closures, had taken its toll on Weimar. Redeveloping the city as a cultural tourism centre was highly attractive, but would require heavy investment. Not surprisingly, therefore, the motive of leveraging funds initially sparked the idea of bidding to host the European City of Culture. The original suggestion came from the GDR's last Minister of Culture and was taken up by the first post-Communist mayor Klaus Büttner, who used his contacts in the west to bring the bid to a successful conclusion.[33] The initial thought was to apply to host the event in 1997, given that the European Union had opened up the bidding with no fixed rotation of member states in mind, but the target soon changed to 1999. This marked the two hundred and fiftieth anniversary of Goethe's birth, the eightieth anniversary of the founding of both the Weimar Republic and the Bauhaus, the fiftieth anniversary of the establishment of the Federal and Democratic Republics of Germany, and the tenth anniversary of the fall of the Berlin Wall – a date, then, that truly had something to offer all interested parties. Although Nuremberg was also interested in staging the festival when it next came to Germany, the government backed the Weimar proposal. The bid was submitted to the Council of Ministers and the city was awarded the title in 1993 (Roth and Frank, 2000, 223, 236, 238).

From the outset, it was recognised that the financial burden of mounting a prestigious international event was too great for Weimar. Indeed, given that the city was effectively bankrupt in 1995 with a debt that stood at £2000 per head of the population,[34] the state of Thuringia and the federal government shouldered the full costs. In fact the latter virtually had to double its initial stake of 16 billion Deutschmarks in 1998 to keep the enterprise afloat (Roth and Frank, 2000, 238). With the change of funding came a shift in the conception of the festival. Rather than having an inclusive notion of culture and seeking local participation, the festival's programme soon switched to one with a high culture agenda that relied on imported virtuosi. This was seen as necessary to attract the international visitors who were vital for the project to prove financially viable and was reinforced by the appointment of a festival director sympathetic to that style of festival (ibid., 232).

The Cultural Capital festival took as its title 'Weimar 1999 – Culture City of Europe, Inc', with a logo that suggested a bag packed for a journey. As the press release (translated in Theile, 2003, 322) put it:

> The package can have as many addresses as this town's history and its hopes provide. It stands for receiving and for sending; it can remain unopened and be left standing. Its contents are no cheap commercial wares, never ready to wear, always different, they can cause a fright, seduce, give joy, or prompt introspection. Its colours and labels change and it is suitable for shipping any sort of goods.

The festival adopted the slogan 'Remind, Visualize and Project', with five sub-themes that encapsulated these ideas: Goethe, Weimar in Europe, the Difficulties of Memories, Ten Years Later, and the New Millennium. The programme comprised over 300 events, with prominence given to the works of those authors and musicians associated with the town. These included Goethe, Schiller, Liszt, Johann Sebastian Bach, Berlioz, Wagner, Richard Strauss, Nietzsche (who died in Weimar) and members of the Bauhaus, such as Gropius, Kandinsky and Klee. The work of other European artists with anniversaries that year, such as Pushkin (born 1799) and Racine (who died in 1699), were also acknowledged. A season of world theatre, the visits of international orchestras and ballet companies, a festival of young filmmakers, and street theatre were also planned. A scheme to build coloured concrete steles by French concept artist Daniel Buren in the Rollplatz, however, met with such ferocious opposition that the project was abandoned (Roth and Frank, 2000, 234–5). The theme of remembrance confronted the stark contrast between the classical age of Weimar and the violence of the Holocaust, as embodied by Buchenwald. Between 1995–9, the former concentration camp opened a series of permanent exhibitions and, at the start of the City of Culture festival, a 'symbolic' path (*Zeitschneise*) was opened connecting Ettersberg Castle in Weimar with the camp. Its route followed an eighteenth-century hunting road and had been used as an orientation line when the camp was constructed.[35]

Conclusion

The final European City of Culture festival of the twentieth century revealed the progress made in 15 years. Athens 1985 was little more than an expression of a broader European initiative, intended to give a gentle start towards developing a community approach to culture. By 1999, the festival had more ambitious aims. The key to its apparent success, like the other major festivals considered in this text, lay in its flexibility. In many ways, it was entirely appropriate for the Weimar organisers to conceive of their festival as a package that could be wrapped and unwrapped in various ways. The permissive rules for the festival had always allowed host cities and their governments to reshape it, almost at will, to fit their agendas. The City of Culture programme had visited small and large cities, offering a vehicle for urban improvement, for encouraging cultural tourists, for altering a city's image, or reaffirming its status among the cultural elite. Research in Weimar (Roth and Frank, 2000, 228–9) showed that local residents generally supported the festival and the environmental improvements that it had brought, especially the restoration of the town's historic fabric. As one observed: 'More than 50 years of neglect are being dealt with in just a few years'.[36] A new Bauhaus museum was opened on the central Theaterplatz in 1995 and in January 1999 the Goethe Museum reopened after being remodelled and redesigned. Nevertheless, residents saw these developments as aimed at tourists rather than benefiting them directly. The proof of its long-term value would only come if these developments helped create a new future for the town.

Weimar 1999, however, was the last time the event would be hosted by a single city for some years. During the 1990s, considerable thought had been expended on diversifying the programme, to allowing more than one city to act as a cultural capital in any given year, and to the special festivals that would be necessary as part of the celebrations of the Millennium. Indeed, these points came together in 2000 when there were no less than nine European Cities of Culture. The next chapter examines the thinking behind that decision, as well as the staging of other forms of international festival in that year.

Notes

1   Quoted by Lisle (1998, 32) from a lecture given by Brian Eno at Sadlers Wells (London) entitled 'Perfume, Defence and David Bowie's Wedding'.
2   These meetings were finally put on a formal footing in June 1984.
3   The value of an ecu ('European currency unit', now known as a 'Euro') to other currencies has varied, but as a rough guide is here taken at £1 = 1.5.
4   *Official Journal*, C153, 22 June 1985, 2.
5   This included Spain and Portugal, who joined in 1986.
6   *Official Journal*, C162/1, 18 May 1990. The title was perhaps misleading in that while it was intended to be a smaller affair, it did not need to be confined to a month. We do not consider the Month of Culture in detail in this text.
7   A new gallery in Pollock Park that housed one of Scotland's greatest private collections. The paintings had been bequeathed to the city in the 1940s.
8   With the exception of Amsterdam 1987, which was administered jointly by an independent promoting company, Holland Festival, and the Netherlands Institute.
9   P. Bruce, 'Revels for a state without a creed', *Financial Times*, 4–5 January 1992.
10 *Antwerp 93 Bulletin*, March–July 1993, n.p.; *Antwerp 93 Bulletin*, July–December 1993, 3.
11 Anon., 'Dreams of leaving Lisbon's slums', *Financial Times*, 15 May 1994.
12 One was a production of *Carmen*, the other an exhibition by the London-based Portuguese contemporary artist Paula Ergo.
13 *Financial Times*, 3 February 1994.
14 Essentially a sentimental popular song form associated with Lisbon; a mix of nostalgia and regret typifies fado songs.
15 Anon., 'Lisbon takes up the laurels', *Financial Times*, 5–6 March 1994.
16 H. Barnes, 'Renaissance takes shape', *Financial Times*, 6 November 1995.
17 H. Barnes, 'Rents remain low', *Financial Times*, 6 November 1995.
18 H. Barnes, 'Shaping the city's future', *Financial Times*, 6 November 1995.
19 M. Hoyle, 'Danes take on Europe', *Financial Times*, 30–31 December 1995; see also http://www.orestad.cc/orestad_eng.html
20 *Europ News*, 5 (1), Spring 1996, 12.
21 H. Barnes, 'Embracing a rich cultural agenda', *Financial Times*, 6 November 1995.
22 See http://www.arken.dk
23 H. Barnes, 'Embracing a rich cultural agenda', *Financial Times*, 6 November 1995.
24 The collapse of Communism had opened up the possibility of enlargement with neutral countries such as Sweden, Finland and Austria, as well as association agreements with the countries of central and eastern Europe.
25 *Official Journal*, C151/1, 16 June 1992; C336/3, 19 December 1992.
26 This was selected in 1992 before the new rules were formulated, whereas the two remaining festivals in the twentieth century, Stockholm (1998) and Weimar (1999), were selected on the new system.

27 Between Aritotelous Square, which opened on to the sea in the social and commercial heart of the old city, and the Platia Dhikastirion, site of the Roman agora.

28 The architects were Aldo and Hannie van Eyck, Finn Geipel, Mario Botta, Alvaro Siza, Coop Himmelbau, Enric Miralles, Rem Koolhaas and Giancarlo De Carlo.

29 C. Mirchell, 'Thessaloniki 1997', *The European Magazine*, 20–27 March 1997, 15.

30 M. Clow, *Independent on Sunday Magazine*, October 1997, 16.

31 Ibid., 19.

32 'Opinion of the Committee of the Regions', 13 March 1998, COM(7)549 final – 97/0290COD.

33 S. Crawshaw, 'Goethe's city rushes to rebuild a broken heritage', *Financial Times*, 22 June 1995. In passing, it is worth noting that Büttner's working methods and grand projects did not endear him to the voters, who believed that ordinary citizens were failing to benefit from council policies. He was replaced as mayor in 1994.

34 S. Crawshaw, 'Goethe – or garbage removal', *Financial Times*, 22 June 1995.

35 The Holocaust was also the subject of a summer school held in Weimar as part of the City of Culture festival. See the Buchenwald website at http://www.emins.org

36 S. Crawshaw, 'Goethe's city rushes to rebuild a broken heritage', *Financial Times*, 22 June 1995.

CHAPTER NINE

The Millennium and After

> The [British] government is hard at work
> imbuing a sense of patriotism into the campaign
> to bring the 2012 Olympics to London. The
> same misplaced Blairite machismo that gave us
> the Millennium Dome is now trying to land us
> with a 16-day logistical nightmare in a city that
> cannot move its population even on a day-to-day
> basis and has no plans to start trying.
>
> Matthew Engel[1]

Few dates in human history have aroused more eager anticipation than the year AD 2000. As the Millennium approached, nations around the world appointed committees, commissions, offices and foundations to take charge of matters and make proposals about appropriate ways to celebrate this auspicious event. There was effectively no precedent on which they could draw. In AD 1000, the only parallel, there was little sense of the beginning of a new era. Indeed it was not until the sixteenth century that stories began to circulate about the apprehension, even terror, apparently felt by tenth-century society about the dawn of the second millennium and the imminence of the apocalypse (Briggs and Snowman, 1996, 3). By the 1990s, however, ideas about chronology and its significance in human history had changed dramatically. The dawn of the third millennium, with the additional 'historical, religious and anthropological freight' that the word 'millennium' now carried (ibid., 1), made this a historical milestone. It positively demanded appropriate recognition.

Understandably, much thought went into commemorating the precise moment at which the second millennium after Christ's birth tipped into the third. For many American cities, the familiar boosterist agenda re-emerged. Parties celebrating New Year's Eve, or perhaps New Millennium's Eve, had to be bigger and better than those offered by rivals. Washington DC, keen for once to outshine the traditional festivities in New York's Times Square, screened an 18-minute collage of panoramic images by Steven Spielberg to an estimated 300 000 spectators. Flashes of light progressively rose to the top of the 555-feet (169-metre) Washington Monument to count down the final seconds of

246

1999.[2] San Francisco spent $3 million on a celebration centred on the Golden Gate Bridge, featuring fireworks and fountains of water. In southern California, an estimated 100 000 people attended the $12 million Millennium Show at Los Angeles' Memorial Coliseum and Sports Arena. This comprised a street festival, a 90-minute audiovisual display leading up to midnight and culminating in fireworks and lasers.

Around the world, matters proceeded in much the same vein. A twelve-hour New Year's Eve party at the Pyramids of Giza featured a concert by Jean Michel Jarre, concluding with fireworks and the addition of a 30-feet (9-metre) cap to the Great Pyramid to restore it to its original height. Sydney employed its distinctive Harbour Bridge as the centrepiece for a lavish firework display. The same logic of turning internationally known landmarks into focal points for firework displays appealed to the Parisian authorities, who mounted a spectacular show centred on the Eiffel Tower. An hour later, following the unfolding of the world's time zones, it was London's turn to offer fireworks, with a display that supposedly concluded with a 'wall of fire' moving upstream along the river Thames at the same speed as the earth's rotation.[3] Further north in Scotland, Edinburgh's city council assimilated the Millennium celebrations into its seventh annual Hogmanay festivities; closing the city centre to traffic and mounting a huge street party with music, entertainments and a massive firework display on the Castle Mound.

Yet even if the Christian dimension of the occasion remained surprisingly muted given what the date commemorated, the deeper significance of the Millennium called for more lasting reminders than transitory pyrotechnics and street parties. Three strategies readily occurred to those charged with finding suitable forms of commemoration. The first was to bury time capsules – sealed receptacles that contained suitably chosen, durable artefacts to convey a sense of the present to people in the far future.[4] Most were modest affairs, prepared and packed by local community, schools or voluntary associations. Others had altogether grander ambitions. A stainless steel version designed by Santiago Calatrava, for example, went on permanent display outside the American Museum of Natural History in Manhattan (New York). The flower-like capsule, contained in a 1.5-metre high structure and mounted on a granite plinth, was to be sealed until the year AD 3000. Its contents included 27 hair samples, selected books, a transcript of Martin Luther King's 'I have a dream' speech, a pack of Post-It sticky notes, and an issue of *Business Week* (RIBA, 2001).

The second strategy for celebrating the Millennium was to construct memorials. The late 1990s saw the publication of a rich assortment of schemes for spectacular arches, pyramids, towers, spires and domes. Most were exercises in fantasy and, sometimes, whimsy. Atlanta, for example, entertained a proposal for a 721-feet (220-metre) steel 'Leap of Faith' monument. This would have resembled a letter 'A' with the top truncated and replaced by the silhouette of a person jumping. Paris, spurred by its inherent competition with London, toyed with ideas for a Millennium Ferris wheel that would be larger, 'if only by a metre', than that planned for London. Other ideas included placing a giant luminous egg under the Eiffel Tower and building a 650-feet (210-metre) wooden tower (the Tour de la Terre) alongside the Seine in the city's eastern district at a cost of £25 million (Hanna, 1999, 120–1). Alexandria (Egypt) entertained the prospect of Pierre Cardin's planned rebuilding of the lighthouse that was one of the Seven Wonders of the classical world. Wellington (New Zealand) considered excavating a cavernous time vault crowned either by a pyramid or a 90-feet (28-metre) statue of a Golden Girl (ibid.).

Predictably none of these schemes materialised, but those allying memorialisation with something approaching need enjoyed greater success. Dublin filled the site in O'Connell Street once occupied by the 134-feet (43-metre) Nelson's Pillar with a tapering minimalist 393-feet (120-metre) stainless steel spire.[5] Properly known as the 'Spire of Dublin' but locally nicknamed the 'Spike' and the 'Stiletto in the Ghetto', this delayed Millennium project was completed in early 2003. Boston (Massachusetts) harnessed a message that was both environmentalist and historical in its Boston 2000 project by planting a commemorative tree on the site of the original Liberty Tree and building a new park along the Charles River (Hanna, 1999, 237). The United Kingdom offered perhaps the most comprehensive programme. Working with local authorities and making use of funding from the National Lottery and private sponsorship, projects proliferated throughout the country, particularly in London. A mile-long strip alongside the river Thames, for example, saw the construction of the Millennium Bridge (a new foot-crossing south of St Paul's Cathedral), renovation of the former Bankside power station to house the Tate Gallery of Modern Art, and the installation of the world's largest Ferris wheel, the 500-feet (135-metre) high 'London Eye'.

The third strategy for reflective commemoration of the Millennium, as for so many previous anniversaries, was to arrange festivals. They came in all shapes and sizes and varied in duration from several days to year-long events. Some were ad hoc events, conceived specifically for the Millennium celebrations. Of these, none was more spectacular in its venue or ambition than the 'Millennium Experience' held at Greenwich in southeast London (see below). Others took advantage of recurrent events. The year AD 2000 would see examples of all three major festivals considered here, with a BIE-approved international exposition at Hanover (Germany), a summer Olympics at Sydney (Australia), and an extraordinary nine-city version of the European Cities of Culture programme. Each could easily be rebranded as a 'Millennium event' and made to take advantage of the reflective nature of the time.

Expo 2000

The Millennium Exposition at Hanover in Lower Saxony (Germany) was a case in point. The organisers of Expo 2000 positively oozed *fin-de-siècle* environmental consciousness, making direct reference to the principles of Local Agenda 21 from the 1992 Rio 'Earth Summit' in their approach to staging the exposition. Expo 2000 took advantage of an existing trade fairground. Its new buildings would be designed to the highest environmental standards and reuse after the festival in line with the long-term interests of the city and its region was paramount. This theme was both topical and politically expedient, in that German unification took place during the period of the festival's production cycle. The exposition's title, 'Humankind–Nature–Technology', and sober environmental message were appropriate to the newly unified German republic, stressing its sense of responsibility and lack of connection with its historic predecessor. It was perhaps ironic that this festival should produce one of the largest budgetary deficits in exposition history.

The project started in the late 1980s, with Hanover, Toronto and Venice seeking to earmark the date for an exposition as early as 1988 (Findling and Pelle, 1990, 410). With Venice having dropped out, the general meeting of the BIE on 14 June 1990 voted in favour of Hanover by one vote. Expo 2000 at Hanover was unusual in that it was only the sixth exposition – after Paris (1937), Brussels (1958), Montreal (1967), Osaka (1970) and Seville (1992) – to receive the coveted imprimatur of the BIE's 'universal exhibition' status. It was, however, held at a time when the international exposition's standing was steadily sinking. For example, the US federal government, so long a bastion of support for international expositions, had decided not to support official pavilions at such events after Seville (see also Chapter 5). There were also profound doubts about the continuing purpose of expositions. Their mid-nineteenth century function of codifying and classifying knowledge about industrial processes and products had long faded. The days of imperial nations showing colonial conquest, ethnographic exhibits of 'inferior peoples', and Cold War displays of ideological rivalries had also passed. The message of science-as-progress, especially in its more utopian manifestations, holds little credibility to a world suffering the environmental consequences of industrialisation.

The city of Hanover and its region, however, had good reason to look to the perceived benefits of international expositions to stimulate the local economy. It had an industrial structure dominated by traditional manufacturing, with a higher unemployment rate and smaller proportion of business services than elsewhere in Germany. From the outset, the exposition proposal carried hopes for structural change and much-needed modernisation of infrastructure, as well as an attempt to develop the town's future potential for cultural tourism. The initial ideas for an exposition on 'Man, Nature, Technology' came from the supervisory board of the Deutsche Messe und Ausstellungs AG (German Trade Fair and Exhibition Company), the body that had run Hanover's trade fair and conference centre since 1947. The board, which included Lower Saxony's minister of finance and the mayor of Hanover, persuaded the federal government to make the application to the BIE. No attempt was made during the preparatory stage to involve the local population in the bid, nor to situate it in a 'well-thought-out city marketing concept conceived for the long-term' (Krantz and Schätzl, 2000, 485). A local referendum in June 1992 narrowly approved the proposal by 51.5 to 48.4 per cent.

The company established to run the exposition drew its capital primarily from public funds, with the federal government supplying 40 per cent, the state of Lower Saxony 30 per cent, business 20 per cent, the city 6 per cent, the district of Hanover 2 per cent and the association of municipalities 2 per cent. Costs were reduced as far as possible by using existing facilities. The fairground, therefore, integrated the existing 216-acre (90-hectare) trade fair site with its exhibition halls, along with an additional 169 acres (70 hectares) for pavilions and 40 acres (17 hectares) for parking. The fairground comprised three main areas. The west primarily contained the pavilions of Latin American, Near and Far Eastern countries and would be cleared after the exposition. The central area incorporated the original trade fairground and exhibition halls owned by Deutsche Messe AG. The eastern area contained about 30 newly built pavilions, primarily occupied by European countries, which would be turned into a business park after the exposition (DCH, 2002). A six-storey tower, resembling a postbox, provided the show's vertical feature and observation deck. The plan also incorporated a scheme for a settlement of 2500 dwellings, intended to show new techniques of environmental sustainability, which would be sold for housing after the exposition. As usual, the associated infrastructural projects absorbed the bulk of investment. Improvements to the motorway network, a new terminal at Langenhagen airport, extensive remodelling of the main railway station, and a new station at the fairground serviced by Germany's high-speed train network drastically raised aggregate costs. Even on the best estimates, break-even or deficit financing was likely (Krantz and Schätzl, 2000, 487–89).

Expo 2000 was widely touted as the 'largest ever', which it certainly merited on the grounds of participating nations. A total of 184 countries and organisations attended, with 51 nations building pavilions and the rest having their exhibit spaces in the trade fair halls. The central area housed five theme pavilions after the fashion of Expo 67. These offered thematic exhibitions on eleven subjects – mobility, future of work, knowledge, energy, health, food, basic needs, environment, humankind, planet of visions, and the twenty-first century. Seminars or 'dialogues' explored issues of religion, faith and spirituality. The organisers invited participant countries to present their own cultural programme on their national days (DCH, 2002). Besides the formal Expo events, an associated cultural and events programme offered 18 000 performances over the festival period. These included dance, theatre, film and sports festivals.

Alarm bells started to ring almost as soon as the exposition opened. Although 150 000 visitors attended on the opening day, daily totals stabilised at 70 000 instead of the anticipated 300 000–400 000. Estimates of total attendances were revised downward from 40 million to 14 million, with commensurate revision of the likely deficit. After six weeks, prices were dropped to attract larger numbers of visitors, but even by the final month (October), daily visitor totals had only reached around 160 000. The final total of 18.1 million visitors was barely 45 per cent of the original forecast. Average spending per visitor was also less than forecast, given that only between 10 and 15 per cent of visitors were non-German rather than the anticipated 35 per cent. With sponsorship failing to raise its targets, the aggregate debt mounted. Allowing for subsequent adjustments in the light of long-term or imputed items, Expo 2000 lost a total of DM2.4 billion (£700m), roughly six times what was budgeted (Hooper, 2000).

Critics offered a wide variety of reasons for this outcome. In their evaluation, the organisers stressed deficiencies in marketing strategy, with the event passing almost unnoticed outside of Germany; failure to involve German diplomatic services in the process; poor press relations; insufficient encouragement to local people to identify with the event; and high admission charges (cited in DCH, 2002). Others emphasised the limited attraction of Hanover as a festival location, transport difficulties and, not surprisingly, poor economic forecasting and financial planning. Yet underlying these criticisms were questions about expositions in general. The commentator in the *Frankfurter Allgemeine Zeitung* (quoted in Kettmann, 2000), for example, argued:

> The bottom line is that World Fairs hardly make sense these days. Information about new products and machinery is passed on through other channels, or through trade fairs. The digital images which have deluged the public at recent expos can now be downloaded elsewhere.

The British journalist John Hooper (2000) agreed that people no longer needed to gather physically to be introduced to new concepts, but also ruminated on the fact that people had traditionally visited expositions to marvel at technologically-driven progress. Expo 2000's powerful environmentalism had tried to counter that theme but had left 'people with precious little to marvel at'. Put another way, the exposition was worthy but lacked the type of spectacle that the famous expositions of the past had achieved. The end product failed to stir the press or enthuse visitors sufficiently to encourage further attendance through word of mouth. If there is one thing worse for exposition organisers than running up a large deficit, it is running up a large deficit for an event that fails to be noticed.

Yet having said this, the international exposition is far from dead as a festival. Despite the growing indifference from European and American cities, the withdrawal of support from the US federal government, and the financial vicissitudes of recent hosts, further events are planned. In line with Japan's more positive experience of expositions, the BIE has registered Expo 2005 for Aïchi (Nagoya, Japan) as a specialised exposition on the theme of 'Nature's Wisdom'. At the time of writing, the bureau is processing an application from Shanghai (China) for 2010 on the theme of 'Better City, Better Life'. It remains perfectly possible that the international exposition has a continuing role outside of the cities and geographical regions that monopolised such events before 1970. The resulting expositions may well be different but, given the failure of recent events, will not necessarily be any the worse for that.

Sydney 2000

By contrast with Expo 2000, the Sydney Olympics were always guaranteed high-visibility coverage as perhaps the year's most anticipated international festival. The Australian Olympic Committee (AOC) chose Sydney in March 1991 as the Australian candidate city for the Millennium Olympics against two competitors, Brisbane and Melbourne. It was, in a sense, Sydney's turn. The AOC had previously selected Brisbane and Melbourne, respectively, for the 1992 and 1996 games. Both those bids were unsuccessful, but their applications provided important groundwork for the Sydney bid, especially by convincing the IOC of the need to bring the Olympics back to the southern hemisphere. Sydney's bid for the Olympics had been in gestation since the late 1960s. The city made feasibility plans for both the 1972 and 1988 games. The latter centred on making use of Homebush Bay in the Parramatta district, approximately nine miles (14 kilometres) upstream from Sydney's city centre, as an Olympic park.

Originally consisting of tidal wetlands and scrub, Homebush Bay at various times had housed Sydney's racecourse, a saltworks, the British Commonwealth's largest abattoir, the state brickworks and a naval munitions store. In the 1930s, the bay had regularly spawned algal blooms through contamination by waste products from the slaughterhouses, with severe pollution thereafter from depositing household and industrial waste in landfill sites. Work began in the 1980s to clean up and redevelop the area, with controls placed on dumping waste. A private consortium constructed a business park, the Australia Centre. The state government had already commissioned the State Sports Centre (opened in 1984) and authorised reclamation of an area of land as Bicentennial Park. An Olympic bid would help regenerate the remainder of the site, tackle its severe environmental problems, supply the city with a replacement for the Royal Agricultural Society's outmoded showground at Moore Park, and provide a cluster of modern world-class sports facilities.

Any bid would involve the state and federal governments as funding agencies and as the owners of the land, as well as the city.[6] Their participation brought three agendas to bear on the games. First, the organisers claimed these would be a 'green games' expressing, like Expo 2000, an environmental consciousness in use of resources and design of facilities. Secondly, the Sydney games were a national project, celebrating the 'entire continent of Australia' rather than just the host city. The aim was to show the beauty and variety of Australian landscapes and wildlife, the culture of the country and its history in a manner that would place Australia on the world map and attract business and tourists. This reiterated themes raised by Melbourne's bid almost half-a-century earlier (see Chapter 7). Thirdly, and related, capturing the games would allow the organisers to highlight the profound changes that had taken place in the 44 years between the two games. The most important contrasts lay in constructions of national identity. The staging of the games, their ceremonies and the cultural Olympiad would allow Australia to present itself as a multicultural society rather than one wishing to perpetuate the nation's traditional white, Anglocentric image. Relations with the indigenous population were paramount here. Culturally denigrated as primitive, the Aborigines continued to suffer loss of traditional lands, segregation, disenfranchisement and abuse of human rights into the 1960s, with 'common sense' prejudices still in evidence in the 1990s. The Australian Bicentennial in 1988, with its accompanying narratives of European conquest, produced severe intercommunal frictions. By contrast, the Olympics might help the process of rapprochement with the Aboriginal populations, provided that they felt this was a project to which they could give support.

Sydney's bid won approval from the AOC in March 1991. The New South Wales government quickly formed a bid committee drawn from the worlds of business, politics and sports, from whom came the membership of a public company called Sydney Olympics Bid Limited (SOBL). This handled the task of collecting funds and preparing and promoting the bid to the IOC. In line with the games' domestic political goals, SOBL made efforts to gain the support of Australia's Aboriginal communities. The New South Wales Aboriginal Land Council, for example, twice voted unanimously in 1992 to support the bid and expressed their hopes that a games held in Australia might lead to more Aboriginal competitors and better employment opportunities for indigenous Australians within the games organisation. During the bid, SOBL employed an Aboriginal liaison officer, with a senior Aboriginal spokesperson Burnum Burnum writing to IOC members urging them to vote for Sydney (SOCOG, 2000). Symbolically, the games logo, designed by Aboriginal artist Ron Hurley, would later feature the outline of the Sydney Opera House in Olympic colours in an indigenous painting style.

The IOC officially nominated Sydney for the 2000 games at its Monte Carlo meeting in September 1993 against competition from Beijing, Manchester, Berlin and Istanbul. Key elements in its candidacy were the promises to concentrate the Olympic venues in one central park, to accommodate all athletes in one village adjacent to the Olympic park, to assist athletes and officials with transport costs, to ensure security for participants, to arrange a four-year arts festival programme with a particular focus on Australia's indigenous and multicultural heritage, and to ensure 'environmental friendliness' (ibid.). The games masterplan, published in 1996, established the concept of a built core surrounded by parklands. In the words of Chris Johnson (1999, 39), the chair of the Olympic Design Review Panel:

> In the urban core, the orthogonal grid of the abattoir fields carried across the site to be sliced through by a new Olympic Boulevard. The Boulevard had to fit between the Australia Centre and the now constructed Aquatic Centre. The plan called for two types of buildings – object buildings and street edged buildings. The object buildings were clearly the stadia with the rest of the buildings

designed to reinforce the street edge. ... On the basis of this plan, the major buildings were allocated through a tender process either to contractors or to designers. Where the state was funding facilities, such as the showground replacement buildings or the railway station, the process was initially to select architects. Where the private sector was to fund all, or part of the facilities such as the stadium, or the village, the selection process was for finance, building and architectural design.

Funding for the main Olympic venue, named Stadium Australia, came from a mixture of public funds and 30-year membership and corporate packages giving access to the stadium's sporting calendar (Margalit, 1999, 70). Designed to hold 110 000 spectators during the games, its capacity would be reduced to 80 000 for its subsequent life as a rugby and Australian Rules football stadium. The other major stadia in the Homebush Olympic Park were the Hockey Centre, Superdome (basketball and artistic gymnastics), International Athletics Centre (warm-up facilities), Tennis Centre, the Aquatic Centre (swimming and diving) and the Archery Park. The Olympic village, on the site of the former munitions depot, accommodated all 15 300 participants at a single centre for the first time. The village comprised a mixed development of apartments, town houses and villages, arranged into three precincts, designed to ecologically sustainable guidelines. Provision of a school and commercial precinct looked ahead to the area's post-games future as a residential suburb of Sydney. A small number of other Olympic facilities, particularly those associated with rowing and sailing, were located within the Sydney city region at a maximum distance of 60 miles (100 kilometres) from Homebush Bay.

The opening ceremony on 15 September 2000 at Stadium Australia reflected the complex agenda of international projection of Australia and domestic reconciliation mentioned above. The bill of fare, as shown in Table 9.1, carefully observed the proprieties of multiculturalism. The ceremony opened with an encounter between indigenous and white Australians, emphasising the antiquity of indigenous culture, its diversity, myths, legends and spirituality. The Aborigines emerged as managers of the land, in contrast to the depiction of what the official report described as the European period of 'vitality and violence' (SOCOG, 2000). A total of 2500 performers, representing postwar immigrants from around the world, portrayed multicultural Australia and arranged themselves into the five Olympic rings (symbolising the world's continents). At the end of the presentation all the performers formed up into the 'Bridge of Life' to signify reconciliation. Yet notwithstanding the serious-minded tone of this political message, the organisers also superimposed a notion of Australian identity on the

Table 9.1   Key elements in the opening ceremony, 27th summer Olympics, 15 September 2000

Content
1   Welcome – lone horseman followed by 120 'bush cavalry' form 5 Olympic rings (to the music of 'The Man from Snowy River') – G'Day banner
2   Arrival of the governor general and dignitaries; swinging trumpet fanfare (James Morrison) and Swing City Band
3   National anthem (Human Nature and Sydney Symphony Orchestra)
4   Narrative sequence taking a journey through Australia's past: Deep sea dreaming – transformed the area into a 3D deep ocean with sea creatures swimming through the air – 800 performers Awakening – exploration of the diversity and unity of Australia's indigenous past – traditional dances and ceremonies – rebirthing the land, awakening spirits, cleansing and welcome Fire – the ancestral creation spirit Wandjina hurls a lightning bolt to ignite a bushfire – fire-breathers, flaming stilt-walkers, flaming club-swingers, 110 000 spectators waving lights Nature – regeneration after fire – plants, animals, water, celebrating Australia's unique natural environment through dance and puppetry Tin Symphony – European colonisation, the Endeavour Horse fire-breathing steel horse made of agricultural machinery, ending with lawnmower ballet Arrivals – celebrating postwar immigration from around the world – 2500 performers Eternity – over 1000 tap dancers, ending with the Bridge of Life – reconciliation
5   Sydney 2000 Olympic Band – from 20 countries
6   Parade of the athletes – 10 500 athletes, 5000 officials – John Farnham and Olivia Newton-John sang 'Dare to Dream'

Table 9.1 *concluded*

Content
7	Speeches of welcome; Sir William Deane declared the games open
8	Olympic flag passed over the heads of spectators and assembled athletes – Vanessa Amorosi sang 'Heroes Live Forever'
9	Official Olympic flag carried into the arena by Australian Olympians; raising of the flag; 200 Millennium children's Choir of the Greek Archdiocese of Australia sang Olympic hymn in Greek.
10	Olympic oath athletes and officials
11	Entry of the Olympic flame – carried by female Australian athletes to celebrate a century of women's participation in the games; Tina Arena sang 'The Flame'; Cathy Freeman lit a ring of fire

Source: after SOCOG (2000).

opening ceremony that tried to encompass irreverence, wit, mistrust of authority, energy, innovation, egalitarianism, informality, sport-loving, and true Olympism (the Australians had been at every games since 1896). Singers injected pop songs into the proceedings and traditional Olympic fare such as the 'Ode to Joy' featured in new forms (played by a 2000-piece marching band). The final narrative section celebrated Arthur Stace, a reformed alcoholic who spent the last 35 years of his life writing the word 'eternity' in chalk on pavements and buildings in Sydney. The presentation of the torch relay also emphasised identity and reconciliation. After travelling though Greece, it toured the Pacific ending up in New Zealand before arriving in Central Australia at Uluru (Ayers Rock) – the spiritual and geographical centre of Australia. The first torchbearer was Aboriginal Olympian Nova Peris-Kneebone, with her compatriot Kathy Freeman lighting the flame when the torch relay reached the Olympic stadium. The ceremony attracted an estimated global audience of 3.7 billion.[7]

The arts programme spanned the Olympiad and comprised four major festivals intended to show indigenous culture, create lasting works of art, and attract new and more diverse audiences. All the festivals featured multiple art forms with the first, the Festival of the Dreaming (15 September–5 October 1997), perhaps the most innovative. Based in the Sydney area, this was Australia's first major festival of Aboriginal art. It involved over 700 indigenous artists principally from Australia, but with contributions from New Zealand, Canada, Greenland, USA, Korea and Oceania that made connections with the experience of indigenous peoples in different parts of the world. Performances included Samuel Beckett's *Waiting for Godot* presented in Bunjalung dialect and the first Aboriginal company to have a season at the Sydney Opera House. The second festival 'A Sea Change' ran for over eight months in 1998, with 122 events in 60 communities across Australia. This focused on postwar Australia with, for example, 'Tears, Fears and Cheers' at the National Maritime Museum examining the social impact of migration. The third festival, 'Reaching the World' (December 1998–January 2000), comprised a series of exhibitions designed to showcase Australian culture abroad. The programme then culminated in the Sydney 2000 Olympic Arts Festival (18 August–1 October 2000), a six-week festival to coincide with the summer games and paralympics. This contained nearly 400 events involving 4000 artists. The performing arts events attracted 260 000 attendances, with over 300 000 people attending the visual arts events. This festival primarily showcased Australian culture, with the Olympic ideal of examining the relationship between sport and art directly tackled in just five exhibitions: '1000 years of Olympic Games'; 'Sydney 2000: Olympic Design of the new Millennium'; 'Body Language – Art Sport and Cyber Conversation'; 'Shutter Speed' (sports photography); and the IOC Art and Sport Exhibition showing the work of 16 finalists in the first Olympic art competition staged since 1948.[8] Although the cultural programme was impressive and well attended over the four years, the public may not necessarily have connected it with the Olympics. It was also difficult to fund these arts projects sufficiently to achieve maximum impact. In the case of 'A Sea Change' and 'Reaching the World', for example, lack of resources meant the festival director having to buy into events that had already been scheduled

The Olympics' closing ceremony was different in degree to previous events. Closing ceremonies were already less formal than opening ceremonies, a trend that Australia could be said to have initiated at the Melbourne games when abolishing the athletes formally marching in groups. Besides the elements of Olympic ritual – the extinguishing of the flame, the lowering of the Olympic flags and the valedictory speeches – was a presentation that celebrated and frequently mocked aspects of Australian popular culture. This included celebrities entering the arena with references to their activities: the supermodel Elle McPherson arriving aboard a large camera with a telescopic lens, flanked by 20 female models and 12 photographers; the actor Paul Hogan making his entrance on top of a giant Crocodile Dundee hat, surrounded by crocodiles on skates, prawns on bicycles, water buffalo on scooters and lizards on unicycles (SOCOG, 2000). Yet, for some critics, this merely highlighted the continuing tensions in Australian identity. As Craig Hassel of the Olympic Arts Festivals noted, 'Crocodile Dundee and the outback' is 'not what and who we are' (Good, 1999, 163). The ceremony ended in a manner similar to Sydney's New Year's Eve celebrations. An enormous fireworks display moved from the stadium down the Parramatta river to Sydney Harbour to the strains of Wagner and Mahler, where the harbour bridge staged a 20-minute display of gold, silver and bronze fireworks.

The immediate impact of the games suggested that the profile of Australia had indeed been raised. Australian Tourist Commission research in the USA revealed that 75 per cent of the Americans surveyed had seen pictures and stories concerning Australia as a holiday destination as part of the Olympic coverage and half reported that they were more interested in Australia as a destination (Morse, 2001, 102). Locally, the games passed off well. Potential demonstrations about homelessness, the plight of Aborigines, ticketing, and the claimed misuse of public funds did not occur. An economic analysis by Jill Haynes (2001) argued that the total cost of the games at A$6.5 billion was roughly neutral in that it was covered by an equivalent amount in extra economic activity in Australia between 1994–95 and 2005–06, of which A$5.1 billion would accrue in New South Wales. For this price, Sydney had achieved the regeneration of a severely blighted industrial region, gained significant improvements to infrastructure, improved its tourist standing, and gained world-class sport facilities. For the Olympic movement, it again showed the value of a festival largely held at a central venue rather than the dispersal and logistic nightmare of Atlanta. Despite the peaks and troughs of summer Olympic events over the course of the twentieth century, the movement remained in good heart as it looked towards Athens (2004).

Nine Cities of Culture

The thought about the value of having one central location might well be applied to the Millennium European Cities of Culture festival or, more strictly, festivals.[9] The year 2000 simultaneously represented something of a belated success and a warning for the European City of Culture programme. It was successful in that cultural activity was finally put on a more coherent and secure footing by the adoption of the First European Community Framework Programme in Support of Culture, 2000–2004. It was belated, in that the programme did not come into force until March 2000, due to acrimonious disputes between the Council of Ministers and the European Parliament, as well as within the Council of Ministers (Fisher, 2001, 24). However, it was also a warning in the sense that the City of Culture festivals in 2000, with no less than nine cities receiving the title, showed up weaknesses in the event.

The First European Community Framework Programme in Support of Culture 2000–2004, known as 'Culture 2000', brought together formerly disparate activities into a single programme of action and provided funding of 167 million (since extended to 2006 with an additional 69.5 million). In the words of article 1, it would 'contribute to the promotion of a cultural area common to the European people, supporting cooperation between creative artists, cultural operators and the cultural institutions of the member States'. The programme highlighted common cultural heritage, creativity, promotion of cultural diversity, contribution to socio-economic development, spreading European cultures into non-member countries, and dialogue with other world cultures. It envisaged three types of action: specific innovative and experimental projects, integrated actions, and special cultural events. This last activity, the category that contained the Cities of Culture festival, was to be 'substantial in scale and in scope, should strike a significant chord with the people of Europe and help increase their sense of belonging to the same community as well as making them aware of the cultural diversity of Europe'.[10]

The intergovernmental approach to selecting the cultural capital ran into difficulty as fresh applicants joined Bologna, Avignon and Prague – three cities that failed to be designated for the 1998 and 1999 events – as candidates for 2000. As early as 1993, the Council of Ministers hinted that one way round the problem was to designate a larger number of cities for 2000 given the 'symbolic importance' of the year. At their meeting in Madrid in October 1995, they agreed on the principle of 'many cultural capitals'[11] and in November they conferred the accolade to no less than nine cities. This offered a rationale for what was essentially, at best, a compromise. The full list comprised Bologna (Italy), Avignon (France), Prague (Czech Republic), Bergen (Norway), Brussels (Belgium), Helsinki (Finland), Reykjavik (Iceland), Santiago de Compostela (Spain) and Cracow (Poland). Reaction to the multiple designations among the chosen cities included shock, amazement and disappointment, while previous Cities of Culture expressed the view that the original concept of the event had been abandoned (Cogliandro, 2001, 26). To bring some coherence to this situation, the Council of Ministers required the nine cities to coordinate their programmes, define a common theme and act together to create a 'European cultural space' for the Millennium (ibid., 74). They responded by agreeing the individual themes for their festivals jointly in order to create a 'common message' (see Table 9.2). They also decided that each city should lead a joint project that would involve all nine cities and encouraged further bilateral collaborations involving two or more cities. This resulted in twelve joint projects and over sixty bilateral collaborations. Moreover, the three Scandinavian cities of Bergen, Helsinki and Reykjavik developed a Nordic Programme to celebrate their common roots and

Table 9.2   European Cities of Culture, 2000

City	Population	City theme	Joint project	Total budget( )
Avignon	88 000	Art and creativity	Technomade	21 084 068
Bergen	220 000	Art, work and leisure	Coast and waterways	13 536 600
Bologna	400 000	Culture and communication	Cafe9.net Bologna Gala Dinner	33 897 000
Brussels	1 000 000	The city	Walk about/ Stalk; The House of the 9 Cities	33 325 000
Cracow	800 000	Thought, spirituality and creativity	Codex Calixtinus	5 697 519*
Helsinki	500 000	Knowledge, technology and the future	Communication Voices of Europe Cafe9.net Kide	58 000 000
Prague	1 250 000	Cultural heritage	Citylink	18 800 000
Reykjavik	170 000	Culture and nature	Voices of Europe	7 900 000
Santiago de Compostela	120 000	Europe and the world	Faces of the Earth	34 863 094

* If the four festivals leading up to 2000 are included, the total expenditure was 12 290 710.

Source: after Cogliandro (2001).

put the region on the European cultural map by staging four major projects and a number of smaller projects. The major projects were 'Baldur', a musical drama inspired by Nordic mythology; 'Nordic Light 2000', artwork inspired by light and using different lighting techniques; 'Futurice', a Nordic fashion show; and 'Art Naust' (Boathouses), a contemporary art project (Cogliandro, 2001, 27, 106, 107).

The challenge of arranging collaboration between such a range of cities required special mechanisms. Regular meetings between the cities started in 1996 and in 1998 they established the Association of the European Cities of Culture of the year 2000 (AECC). This formalised the interaction between the cities and established a small secretariat, with two posts, in Brussels. The secretariat helped with European Union lobbying, funding applications and promotion. It also set up an intranet scheme to ease communication between staff in the nine cities although, due to operational difficulties, it was little used. One further weakness of the collaboration was that there were too many meetings between the cities' mayors and not enough between the 'real actors', the arts administrators (Cogliandro, 2001, 76 et seq.). The AECC was wound up in March 2001.

Efforts to act jointly included the design of a logo, marketing and sponsorship – again not altogether successful. The City of Culture event had evolved as a series of events firmly under the control of the host city, and the desire to control the event at the local level remained far greater than the ability to act jointly. Moreover, as Table 9.2 shows, the financial resources of the nine programmes varied considerably. A Spanish designer created a joint logo in the shape of a star (to symbolise Europe) with personalised versions for the nine cities, but only three (Helsinki, Reykjavik and Santiago de Compostela) chose to base their own logos on the design. Marketing also resulted in a mixed response. The nine cities produced a joint brochure for the event, but only issued 5000 per city. There were also joint folders (100 per city), a poster and a video suitable for display to air travellers and on television. By contrast, they failed to produce a common brochure outlining the cultural programme or establish a joint website, settling instead for links between city sites, which according to a Finnish survey in February 2000 were of variable quality.[12] They also failed to act jointly at trade fairs, choosing instead to have their own stands.

The cities were keen to obtain a common sponsorship and licensing programme to complement activity at the city level. In July 1997 Thue and Selwaag, a Norwegian firm, was appointed to advise in this area. They proposed targeting companies in the soft drinks, credit cards, and rental car sectors and in February 1998 were awarded a contract to initiate the sponsorship campaign. This resulted in total failure for several reasons but particularly because, first, the campaign was too late in view of the wealth of other sponsorship opportunities available in 2000 and, second, because the 'product' on offer was insufficiently distinct.[13] While established cultural centres within their own countries, the nine cities hosting the 2000 event were diverse. All but two of the nine either were, or contained, World Heritage Sites and four were capital cities. As Table 9.2 shows, they ranged in size from Avignon's population of 88 000 to Prague with 1.25 million. Four of the cities were outside the European Union (Reykjavik, Bergen, Cracow and Prague). Three were part of the Nordic Union (Reykjavik, Bergen and Helsinki). Understandably, their agendas varied enormously. For Helsinki and Bergen, the event was part of a strategy to develop the city's cultural profile. Major cultural infrastructure was opened for the festivals in Bergen, Bologna (spending $100 million), Brussels, Helsinki and Reykjavik, with major restorations and urban improvements taking place in Prague, Bologna and Brussels. Virtually all the cities used the event to improve their image or raise their profiles on the international stage. Avignon, already famous for its theatre festival, aimed to spread its visitors more evenly throughout the year. Bologna wanted to develop cultural tourism to complement its established business tourism sector. The civic authorities in Santiago de Compostela wanted to present their city as being modern, as well as a pilgrimage city and historical centre. Cracow and Prague saw their festivals as symbolic of their nations moving politically closer to the European Union. For Brussels the event had the added importance of bringing together the Flemish-speaking and French-speaking communities in a single festival for the first time, with the hope that this would help longer-term collaborations between the two groups. For Reykjavik, with its population of 170 000 comprising almost half of the country's 272 000 population, the festival was a national celebration – reminiscent of Luxembourg's approach in 1995.

Helsinki certainly devoted the largest budget and displayed the greatest commitment to the event.[14] The city identified the event as part of a culture-based regeneration strategy directly focused on image building and place marketing, tourism and the cultural industries. It also had possible spin-offs for Helsinki's policies of promoting science-based industries, acquiring knowledge-based industries, and developing its role as a communications hub between east and west. This strategy stemmed not from industrial decline as in many west European cities, but from the collapse of the Soviet Union, an internal banking crisis, and a decrease of over 10 per cent in the country's GNP between 1991–93. The idea of applying for the City of Culture originated in 1993 and symbolised Finland's new-found independence in the sphere of foreign policy and relations with the European Union (Heikkinen, 2000, 203).[15]

In 1994 a commissioned report from the consultancy Comedia examined Helsinki's image, showing particularly negative associations among those who had never visited the city (dark, cold, desolate, sad, empty and lonely tinged with drunkenness). Even those familiar with the city could not imagine living and working there, citing the relative isolation, harsh climate, the language and Finnish mentality as reasons (ibid., 207). The report recommended that the city had to find ways of 'repositioning' Helsinki to foreigners, stressing the value of the European City of Culture for this purpose. The ensuing festival took the theme of 'knowledge, technology and the future', with Helsinki presented as a young, modern, technologically aware city. The programme stressed innovation, including media art and future communications technology. Two joint projects led by Helsinki enhanced this strategy. Kide (Crystal) consisted of nine large glass blocks – one for each City of Culture. These combined light and sound, lit up when touched and, with the aid of a nearby monitor, provided a visual connection between the nine cities. Cafe9 was a chain of internet cafes, again one for each city, with network and video-conferencing links between the nine cities. In the final event, however, Santiago and Cracow had to drop out of the project through lack of funds.

Cracow, by contrast, had the smallest budget in 2000, although few European cities had made more determined efforts to harness cultural festivals. Cracow was the first city from central Europe to embrace the European festival concept, being nominated to host the first European Cultural Month in 1992. The city hosted a series of themed festivals starting in 1996 and culminating in 2000. In 1996, it staged the Year of Film and Theatre, 1997 the Year of Poetry, 1998 the Year of Music, and in 1999 a mixed programme anticipating the major festival of 2000. The authorities aimed to promote and raise the profile of their city, strengthen its tourist base and confirm Poland's European credentials in the lead-up to membership of the European Union (Hughes et al., 2002, 135). The adopted theme of 'thought spirituality and creativity' was intended to resonate with Polish culture and identity. The programme featured a considerable amount of 'high art' and international names, partly to prove that Cracow could attract the best and partly because this was thought the best way to attract international tourists. The marketing effort, however, was not commensurate with this aim. Moreover, the small budget meant there was no opportunity to create new performance spaces, commission new works, promote unknown talent or develop local audiences (ibid., 136–7).

The experience of the cities for 2000 confirmed the general feeling that designating nine cities simultaneously as Cities of Culture was a mistake that should not be repeated. During 2000, negotiations finally reached agreement on the third phase of the programme starting in 2005. The event was renamed the European Capital of Culture and returned to the principle of establishing a 'predictable, consistent and transparent rotational system', setting out the order in which the member states would host the festival for the years 2005–19 (see Table 9.3). Non-member states could now nominate one city, although the final choice rested with the Council's unanimous vote, with the expectation that the European Union would collaborate with any such city nominated as Cultural Capital. The new rules placed the onus on the Cultural Capital to make links with any other designated city and outlined in greater detail the aims and objectives of the new programme, recognising the diverse economic, urban and cultural goals of the programme and emphasising the European dimension. The commission would also review the Cultural Capital event annually.[16]

Although the timing of these new rules was not directly prompted by the unsatisfactory resolution of the 'Millennium problem', it recognised that the City of Culture festival had proven resilient and popular over its first sixteen years and needed protection from devaluation by overuse. Little long-term damage appears to have occurred. National governments and their nominated host cities increasingly clamour to stage the event, as exemplified by no less than twelve British cities submitting bids for the privilege of winning the nomination to become the United Kingdom's European Cultural Capital for 2008. In addition, the concept of the City of Culture has been copied elsewhere. The 35 members of the Organisation of American States decided in 1997 to initiate an American Capital of Culture. In the same manner, the federal district of the Volga (Russian Federation) has also developed an event based on the European Cities of Culture in 2001.[17] It provides a striking endorsement of an idea that has added a new dimension to the business of staging international festivals.

A Dome Too Far?

There are few certainties in the world of international festivals, as these examples from the year 2000 clearly show. As the latest in a series of events that had oscillated from triumph to disaster over more than a century, the well-run and popular Sydney Olympics contrasted favourably with the organisational problems and obtrusive commercialism of Atlanta. The festival had paid for itself, even after taking account of the accompanying urban regeneration and infrastructural improvements. The sensitive problems over identity and culture had been resolved and the accompanying cultural programme

Table 9.3   European Cultural Capitals, 2000–19

Cities of Culture

2000   Avignon (France)
          Bergen (Norway)
          Bologna (Italy)
          Brussels (Belgium)
          Cracow (Poland)
          Helsinki (Finland)
          Prague (Czech Republic)
          Reykjavik (Iceland)
          Santiago de Compostela (Spain)
2001   Porto (Portugal)
          Rotterdam (Netherlands)
2002   Bruges (Belgium)
          Salamanca (Spain)
2003   Graz (Austria)
2004   Genoa (Italy)
          Lille (France)

European Cultural Capitals

2005   Cork (Eire)
2006   Patras (Greece)
2007   Luxembourg
2008   Liverpool (United Kingdom)
2009   Austria
2010   Germany
2011   Finland
2012   Portugal
2013   France
2014   Sweden
2015   Belgium
2016   Spain
2017   Denmark
2018   Netherlands
2019   Italy

---

was seriously tackled – even if the festival as a whole remained far short of the panegyris of Coubertin's hopes. That experience differed radically from the outcome of Hanover's Expo 2000. Like Seville 1992, it posted huge debts caused primarily by accompanying infrastructural improvements but, unlike Seville, it failed to attract visitors in any substantial numbers. Indeed at 18.1 million, it drew scarcely half the 34 million visitors who attended Paris 1937, the previous lowest aggregate attendance for a BIE-registered Universal Exposition. Although further international expositions remain in the pipeline, the continuing erosion of the underlying rationale of this form of festival makes its future, at best, problematic. The 2000 European Cities of Culture showed how a sound idea could be briefly clouded by ill-conceived application. The indecision that led to nine designated cities left those cities trying to make sense of the poisoned chalice that they had been given. Despite attempts to establish shared projects and common themes, the European Union fully recognised that it was impossible to give proper support to the host cities, where the festivals mostly passed off without attracting significant international attention. The return in the future to more conventional designations draws a line under an unsuccessful experiment, generally perceived to have done no lasting damage to the Cities of Culture scheme.

All three festivals, however, shared the characteristic of competing in an unusually crowded market. Besides the regular diet of arts and cultural festivals, the year 2000 also led, as noted earlier, to an extraordinary profusion of ad hoc festivals. One of these, London's Millennium Experience, provides a valuable postscript to the discussion here, both because it shared many of the characteristics of the international festivals and because, like Expo 2000, it had claims to commemorate the sesquicentenary of the movement initiated by the 1851 Great Exhibition. The project traces its origins back to the Conservative Party's general election manifesto of 1992. Floating the idea of establishing a National Lottery, it suggested that one use for revenues might be to establish a lottery-based Millennium Fund to sponsor worthwhile projects. Although framed mainly in terms of restoring historic buildings and encouraging sport, the manifesto specifically proposed that one use of the fund might be for holding a Millennium 'international trade fair to be a showcase of British innovation for the twenty-first century' (quoted in Nicolson, 1999, 9). After setting up the National Lottery and the Millennium Commission in 1994, thoughts turned to the form that the fair, now commonly called an 'exhibition', might take. In May 1995, it was proposed that the 'exhibition' would last from 1 January to 31 December 2000. After considering four possible sites, the choice was a derelict and heavily polluted 130-acre (53-hectare) site on the Greenwich Peninsula in southeast London, formerly occupied by a gasworks.[18]

Greenwich had culture and history on its side. The Royal Observatory, established at Greenwich in 1675, had a long association with groundbreaking astronomical observations. In 1884, the International Meridian Conference recognised Greenwich as Prime Meridian of the world and therefore the fulcrum of the earth's longitudinal system and time zones (Irvine, 1999, 3). This close association with world time provided an opportunity to create a unique year-long festival that, it was argued, would draw favourable attention to the United Kingdom and boost international tourism. It was located in London and, in many ways, could be presented as a successor to the 1851 Great Exhibition – the sesquicentenary of which would fall the following year. Moreover the site was vacant and ripe for regeneration in a borough that had lost 500 companies and 10 000 jobs between 1991–93. The prospects of creating 10 000 badly needed jobs, a neatly equivalent figure, in this area of high unemployment and urban decay was a clinching factor in the calculations of net benefits (ibid., 45). The scheme would also help justify the long awaited extension to the Jubilee line on London's underground (metro) rail system.

The chosen venue for the 'Millennium Experience' would be a single umbrella structure, as innovative in its time as the Crystal Palace had been in the 1850s. Although threatened many times with cancellation, construction began on the specially commissioned Millennium Dome in July 1997. The Dome was a cable-net structure with a translucent roof, 165 feet (50 metres) in height, 0.6 mile (one kilometre) in circumference, and enclosing over 20 acres (8.5 hectares) (Wilhide, 1999, 9). The exhibition inside would be organised by the New Millennium Experience Company, a government-sponsored body run by an executive and a nominated council. Their extended deliberations over its contents led eventually to an exhibition that partly resembled the 1951 Festival of Britain. The Millennium Experience focused on key elements of national life and explorations of the future. The organisers arranged it around three broad principles – 'who we are, what we do and where we live' – which, in turn, were explored in 14 zones.[19] The exhibition, however, broke with the practices of the international expositions by placing entertainment literally centre-stage. Using the vertical dimension of the Dome's central arena to telling effect, the organisers commissioned a circus-style rock musical extravaganza that was performed six times daily.

The site attracted 6.5 million visitors, making it the country's top tourist attraction during 2000, but earned a reputation that, in the short term at least, has seen it elevated to the list of 'Great (British) Planning

Disasters' (cf. Hall, 1980). Critics from across the political spectrum had castigated the Dome project from the outset. The right campaigned against interventionism and incurring public expenditure. The left claimed that it pursued a middle-class agenda and made too little connection with the working-class communities in the area. Its planning was dogged by lack of direction, tortuous negotiations between interested parties, endless conflicting consultants' reports, and changes of minister and senior personnel. It would attract further opprobrium for its heavy costs overruns, eventually costing over £800 million against initial estimates of £337 million. The 6.5 million visitors were scarcely half of the 12 million visitors forecast and far too few to carry the project's bloated costs. It proved difficult to find sponsors, as planned, for many of the themed zones. Even while operating, and therefore bringing in revenue, it twice required cash infusions to stave off bankruptcy. Yet ironically, despite the expenditure, various aspects of the Millennium Experience were condemned as being cheap, uninspiring and in poor repair.

The problems did not end with closure. Somewhat astoundingly, there were no firm plans for converting the site to its post-festival state. No buyer could be found when the festival finished, forcing English Partnerships, the government's regeneration arm, to take over the site in July 2001. The losses continued to mount. The upkeep of the shell alone cost £0.25 million a month.[20] Between July 2001 and the start of January 2003, the Dome and its surrounding site drained a further £16.7 million from the public purse, comprising £4 million on maintenance and security, £6 million on efforts to sell the Dome and a separate £6.7 million on a failed competition to find a use for the attraction.[21] Meanwhile the building remained empty and its future as uncertain as ever. Current estimates suggest it is unlikely to reopen before 2007.[22] Plans to turn the site into housing, commercial and retail uses have run into difficulty over the proportion of 'affordable' (cheap) houses that developers are willing to create. Plans to turn the Dome into a major multipurpose arena have foundered on the extent to which southeast London actually needs a new large concert hall and the difficulty of finding a sports usage that would attract large audiences on a regular basis to an indoor venue. The idea that it would stage the basketball and gymnastics events if Britain hosts the 2012 Olympics begs many questions. For the short-term, even the project's regeneration credentials remain in doubt.

The problems encountered at Greenwich led to much political soul-searching. The process of damage limitation had begun long before the festival closed. Speaking to the Labour Party conference in October 2000, the Prime Minister Tony Blair ruminated: 'Hindsight is a wonderful thing, and if I had my time again I would have listened to those who said governments shouldn't try to run tourist attractions'. In doing so, he sensed an opportunity to show humility to the electorate before the imminent 2001 General Election and pacify the press. He was on safe ground. The Dome exercise was self-contained and finite and, in any case, the Conservative Party shared some of the blame since they had initiated the project when they were in office. Yet the description of the scheme as a 'tourist attraction' does little justice to the plural aims that it embraced. This was a project that saw returns stemming from boosts to tourism, creative design, national prestige, infrastructure and employment, as well as accomplishing the regeneration of a large, but difficult, site within easy reach of central London. Should the regeneration process eventually turn out to be a success, as is perfectly possible given its location, the final analysis may yet prove less damning than the current arithmetic would suggest.

Moreover, Blair's reaction hardly squared with the government's backing for London's bid to capture the Olympic Games in 2012 or its systematic approach to selecting cities for the 2008 European Cultural Capital. The history of international festivals clearly shows that poorly conceived and badly executed schemes seldom deliver the desired results. Adopting over-ambitious designs for buildings and fairgrounds, overloading festivals with huge indirect costs from urban regeneration, and failing to carry out rigorous economic forecasts usually leads to festivals being reluctantly bailed out by the public purse. Cost overruns have long been the rule rather than exception for the events discussed in this book and the comparatively rare examples of profitability often owed something to the method of accountancy. Nevertheless, these events beget their own logic. They offer the prospect of high direct and indirect returns spread over a wide spectrum and are supremely malleable to the agendas of their host cities. Although there may be specific disenchantment in western nations with traditional expositions, the conviction remains that if tackled successfully, large international festivals are golden opportunities to kick-start sluggish economies, knock years off the normal development cycle for infrastructural improvement, reposition a city in the global tourist market, create vibrant cultural quarters, and generally steal a march on rivals. Having the right leadership and policies, it is commonly believed, ameliorates the known risks. In a world in which capitalising on culture has too often assumed the status of a panacea for all urban ills, that illusion may seem irresistible.

Notes

1   M. Engel, 'Don't cry for me, Wendell Sailor', *The Guardian*, 'Sport' section, 22 November 2003, 4.
2   *Washington Post*, 1 January 2000.
3   There remains considerable debate as to whether this ever materialised.
4   Detailed handbooks had long existed for those who needed further guidance (for example, see Matsushita Electric, 1980; Lorne, 1995).
5   The IRA blew up Nelson's Pillar in 1966 for its associations with Great Britain.
6   The state government owned the state brickworks and abattoir, with the national government owning the land occupied by the munitions facility.
7   *The Independent*, 16 September 2000.
8   In passing, it is worth noting that this exhibition was shown in David Jones department store, which scarcely qualified as a major venue.
9   Although there is confusion in the literature, strictly speaking the official title 'City of Culture' did not change to 'Cultural Capital' until 2005.
10 'The First European Community Framework Programme in Support of Culture, 2000–2004', COM (1998) 266, *Official Journal*, C211, 7 July 1998.
11 Anon., 'European cities of culture set to multiply', *Financial Times*, 21–22 October 1995.
12 Helsingin Sanomat (2000), http://www.helsinki-hs.net (accessed 30 October 2003).
13 Indeed there was *no* 'brand recognition' at the European level. Thue and Selwaag recommended that a common logo be used for all future European Cities of Culture and that sponsorship should be made for a five-year period to remedy this situation.
14 Anthony Thorncroft, 'Finland's capital senses that its time has come', *Financial Times*, 22–23 January 2000.
15 Its neutral status and relationship to the Soviet Union previously precluded it from any association with the European Union.
16 'Decision establishing a Community action for the European Capital of culture event for the years 2005 to 2019', 1419/1000/EC, *Official Journal*, L166/1, 1 July 1999.
17 http://europa.eu.int/comm/culture/eac/sources_info/brochures/capitales/page3_en.html (accessed 30 October 2003).
18 The other three sites were at Stratford (east London), Derby in the East Midlands, and the National Exhibition Centre in the West Midlands.
19 These were spirit, national identity, body, mind, local, play, work, learn, transaction, global, rest, living island, communicate and mobility.
20 K. Maguire and D. Teather, 'The dome: new delay, new doubts', *The Guardian*, 29 July 2003.
21 *Metro*, 14 April 2003.
22 K. Maguire and D. Teather, 'The dome: new delay, new doubts', *The Guardian*, 29 July 2003.

Bibliography

The references listed in this bibliography include both the primary and secondary sources used in writing this book. Full publication details are not always given on sources published before 1900, since many were privately published and bear only the names of their printers.

Adamson, J., ed. (1999) *The Princely Courts of Europe: ritual, politics and culture under the 'Ancien Regime', 1500–1750*, London: Weidenfeld and Nicolson.

Agnew, J., Mercer, J. and Sopher, D. (1984) 'Introduction', in J. Agnew, J. Mercer and D. Sopher, eds, *The City in Cultural Context*, Boston: George Allen and Unwin, 1–30.

Agulhon, M. (1981) *Marianne into Battle: Republican imagery and symbolism in France, 1789–1800*, translated by J. Lloyd, Cambridge: Cambridge University Press.

Alden, J. and da Rosa Pires, A. (1996) 'Lisbon: strategic planning for a capital city', *Cities*, 13, 25–36.

Allan, K. (1998) *The Meaning of Culture: moving the postmodern critique forward*, Westport, CN: Praeger.

Allan, T. (1990) 'Appendix A: Bureau of International Expositions', in J.E. Findling and K.D. Pelle, eds, *Historical Dictionary of World's Fairs and Expositions, 1851–1988*, Westport, CN: Greenwood Press, 372–74.

Allen, R. (1995) *Projecting Illusion: film spectatorship and the impression of reality*, Cambridge: Cambridge University Press.

Allwood, J. (1977) *The Great Exhibitions*, London: Studio Vista.

Altick, R.D. (1978) *The Shows of London*, Cambridge, MA: Belknap Press.

Anon. (1851) 'The World's Great Assembly (1851)', http://65.107.211. 206/1851/crystal1.html (accessed 18 September 2002).

_____ (1904) *Universal Exposition, Saint Louis 1904, Preliminary Programme of Physical Culture, Olympic Games and World's Championship Contexts*, St Louis.

_____ (1963) 'Variations on a theme', *Canadian Architect*, 8(7), 5, 7.

_____ (1967) 'How the Fair was planned', *Progressive Architecture*, June, 123.

_____ (2002a) 'Festival of the Federation', *Catholic Encyclopedia*, http://www.newadvent.org/cathen/13009a.htm (accessed 22 September 2002).

_____ (2002b) 'Jacques-Louis David', http://www.ibiblio.org/wm/paint/auth/david (accessed 22 September 2002).

_____ (2003) 'Medieval sourcebook: accounts of medieval fairs and markets', http://www.fordham.edu/halsall/source/1248Westmnst.html

AOC (1936) *Report of the American Olympic Committee: Games of the XIth Olympiad, Berlin Germany*, New York: American Olympic City.

Applebaum, S. (1977) 'Introduction', in R. Werts, ed., *The New York World's Fair, 1939–1940*, London: Constable, x–xviii.

Arbena, J.L. (1996) 'Mexico City: the Games of the 19th Olympiad', in J.E. Findling and K.D. Pelle, eds, *Historical Dictionary of the Modern Olympic Movement*, Westport, CN: Greenwood Press, 139–47.

Arendt, H. (1978) *The Life of the Mind*, New York: Harcourt Brace Jovanovich.

Arnold, B. (1992) 'The past as propaganda', *Archaeology*, July/August, 30–37.

Arvidsson, A.A. (2000) 'Fascist spectacle: the aesthetics of power in Mussolini's Italy', *Sociologisk Forskning*, 37, 103–8.

Ashdown, P. (1990) 'Seattle 1962: Seattle World's Fair (Century 21 Exposition)', in J.E. Findling and K.D. Pelle, eds, *Historical Dictionary of World's Fairs and Expositions, 1851–1988*, Westport, CN: Greenwood Press, 319–21.

Atkinson, D. and Cosgrove, D. (1998) 'Urban rhetoric and embodied identities: city, nation and Empire at the Vittorio Emanuele II monument in Rome, 1870–1945', *Annals of the Association of American Geographers*, 84, 28–49.

Auerbach, J.A. (1999) *The Great Exhibition of 1851: a nation on display*, New Haven, CN: Yale University Press.

Avery, P. (2000) 'City cultures as the object of cultural tourism 2000', in M. Robinson, R. Sharpley, N. Evans, P. Long and J. Swarbrooke, eds, *Reflections in International Tourism: developments in urban and rural tourism*, Sunderland: Business Education Publishers, 21–51.

Baculo, A., Gallo, S. and Mangone, M. (1988) *Le Grandi Esposizioni nel Mondo, 1851–1900: dall'edificio citta di edifici dal Crystal Palace alla White City*, Naples: Liguori Editore.

Badger, R.R. (1990) 'Chicago 1893: World's Columbian Exposition', in J.E. Findling and K.D. Pelle, eds, *Historical Dictionary of World's Fairs and Expositions, 1851–1988*, Westport, CN: Greenwood Press, 122–32.

Baker, J. (1967) 'Expo and the Future City', *Architectural Review*, 142, 151–4.

Bal, M. (2003) 'Visual essentialism and the object of visual culture', *Journal of Visual Culture*, 2, 5–32.

Balfour, A. (2001) *New York*, Chichester: Wiley-Academy.

Bancroft, H.H. (1893) *The Book of the Fair; an historical and descriptive presentation of the world's science, art, and industry, as viewed through the Columbian Exposition at Chicago in 1893, designed to set forth the display made by the Congress of Nations, of human achievement in material form, so as the more effectually to illustrate the progress of mankind in all the departments of civilized life*, Chicago: Bancroft Company.

Banham, P.R. (1962) 'Seattle's World's Fair', *Architectural Review*, 132, 134–5.

_____ (1976) *Megastructures: urban futures of the recent past*, London: Thames and Hudson.

Barnett, C. (2000) *Towards Culture 2000: the evolution of cultural policy in the European Union in the 1990s*, Geographical Paper 149, Department of Geography, University of Reading.

Barnett, C.R. (1996) 'St. Louis 1904: the Games of the 3rd Olympiad', in J.E. Findling and K.D. Pelle, eds, *Historical Dictionary of the Modern Olympic Movement*, Westport, CN: Greenwood Press, 18–25.

Barney, R.K. (1996) 'Prologue: the ancient games', in J.E. Findling and K.D. Pelle, eds, *Historical Dictionary of the Modern Olympic Movement*, Westport, CN: Greenwood Press, xix–xl.

Barrett, D. (2000) 'Sport and spectacle in the Bronze Age', paper given to the symposium on 'Sport and spectacle in the Ancient World', Department of Classics and Ancient History, University of Queensland, Australia.

Bassett, K. (1993) 'Urban cultural strategies and urban cultural regeneration: a study and a critique', *Environment and Planning A*, 25, 1773–88.

Bauman, R., Sawin, P. and Carpenter, I.G. (1992) *Reflections on the Folklife Festival: an ethnography of participant experience*, Special Publications of the Folklore Institute, 2, Bloomington: Indiana University Press.

Beacham, R.C. (1991) *The Roman Theatre and its Audience*, London: Routledge.

_____ (1999) *Spectacle Entertainments of Early Imperial Rome*, New Haven, CN: Yale University Press.

Beard, M., North, J. and Price, S. (1998) *Religions of Rome*, vol. 1, Cambridge: Cambridge University Press.

Beaver, P. (1970) *The Crystal Palace, 1851–1936: a portrait of Victorian enterprise*, London: Hugh Evelyn.

Behagg, C. (1991) *Labour and Reform: working class movements, 1815–1914*, London: Hodder and Stoughton.

Belfer, L. (1999) *City of Light*, London: Hodder and Stoughton.

Benedict, B. (1983) 'The Anthropology of World's Fairs', in B. Benedict, ed., *The Anthropology of World's Fairs: San Francisco's Panama–Pacific International Exposition of 1915*, London: Lowie Museum of Anthropology in association with Scolar Press, 1–65.

———— (1990) 'San Francisco 1915: Panama–Pacific International Exposition', in J.E. Findling and K.D. Pelle, eds, *Historical Dictionary of World's Fairs and Expositions, 1851–1988*, Westport, CN: Greenwood Press, 219–26.

———— (1994) 'Rituals of representation: ethnic stereotypes and colonised peoples at World's Fairs', in R.W. Rydell and N.E. Gwinn, eds, *Fair Representations: World's Fairs and the Modern World*, Amsterdam: VU University Press, 28–61.

Benjamin, M. (1996) 'Sliding scales: microphotography and the Victorian obsession with the minuscule', in F. Spufford and J. Uglow, eds, *Cultural Babbage: technology, time and invention*, London: Faber and Faber, 99–122.

Bennett, T. (1995) *The Birth of the Museum*, London: Routledge.

———— (1996) 'The exhibitionary complex', in R. Greenberg, B.W. Ferguson and S. Nairne, eds, *Thinking about exhibitions*, London: Routledge, 81–112.

Berger, J. (1972) *Ways of Seeing*, Harmondsworth: Penguin.

Bergmann, B. (1999) 'Introduction: the art of ancient spectacle', in B. Bergmann and C. Kondoleon, eds, *The Art of Ancient Spectacle*, Washington, DC: National Gallery of Art, 8–35.

Berlyn, P. (1851) *A Popular Narrative of the Origin, History, Progress and Prospects of the Great Industrial Exhibition, 1851*, London: James Gilbert.

Berman, M. (1983) *All that is Solid melts into Air: the experience of modernity*, London: Souvenir Press.

Bertelli, S. (1986) 'The courtly universe', in S. Bertelli, F. Cardini and E.G. Zorzi, eds, *Italian Renaissance Courts*, trans. M. Fitton and G. Culverwell, London: Sidgwick and Jackson, 7–37.

Bianchini, F. and Parkinson, M., eds, (1993) *Cultural Policy and Urban Regeneration: the West European experience*, Manchester: Manchester University Press.

BIE (Bureau International des Expositions) (2002) 'The BIE', http://www.bie-paris.org/eng/index3.htm

Billinge, M. (1993) 'Trading history, reclaiming the past: the Crystal

Palace as icon', in G. Kearns and C. Philo, eds, *Selling Places: the city as cultural capital, past and present*, Oxford: Pergamon Press, 103–31.

BOA (British Olympic Association) (1936) *The Official Report of the XIth Olympiad Berlin 1936*, London: British Olympic Association.

Bodel, J. (1999) 'Death on display: looking at Roman funerals', in B. Bergmann and C. Kondoleon, eds, *The Art of Ancient Spectacle*, Washington, DC: National Gallery of Art, 259–81.

Bondanella, P. (1987) *The Eternal City: Roman images in the modern world*, Chapel Hill: University of North Carolina Press.

Boniface, P. (1994) 'Theme park Britain: who benefits and who loses?', in J.M. Fladmark, ed., *Cultural Tourism*, Wimbledon: Donmark, 101–9.

Bonnemaison, S. (1998) 'Moses/Marianne parts the Red Sea: allegories of liberty in the bicentennial of the French Revolution', *Environment and Planning D: Society and Space*, 16, 347–65.

Booker, C. (1981) *The Games War: a Moscow journal*, London: Faber and Faber.

Booth, P. and Boyle, R. (1993) 'See Glasgow, see culture', in F. Bianchini and M. Parkinson, eds, *Cultural Policy and urban regeneration: the West European experience*, Manchester: Manchester University Press, 21–47.

Borden, I., Kerr, J., Pivaro, A. and Rendell, J., eds (1996) *Strangely Familiar: narratives of architecture in the city*, London: Routledge.

Borsay, P. (1984) 'All the town's a stage: urban ritual and public ceremony, 1660–1800', in P. Clark, ed., *The Transformation of English Provincial Towns, 1600–1800*, London: Hutchinson, 228–58.

Boyer, M.C. (1994) *The City of Collective Memory: its historical imagery and architectural entertainments*, Cambridge, MA: MIT Press.

Boyle, M. and Hughes, G. (1994) 'The politics of urban entrepreneurialism in Glasgow', *Geoforum*, 25, 453–70.

Bramen, C.T. (2000) 'The urban picturesque and the spectacle of Americanization', *American Quarterly*, 52, 444–77.

Brendon, P. (1991) *Thomas Cook: 150 years of popular tourism*, London: Secker and Warburg.

Brewer, J. (1997) *The Pleasures of the Imagination: English culture in the nineteenth century*, London: HarperCollins.

Brichford, M. (1996) 'Munich 1972: the Games of the 20th Olympiad', in J.E. Findling and K.D. Pelle, eds, *Historical Dictionary of the Modern Olympic Movement*, Westport, CN: Greenwood Press, 148–52.

Briggs, A. (2000) 'Exhibiting the nation', *History Today*, 50(1), 16–25.

Briggs, A. and Snowman, D. (1996) 'Introduction', in A. Briggs and D. Snowman, eds, *Fins de siècle: how centuries end, 1400–2000*, New Haven, CN: Yale University Press, 1–5.

Brown, E.A.R. and Regalado, N.F. (1994) '*La grant feste*: Philip the Fair's celebration of the knighting of his sons in Paris at Pentecost of 1313', in B.A. Hanawalt and K.L. Reyerson, eds, *City and Spectacle in Medieval Europe*, Medieval Studies at Minnesota, 6, Minneapolis: University of Minnesota Press, 56–86.

Bruss, E.W. (1982) *Beautiful Theories: the spectacle of discourse in contemporary criticism*, Baltimore: Johns Hopkins University Press.

Buchanan, I. and Mallon, B. (2001) *Historical Dictionary of the Olympic Movement*, Lanham, MD: Scarecrow Press.

Burbank, M.J., Andranovitch, G.D. and Heyling, C.H. (2001) *Olympic Dreams: the impact of mega-events on local politics*, Boulder, CO: Lynne Rienner.

Bureau of Cultural Affairs (n.d.) *Public Art in Downtown Atlanta*, Atlanta: Bureau of Cultural Affairs, City of Atlanta.

Burnett, J. and Tabraham, C.J. (1993) *The Honours of Scotland: the story of the Scottish Crown Jewels*, Edinburgh: Historic Scotland.

Burris, J.P. (2001) *Exhibiting Religion: colonialism and spectacle at international expositions, 1851–1893*, Charlottesville: University Press of Virginia.

Buzard, J. (1993) *The Beaten Track: European tourism, literature, and the ways to 'culture', 1800–1918*, Oxford: Clarendon Press.

———— (1999) 'Then on the shore of the wide world: the Victorian nation and its others', in H.F. Tucker, ed., *A Companion to Victorian Literature and Culture*, Oxford: Blackwell, 438–55.

Cameron, D.K. (1998) *The English Fair*, Stroud: Sutton Publishing.

Canogar, D. (1992) *Ciudades Efímeras: Exposiciones Universales, espectáculo y tecnología*, Madrid: Anjana Ediciones.

Carreras, C. (1995) 'Mega-Events: local strategies and global tourist attractions', in A. Montanari and A.M. Williams, eds, *European Tourism: regions, spaces and restructuring*, Chichester: John Wiley, 193–205.

Casson, L. (1974) *Travel in the Ancient World*, London: George Allen and Unwin.

Chandler, A. (1990) 'Paris 1937: Exposition Internationale des Arts et des Techniques Appliqueés à la Vie Moderne', in J.E. Findling and K.D. Pelle, eds, *Historical Dictionary of World's Fairs and Expositions, 1851–1988*, Westport, CN: Greenwood Press, 283–90.

Chase, K. and Levenson, M. (2000) *The Spectacle of Intimacy: a public life for the Victorian family*, Princeton, NJ: Princeton University Press.

Chisholm, D. and Brazeau, R. (2002) 'Introduction – special issue: the other city, (de)mystifying urban culture', *Journal of Urban History*, 29, 3–5.

Clark, K. (2000) 'Beyond spectacle: critically examining the Olympics industry', http://www.monkeyfist.com/articles/678 (accessed 6 November 2003).

Coates, J.R. (1996) 'London 1908: the Games of the 4th Olympiad', in J.E. Findling and K.D. Pelle, eds, *Historical Dictionary of the Modern Olympic Movement*, Westport, CN: Greenwood Press, 35–40.

Cogliandro, G. (2001) *European Cities of Culture for the Year 2000 – a wealth of urban cultures celebrating the turn of the century, Final Report*, Brussels: European Commission.

Cole, A. (1995) *Art of the Italian Renaissance Courts: virtue and magnificence*, London: George Weidenfeld and Nicolson.

Cole, H. (1853) 'On the international results of the exhibition of 1851', in *Lectures on the Results of the Great Exhibition of 1851, delivered before the Society of Arts, Manufactures and Commerce, at the Suggestion of H.R.H. Prince Albert, President of the Society*, second series, London: David Bogue, 419–51.

Collier, P. (1985) 'Nineteenth-century Paris: vision and nightmare', in E. Timms and D. Kelley, eds, *Unreal City: Urban Experience in Modern European Literature and Art*, Manchester: Manchester University Press, 25–44.

Conrads, U. and Sperlich, H.G. (1963) *Fantastic Architecture*, trans. C.C. Collins and G.R. Collins, London: Architectural Press.

Cooper, J.I. (1969) *Montreal: a brief history*, Montreal: McGill-Queen's University Press.

Coubertin, P. de (1889) *L'Education en Angleterre*, Paris: Hachette.

_____ (1890) *Universités Transatlantiques*, Paris: Hachette.

Couldry, N. (2000) *Inside Culture: re-imagining the method of cultural studies*, London: Sage.

Cox, J.C. (1911) 'Forestry', in W. Page, ed., *The Victoria History of the County of Middlesex*, vol. 2, London: Constable, 223–51.

Crandell, G. (1993) *Nature Pictorialized: 'the view' in landscape history*, Baltimore: Johns Hopkins University Press.

Crane, S.A. (2000) 'Curious cabinets and imaginary museums', in S.A. Crane, ed., *Museums and Memory*, Stanford, CA: Stanford University Press, 60–81.

Crary, J. (1989) 'Spectacle, attention, counter-memory', *October*, 50, 96–107.

_____ (1990) *Techniques of the Observer: on vision and modernity in the nineteenth century*, Cambridge, MA: MIT Press.

Cumming, J. (1851) *The Great Exhibition: suggestive and anticipative*, London: John Farquhar Shaw.

Cunningham, H. (1977) 'The metropolitan fairs: a case study in the social control of leisure', in A.P. Donajgrodzki, ed., *Social Control in Nineteenth Century Britain*, London: Croom Helm, 163–84.

――――― (1980) *Leisure in the Industrial Revolution*, London: Croom Helm.

Cusker, J.P. (1980) 'The world of tomorrow: science, culture and community at the New York World's Fair', in H.A. Harrison, ed., *Dawn of a New Day: the New York World's Fair*, New York: Queen's Museum/New York University Press, 2–15.

Daly, J.A. (1990) 'Introduction', in J.E. Findling and K.D. Pelle, eds, *Historical Dictionary of World's Fairs and Expositions, 1851–1988*, Westport, CN: Greenwood Press, xiii–xix.

――――― (1996) 'Introduction', in J.E. Findling and K.D. Pelle, eds, *Historical Dictionary of the Modern Olympic Movement*, Westport, CN: Greenwood Press, xviii–xxvii.

Damer, S. (1990) *Glasgow's Going for a Song*, London: Lawrence and Wishart.

D'Arms, J.H. (1999) 'Performing culture: Roman spectacle and the banquets of the powerful', in B. Bergmann and C. Kondoleon, eds, *The Art of Ancient Spectacle*, Washington, DC: National Gallery of Art, 300–19.

Dart, G. (1999) *Rousseau, Robespierre and English Romanticism*, Cambridge: Cambridge University Press.

Davenport, J. (1996) 'Athens 1896: the Games of the 1st Olympiad', in J.E. Findling and K.D. Pelle, eds, *Historical Dictionary of the Modern Olympic Movement*, Westport, CN: Greenwood Press, 3–11.

Davies, E.L. (1996) 'Rome: the Games of the 18th Olympiad', in J.E. Findling and K.D. Pelle, eds, *Historical Dictionary of the Modern Olympic Movement*, Westport, CN: Greenwood Press, 128–34.

Davis, J. (1988) *Reforming London: the London government problem, 1855–1900*, Oxford: Clarendon Press.

Davis, J.R. (1999) *The Great Exhibition*, Stroud: Sutton.

Davis, N.Z. (1971) 'The reasons of misrule: youth groups and Charivaris in sixteenth-century France', *Past and Present*, 50, 41–75.

Davis, S.G. (1985) 'Strike parades and the politics of representing class in antebellum Philadelphia', *Drama Review*, 29(3), 106–16.

DCH (Department of Canadian Heritage) (2002) 'Evaluation of Canada's participation in Expo 2000, Hannover, Germany', http://www.pch.gc.ca/progs/em-cr/eval/2002/2002_17/3_e.cfm (accessed 30 October 2003).

Debord, G. (1967) *La Société du Spectacle*, Paris: Buchet-Chastel, published (1995) as *The Society of the Spectacle*, trans. D. Nicholson-Smith, New York: Zone Books.

Delgado-Moreira, J.M. (2000) 'Cohesion and citizenship in European Union cultural policy', *Journal of Common Market Studies*, 38, 449–70.

Denzin, N.K. (1995) *The Cinematic Society: the voyeur's gaze*, London: Sage.

De Sainte Croix, G.E.M. (1972) *The Origins of the Peloponnesian War*, London: Duckworth.

Dickens, C. (1912) *Sketches by Boz: illustrative of everyday life and everyday people, and other early papers*, London: Gresham (originally published in 1836, London: John Macrone).

Doak, R. (1990) 'Knoxville 1982: Knoxville International Energy Exposition', in J.E. Findling and K.D. Pelle, eds, *Historical Dictionary of World's Fairs and Expositions, 1851–1988*, Westport, CN: Greenwood Press, 352–5.

Doctorow, E.L. (1985) *World's Fair*, London: Michael Joseph.

Dodwell, P.C. (1966) 'Studies of the visual system', in B.M. Foss, ed., *New Horizons in Psychology*, Harmondsworth: Penguin.

Donat, J. (1964) *Architecture in Television and Broadcasting*, London: Royal Institute of British Architects.

Douglas, M. (1966) *Purity and Danger: an analysis of the concepts of pollution and taboo*, London: Routledge and Kegan Paul.

Dowd, D.L. (1948) *Pageant-Master of the Republic: Jacques-Louis David and the French Revolution*, University of Nebraska Studies, New Series 3, Lincoln: University of Nebraska Press.

Downing, T. (1992) *Olympia*, London: British Film Institute.

Dueppengiesser, M. (1995) 'Luxemburg: European Grand Duchy of Culture',
http://www.karl.aegee.org/oem/articles/oe8/luxcul.htm (accessed 17 October 2003).

Duncan, C. (1995) *Civilizing Rituals: inside public art museums*, London: Routledge.

Durick, W. (1996) 'Berlin 1916: the Games of the 6th Olympiad (Never Held)', in J.E. Findling and K.D. Pelle, eds, *Historical Dictionary of the Modern Olympic Movement*, Westport, CN: Greenwood Press, 47–53.

Eames, E. and Goode, J.G. (1977) *Anthropology of the City: an introduction to urban anthropology*, Englewood Cliffs, NJ: Prentice Hall.

Edelman, M. (1988) *Constructing the Political Spectacle*, Chicago: University of Chicago Press.

Edmondson, J.C. (1999) 'The cultural politics of public spectacle in

Rome and the Greek East, 167–166 BCE', in B. Bergmann and C. Kondoleon, eds, *The Art of Ancient Spectacle*, Washington, DC: National Gallery of Art, 77–95.

Edwards, S. (2001) 'The accumulation of knowledge or, William Whewell's eye', in L. Purbrick, ed., *The Great Exhibition of 1851: new interdisciplinary essays*, Manchester: Manchester University Press, 25–52.

Engelstoft, S. and Jorgesen, J. (1997) 'Copenhagen the redistributive city?', in C. Jensen-Butler, A. Shachar and J. van Weesep, eds, *European cities in competition*, Aldershot: Avebury, 209–43.

Eoff, S.M. (1990) 'San Antonio 1968: Hemisfair '68, a Confluence of Cultures of the Americas', in J.E. Findling and K.D. Pelle, eds, *Historical Dictionary of World's Fairs and Expositions, 1851–1988*, Westport, CN: Greenwood Press, 336–8.

Essex, S. and Chalkley, B. (1998) 'Olympic Games: catalyst of urban change', *Leisure Studies*, 17, 187–206.

Evans, G. (2001) *Cultural Planning: an urban renaissance?*, London: Routledge.

Falassi, A., ed. (1987) *Time Out of Time: essays on the festival*, Albuquerque: University of New Mexico Press.

Favro, D. (1999) 'The city is a living thing: the performative role of an urban site in ancient Rome, the Vallis Murcia', in B. Bergmann and C. Kondoleon, eds, *The Art of Ancient Spectacle*, Washington, DC: National Gallery of Art, 204–19.

Fay, C.R. (1951) *Palace of Industry, 1851: a study of the Great Exhibition and its fruits*, Cambridge: Cambridge University Press.

Feldherr, A. (1998) *Spectacle and Society in Livy's 'History'*, Berkeley: University of California Press.

Findling, J.E. and Pelle, K.D., eds (1990) *Historical Dictionary of World's Fairs and Expositions, 1851–1988*, Westport, CN: Greenwood Press.

———— (1996) *Historical Dictionary of the Modern Olympic Movement*, Westport, CN: Greenwood Press.

Finley, G. (1981) *Turner and George the Fourth in Edinburgh 1822*, London: Tate Gallery in association with Edinburgh University Press.

Fisher, R. (2001) 'EU support for culture: separating rhetoric from reality', *Insight Europe*, 1(2), 24–5.

Fleming, W. (1990) *Concerts of the Arts: their interplay and modes of relationship*, Pensacola: University of West Florida Press.

Flynn, M. (1994) 'The spectacle of suffering in Spanish streets', in B.A. Hanawalt and K.L. Reyerson, eds, *City and Spectacle in Medieval Europe*, Medieval Studies at Minnesota, 6, Minneapolis: University of Minnesota Press, 153–68.

Forrest, A. (1994) 'A new start for cultural action in the European Community: genesis and implications of Article 128 of the Treaty of European Union', *Cultural Policy*, 1, 11–20.

Foucault, M. (1973) *The Birth of the Clinic*, London: Tavistock.

Fox, R.G. (2001) 'Urban Culture', http://www.britannica.com/bcom/eb/article/0/0,5716,1182501,00.html (accessed 7 January 2001).

Frampton, K. (1978) 'A synoptic view of the architecture of the Third Reich', *Oppositions*, 12, 54–87.

Furet, F. (1981) *Interpreting the French Revolution*, trans. E. Forster, Cambridge: Cambridge University Press.

Futrell, A. (1997) *Blood in the Arena: the spectacle of Roman power*, Austin: University of Texas Press.

Galopin, M. (1997) *Les Expositions Internationales au XXe Siecle et le Bureau International des Expositions*, Paris: L'Harmattan.

Gandy, M. (2002) *Concrete and Clay: reworking nature in New York City*, Cambridge, MA: MIT Press.

Garber, M., Matlock, J. and Walkowitz, R., eds (1993) *Media Spectacles*, New York: Routledge.

Gardner, D., ed. (1965) *The British Olympic Association Official Report of the Olympic Games 1964*, London: World Sports.

Gaskell, S.M. (1986) *Model Housing: from the Great Exhibition to the Festival of Britain*, London: Mansell.

Gay, P. (1998) *The Bourgeois Experience: Victoria to Freud*, vol. 5 'Pleasure Wars', London: HarperCollins.

Geddes, P. (1887) *Industrial Exhibitions and Modern Progress*, Edinburgh: David Douglas.

Gelernter, D.H. (1995) *1939: the Lost World of the Fair*, New York: Free Press.

Germain, A. and Rose, D. (2000) *Montreal: the quest for a metropolis*, Chichester: John Wiley and Sons.

Getz, D. (1991) *Festivals, Special Events and Tourism*, New York: Van Nostrand.

―――― (2001) 'Festival places: a comparison of Europe and North America', *Tourism*, 49, 3–18.

Gibbs-Smith, C.H. (1981) *The Great Exhibition of 1851*, 2nd edn, London: HMSO.

Gilbert, J.B. (1991) *Perfect Cities: Chicago's utopias of 1893*, Chicago: University of Chicago Press.

Girodano, B. and Twomey, L. (2002) 'Economic transitions: restructuring local labour markets' in J. Peck and K. Ward, eds, *City of Revolution: restructuring Manchester*, Manchester: Manchester University Press, 116–31.

Glasgow City Council (1992) *The 1990 Story: Glasgow Cultural Capital of Europe*, Glasgow: Glasgow City Council.

Glasgow District Council (1990) *The Book – Glasgow 1990: There's a lot Glasgowing on in 1990. The Authorised Tour of the Cultural Capital of Europe*, Glasgow: Glasgow District Council.

Glenn, S.A. (1997) *Female Spectacle: the theoretical roots of modern feminism*, Cambridge, MA: Harvard University Press.

Goksyr, M. (1989) '"One certainly expected more from the savages": the Anthropological Days in St. Louis, 1904, and their aftermath', *International Journal of the History of Sport*, 6, 297–306.

Gold, J.R. (1974) *Communicating Images of the Environment*, Occasional Paper 29, Centre for Urban and Regional Studies, University of Birmingham.

――― (1980) *An Introduction to Behavioural Geography*, Oxford: Oxford University Press.

――― (1997) *The Experience of Modernism: modern architects and the future city, 1928–1953*, London: E. & F.N. Spon/Routledge.

Gold, J.R. and Gold, M.M. (1995) *Imagining Scotland: tradition, representation and promotion in Scottish tourism since 1750*, Aldershot: Scolar Press/Ashgate Press.

Gold, J.R. and Revill, G.E. (2004) *Representing the Environment*, London: Routledge.

Gold, J.R. and Ward, S.V., eds (1994) *Place Promotion: the use of publicity and public relations to sell towns and regions*, Chichester: John Wiley.

Goldberg, S. (1998) 'Plautus and the Palatine', *Journal of Roman Studies*, 88, 1–19.

Goldstein, E.S. (1996) 'Amsterdam: the Games of the 9th Olympiad', in J.E. Findling and K.D. Pelle, eds, *Historical Dictionary of the Modern Olympic Movement*, Westport, CN: Greenwood Press, 68–83.

Good, D. (1999) 'The cultural Olympiad', in R. Cashman and A. Hughes, eds, *Staging the Olympics: the event and its impact*, Sydney: University of New South Wales Press, 159–69.

Gordon, B.F. (1983) *Olympic Architecture: building for the Summer Games*, New York: John Wiley.

Gotham, K.F. (2002) 'Marketing Mardi Gras: commodification, spectacle and the political economy of tourism in New Orleans', *Urban Studies*, 39, 1735–56.

Graham, C.G. (1986) *Leni Riefenstahl and Olympia*, New Jersey: Scarecrow Press.

Greeley, H. (1851) *Glances at Europe in a Series of Letters from Great Britain, France, Italy, Switzerland, &c. during the Summer of 1851, including Notices of the Great Exhibition, or World's Fair*, New York: Dawitt and Davenport.

Green, A.S. (1994) *The Revisionist Stage: American directors reinvent the classics*, Cambridge: Cambridge University Press.

Green, N. (1990) *The Spectacle of Nature: landscape and bourgeois culture in nineteenth-century France*, Manchester: Manchester University Press.

Greenhalgh, P. (1988) *Ephemeral Vistas: the Expositions Universelles, Great Exhibitions and World's Fairs, 1851–1939*, Manchester: Manchester University Press.

———— (1989) 'Education, entertainment and politics: lessons from the Great International Exhibitions', in P. Vergo, ed., *The New Museology*, London: Reaktion, 74–98.

Gregory, D. (1994) *Geographical Imaginations*, Oxford: Blackwell.

Gruneau, R. and Cantelon, H. (1988) 'Capitalism, commercialism and the Olympics', in J.O. Seagrove and D. Chu, eds, *The Olympic Games in Transition*, Champaign, IL: Human Kinetics Books, 345–64.

Gurney, P. (2001) 'An appropriated space: the Great Exhibition, the Crystal Palace and the working class', in L. Purbrick, ed., *The Great Exhibition of 1851: new interdisciplinary essays*, Manchester: Manchester University Press, 114–45.

Habermas, J. (1989) *The Structural Transformation of the Public Sphere: an inquiry into a category of bourgeois society*, trans. T. Burger and F. Laurence, Cambridge, MA: MIT Press.

Hahn, D. (2003) *The Tower Menagerie: being the amazing true story of the Royal Collection of Wild Beasts*, New York: Simon and Schuster.

Hale, J. (1993) *The Civilization of Europe in the Renaissance*, London: Fontana Press.

Hall, C.M. (1989) 'The definition and analysis of hallmark tourist events', *GeoJournal*, 19, 263–8.

———— (1992) *Hallmark Tourist Events: impacts, management, planning*, London: Belhaven.

Hall, J.A. (1993) 'Culture', in W. Outhwaite and T. Bottomore, eds, *The Blackwell Dictionary of Twentieth-Century Social Thought*, Oxford: Blackwell, 129–32.

Hall, J.H. (1990) 'Paris 1889: Exposition Universelle', in J.E. Findling and K.D. Pelle, eds, *Historical Dictionary of World's Fairs and Expositions, 1851–1988*, Westport, CN: Greenwood Press, 108–16.

Hall, P. (1980) *Great Planning Disasters*, London: Weidenfeld and Nicolson.

———— (1998) *Cities in Civilization: culture, innovation, and urban order*, London: Weidenfeld and Nicolson.

Hall, T. and Hubbard, P., eds (1996) *The Entrepreneurial City: geographies of politics, regime and representation*, Chichester: John Wiley.

Hanawalt, B.A. and Reyerson, K.L., eds (1994a) *City and Spectacle in*

Medieval Europe, Medieval Studies at Minnesota, 6, Minneapolis: University of Minnesota Press.

——— (1994b) 'Introduction', in B.A. Hanawalt and K.L. Reyerson, eds, *City and Spectacle in Medieval Europe*, Medieval Studies at Minnesota, 6, Minneapolis: University of Minnesota Press, ix–xx.

Handelman, D. (1990) *Models and Mirrors: towards an anthropology of public events*, Cambridge: Cambridge University Press.

Handwerker, W.P. (2002) 'The construct validity of culture: cultural diversity, cultural theory, and a method for ethnography', *American Anthropologist*, 104, 106–22.

Hanna, N. (1999) *The Millennium: a Rough Guide to the year 2000*, revised edn, London: Rough Guides.

Hannerz, U. (1980) *Exploring the City*, New York: Columbia University Press.

Hansen, M. (1991) *Babel and Babylon: spectatorship in American silent films*, Cambridge, MA: MIT Press.

Hardy, R. (1990) 'Fairs that never were', in J.E. Findling and K.D. Pelle, eds, *Historical Dictionary of World's Fairs and Expositions, 1851–1988*, Westport, CN: Greenwood Press.

Hardy, T. (1894) *Life's Little Ironies: a set of tales with some colloquial sketches entitled 'A Few Crusted Characters'*, London: Osgood, MacIlvanie and Co.

Hargreaves, J. (2000) *Freedom for Catalonia?: Catalan nationalism, Spanish identity and the Barcelona Olympic Games*, Cambridge: Cambridge University Press.

Hart Davis, D. (1986) *Hitler's Games: the 1936 Olympics*, London: Century.

Harvey, P. (1998) 'Nations on display: technology and culture in Expo 92', in S. Macdonald, ed., *The Politics of Display: museums, science, culture*, London: Routledge, 139–58.

Harvie, C., Martin, G. and Scharf, A., eds (1970) *Industrialisation and Culture*, London: Macmillan for the Open University Press.

Hauss-Fitton, B. (1994) 'Futurama, New York World's Fair, 1939–40', *Rassegna*, 60, 55–9.

Haynes, J. (2001) 'Socio-economic impact of the Sydney 2000 Olympic Games', paper given to the 2001 seminar of the International Chair in Olympism, http://www.blues.uab.es/olympic.studies/web/pdf/od013_eng.pdf (accessed 30 October 2003).

Hazan, B. (1982) *Soviet Impregnational Propaganda*, Ann Arbor, MI: Ardis.

Hebbert, M. (1998) *London: more by fortune than design*, Chichester: Wiley.

Heikkinen, T. (2000) 'In from the margins: the City of Culture 2000 and the image transformation of Helsinki', *Cultural Policy*, 6, 201–18.

Heller, A. (1999) *A Theory of Modernity*, Oxford: Blackwell.

Heywood, I. and Sandywell, B., eds (1999) *Interpreting Visual Culture: explorations in the hermeneutics of the visual*, London: Routledge.

Hill, C. (1992) *Olympic Politics*, Manchester: Manchester University Press.

Hiller, H.H. (1990) 'The urban transformation of a landmark event', *Urban Affairs Quarterly*, 26, 118–37.

Hillis, M. (1939) *New York, Fair or No Fair: a guide for the woman vacationist*, Indianapolis: Bobbs-Merrill.

Hobhouse, H. (2002) *The Crystal Palace and the Great Exhibition, art, science and productive industry: a history of the Royal Commission for the Exhibition of 1851*, London: Athlone Press.

Hobsbawm, E. (1995) *The Age of Capital, 1848–1875*, 2nd edn, London: Weidenfeld and Nicolson.

Hodder, I., ed. (1991) *The Meaning of Things: material culture and symbolic expression*, London: HarperCollins.

Holme, B. (1988) *Princely Feasts and Festivals: five centuries of pageantry and spectacle*, London: Thames and Hudson.

Holt, R. and Mason, T. (2000) *Sport in Britain, 1945–2000*, Oxford: Blackwell.

Hooper, J. (2000) 'Is Expo out of steam?', *Guardian Unlimited*, http://www.guardian.co.uk/elsewhere/journalist/story/0,7792,398097,00.html

Hopkinson, A. (1992) 'There's an awful lot of phooey in Seville', *New Statesman and Society*, 12 June, 18–19.

Hornbuckle, A.R. (1996) 'Helsinki 1952: the Games of the 15th Olympiad', in J.E. Findling and K.D. Pelle, eds, *Historical Dictionary of the Modern Olympic Movement*, Westport, CN: Greenwood Press, 109–18.

Howell, R.A. and Howell, M.L. (1996) 'Paris 1900: the Games of the 2nd Olympiad', in J.E. Findling and K.D. Pelle, eds, *Historical Dictionary of the Modern Olympic Movement*, Westport, CN: Greenwood Press, 12–17.

Howes, D., ed. (1991) *The Varieties of Sensory Evidence: a sourcebook in the anthropology of the senses*, Toronto: University of Toronto Press.

Hughes, H.L, Allen, D. and Wasik, D. (2002) 'Culture as a tourist resource in Krakow, European City of Culture 2000', *Tourism*, 50, 131–9.

Hughes, H.M. (1991) 'The year in perspective', in T. Jackson and A. Guest, eds, *A Platform for Partnership: the visual arts in Glasgow,*

Cultural Capital of Europe 1990, Glasgow: Glasgow City Council, 22–32.

Hughes, R. (1992) *Barcelona*, London: Harvill.

―――― (1996) *Barcelona*, New York: Alfred A. Knopf.

Huizinga, J. (1924) *The Waning of the Middle Ages: a study of the forms of life, thought and art in France and the Netherlands in the XIVth and XVth centuries*, London: Edward Arnold.

Inwood, S. (1998) *A History of London*, London: Macmillan.

IOC (International Olympic Committee) (2001) *Olympic Charter*, Lausanne: International Olympic Committee.

Irvine, A. (1999) *The Battle for the Millennium Dome*, London: Irvine News Agency.

Islam, K.M. (1976) *The Spectacle of Death, including glimpses of life beyond the grave*, Lahore: Tablighi Kutub Khana.

Jackson, P. (1989) *Maps of Meaning: an introduction to cultural geography*, London: Unwin Hyman.

Jackson, T. and Guest, A., eds (1991) *A Platform for Partnership: the visual arts in Glasgow, Cultural Capital of Europe 1990*, Glasgow: Glasgow City Council.

Jacobs, M.C. (1997) *Scientific Culture and the Making of the Industrial West*, New York: Oxford University Press.

Jarvis, B. (1994) 'Transitory topographies: places, events, promotions and propaganda', in J.R. Gold and S.V. Ward, eds, *Place Promotion: the use of publicity and public relations to sell towns and regions*, Chichester: John Wiley, 181–93.

Jay, M. (1993a) *Downcast Eyes: the denigration of vision in twentieth-century French thought*, Berkeley: University of California Press.

―――― (1993b) *Force Fields: between intellectual history and cultural critique*, Berkeley: University of California Press.

―――― (2002) 'Cultural relativism and the visual turn', *Journal of Visual Culture*, 1, 267–78.

Jay, R. (1987) 'Taller than Eiffel's Tower: the London and Chicago Tower projects, 1889–1894', *Journal of the Society of Architectural Historians*, 46, 145–56.

Jobbing, I. (1996) 'Melbourne 1956: the Games of the 18th Olympiad', in J.E. Findling and K.D. Pelle, eds, *Historical Dictionary of the Modern Olympic Movement*, Westport, CN: Greenwood Press, 119–27.

Johnson, C. (1999) 'Planning the Olympic site', in P. Bingham-Hall, ed., *Olympic Architecture: building Sydney*, Sydney: Watermark Press, 36–45.

Johnson, D.J. (2003) 'Los Angeles', in S.I. Kutler, ed., *Dictionary of American History*, 3rd edn, vol. 5, 'La Follette to Nationalism', New York: Charles Scribner's Sons, 151–5.

Kaplan, H. (1982) *Reform, Planning and City Politics: Montreal, Winnipeg, Toronto*, Toronto: University of Toronto Press.

Kellum, B. (1999) 'The spectacle of the street', in B. Bergmann and C. Kondoleon, eds, *The Art of Ancient Spectacle*, Washington, DC: National Gallery of Art, 282–99.

Kessing, R.M. and Strathern, A.J. (1998) *Cultural Anthropology: a contemporary perspective*, 3rd edn, New York: Harcourt, Brace and Co.

Kettmann, S. (2000) 'Not all is fair at Expo 2000', http://www.wired.com/news/business/0,1367,36884,00.html (accessed 30 October 2003).

Kidd, B. (1996) 'Montreal 1976: the Games of the 21st Olympiad', in J.E. Findling and K.D. Pelle, eds, *Historical Dictionary of the Modern Olympic Movement*, Westport, CN: Greenwood Press, 153–60.

Killanin, Lord (1983) *My Olympic Years*, London: Secker and Warburg.

Kim, J. and Choe, S.-C. (1997) *Seoul: the making of a metropolis*, Chichester: John Wiley.

Kinchin, P. and Kinchin, J. (n.d.) *Glasgow's Great Exhibitions: 1888, 1901, 1911, 1938, 1988*, Bicester: White Cockade Publishing.

Kondoleon, C. (1999) 'Timing spectacles: Roman domestic art and performance', in B. Bergmann and C. Kondoleon, eds, *The Art of Ancient Spectacle*, Washington, DC: National Gallery of Art, 321–41.

Krantz, M. and Schätzl, L. (2000) 'Marketing the city', in C. Jensen-Butler, A. Shachar and J. van Weesep, eds, *European cities in competition*, Aldershot: Avebury, 468–93.

Kriegel, L. (2001) 'Narrating the subcontinent in 1851: India at the Crystal Palace', in L. Purbrick, ed., *The Great Exhibition of 1851: new interdisciplinary essays*, Manchester: Manchester University Press, 146–78.

Kroeber, A.L. and Kluckhohn, C. (1952) *Culture: a critical review of concepts and definitions*, Cambridge, MA: Peabody Museum.

Kroessler, J.A. (1995) 'World's Fairs', in K.T. Jackson, ed., *The Encyclopedia of New York City*, New Haven, CN: Yale University Press, 1275–6.

Krüger, A. (1993) 'The origins of Pierre de Coubertin's *Religio Athletae*', *Olympika: the International Journal of Olympic Studies*, 2, 91–102.

Kuhn, J. (1995) 'Flushing Meadows-Corona Park', in K.T. Jackson, ed., *The Encyclopedia of New York City*, New Haven, CN: Yale University Press, 420.

Kupar, A. (1999) *Culture: the anthropologist's account*, Cambridge, MA: Harvard University Press.

Kusamitsu, T. (1980) 'Great Exhibitions before 1851', *History Workshop*, 9, 70–89.

Kuttner, A. (1999) 'Hellenistic images of spectacle, from Alexander to Augustus', in B. Bergmann and C. Kondoleon, eds, *The Art of Ancient Spectacle*, Washington, DC: National Gallery of Art, 95–123.

Kyle, D.G. (1998) *Spectacles of Death in Ancient Rome*, London: Routledge.

Lappo, G., Chikishev, A. and Bekker, A. (1976) *Moscow, capital of the Soviet Union: a short geographical survey*, Moscow: Progress Publishers.

Larson, E. (2003) *The Devil in the White City: murder, magic and madness at the Fair that changed America*, New York: Crown Publishers.

Larson, J.F. and Park, H.S. (1993) *Global Television and the Politics of the Seoul Olympics*, Boulder, CO: Westview Press.

Larson, R. and Staley, T. (1998) *Atlanta Olympics: the big story*, in P. Thompson, J.J.A. Tolloczko and J.N. Clarke, eds, *Stadia, Arenas and Grandstands: design, construction and operation*, London: Spon, 276–83.

Lawrence, D.T. (1990) 'New York 1964–1965: New York World's Fair', in J.E. Findling and K.D. Pelle, eds, *Historical Dictionary of World's Fairs and Expositions, 1851–1988*, Westport, CN: Greenwood Press, 322–8.

Leapman, M. (2001) *The World for a Shilling: how the Great Exhibition of 1851 shaped a nation*, London: Headline.

Lebesque, S., ed. (1997) *Between Sea and City: eight piers for Thessaloniki*, Rotterdam: NAi Publishers.

Lefebvre, H. (1991) *The Production of Space*, trans. D. Nicholson-Smith, Oxford: Blackwell.

Lenskyj, H.J. (2000) *Inside the Olympic Industry: power, politics and activism*, Albany: State University of New York Press.

Lewis, R. (2000) *Manufacturing Montreal: the making of an industrial landscape, 1850 to 1930*, Baltimore: Johns Hopkins University Press.

Lindner, R. (2001) 'The construction of authenticity: the case of subcultures', in J. Liep, ed., *Locating Cultural Creativity*, London: Pluto Press, 81–89.

Lisle, T. de (1998) '50 Eno Moments', *The Sunday Review: Independent on Sunday*, 10 May, 16–17, 19–20, 32.

Lloyd, S. (2002) 'Pleasing spectacles and elegant dinners: conviviality, benevolence and charity anniversaries in eighteenth century London', *Journal of British Studies*, 41, 23–57.

Lorne, P. (1995) *The Millennium Planner*, London: Boxtree.

Lovett, C. (1997) *Olympic Marathon: a centennial history of the Games most storied race*, Westport, CN: Praeger.

Luckhurst, K.W. (1951) *The Story of Exhibitions*, London: Studio Vista.

Lury, C. (1996) *Consumer Culture*, Oxford: Polity Press.

Lyon, R. (1987) 'Theme parks in the USA: growth markets and future prospects', *Travel and Tourist Analyst*, 9, 31–43.

MacAloon, J.J. (1981) *This Great Symbol: Pierre de Coubertin and the origins of the modern Olympic Games*, Chicago: University of Chicago Press.

_____ (1984a) 'Introduction: cultural performances, cultural theory', in J.J. MacAloon, ed., *Rite, Drama, Festival, Spectacle: rehearsals towards a theory of cultural performance*, Philadelphia: Institute for the Study of Human Issues, 1–15.

_____ (1984b) 'Olympic Games and the Theory of Spectacle in Modern Societies', in J.J. MacAloon, ed., *Rite, Drama, Festival, Spectacle: rehearsals towards a theory of cultural performance*, Philadelphia: Institute for the Study of Human Issues, 241–80.

McArthur, A. and Kingsley Long, H. (1935) *No Mean City*, London: Longmans Green.

Macaulay, T.B. (1906) *A History of England from the Accession of James II*, vol.1, London: Dent (originally published in 1848).

McDonald, J. and Schumacher, C., eds (1991) *The Citizens' Theatre Season, Glasgow 1990*, Glasgow: Theatre Studies Publications, Department of Theatre Studies, Glasgow University.

MacDonald, S. (2000) 'Defining a decade: Glasgow and the 1990 City of Culture', *Locum Destination Review*, 9, 51–2.

Mackenzie, M. (2003) 'From Athens to Berlin: the 1936 Olympics and Leni Riefenstahl's *Olympia*', *Critical Inquiry*, 29, 302–36.

McLaughlin, M. (2002) 'Reconsidering the East St. Louis race riot of 1917', *International Review of Social History*, 47, 187–212.

McMahon, J.A. (1995) *Education and Culture in European Community Law*, London: Athlone Press.

_____ (1999) 'Article 128: a community contribution to the cultural policies of the member states?', in S.V. Konstadinidas, ed., *A People's Europe: turning a concept into content*, Aldershot: Ashgate, 183–210.

Macy, C. and Bonnemaison, S. (2003) *Architecture and Nature: creating the American landscape*, London: Routledge.

Mainardi, P. (1996) 'International Exhibition', in J. Turner, ed., *The Dictionary of Art*, vol. 15, London: Macmillan, 883–5.

Malcolmson, R. (1973) *Popular Recreations in English Society, 1700–1850*, Cambridge: Cambridge University Press.

Mallon, B. (1998) *The 1900 Olympic Games: results for all competitors in all events with commentary. Results from the Early Olympics 2*, Jefferson, NC: McFarland and Company Inc.

_____ (1999a) *The 1904 Olympic Games: results for all competitors in all events with commentary. Results from the Early Olympics 3*, Jefferson, NC: McFarland and Company Inc.

_____ (1999b) *The 1906 Olympic Games: results for all competitors in all events with commentary. Results from the Early Olympics 4*, Jefferson, NC: McFarland and Company Inc.

Mallon, B. and Buchanan, I. (2000) *The 1908 Olympic Games: results for all competitors in all events with commentary. Results from the early Olympics 5*, Jefferson NC: McFarland and Company Inc.

Mallon, B. and Widlund, T. (1998) *The 1896 Olympic Games – Results for all competitors in all events with commentary. Results from the Early Olympics 1*, Jefferson, NC: McFarland and Company Inc.

Maloney, L. (1996) 'Barcelona 1992: the Games of the 25th Olympiad', in J.E. Findling and K.D. Pelle, eds, *Historical Dictionary of the Modern Olympic Movement*, Westport, CN: Greenwood Press, 185–93.

Mandell, R.D. (1976) *The First Modern Olympics*, London: Souvenir Press.

Manning, F.E., ed. (1983) *The Celebration of Society: perspectives on contemporary cultural performance*, Bowling Green, OH: Bowling Green University Popular Press.

Manning, M. (1990) 'Osaka 1970: Japan World Exposition (Expo '70)', in J.E. Findling and K.D. Pelle, eds, *Historical Dictionary of World's Fairs and Expositions, 1851–1988*, Westport, CN: Greenwood Press, 339–46.

Margalit, H. (1999) 'Stadium Australia', in P. Bingham-Hall, ed., *Olympic Architecture: building Sydney*, Sydney: Watermark Press, 68–83.

Marsh, J. (1999) 'Spectacle', in H.F. Tucker, ed., *A Companion to Victorian Literature and Culture*, Oxford: Blackwell, 276–88.

Marshall, T. (1996) 'Barcelona: fast forward?', *European Planning Studies*, 4, 147–65.

Martorell, J., Bohigas, O., Mackay, D. and Puigdomènech, A. (1992) *The Olympic Village: architecture, parks, leisure, port*, 2nd edn, Barcelona: Gustavo Gili.

Mason, G. (2002) *The Spectacle of Violence: homophobia, gender and knowledge*, London: Routledge.

Matsushita Electric (1980) *The Official Record of Time Capsule Expo 70: a gift to the people of the future from the people of the present day*, Osaka: Matsushita Electric Industrial Co. Ltd.

Mattie, E. (1998) *World's Fairs*, Princeton, NJ: Princeton University Press.

Maxwell, R. (1995) *The Spectacle of Democracy: Spanish television, nationalism and political transition*, Minneapolis, MN: University of Minnesota Press.

Mayhew, H., with G. Cruikshank, illustrator (1851) *1851: or, the adventures of Mr. and Mrs. Sandboys and Family, who came up to London to 'enjoy themselves' and visit the Great Exhibition*, London: Henry Newbold.

Mayne, J. (1993) *Cinema and Spectatorship*, London: Routledge.

Merback, M.B. (1999) *The Thief, the Cross and the Wheel: pain and the spectacle of punishment in Medieval and Renaissance Europe*, London: Reaktion Books.

Messaris, P. (2001) 'Visual culture', in J. Lull, ed., *Culture in the Communication Age*, London: Routledge, 169–92.

Metz, C. (1977) *Le Signifiant Imaginaire: psychoanalyse et cinéma*, Paris: Union Générale d'Editions, trans. C. Britton, A. Williams, B. Brewster and A. Guzzetti (1982) as *Psychoanalysis and Cinema: the imaginary signifier*, London: Macmillan.

MIC (Melbourne Invitation Committee) (1948) *The Melbourne Invitation Committee extends a most cordial Invitation to the esteemed International Olympic Committee to celebrate the XVI Olympiad in Melbourne, Australia in 1956*, Melbourne: G.W. Grant and Sons.

Migliazzo, A.C. (1990) 'Spokane 1974: Expo 74: the International Exposition of the Environment', in J.E. Findling and K.D. Pelle, eds, *Historical Dictionary of World's Fairs and Expositions, 1851–1988*, Westport, CN: Greenwood Press, 347–9.

Miles, M., Hall, T. and Borden, I., eds (2000) *The City Cultures Reader*, London: Routledge.

Miller, J. (1967) 'Expo '67: a search for order', *Canadian Architect*, 12(5), 45–6.

Milns, B. (2000) 'The Ancient Olympic Games', http://www.library.uq. edu.au/olympics/milns.html

Mitchell, S. (1990) 'Festivals, games, and civic life in Roman Asia Minor', *Journal of Roman Studies*, 80, 183–93.

Mitchell, T. (1991) *Colonising Egypt*, Berkeley: University of California Press.

Moeller, W.O. (1970) 'The riot of 59 AD at Pompeii', *Historia*, 19, 84–95.

Monaghan, F. (1939) *New York: the world's fair city*, Garden City, NY: Garden City Publishing Company.

Moore, K. (1991) 'A neglected imperialist: the promotion of the British Empire in the writing of John Astley Cooper', *International Journal of the History of Sport*, 8, 256–69.

Morris, J. (1982) *The Spectacle of Empire: style, effect and the Pax Britannica*, London: Faber.

Morse, J. (2001) 'The Sydney 2000 Olympic Games: how the Australian

Tourist Commission leveraged the games for tourism', *Journal of Vacation Marketing*, 7, 101–7.

Mullen, M. (1990) 'New York 1939–1940: New York World's Fair', in J.E. Findling and K.D. Pelle, eds, *Historical Dictionary of World's Fairs and Expositions, 1851–1988*, Westport, CN: Greenwood Press, 292–300.

Müller, A., ed. (2000) *Pierre de Coubertin, 1893–1937: Olympism, selected writings*, Lausanne: International Olympic Committee.

Mumford, L. (1938) *The Culture of Cities*, London: Secker and Warburg.

_____ (1961) *The City in History: its origins, its transformations, and its prospects*, Harmondsworth: Penguin.

Myerscough, J. (1988) *Economic Importance of the Arts in Glasgow*, London: Policy Studies Institute.

_____ (2003) 'Luxembourg, Topic 3: Cultural Identities', http://www.planum.net/4bie/main/m-4bie-luxembourg.htm (accessed 30 September 2003).

Newburg, V.E. (1973) 'The literature of the streets', in H.J. Dyos and M. Wolff, eds, *The Victorian City: images and realities*, vol. 1, 'Past and Present/Numbers of People', London: Routledge and Kegan Paul, 191–209.

Nicolson, A. (1999) *Regeneration: the story of the Dome*, London: HarperCollins.

North, J.A. (1992) 'Deconstructing stone theatres', in *Apodosis: essays presented to Dr. W.W. Cruickshank to mark his eightieth birthday*, London: St Paul's School, 75–83.

Nye, D.E. (1990) *Electrifying America: social meanings of a new technology, 1880–1940*, Cambridge, MA: MIT Press.

Ogata, A.F. (2002) 'Viewing souvenirs: peepshows and the International Expositions', *Journal of Design History*, 15, 69–82.

O'Leary, K.P. (1988) 'Expo 67 and Expo 86', in J.H. Marsh, ed., *The Canadian Encyclopedia*, vol. 2, Edmonton: Hurtig, 738–9.

Olympic Games (1948) *Olympic Games. London, 1948. Official souvenir*, London: Futura Publications.

Organising Committee (1928) *The Ninth Olympiad, Amsterdam 1928: Official Report*, Amsterdam: R.H. de Bussig Ltd.

_____ (1936) *The XI Olympic Games Berlin 1936: Official Report*, Berlin: Wilhelm Limpert.

_____ (1948) *The Official Report of the Organising Committee for the XIV Olympiad: London 1948*, London: British Olympic Association.

_____ (1960) *The Official Reports of the Olympic Committee for the Games of the XVII Olympiad*, Rome: Olympic Committee.

_____ (1964) *The Official Reports of the Olympic Committee for the Games of the XVIII Olympiad*, Tokyo: Olympic Committee.

_____ (1969) *1968 Mexico Official Report*, Mexico City: Olympic Committee of the XIX Olympiad.

_____ (1972) *The Official Report of the Olympic Committee for the Games of the XX Olympiad, Munich 1972*, Munich: Pro-Sport Munchen.

_____ (1976) *Official Report of the Games of the XXI Olympiad*, Ottawa: COJO–76.

_____ (1980) *Official Report of the Organising Committee for the Games of the XXII Olympiad*, Moscow: Progress Publishers.

_____ (1985) *Official Report of the Games of the XXIII Olympiad, Los Angeles 1984*, Los Angeles: Los Angeles Olympic Organising Committee.

_____ (1989) *Official Report of the Games of the XXIV Olympiad*, Seoul: Seoul Olympic Organising Committee.

_____ (1992) *Official Report of the Games of the XXV Olympiad*, Barcelona: COOB'92.

_____ (1996) *Official Report of the Games of the XXVI Olympiad*, Atlanta: Atlanta Committee for the Olympic Games.

Osborne, P.D. (2000) *Travelling Light: photography, travel and visual culture*, Manchester: Manchester University Press.

Ozouf, M. (1988) *Festivals and the French Revolution*, trans. A. Sheridan, Cambridge, MA: Harvard University Press.

Palenski, R. (1996) 'Seoul 1988: the Games of the 24th Olympiad', in J.E. Findling and K.D. Pelle, eds, *Historical Dictionary of the Modern Olympic Movement*, Westport, CN: Greenwood Press, 178–84.

Palmer, T. (1990) 'Seville 1929–1930: Exposicion Ibero-Americana (Ibero-American Exposition)', in J.E. Findling and K.D. Pelle, eds, *Historical Dictionary of World's Fairs and Expositions, 1851–1988*, Westport, CN: Greenwood Press, 255–7.

Pamboukian, S. (2001) '"Looking radiant": science, photography and the x-ray craze of 1896', *Victorian Review*, 27, 387–409.

Pantell, M. (1999) 'Unity-in-diversity: cultural policy and EU legitimacy', in T. Banchoff and M.P. Smith, eds, *Legitimacy and the European Union: the contested polity*, London: Routledge, 46–65.

Park, S.J. (1991) *The Seoul Olympics: the inside story*, London: Bellew.

Parker, H.N. (1999) 'The observed of all observers: spectacle, applause, and cultural poetics in the Roman theatre audience', in B. Bergmann and C. Kondoleon, eds, *The Art of Ancient Spectacle*, Washington, DC: National Gallery of Art, 162–79.

Parpola, S., ed. (1993) *Letters from Assyrian and Babylonian scholars*, Helsinki: Helsinki University Press.

Peabody, S.H. (1902) *World's Fairs, Universal Expositions: the milestones along the highway of human progress*, St Paul, MN.

Peck, J. and Ward, K. eds (2002) *City of Revolution: restructuring Manchester*, Manchester: Manchester University Press.

Pender-Gunn, K. (1999) 'Crystal Palace: on a hot summer's day', http://crystal.dircon.co.uk/mrskpg.htm (accessed 20 December 2002).

Pieroth, D. (1996) 'Los Angeles 1932: the Games of the 10th Olympiad', in J.E. Findling and K.D. Pelle, eds, *Historical Dictionary of the Modern Olympic Movement*, Westport, CN: Greenwood Press, 75–83.

Pilling, P. (1960) 'The biggest ever ... perhaps the best ever', in British Olympic Association, *Official Report of the Olympic Games of the XVIIth Olympiad Rome 1960*, London: World Sports.

Pinder, D. (2000) '"Old Paris is no more": geographies of spectacle and anti-spectacle', *Antipode*, 34, 357–86.

Pipan, T. and Porsander, L. (2000) 'Imitating uniqueness: how big cities organize big events', *Organization Studies, Annual, 2000*, http://www.findarticles.com/cf_dls/m4339/2000_Annual/63543386/p3/article (accessed 8 October 2003).

Plass, P. (1995) *The Game of Death in Ancient Rome: arena sport and political suicide*, Madison: University of Wisconsin Press.

Polley, M. (1996) '"No business of ours?": The Foreign Office and the Olympic Games 1896–1914', *International Journal of the History of Sport*, 13, 96–113.

Pollitt, J.J. (1986) *Art in the Hellenistic Age*, Cambridge: Cambridge University Press.

Prior, N. (2002) *Museums and Modernity: art galleries and the making of modern culture*, Oxford: Berg.

Promyslov, V. (1980) *Moscow: past and present*, Moscow: Progress Publishers.

Proudfoot, P., Maguire, R. and Freestone, R., eds (2000) *Colonial City, Global City: Sydney's International Exhibition 1879*, Darlinghurst, NSW: Crossing Press.

Purbrick, L. (2001) 'Introduction', in L. Purbrick, ed., *The Great Exhibition of 1851: new interdisciplinary essays*, Manchester: Manchester University Press, 1–25.

Purcell, N. (1999) 'Does Caesar mime?', in B. Bergmann and C. Kondoleon, eds, *The Art of Ancient Spectacle*, Washington, DC: National Gallery of Art, 180–91.

Putnam, J. (1990) *Egyptology: an introduction to the history, art and culture of ancient Egypt*, New York: Crescent Books.

Quennell, M. and Quennell, C.H.B. (1957) *Everyday Things in Ancient Greece*, London: Batsford.

Ray, L. and Sayer, A. (1999) 'Introduction', in L. Ray and A. Sayer, eds, *Culture and Economy after the Cultural Turn*, London: Sage, 1–24.

Redmond, G. (1988) 'Toward modern revival of the Olympic Games: the various pseudo-Olympics of the 19th century', in J.O. Seagrave and D. Chu, eds, *The Olympic Games in Transition*, Champaign, IL: Human Kinetics Books.

Renson, R. (1996) 'Antwerp 1920: the Games of the 7th Olympiad', in J.E. Findling and K.D. Pelle, eds, *Historical Dictionary of the Modern Olympic Movement*, Westport, CN: Greenwood Press, 54–60.

RIBA (Royal Institute of British Architects) (2001) *RIBAWorld*, 171, http://www.RIBAWorld@inst.riba.org (accessed 25 September 2001).

Richards, G., ed. (2001) *Cultural Attractions and European Tourism*, Wallingford: CAB International.

Richards, J.M. (1967) 'Multi-level city: towards a new environment in downtown Montreal', *Architectural Review*, 142, 89–96.

Riordan, J. (1984) 'The Workers' Olympics', in A. Tomlinson and G. Whannel, eds, *Five Ring Circus: money, power and politics at the Olympic Games*, London: Pluto Press.

———— (1996) 'Moscow 1980: the Games of the 22nd Olympiad', in J.E. Findling and K.D. Pelle, eds, *Historical Dictionary of the Modern Olympic Movement*, Westport, CN: Greenwood Press, 161–8.

Roche, M. (1992) 'Mega-events and micro-modernisation: on the sociology of the new urban tourism', *British Journal of Sociology*, 43, 563–600.

———— (2000) *Mega-Events and Modernity: Olympics and Expos in the growth of global culture*, London: Routledge.

Rock, H.B. and Moore, D.D. (2001) *Cityscapes: a history of New York in images*, New York: Columbia University Press.

Roth, R.O. (1990) 'New York 1918: Bronx International Exposition', in J.E. Findling and K.D. Pelle, eds, *Historical Dictionary of World's Fairs and Expositions, 1851–1988*, Westport, CN: Greenwood Press, 230–1.

Roth, S. and Frank, S. (2000) 'Festivalization and the media: Weimar, Cultural Capital of Europe 1999', *Cultural Policy*, 6, 219–41.

Roy, G. (1982) *Le Véritable Histoire de Jean Drapeau*, Montreal: Québecor.

Rürup, R., ed. (1996) *1936: die Olympischen Spiele und der Nationalsozialismus: eine Dokumentation*, Berlin: Argon.

Rutheiser, C. (1996) *Imagineering Atlanta: the politics of place in the city of Atlanta*, London: Verso.

Rydell, R.W. (1984) *All the World's a Fair: visions of Empire at American International Expositions, 1876–1916*, Chicago: University of Chicago Press.

_____ (1993) *World of Fairs: the Century-of-Progress Expositions*, Chicago: University of Chicago Press.

Rydell, R.W., Findling, J.E. and Pelle, K.D. (2000) *Fair America: World's Fairs in the United States*, Washington, DC: Smithsonian Institution Press.

Rykwert, J. (1976) *The Idea of a Town: the anthropology of urban form in Rome, Italy and the ancient world*, London: Faber and Faber.

Safdie, M. (1970) *Beyond Habitat*, J. Kettle, ed., Cambridge, MA: MIT Press.

Safdie, M. and Kohn, W. (1997) *The City after the Automobile: an architect's vision*, Toronto: Stoddart.

Saint-Exupéry, A. de (1939) *Terre des Hommes*, trans. L. Kidson (1990) as *Wind, Sand and Stars*, London: Folio Society.

Samuels, M. (2002) 'Realizing the past: history and spectacle in Balzac's "Adieu"', *Representations*, 79, 82–99.

Sandell, T. (2002) 'Cultural issues, debate and programmes', in J. Gower, ed., *The European Union Handbook*, London: Fitzroy Dearborn, 256–67.

Santomasso, E.A. (1980) 'The design of reason: architecture and planning at the 1939/40 New York World's Fair', in H.A. Harrison, ed., *Dawn of a New Day: the New York World's Fair*, New York: Queen's Museum/New York University Press, 29–41.

Schelling, V. (1999) '"The People's Radio" of Vila Nossa Senhore Aparecida: alternative communication and cultures of resistance in Brazil', in T. Skelton and T. Allen, eds, *Culture and Global Change*, London: Routledge, 167–79.

Schroeder-Gudehus, B. and Cloutier, D. (1994) 'Popularising science and technology during the Cold War: Brussels 1958', in R.W. Rydell and N.E. Gwinn, eds, *Fair Representations: World's Fairs and the Modern World*, Amsterdam: VU University Press, 157–80.

Schwarcz, L.M. (1999) *The Spectacle of the Races: scientists, institutions and the race question in Brazil, 1870–1930*, trans. L. Guyer, New York: Hill and Wang.

Schwartz, L. (2000) 'London 1700–1840', in P. Clark, ed., *The Cambridge Urban History of Britain*, vol. 2 '1540–1840', Cambridge: Cambridge University Press, 641–71.

Scott, W. (1822) *Hints addressed to the Inhabitants of Edinburgh, and Others, in Prospect of His Majesty's Visit, by an Old Citizen*, Edinburgh.

Senn, A.E. (1999) *Power, politics and the Olympic Games: a history of the power brokers, events and controversies that shaped the Games*, Champaign, IL: Human Kinetics.

Sennett, R. (1994) *Flesh and Stone: the body and the city in Western civilization*, London: Faber and Faber.

Sereny, G. (1995) *Albert Speer: his battle with the truth*, London: Macmillan.

Shaikin, B. (1988) *Sport and Politics: the Olympics and the Los Angeles Games*, New York: Praeger.

Sheil, P. (1998) *Olympic Babylon*, Sydney: Pan Macmillan.

Simson, V. and Jennings, A. (1992) *The Lord of the Rings: power, money and drugs in the modern Olympics*, Toronto: Stoddart.

Sinn, U. (2000) *Olympia: cult, sport and ancient festival*, Princeton: Markus Wiener Publishers.

Smith, J.A. (1999) 'The denigration of vision and the renewal of painting', in I. Heywood and B. Sandywell, eds, *Interpreting Visual Culture: explorations in the hermeneutics of the visual*, London: Routledge, 162–82.

Smith, P. (2001) *Cultural Theory: an introduction*, Oxford: Blackwell.

SOC (Stockholm Organising Committee) (1913) *The fifth Olympiad; the official report of the Olympic games of Stockholm, 1912. Issued by the Swedish Olympic Committee*, ed. E. Bergvall and trans. E. Adams-Ray, Stockholm: Wahlstrom and Widstrand.

SOCOG (Sydney Organising Committee for the Olympic Games) (2000) *Official report of the XXVII Olympiad*, http://www.gamesinfo.com.au/postgames (accessed 19 August 2003).

Spa, M.A.M, Rivenburgh, N.K. and Larson, J.F. (1995) *Television in the Olympics*, London: John Libby.

Spezia, G. (1992) *Eventi e Turismo*, Bologna: Editore Calderini.

Spierenburg, P. (1984) *The Spectacle of Suffering: executions and the evolution of repression, from a preindustrial metropolis to the European experience*, Cambridge: Cambridge University Press.

Stanton, J. (1997) 'Building Expo 67', revised version, http://naid.sppsr.ucla.edu/expo67/map-docs/buildingexpo.htm (accessed 11 November 2002).

Starobinski, J. (1988) *Jean-Jacques Rousseau: transparency and obstruction*, Chicago: University of Chicago Press.

Steinberg, M.P. (1990) *The Meaning of the Salzburg Festival: Austria as theatre of ideology, 1890–1938*, Ithaca, NY: Cornell University Press.

Stern, R.A.M., Mellins, T. and Fishman, D. (1995) *New York 1960: architecture and urbanism between the Second World War and the Bicentennial*, New York: Monacelli Press.

Stewart, D. (1822) *Sketches of the Character, Institutions and Customs of the Highlands of Scotland*, Edinburgh.

Stokes, I.N.P. (1939) *New York: past and present*, New York: New York Historical Society.

Strong, R. (1973) *Splendour at Court: Renaissance spectacle and illusion*, London: Weidenfeld and Nicolson.

Stump, A.J. (1988) 'The Games that almost weren't', in J.O. Seagrove and D. Chu, eds, *The Olympic Games in transition*, Champaign, IL: Human Kinetics Books, 191–9.

Sullivan, J.E. (1905) 'Olympic Games', *Spalding's Official Athletic Almanac for 1905*, 18 (217).

Summerson, J. (1978) 'London, the artifact', in H.J. Dyos and M. Wolff, eds, *The Victorian City: images and realities*, vol. 2, 'Shapes on the Ground/A Change of Accent', London: Routledge and Kegan Paul, 311–32.

Susman, W. (1980) 'The people's fair: cultural contradictions of a consumer society', in H.A. Harrison, ed., *Dawn of a New Day: the New York World's Fair*, New York: Queen's Museum/New York University Press, 16–27.

Theile, G. (2003) 'The Weimar myth: from city of the arts to global village', in B. Henke, S. Kord and S. Richter, eds, *Unwrapping Goethe's Weimar: essays in cultural studies and local knowledge*, Rochester, NY: Camden House, 310–27.

Thorold, P. (1999) *The London Rich: the creation of a great city, from 1666 to the present*, New York: St Martin's Press.

Tisdall, B. (1956) 'Lighter moments', in S. Tomlin, ed., *Olympic Odyssey*, Croydon: Messrs Bovril Ltd/Modern Athlete Publications Ltd, 31–32.

TOC (Tenth Olympic Committee of the Games of Los Angeles) (1933) *Xth Olympiad – Los Angeles 1932 Official Report*, Los Angeles: TOC.

Tolstoy, V., Bibikova, I. and Cooke, C., eds (1990) *Street Art of the Revolution*, trans. F. Longman, F. O'Dell and V. Wankov, London: Thames and Hudson.

Tomlinson, A. (2000) *The Game's Up: essays in the cultural analysis of sport, leisure and popular culture*, Aldershot: Ashgate.

――――― (2002) 'Theorising spectacle: beyond Debord', in J. Sugden and A. Tomlinson, eds, *Power Games: a critical sociology of sport*, London: Routledge, 44–60.

Toohey, K. and Veal, A.J. (2000) *The Olympic Games: a social science perspective*, Wallingford: CAB International Publications.

Turbayne, C.M. (1971) *The Myth of Metaphor*, rev. edn, Columbia: University of South Carolina Press.

Turner, V. (1972) 'Symbols in African ritual', *Science*, 179 (16 March), 1100–05.

――――― (1984) 'Liminality and the performative genres', in J.J. MacAloon, ed., *Rite, Drama, Festival, Spectacle: rehearsals towards a theory of cultural performance*, Philadelphia: Institute for the Study of Human Issues, 19–41.

Tylor, E.B. (1871) *Primitive Culture: researches into the development of mythology, philosophy, religion, language, art and custom*, London: John Murray.

Ueberroth, P. (1986) *Made in America: his own story*, New York: Morrow.

UNESCO (2003) 'World Heritage Sites', http://whc.unesco.org/sites/846.htm (accessed 8 October 2003).

Urry, J. (2000) 'Sensing the city', in D.R. Judd and S.S. Fainstein, eds, *The Tourist City*, New Haven, CN: Yale University Press, 71–86.

——— (2002) *The Tourist Gaze*, 2nd edn, London: Sage.

USHMM (United States Holocaust Memorial Museum) (2003) 'Berlin Olympics 1936', http://www.ushmm.org/Olympics/zcc034a.htm (accessed 1 January 2003).

Varley, A. (1992) 'Barcelona's Olympic facelift', *Geographical Magazine*, 64 (July), 20–24.

Vickers, M. (1989) *Ancient Rome*, Oxford: Phaidon.

Voeltz, R.A. (1996) 'London 1948: the Games of the 14th Olympiad', in J.E. Findling and K.D. Pelle, eds, *Historical Dictionary of the Modern Olympic Movement*, Westport, CN: Greenwood Press, 103–8.

Walford, C. (1883) *Fairs, Past and Present: a chapter in the history of commerce*, London: Elliot Stock.

Walker, J.A. and Chaplin, S. (1997) *Visual Culture: an introduction*, Manchester: Manchester University Press.

Walton, J.M. (1987) *Living Greek Theatre*, New York: Greenwood Press.

Ward, S.V. (1996) 'Place marketing: a historical comparison of Britain and North America', in T. Hall and P. Hubbard, eds, *The Entrepreneurial City: geographies of politics, regime and representation*, Chichester: John Wiley, 31–53.

——— (1998) *Selling Places: the marketing and promotion of towns and cities, 1850–2000*, London: Spon.

Warner, P.M. (1990) 'Montreal 1967: Expo 67, Universal and International Exhibition of 1967', in J.E. Findling and K.D. Pelle, eds, *Historical Dictionary of World's Fairs and Expositions, 1851–1988*, Westport, CN: Greenwood Press, 329–35.

Weinreb, B. and Hibbert, C., eds (1993) *The London Encyclopedia*, rev. edn, London: Macmillan.

Weir, A. (2002) *Henry VIII: king and court*, London: Pimlico.

Welch, P.D. (1996) 'Paris 1924: the Games of the 8th Olympiad', in J.E. Findling and K.D. Pelle, eds, *Historical Dictionary of the Modern Olympic Movement*, Westport, CN: Greenwood Press, 61–67.

Wendt, G. (1939) *Science for the World of Tomorrow*, New York: W.W. Norton.

Westwood, S. and Williams, J., eds (1997) *Imagining Cities*, London: Routledge.

Whitehead, J. (1989) *The Growth of St Marylebone and Paddington*, London: Jack Whitehead.

Whitelegg, D. (2000) 'Going for gold: Atlanta's bid for fame', *International Journal of Urban and Regional Research*, 24, 801–17.

Wilhide, E. (1999) *The Millennium Dome*, London: HarperCollins-Illustrated.

Williams, H.M. (1929) *Memoirs of the Reign of Robespierre*, London: John Hamilton (originally published 1795).

Williams, R. (1976) 'Culture', in R. Williams, *Keywords: a vocabulary of culture and society*, London: Fontana, 76–82.

Wilson, D.M. (2002) *The British Museum: a history*, London: British Museum Press.

Wilson, W. (1996) 'Los Angeles 1984: the Games of the 23rd Olympiad', in J.E. Findling and K.D. Pelle, eds, *Historical Dictionary of the Modern Olympic Movement*, Westport, CN: Greenwood Press, 169–77.

Wimmer, M. (1976) *Olympic Buildings*, Leipzig: Edition Leipzig.

Winkler, M.M., ed. (1991) *Classics and Cinema*, Lewisburg, PA: Bucknell University Press.

_____ (2001) *Classical Myths and Culture in the City*, New York: Oxford University Press.

Winsberg, M.D. (1992) 'Walt Disney World, Florida: the creation of a fantasy landscape', in D.G. Janelle, ed., *Geographical Snapshots of North America*, New York: Guilford Press, 350–53.

Wordsworth, W. (1850) *The Prelude, or Growth of a Poet's Mind: an autobiographical poem*, London: Edward Moxon.

Worsley, P. (1999) 'Classic conceptions of culture', in T. Skelton and T. Allen, eds, *Culture and Global Change*, London: Routledge, 11–21.

WOS (Wenlock Olympian Society) (2003) 'Shropshire Olympics', http://www.wenlock-olympian-society.org.uk (accessed 1 January 2003).

Wyke, M. (1997) *Projecting the Past: ancient Rome, cinema and history*, London: Routledge.

Yew, W. (1996) *The Olympic image: the first 100 years*, Edmonton, Alberta: Quon Editions.

Young, D.C. (1987) 'The origins of the modern Olympics: a new version', *International Journal of the History of Sport*, 4, 271–300.

_____ (1996) *The Modern Olympics: a struggle for revival*, Baltimore: Johns Hopkins University Press.

Young, K. and Garside, P. (1982) *Metropolitan London: political and urban change, 1837–1981*, London: Edward Arnold.

Zanker, P. (1988) *The Power of Images in the Age of Augustus*, trans. A. Shapiro, Ann Arbor: University of Michigan Press.

Zorzi, E.G. (1986) 'Court Spectacle', in S. Bertelli, F. Cardini, and E.G. Zorzi, eds, *Italian Renaissance Courts*, London: Sidgwick and Jackson, 127–87.

Zukin, S. (1996) *The Culture of Cities*, Oxford: Blackwell.

Index